THERE'S A HOLE IN MY LOVE CUP

THE BADASS COUNSELING® METHOD FOR HEALING THE SOUL AND UNLEASHING GREATNESS

Sven Erlandson, MDiv, BA

EKSJÖ YARD PUBLISHING, NEW YORK

ISBN: 978-1-62550-538-5
978-1-62550-539-2

- to Karen,
one helluva woman

THE SIX HARDENED TRUTHS
OF THE BADASS COUNSELING METHOD

1) Transformation can be immediate,
if you go deep enough.

2) Change will not occur,
until the pain gets bad enough.

3) Creation is invariably
preceded by destruction.

4) No man is truly free,
until he can live as though his father is dead.

5) At the deepest level, the voice of the Universe/God
is indistinguishable from the voice of your own soul.

6) Until you have the stillness and solitude
necessary to hear the voice of the soul,
until you have the courage to heed that voice,
and until you can let go of needing specific results,
there will be no true joy, no lasting peace, no inimitable power, and
no sense of purpose.

ACKNOWLEDGMENTS

First and foremost, I give thanks to the gods/God/Universe/the Force/Energy/my own soul. In my lifetime, I have always been a bit of an atheist intellectually, but on the experiential level a believer in unexplained forces and energies that science is clueless to explain. It is these energies and the calling of my soul that have brought me to this point, inspired me to write this book, and drawn me to endeavor all I have. I have followed you all the days of my life, often to great success, often to monumental and overwhelming loss, always to deep learning and growth.

Thanks to my parents, Rev. LeRoy and Charlotte Erlandson for a lifetime of Solomonic wisdom, deep questioning, contrarian thinking, effusive love coupled with required responsibility and hard work. Mostly, thanks for your love of people, assiduously honoring the call of the spirit in your lives, and graciously serving humanity. We all stand on the shoulders of giants; I yours.

Thanks to Colbjorn and Svea, my little mutts. Colbjorn, the sheer embodiment of gritty hard work and big laughter. Svea, the intense one with high ideals. I work at this so that you two will have solid shoulders to stand on, doing far more than I ever could.

Thanks to Dr. Jay Bland, Todd Rens, John Erlandson, and Lisa Louise Koger for a lifetime of both bemusement by and encouragement of my unusual path.

A big thanks to my clients, who trust me with their life problems, trust my lead, aggressively pursue growth (a treat for any teacher), and teach me so much with their thoughts, feelings, new turns of phrase, experiences and insights – all of which challenge me to find new patterns and new anomalies.

Lastly, a most heartfelt thank you to Karen Camporeale, with whom I listen to 'Writer's Almanac,' eat oysters with beers by the water, attend the symphony, and go overboard with Christmas decorations; with whom I share my latest ideas, who challenges and questions my concepts, yet trusts me; and who with profound patience pushes me to never have clipped wings, but to pound at life at full wingspan – being the most complex, hard-hitting, and ridiculous Sven I can be. You're one of the finest human beings I've ever met or known! Hell, you can tolerate *me*; so what does that say?

STRONGLY RECOMMENDED READING LIST

I know it is unusual to put a bibliography at the beginning of a book, but there are a few books that I highly, highly recommend to nearly every one of my clients. Even if you never finish my book, read these. There is so much wisdom in them that helps me, each year. I know they will help you, too.

1. *The Sedona Method*, by Hale Dwoskin. I cannot recommend this book enough. It's not a book of concepts, but a method. The more self-discipline you have, the more powerful the book.

2. *Living in the Light*, by Shakti Gawain. My bible in so many ways.

3. *Radical Acceptance*, by Tara Brach. Just a wonderfully accessible, yet rich read that I keep coming back to. An insightful book for daily devotions/meditation.

4. *Reflections on the Art of Living*, by Joseph Campbell. Campbell is the master. My guru. This book is rooted in his other books, of particular note *The Power of Myth*. But this is the condensed book for everyday reflection.

5. *The Untethered Soul*, by Michael Singer. Dense and deep.

6. *The Artist's Way*, by Julia Cameron. Bestseller classic. So great for opening the soul.

7. *The 5 Love Languages*, by Gary Chapman. Classic bestseller. Short. The God-stuff included in the book is not too much, even for an atheist.

8. *Illusions*, by Richard Bach. The book that, at 19, started my entire deliberate spiritual journey.

9. *The Dark Side of the Light Chasers*, by Debbie Ford. It's Carl Jung meets today's language. A truly great book that will move you along further on your journey to full relationship with self.

TABLE OF CONTENTS

Introduction   i

THE CORE

Chapter 1   Therapy Just Doesn't Work For Me!   1
Chapter 2   Becoming Truest Self And Unleashing Greatness   17
Chapter 3   You're Running!   25
Chapter 4   Change Will Not Occur 'Til The Pain Gets Bad   33
             Enough
Chapter 5   Your Love Cup   37
Chapter 6   Around The Dinner Table   49
Chapter 7   A Ship Crossing The Ocean   57
Chapter 8   The Wet Cement Of Your Soul   61
Chapter 9   The 3 Binary Gates   67
Chapter 10   Growing Rods And Video Surveillance   87
Chapter 11   Empty Love Cups Produce Relationship Camels   93
Chapter 12   The Bag Of Rocks On Your Back   103
Chapter 13   Who Owns You?   107
Chapter 14   Y'KNOW WHAT YOUR PROBLEM IS!?!?!?   113
Chapter 15   "Are You Sure?" His Mother Asked, All His Life   117
Chapter 16   We Are Constantly Being Led To Higher Ground   123
Chapter 17   'When Did You Know?'   129
Chapter 18   Your Addiction To Busyness. And The 3 Steps Of   139
             The Spiritual Life
Chapter 19   Every Morning, Life Is Whispering Two Questions   163
             In Your Ear
Chapter 20   How Do I Become Me When I Don't Even Know   165
             Who I Am?
Chapter 21   Diamonds And Raw Sewage   171
Chapter 22   The Computer Chip Of Your Soul   195
Chapter 23   Your Life Messages, Part 1   203
Chapter 24   Your Life Messages, Part 2: The Golden Child,   207
             The Sibling, And The Special-Needs Kid
Chapter 25   Your Life Messages, Part 3: 'The World Is Your   219
             Oyster'
Chapter 26   The Truth Is Obvious   223

THE TURN

Chapter 27	The Pilot Light Of Greatness Burning Deep Inside You	235
Chapter 28	Three Things Happen As You More Become Your Truest Self	239
Chapter 29	Jumping Ship	245
Chapter 30	Every Decision In Life Boils Down To Two Things	249
Chapter 31	The Power Of The Third Path	253
Chapter 32	'You'll Know'	261
Chapter 33	Closed Doors Are Greater Blessings Than Open Ones	265
Chapter 34	Dumbest Exercise EVER...But It Works!	269

PARENTING

Chapter 35	Even Good Parents Can Seriously Harm A Child's Soul	275
Chapter 36	Children Love Parents More Than Parents Love Children	285
Chapter 37	Grandma Charlotte's Wisdom On Parenting The Soul	293
Chapter 38	Motivation And Your 22 Year-Old Son (Or Your 35 Year-Old Self)	297

RELATIONSHIPS

Chapter 39	Every Shared Experience Is A Cord Binding Two People Together, Making Unbinding Tricky	307
Chapter 40	Unhealthy People Come In Twos	313
Chapter 41	The Impasse Between Two People	319
Chapter 42	NCAA Possession Arrow & Death By A Thousand Cuts	325
Chapter 43	When 'Should I Leave?' Becomes 'I'm Done!'	333
Chapter 44	Breakup Myths: 'It Was Mutual' And 'Let's Be Friends'	337
Chapter 45	Surprise!	347

BONUS TRACKS

BT 1	The Root Of All Depression & Anxiety	BT1-1
BT 2	Why Telling An Adult to "Just Get Over It And Move On" Is The Dumbest Thing Ever	BT2-1
BT 3	People Shout Loudest When Feeling Heard Least	BT3-1
BT 4	Naming The Beast Is Half The Problem	BT4-1
BT 5	Pouring Out The Love Cup Onto The Ground	BT5-1
BT 6	The Greatest Fears In Life	BT6-1
BT 7	The Dog And The Electric Fence	BT7-1
BT 8	The Purpose Of The 'Why'	BT8-1
BT 9	Non-Negotiables, I-Don't-Give-A-Craps, And The Power Of Percentages	BT9-1
BT 10	When Positive Energy Sources Turn Negative	BT10-1
BT 11	Effortlessness And Flow	BT11-1
BT 12	Words Speak Louder Than Actions, Not Vice Versa	BT12-1
BT 13	When The Soul Burps Gold	BT13-1

INTRODUCTION

In 1956, legendary filmmaker Cecil B. DeMille and Paramount Pictures released what is arguably one of the epic cinematic masterpieces, of all time. The film, *The Ten Commandments*, starred American icon, Charlton Heston, and depicted the millennia-old story from Jewish Scripture about the life and heroic adventures of Moses, particularly his actions in saving the Hebrew people from slavery in Egypt. It is a movie roundly considered one of the greatest – certainly one of the most enduringly popular – in all of American filmography.

Perhaps most interesting in the entire narrative of *The Ten Commandments* is the oft-overlooked and easily forgotten part of the Moses odyssey (relative to the later high drama of 12 plagues and a sea cut in two) known as the calling, more formally referred to as the story of 'The Burning Bush'. Moses, you may recall from your own religious training as a child, was tending the sheep of his father-in-law, Jethro on Mount Horeb when he, quite unexpectedly encountered a bush that was consumed by flame but did not burn up. And, to the awe and delight of children through the ages, God spoke to Moses from the burning bush.

What is most fascinating – relative to the purposes of this book – however, is not that God spoke to Charlton Heston (er, Moses) through the burning bush, or even that there is a god, at all, (though, that is kind of a biggy), but what God said, in that moment. For, it dictates precisely both the ethos of this book and the most frequently missed necessity for great relationships – be it relationships with one's partner, one's friends and family, or, most significantly, with oneself. In that moment of Divine revelation, the very first words God speaks to his soon-to-be-new-messenger are not the unforgettable calling itself ("Go to Egypt...set my people free") but a conversational precursor, a simple command for recognition of the power of the physical space Moses was now occupying. Moses had just stepped into the presence of the Divine. As such, protocol changed. In this unusual space, everything was different; old rules did not apply. Establishing that, God said to Moses,

i

*"Take off your shoes
This is sacred ground."*

And with that small statement of expectations between parties the die is cast for what must happen – what must always happen – when one stands before the Divine, when one stands before that which burns with a most powerful truth. One of greatest mistakes made in relationships is the failure to recognize when one is standing before the very gods themselves, the failure to recognize when one is about to walk into and onto the sacred ground of another person.

It is at the moment that one person opens up the doors to the darkest corridors of the soul, revealing the presence and voice of the Divine speaking from within, that the other person must remove her shoes, that the other person must tread gingerly, fully acknowledging and living in the sacredness of what is being shared. It is in that moment that the dreams, fears, burdens, aspirations, and wounds that are unique to that individual are brought forth that the one being trusted with these revelations must grasp and fully acknowledge the gravitas of the situation.

The big mistake people make in relationships is that they treat the sacred as banal. They treat conversations and topics of holy ground as just another grocery list or just another daily conversation. There is no shift in countenance or comportment, not to mention communication. It falls on the one sharing deepest truth to indicate for the listener that this is, indeed, sacred ground and needs to be treated as such. And it falls on the hearer to remove his or her shoes, metaphorically speaking, to begin to tread ever so gently.

Far, far worse, however, and at the root of all other problematic relationships, is that most people do not treat their relationship with their own self, with their own soul, as anything more than an afterthought. For most people, relationship with the true self is something to be done after security is established, the house is built, the children are born and grown, and the bank account is stocked. For, it's usually about that time, somewhere in their 30s or 40s, that they realize how much life they've missed, how disconnected and unhappy they've become. It manifests as depression or anxiety, general malaise or discontent, but it's there, and it has grown and grown, over the years. Because they've never treated their own soul as sacred, giving it the homage and discipline necessary for its expansion and fertility, they become empty inside. Sadly, it's only when the soul has grown empty and arid that its significance is recognized. Often, a grief over the loss of time and life follows in its wake.

This book is entirely about that sacred ground of the soul. It is about the depth, gravitas, fear, and longing that are at the root of your madness, your scheming, your obsessions, your depression, your anxiety, and that incessantly churning mind you so wish to shut off. The fundamental operating principle of this book and my life's work is that at the core of the soul your voice and the voice of the Divine/Universe/God/Higher Self are indistinguishable. The still, small voice speaking from within, when heard, is the only true and lasting source of joy and peace in life. Yet, most people have never heard it; they cannot hear it. The sacred space of their soul has forever been cluttered with the garbage and false messages of everyone, particularly the most well-intentioned of parents and significant influences. When this still, small whisper of the Divine is unheard and blocked by fears and negative beliefs life becomes nothing more than anxiety, depression, and a mad desire to forever seek escape, in one form or another.

But when the blockages are removed, when the clutter of decades of fear and debilitating lies are removed, the soul breaks forth, enveloping the host body and mind, and manifesting in an external life of great joy. For the person who has the courage to clear the dross and commence a real relationship with their own self the reward is an integrated life – outer and inner become indistinguishable. No longer is there a grating, mid-chest, between who you are inside and who everyone sees outside. Depression and anxiety float away, which are the result of that grating of inner and outer worlds. Your soul, which has been fighting to be released onto your life, is finally set free, no longer constrained. And joy follows. Peace follows. Lightness of being follows. Great, great things, great actions, great callings, great purposes, grand endeavors all follow.

The sacred space of your soul is the alpha and the omega. Everything begins and ends here, down where your beliefs reside – not the beliefs you hold, but the beliefs you don't even know you hold, the beliefs that are controlling your life (more on that as we go). Heal it and you will never be the same. So, please, let me help you do so.

A few quickie notes:

- Illustrations note: I have deliberately not computer-generated the illustrations in this book, but drew them the same as I do in session with clients, every day, so as to keep the reader experience as true to counseling as possible. They're primitive, but clear.
- I don't care what you believe about God/gods, the Universe, Higher Power, or what have you. That's between you and your god or your own self. I have clients who are atheists, agnostics, Orthodox Jews, hardcore Christians, avowed Hindus, pantheists, panentheists, and more. I use god terms interchangeably with soul. You'll understand as you go.
- This book is two books. The main body and then Bonus Tracks in the back that are recommended at the end of certain chapters. The Bonus Tracks (BTs) are totally optional.
- I've added journaling, reading, and specific song recommendations at the end of some chapters to expand your interaction with the meat we are chewing on in that particular chapter.
- This book is based on 25 years as a spiritual counselor, which were, in turn, based on the previous 25 years as the son of a pastor father and spiritual counselor/educator mother, as well as four uncles who were clergy. Additionally, my bachelor's and master's degrees are in religion and spirituality (and mathematics). Quite literally, spirituality is my entire life. This is what I do. This is who I am. My life has been about finding the patterns in human spirituality and what it takes to bring healing to bruised and broken lives. A very large portion of my life's work and what I cover in counseling with clients are in this book. I liken this book to back in 1988 when the game show, *Wheel of Fortune*, started automatically giving contestants in the bonus round the letters R S T L N E in their puzzles, because most contestants already guessed those common letters, anyway. I'm giving you here what is

nearly always covered in my spiritual counseling work, so that my clients may be prepared before we even begin our work and so that non-clients may do much of the work themselves.

So come, let us find you some peace, clarity, power, and a whole lot of happiness!

Skol!

Sven
Winter 2018
Manhattan & Connecticut

THE CORE

CHAPTER 1

THERAPY JUST DOESN'T WORK FOR ME!

So there's this story I was told several times, as a kid. It's the story of a man who lived his entire life in a forest in a valley between giant mountain ranges. Deep, deep into those woods was his small cottage. There was a heavy wooden door, canopy of the high tree tops, and high mountains forever shrouding his home and vast environs in darkness. Always darkness.

He would venture out of his hermitage each day dressed in his big overcoat, whether to chop wood for the fire, kill an animal to eat or just to work this quiet, dark life he had carved out for himself. Some days his wanderings weren't far, some days quite far.

On one particular day, his hunt took him far from his cottage, farther than he had ever been. After a full morning of walking and stalking animals, he laid himself down to rest before commencing his return. As he slept, the strangest thing happened, an altogether new sensation took over his body. He awoke from his slumber to find it very bright. There was, it seemed, an opening in the canopy of the forest and a break in the mountain range beyond it, and through it came something he had never experienced before – a light as bright and warming as the very fires he would gather would to create. It stayed for only a brief period of time, but the brightness and warmth were completely new and bewildering. He liked it, but simultaneously was somewhat afraid, as it was something he had never experienced before in his life.

He returned home that afternoon, all the while thinking about that peculiar yet wonderful experience he had just had. In fact, that experience rather consumed his thoughts for a great many days, to come. So much so that he finally resolved to go back. And so he did, one day, then again another day, each time growing more fond of that brief brightness and heat. Yet one day, so mesmerized was he by the experience, he resolved to bring with him extra food and a blanket so that he might walk farther, perhaps discovering more of this brightness and warmth, prepared to stay the night, if necessary.

Find it he did. The following day, he discovered an open field covered in only tall, wild grasses. For the first time in his life he encountered something other than the dense, dark forest. Open space. And as he gazed up in wonderment at not only the full sky but the two mountain ranges of his valley, he noticed the light moving across one of the ranges, slowly, making the sky brighter, warming the air. He watched with bated breath as this first dawning of light swept across his entire landscape and colors seemed to spring to life. He removed his overcoat, as its heat was no longer necessary. Before long, the light had not only run over him and warmed his body and face completely, but became so bright that he had to shield his eyes. The whole experience was the most glorious thing he had ever felt. And there, in the grasses, he fell into a new, deep slumber, as he had never experienced before.

However, he knew he could not stay long. He had not brought provisions for two nights away. And he missed the safety of his tiny, dark cottage. So, after his warm nap, he walked back to the edge of the forest and with one last backward glance at the marvel of it all, he ducked back into the wood and began his long trek back to his cottage deep inside the canopy of the dark forest. It was an arduous journey to be done in one day and his overcoat seemed hotter and heavier than normal, even unnecessary, having been heated by the light. But stoked by a head full of new thoughts and even more questions, it was as if time did not exist. He was home before he knew it. Opening the thick, solid front door he gazed inside to his familiar everything, and for the first time in his life had a sensation of how small his home really was. The table he had hewn as a boy, the chair, the rug he had weaved with his own hands. All of it was warm in its own way, but...small. Tight, even.

For many days after, as he worked or hunted or ate his meals in silence, his mind forever returned to the field, the soaring mountains, the absence of darkness, and that mesmerizing, warm (even hot) light. Knowing he had to return and experience it again and confident he could do it in a day, now that he knew the way, he planned his trip. Just a day's provisions, and his lighter coat so that he might move quicker, particularly on his return. And depart he did, leaving very early; arriving earlier than last time, staying slightly longer, and, as last time, arriving to the door of his little cottage, even hitting his head on the top of the door frame as he entered. "That's odd. I've never done that before," he thought. While he knew his cottage had not actually shrunk, except in his perception, he realized it could only have happened because he was, quite strangely, standing taller, upright. Odd.

And this began his journeys. His day treks started earlier and earlier; his departure from the open field and its light got later and later, til one time the brightness had actually begun to slide past the other mountain range. That one was a more difficult hump back to the cottage. While energized by the light, it was also just a very long day. But he made it...and yet again, for the seemingly hundredth time, he hit his head as he entered his ever-littler home. Eventually, he started bringing two-day provisions, so that he could overnight near the field, just inside the canopy of the forest, as the safety of the woods was all he ever knew. He would spend two days in the light, then return. Two became four, after he had erected a lean-to at the edge of the woods, now part in the woods and part in the field. And before long he had brought his hunting pieces and a basket for gathering the richest berries and seeds, which he had found on the yonder side of the field.

And one day, as he lay in his makeshift grassy bed, clothed in the warmth and radiance of the light alone, he had the most startling epiphany. He realized he had everything. More, he realized there was nothing – not one thing, except sheer familiarity – left to draw him back to his hermitage. There was simply nothing he wanted anymore that that small, yet familiar past home held for him. He had not only found a new home but a new life, a whole new body of experiences.

So, for the last time, he took what had become a very, very long walk back to the cottage. For the next day or two, he assembled the one or two things left in his food stores. But everything else, the chair, the table, the rug. Well, they were the past and he knew it. The next morning, he slept in, woke, ate, dressed lightly, placing his old overcoat on the bed, made sure the fireplace was completely wet, and walked out, closing the old wood door behind him, running his hand over it's dark lumber. And with a smile, he turned and left, never to set eyes upon this tiny house again. Never, ever again. That day, his new life fully and finally began.

Living in The Light

This is the journey from darkness to light. This is what it is to finally come alive in this lifetime. Done rightly, this movement from a life of darkness to one of light is what the therapy experience is supposed to be. Whether it comes at the hands of a psychologist, a priest/pastor, a gifted friend or some other source of wise counsel, this movement from dark, small and hidden to open, warm, bright and fully ALIVE is the goal of introspection, courage, and a life lived deliberately.

Unfortunately, there seems to be a dearth of people, whether professional or lay, who possess both the personal experience and the capacity to transform others necessary to facilitate movement from darkness to light. Yet, this is very much what is most needed. This is, indeed, the great longing in our society – the longing to live in the light and to have people who actually possess the ability to help us get there, who know the journey of the dark forest, who can come back in and help us get out, who can, in short, set our soul free, who can take us from pain and darkness to joy, peace, and light.

I believe this is spirit work, not as normally construed by those typically charged with tending spiritual matters – i.e. religion. I believe what is most necessary for the liberation of so many caught in the darkness of unhappiness and even misery, despite all the possessions and accoutrements of supposed happiness in America, is the deepest inner work of the soul.

If there's one thing I have learned as a spiritual counselor for 25 years, speaking and lecturing at the graduate and undergraduate levels in the fields of spirituality and sociology of religion; if there's one thing I've learned as the son of two spiritual leaders (one pastor, one seminary professor), the nephew of a four clergy uncles, and the grandson of a woman who told her country pastor to 'stick it' and started her own church, in the 1940s; if there is one thing I have a learned as a man who has committed his life to his own spiritual journey and facilitating the spiritual growth of others, it is this:

4

Life is fair
...very, very fair.

Despite the nearly ubiquitous belief to the contrary, despite the incessant 'life's not fair' caterwauling of so many people who haven't won some life lottery yet, the old spiritual maxim rings true, "The rain falls on the just and the unjust," the rich and the poor, the old and the young. Specifically, life is unflinchingly fair when it comes to pain. No one escapes life without pain, without suffering, without anxiety and emptiness of the soul. No one goes through life without some form of spiritual depression. No one goes unscathed. No one.

Back on point, pain is what unites us all. That sounds a bit morbid, perhaps, but it's not. It's just truth. And it is that unity in pain that binds us, that brings out our compassion for each other, and that galvanizes human endeavors toward the same goal: to be loved and to be happy, to fight together the ugly animal of pain (and her brother, the fear of pain) seeking to pull us down into despair and deadness of the soul. So, if that be true, then the real challenge of life is getting from pain to love and happiness.

Getting There

Tragically, the elements of society that have grown up over time to meet or, at the very least, assuage that spiritual longing inside have largely failed us. Religion has fallen out of esteem and become inept for a great many people, even many of the religious, themselves. I'm a former pastor and know what religion, done well, is capable of. But it has fallen into such a sad state of disrepair in America. And psychology, whose business is internal pain and which I also have respect for, continues to disappoint a lot of people. And so, the longing and emptiness persist. From one day into the next, year after tumbling year.

What I'm getting at and what really needs to be spoken for us to start together on a solid base in our spiritual work together is that, if we're completely honest, for a great many of us there is no healing, no path to the light. There is nothing, it seems, that really makes the numbness and happiness of life go away, permanently. There are quick fixes and mild things that paper over the gnawing unhappiness. But there is no permanent fix, or so it feels. Whether it's in the confessional booth or pastor's study of your local church, or whether it's in the office of your marriage and family counselor or your psychologist, for a great many people therapy just doesn't hit the nail. This means we have a country full of people who are not making the transition from fear to happy and from pain to love, both outside and inside.

You're stumbling through life, hurting on the inside, fumbling relationships and careers, running from the tidal wave of emotions, staying as busy as you can. You keep struggling for control of life. You've created a great illusion on the outside: good career, good family, good kids, good title, good spouse, and good financial picture, even. Perhaps it's not just good, but great. All of your willpower and control have made a life that looks very presentable on the outside. But your illusion of control stops at your skin. Once the story moves inside, everything is out of control, isn't it? You've reached out to friends, to clergy perhaps, and of course to therapists (perhaps several therapists). Or, maybe like many of my most successful clients, you've reached out to no one, but just kept running from it, denying it, or stuffing it down.

Yet, nothing helps or you're sick of running. Tiny gains are regularly outweighed by massive frustrations, not to mention the loss of money, time and energy from ineffective therapy. And, all the while, your ever-churning mind rages on and on with confusion, self-doubt, longing to know your true self, self-loathing, and brief spurts of willpower that later get bogged down by lethargy, anger, or just plain exhaustion. A hearty mix of anxiety and depression, in one form or another, rule your life, even when you're able to keep them well-hidden, even when you stay medicated or self-medicated. You're just a hair's breadth away from losing it at any moment, aren't you?

And nothing – nothing! – seems to help, especially the one thing that is supposed to make this very unhappiness go away: therapy.

Some people have good experiences in therapy. But sadly, a great many people don't. And so, you're left feeling stuck. You can't get yourself out of your own problems and you can't seem to find anyone who can help you. There are countless reasons it may not work for you. For example:

- **If you're a guy**, therapy stinks because it feels like therapists have it in for you before you even ever walk in the door.

Heck, therapy as a profession, as well as science and society are convinced that men are utterly devoid of feelings, less developed emotionally, and purely incapable of expressing feelings (all of which are asinine beliefs, patently untrue; if anything, I've found men to often be my most honest, open, and highly sensitive clients, if and only if they have a therapist they both trust and respect). How many times have you heard, "Girls develop emotionally faster than boys," and "Men don't express their feelings well"? Such condescending beliefs have become this giant cultural myth. So, you're deemed an emotional invalid before the first conversation even starts and are forever dogged by the feeling that you are looked down upon. Or, if that's not always the case, the industry is so rampant with this belief system that men are quite reasonably skeptical of the field, thereby unwilling or unable to conjure the trust upon which great therapy is predicated.

- **Perhaps you're a woman** for whom therapy stinks because you get 8-10 sessions into it, – telling your life story and revealing all your pain – before you realize your psychologist blows, because she has nothing original. She has no deep insights, no challenging questions – with which to push you and encourage growth, nothing to contribute, at all. You realize you're paying someone to do nothing but sit back and listen to you, as if you are able to self-direct your therapy, failing to realize that if you knew how to fix your doggone self you wouldn't be seeing a therapist, to begin with. And what's worse is that you then leave that therapist and move on to the next therapist, who was recommended by some friend, only to discover (8-10 sessions in) that this one isn't even one ounce better than the last. And so, you're stuck in this ugly, wasteful, frustrating chapter upon chapter of spilling your guts and getting nowhere.

- **Or,** almost worse than that, you stay in a counseling relationship that isn't getting you anywhere and you know it isn't getting you anywhere, but you stay because it's familiar and it's safe, never pushing you very hard out of your comfort zone, yet allowing you to live in the illusion that you're actually doing something to solve your life problems. Perhaps you are withholding large chunks of truth from your therapist, fearing what she will think of you, fearing the ramifications of admitting your truth, or fearing the seemingly great unknown if you were to really start opening up.

- **Worse still** – and it's far more common than you'd think – a great many folk actually flat out lie to their therapists. Yes, they pay someone to help them, but then give disinformation, preferring to stay deeply rooted in their own inertia and fears. And sadly, most therapists have no idea how to break through the lies and the fear that keep people from opening up.

But, interestingly, the real problem isn't just that you dislike therapy (or maybe you like it but are very, very discontent with the whole thing). *The real problem is that therapy so often doesn't work.* Let's be clear, if your therapy actually powerfully and permanently worked, you likely wouldn't be reading this book. There would be no need.

And so, in the end, what this really means is that you're just craving something that can actually, fully, and finally HELP YOU!!! Right? I mean, isn't what you really want, more than anything, to be over the crud that you know is there in you and in your life? Isn't what you really want to be healed, finally and definitively? Isn't what you really want to know peace, know purpose, know true clarity of life, and to know actual happiness when you wake up in the morning?

Well, I'm here to tell you it's not only possible, it's quite doable and doable quickly. But, it means going into some heavy stuff, perhaps the very stuff you've been avoiding your entire life; you know, the stuff you've been running from. B'cuz, until you look at, sit in, and deal with the real stuff of your past and your life and your fears, you ain't never going anywhere. (Ignore the double-negatives throughout the book. You get the point.) You're going to stay stuck, just making new iterations of the same problem, for years, for decades. And you'll get into your 50s, 60s, and 70s with nothing more than resigned regret.

And, truth is, you don't want that, do you? Of course not. You want life. You want to finally feel fully alive, not just once, not just 'til the weekly therapy session wears off, but daily, permanently.

Badass Counseling

My method, Badass Counseling®, is the rather organic result of my belief that I could do it better. Decades ago, having been raised by a family of spiritual leaders, who succeeded, failed, and succeeded, many times over, I began to explore what would need to happen to create highly effective spiritual counsel and leadership. This required going deep into my own spiritual crud – where all good spiritual journeys start – wrestling with it all, clearing it out, and beginning to craft spiritual solutions from the soil up.

My method is nearly three decades of work condensed into a very tight, very fast, very overwhelming, and very effective technique for taking very highly successful individuals, couples, families, and even organizations/groups from pain to happiness and from fear to love. It's the fusion of wisdom, spirituality, athleticism, creativity and academic traditions, and a big ol' dose of fire, violence of the soul, and hard work.

The rain falls on the unjust and just. We all do suffer in life. Pain is as integral to life as sunshine and water. Most people make the mistake of running from it, rather than to it. But, I come from athletics and military, where the most difficult, painful, violent, challenging, failure-filled workouts yield the greatest fruit.

Over the past 25 years, weaving that military and athletics past into my lifetime of religion and spirituality as a pastor's kid and later a pastor myself, I radically changed my understanding of God. When I was an NCAA Head Coach for Strength, my teams would come into my gym for the express purpose of being made stronger, faster, bigger, and, most importantly, mentally tougher. But muscle growth (and mental growth) does not occur during the workout. Muscles are, essentially, torn down *during* the workout. Muscle growth occurs in the period of rest *after* the workout. But if the athlete, whether novice or professional, is not first taken to failure, fatigue, and extreme hardship, the athlete will not ever become stronger, faster, meaner, and bigger. Ever. Muscle growth is 100% dependent upon being torn down first.

Somewhere in the last 20 years, I had the epiphany that *that* is exactly how God works. Thanks to the research of Joseph Campbell, we know that one of the meta-themes extending across nearly all religions and sacred scriptures, past or present, is this notion that the gods send trials, not as punishment but as strengthening agents. Particularly in the Judeo-Christian gospel and history, there is an abundance of evidence that God uses 'bad' to create good. It's not just that God redeems bad created by humanity, but actually sends it for the up-building of humanity. One need look no further than the central Christian story: God sent his son – knowing full well in advance that the boy would suffer and die – so that humanity would forever have new life. God uses supposed 'bad' to create good. The things we perceive to be painful are meant for our growth and strength, so that we may further become instruments of God's love in the world. Just as my athletes would hate me at the end of their workouts and you likely hate your trainer or coach at the end of leg day, we at times hate God or at least hate what we perceive to be God's recriminations and scorching of our lives. God is, effectively, the Great Coach in the Sky, so to speak. Everything, even perceived pain, is for your growth. Everything.

This is why so much therapy – whether psychological, spiritual, or even life coaching, yoga, and energy healing – just isn't that effective. Either it fails to go deep enough to the root sources of an individual's pain, which are usually found in childhood; or it seeks only to release the physical and emotional pain associated with the initial wounding. But the point of soul work isn't the pain you experienced but what that experience taught you about yourself. It's not enough to release the pain. It is to ask the pain what it was sent – either by the Universe, God, or your own soul – to teach you about yourself and about life. The purpose of going into the crud from your past is also to discern the affect those negative experiences had on your core belief system about yourself. And very, very few people can do that work on their own, unguided by a teacher. One of the purposes of this book is to both purge your pain and help you discern what that pain has been trying to teach you.

Your problem – or one of them – is simply that you've been framing pain wrongly. You've been incorrectly taught that the pain of your life was either completely random (bad luck, if you will, as if completely outside the scope of God and God's power), your fault, or God's punishment, all of which are wrong. Whether you like it or not, everything is to make you stronger and wiser. And the sooner you see it as such – i.e. the sooner you stop running from your pain and start asking the pain and the gods in what ways this hardship is the greatest blessing of your life – the sooner you become a more powerful and more compassionate agent of God's love in the world.

God is love and a loving God. Unfortunately, far, far too many lay people, pastors, and theologians make the grand mistake of wanting 'loving God' to mean 'nice God'. People repeat the ridiculous and ill-begotten nonsense, "God doesn't send pain" or "God would never hurt humanity or me." But there is no Biblical precedent for such thinking. Heck, there ain't nowhere in any religion's scripture where God is pitched as 'nice.' Just like the great coaches in any sport, God kicks our butts to strengthen us; and sometimes that ass-whuppin' doesn't feel 'nice' and even hurts. Those who've sought to dispel the maxim 'no pain, no gain' in the athletic world would be quite uncomfortable and out-of-sorts with honest spirituality. God ain't nice, and God never was. And 'loving' never meant 'always nice.'

What feels like the incessant pain of life is God forever trying to grow you, push you, challenge you, knock you around, rattle you, and shred you....all for your pruning, your growth, your depth, your strength, and the long-lasting oxytocin release of true peace. And you've been running from it! You've been running from the greatest instrument of your growth, the greatest conduit to your happiness, like a lazy man or a coward runs from hard workouts or avoids the gym.

My work is with those who are looking for something different, those for whom regular counseling, religion, and psychology just don't work, those who feel marginalized by the process, and those individuals who aren't just having problems in their head but whose souls are hurting, who have pain and emptiness inside. My work is like the hardest leg day in the gym – painful, especially in the beginning, but immensely fruitful after the crud and pain are cleared away. And, lastly, my work is with people who are looking for a counselor who is, on a personal level, a different animal, not your average counselor type, not your average spiritual type. For, again, any good counsel grows out of the woman (or man) herself – who she is, where she has been, the dragons she has slayed, and the wisdom she has mined from her suffering. It's a bit of that *When Harry Met Sally* one-liner, "I'll have what she's having." People want the peace, power, purpose, and happiness they see lived in the life of a great counselor. Would you take investment advice from someone ever poorer than you? Training advice from someone ever weaker or slower than you? So why, for the love of God, would you take soul advice and life counsel from someone whose message is canned, from a book, and clearly not implemented in the person's life?

So, I'm asking you to take a ride with me. Trust me. Let me carry you. Open. Do the stuff I tell you to do. Read the books and listen to the songs I tell you to. Meditate on what I lay before you. Hear my words. And, above all else, have the courage to go into yourself and sit in that which you've formerly run from.

As you do this, begin to feeeeeel your truth. The goal is to begin to be, say, do and become that which you truly are. Do not let the pain you have experienced become your reason for distrusting the Universe/God/soul work. For, everyone is suffering, not just you. Pain is universal; what you do with it – specifically what you let it teach you about life and yourself – is what determines the trajectory of your life and the power of your communion with the spirit of the Universe, as it whispers to you from deep within your own soul.

To finally become your truest self and find your greatest happiness you must let go of the not-so-great life you've been holding on to, not just the pain but the fears and the craving for security, above all else. You must allow the grasp of that which is merely familiar to release you to find and live in the light and the warmth. You must let go of the neurotic longing for control. You must let yourself fall into the arms of the Universe. It is speaking to you from within, always has. And life doesn't truly begin, until you begin to listen to that quiet inner voice and trust it – trust what it's leading you to, trust what it's leading you away from, and trust that, no matter what happens, you'll be okay.

Once you have the courage to trust, you then have the courage to be, say, do, become, have, and believe that which you truly are. That's when everything changes, and stuff begins to fall out of the sky. Stuff you can't even begin to imagine. I've seen it, daily, weekly, consistently, both in my own life and in the lives of nearly all of my clients. I know it sounds hokey as heck, but I see magical, completely unexpected stuff happen in clients' lives as they clear the underbrush of the soul and begin to live their truth. Once you break through that wall that is the fear of revealing who you really are to the world, amazing things begin to happen in the most unexpected and glorious ways.

Song Recommendation

Throughout the course of this book, I will be offering songs for you to buy and use as part of your reading and meditation process. This is heavy stuff we're chewing on in this book. And, sometimes, getting the messages through music has the effect of feeling them more deeply, experiencing them more profoundly, and engaging them more meaningfully. In that vein, I commend to your listening pleasure and spirit work the powerfully intense music and lyrics of **Evanescence**, *Bring Me To Life*.

https://www.youtube.com/watch?v=3YxaaGgTQYMBRINGMETOLIFE

Journaling Recommendation

Alright, now we get into some really deep work. Take out a pad of paper and pen, or sit at your laptop, or perhaps even thumb-type in the notes section of your cell phone. I'm a big believer in pen and paper, but call me 'old school.' We're going to do some heavy journaling here. If you've never really journaled, great. If you have, terrific. Doesn't matter. What we're getting into isn't journaling about the color of the sky and how pretty the trees and flowers are today. What we're journaling about is the real stuff going on inside you, the stuff you've been running from. Until you reach the state of lasting bliss, you oughta be journaling daily. Heck, multiple times a day.

The simplest way I have found to get my mind going, when journaling, is simply to write a question at the top of the page, then spend a page or ten, fleshing out my answers to that question. Just keep journaling until your mind and soul are empty, or until a new or deeper question comes up. Then go in the direction of answering that question, or even coming back to a question from days or weeks earlier.

There are no right or wrong answers, as long as you're flushing out your feelings, not just your thoughts. Both. Just keep flushing it out of you. And there are certain default questions you should always be coming back to, even if the questions of the day were something completely different. Keep coming back to the questions:

1. What do I really, really feel about this, if I were to be totally honest?
2. Why?
3. What's really eating at me about this situation?
4. Why am I so angry? So sad? So afraid?
5. What's the single biggest and most powerful FEAR driving this whole equation?
6. Is there one person I'm having strong feelings about? Who?
7. What are those feelings – anger, love, happiness, frustration, disappointment?
8. How is this hardship or pain I'm experiencing the single greatest blessing that could have ever happened to me? What are the gods trying to teach me with this pain? What am I still not learning or still resisting that the ongoing pain keeps trying to get through to me?
9. In what ways am I feeling called to be an instrument of stronger love and compassion in the world? How has the past pain – the past workouts in the spiritual gym with the badass coach in the sky – perfectly prepared me for the work ahead?

But, for today's question at the top of your page I want you to start with either these few questions or just put each of the questions (below) at the top of a different page and simply journal and journal, until you're done for this day or this moment.

1. In your journal, list the five most persistent irritants in your life. These are not the giant pain sources in your life. These are the incredibly small, yet ever-present drains on your focus, energy, or happiness that are always there.
2. Now, write out why each of these is such an irritant and how your life would be different (be as specific as possible) if each of these, item by item, were not in your life.
3. Next, tell me the story in your journal of the single most traumatic even in your life. Use as much detail as possible,

as well as the most graphic, strong, even offensive language you can, if that is what you feel when writing it.

4. Lastly, journal out the one decision, above all else, you most regret making in your entire life.

CHAPTER 2

BECOMING TRUEST SELF AND UNLEASHING GREATNESS

So where are we? What the heck is really going on inside each one of us? What is it that really, really, REALLY drives us to therapy? What is it we really seek?

It's not the desire for security, though that is a big driver in many lives. It's really not wealth, though that has appeal, too. Further, what we really seek is not even the meaning of life.

As we age, inch by inch, year into year, we realize that what we really seek from this life is the experience of ALIVENESS. We want to feel fully alive, just once. Or, we long to maybe even feel on fire and passionate about life, for a long time, maybe even for good. And, by the time we get around to wanting therapy we realize how much aliveness we've lost, whether we've lost time, lost energy, or just lost our own self and sense of being REAL.

It is that sense of invigoration that we seek; that vitality, and feeling truly on fire for life and all that it holds. It's more than mere joy or even inner peace. Aliveness includes happiness and peace, yet also includes this flair of true excitement. Not every minute of every day, but an over-arching feel, day in and out, that life is finally, truly, fully in blossom – simultaneously exciting, calm, and largely effortless. That's what we're all really seeking. Aliveness!

Where ALIVENESS Isn't

With my more rogue clients – those who aren't as comfortable with the fuzzy spiritual language, which is the greater preponderance of my clientele – I describe it as the desire we all have to get high. We are all trying to get high in life. We really are. That's why we gamble, acquire more and more possessions, go out to eat incessantly, over-work, do drugs, have kids, get into religion, book vacations, over-exercise, go to every Springsteen or Phish concert, and do almost every manner of human activity. Everything is an attempt to, in some form or another, get high. But, why?

Generally, we seek to get high because life sucks so badly that we seek escape. It bores us, numbs us, or just bleeds all life from us. So we desire to feeeeeel something. Anything! We're seeking something lasting in the arms of something temporary. Or, life is so intense or painful that we seek to get numb, check out, or forget for a minute all that afflicts us...so we can finally breathe, for a moment.

It is why people get hyper-addicted to sports teams or even horror movies, for instance. It is the desire to feeeeel something. It is the reason people gamble or become over-involved in their children's lives, either living vicariously through them – pushing them to get new achievements, which the parent can then draft off of – or enmeshing in them, using them for affection needs and/or even emotional approval and problem-solving.

This is a big reason people cheat in relationships, do drugs/drink heavily, or engage in the several hours of bingeing and purging of bulimia, for example. For those brief hours, the incessant churning of the mind – the constant negative thoughts, beliefs, and other life-killing energies – gets turned off. There is release, albeit momentary. And when these activities, such as bingeing and purging or excessive pot-smoking or gambling become life-consuming (when the quest for escape is literally unceasing), it becomes very easy to focus on that behavior as the problem in your life, as if the addiction, itself, is the real problem. Most therapies try to get rid of the addiction or bad behaviors, so that the person can be more ensconced in his or her life, when it was that life that drove 'em to the bad behaviors, in the first place.

However, the real problem is the underlying belief system you have about yourself. That is what's driving the problem. Those mad escape activities have been your friend, in a manner of speaking, getting you through the very hard life of living with what's going on inside you. Those messed-up and consuming behaviors will almost effortlessly go away, if the real root of the problem is addressed and taken care of. Destroy the debilitating core beliefs and new creation follows in its wake. You no longer need to run from or numb yourself from life, because you have created a life that you want to be engaged in, more and more. But again, that only happens when you have gone down to the very bedrock of your soul where the self-destructive core beliefs are pressed into the firmament of your existence. Anything less will be a half-solution created by not going deep enough. And half-solutions look pretty for a while, but eventually feel forced and fall flat, long term.

Continuing in this thread of 'where aliveness isn't', far too easily in America we wrap happiness only in terms of the standard American Dream sort of things: house, family, cars, title, great career, vacations, and dinners out. "If I can just get everything – *have* everything – then I'll be happy and have peace." We think, "Once I get success and money, THEN I can be who I want to be and do the things I want to do." And that thinking is always driven by someone trying to prove themselves to someone else, first, and *then* being who they really want to be. Mistakenly, though they're not aware of it, they think approval must precede authenticity, as if permission to be real must be (first) given by an external source.

That thinking is always, at its core, driven by the fear of living authentically NOW: "Only when I've proven my worth (to others) can I live my truth (for me)." And that's a path that rarely ends well or comes without pain, no matter how much we're sold on its merits by society. This absorption into the American Dream and it's supposed promise of happiness can last decades. But, eventually the veneer fades, the promise we thought it held erodes. Whether we can articulate it as such, or not, we realize that the things we seek to have get us high for only a short time.

Now, I'm all for the American Dream, but not as a primary source of happiness and love. American Dream-related acquisitions are never enough to satiate what we really seek, deep down. One of the grand clichés in my work is the number of people who have the house, boat, title, vacations, great kids, great spouse, great career, etc, and yet are utterly empty inside and numb.

We long for ALIVENESS, now. Yet, very young, we begin getting our wings clipped, bit by bit, year by year. People want to rein us in, control us, make us easier for them to tolerate, deal with, or manipulate to their ends. But our soul calls out to us, each day, longing to be set free, longing to fly at full wingspan, longing for that lasting happiness and peace, today, now, in the present, not in some distant future. Essentially, the soul is calling you to proclaim and live your worth now, rather than waiting to somehow gain approval and worth from some arbitrary figure from your past (or present) – a waiting that rarely yields the fruit it desires. (And, the simple truth is that ain't nobody else gonna fall in love with you 'til you fall in love with you.)

Not only that, we seek flow – that feel that life has picked up positive momentum that carries us along, that we no longer have to grind the pedals one more crank to get the bike to move just a few more feet.

Hangover vs. Carry-over

What we further discover, with age, is that nearly all of the attempts to get high end. We seek something lasting, but keep running into highs that burn out. And, more often than not, we crash. There's a hangover. Whether it's gambling, cheating, smoking grass, boozing, absorption in your children, excessive fitness or yoga, sports obsession, or just about anything else, there's always a hangover, a come-down or grand letdown. The high, it seems, never lasts.

We discover that what we really want is a high that has no hangover, but has *carry-over*, from one day to the next, perhaps even from one year to the next. And if we've really done our life homework – releasing the pain of the past and changing our core beliefs – we no longer need a high that enables us to escape the past. We grow quite content with a high that is not so sharp and vertical, perhaps less high but more enduring, more lasting. We seek that vigor and excitement, with flow, with inner calm, and without the crash. That desire to never come down is what drove the escalation of your obsessions, in the first place – always more, always higher, always something to drag you out of tomorrow's inevitable crash.

The desire for a high with carry-over
– that carries over from day to day, without hangover –
is what we all seek,
whether we're consciously aware of it or not.

And it is not only possible, but necessary for feeling like life is well spent.

How?

A sense of true ALIVENESS in this life is very doable, but it demands doing a bit of work; three things, in particular. First, every piece of your past that created the crud in your soul is a memory, right? But each memory has an emotional charge, either positive, negative, or neutral, sort of like every atom comes with a charge. That's why some memories come with positive feelings, some have the power to make you feel yucky, and some are just memories – thoughts – without any affect, or feeling, at all. And it is the charge, not the memory itself, that is doing the damage to your soul and life. Negatively charged memories have a weight to them that drags you down from the inside. The greater the accumulation, the greater the heaviness. Thus, the first step toward aliveness is to de-charge the memories, to remove the negative charges they carry. Can you imagine having lots of memories of different life events but not getting agitated inside or sad, mad, or frustrated when you recall that memory? Can you imagine just having a lifetime of memories without the heaviness many of them bring? It is tremendously freeing and light.

But that quest for lightness of the soul also means selectively releasing the positively charged memories, too. Why? Think about it. Positively charged memories actually have the power to hold you back, slow you down, and keep you looking backward, rather than forward. We've all had the experience of thinking back on the loving memories of an ex-boyfriend or ex-girlfriend, and to find ourselves obsessing and thinking 'what if.' We've all experienced life stopping (or love life stopping) because we're so consumed with loving, warm, happy, positive thoughts of some ex. Well, that is a perfect example of positively charged memories actually being destructive to our life, our forward movement, and our growth.

Another example, we often make life harder today by focusing on how great life used to be. The destruction wrought by relative success and relative happiness comes not from comparing ourselves to those around us (as is too often the case with many people) but to a past, happier version of ourselves or a past version who seemed to have so many more opportunities in front of him or her. Or, we stay fixated on a childhood home, or the glory days of college, or previous successes.

Second, and far more importantly, true aliveness demands destroying the impact of those past negative experiences, particularly the impact on your core beliefs. This is huge! HUGE! Your core beliefs are fundamentally the operating system that drives your entire life, whether you're aware of them or not. Most people aren't. We have stories, memories, and values about life that we remember, know, and consider part and parcel of our being and existence. But below that are the imprints, beliefs, and non-memories (events that occurred and messages that were received, but none of which are remembered or consciously understood) that are innate to who we are, but are completely unknown to our conscious mind. Unearthing, identifying, and, hopefully, changing these core beliefs requires either a spiritual (not religious) pro or a disciplined commitment of time and energy to do it oneself, using proper tools.

However, the absolute core and most important element of spiritual counseling is the changing of one's core beliefs. Without that most fundamental change, nothing else changes or even matters.

Third, moving into a state of true aliveness also demands living in full concert with your own intuition, tuning into your body, your feelings, and what feels right inside of you, no longer allowing your power source to be outside of you in someone else – be it parents, spouse, boss, children, friends, or society. It is to finally be governed by the quiet whisper of your soul and not the fears tumbling around in your head or the negativity and expectations of those around you.

At the core of your being is your truest self. And down there it finds union with the pulse of the universe, itself. Whether you're aware of it or not, what's most missing in your life is a relationship with your own self. To fully commune with your own deepest and truest self is what it means to finally be fully alive. Deadness comes from disconnect from your true self, as written on your soul. All the external trappings of life cannot come anywhere near the life satisfaction that comes from full communion with the spirit of the Universe lying deep inside you, whispering, in a voice indistinguishable from your very own.

Finding The Patterns

For decades, I have counseled some of the worlds wealthiest people, as well as street people. I have counseled faculty at the top universities in the world, as well as struggling teens/20s. Top Olympians and the physically infirm. The boldest and the most afraid. The oldest and the youngest.

The intrepid and the intimidated. The successful and the struggling. As well as couples struggling so valiantly to save or fight for their relationship.

Additionally, 30 years ago, I was a math major and religious studies major in college, and my Master's degree is in divinity – spirituality. If there's one thing my math/science history gave me, it's a nose for patterns. And if there's one thing the decades in spirituality and religions brought, it's my love for the human soul. This book is a compilation of the patterns I've seen in human nature and neglect of the soul. My whole life, including my own deepest inner work, is about seeing patterns in the human experience and using these to bring people into greater experience of the spiritual side of life, which starts and ends inside, and which is tapped into through your intuition. It is found in solitude, quiet, and times of reconnecting to your own source energy. It is this spiritual side, and only this side, that has the power to yield the true fruit you seek – flow, happiness, peace, carry-over...ALIVENESS. For that truly is the point of it all.

Lastly

I know you feel weak. I know you want to give up. It's not time. No. Not now. It's time to change you. It's time for me to give you what I've been given. It's time to turn all that crud around. Now. Today. This week. This month. It's time.

Song Recommendation

1) I love this kickass song of hope and the great opening of the soul. Download and dig this upbeat tune and monster lyrics of *Unwritten*, by **Natasha Bedingfield**.

https://www.youtube.com/watch?v=b7k0a5hYnSIUnwritten2

2) Download *Till I Collapse*, by **Eminem**. It's great on YouTube with the video from the *Real Steel* movies. But the song, by itself, is monster.

https://www.youtube.com/watch?v=ytQ5CYE1VZwTillICollapse

Bonus Tracks

For the reader looking for more, check out Bonus Track 1: The Root Of All Depression And Anxiety. It's in the back of the book.

CHAPTER 3

YOU'RE RUNNING!

Do you want to know the reason you're:

- Smoking so much weed?
- Addicted to lots and lots and lots of sleep?
- Surrounding yourself with incessant commotion, from crazy kid schedules to lots of dogs/animals, from constant appointments to an ever-demanding career?
- So addicted to your sports teams?
- Holed up in bed, away from kids, responsibilities, spouse, and life?
- Having sex with and concomitantly obsessing over another woman's husband (or another man's wife), as well as subsequently lying about it?
- Constantly looking forward to the next vacation, trying to constantly get away?
- Shopping, shopping, shopping, shopping and more shopping?
- Pasted to the couch, watching insane amounts of TV?
- Drinking 3-4 cocktails every night?
- Working four jobs?
- Seriously OD-ing on porn?
- Working crazy hours, week in and week out, year in and year out?
- Betting so much money on football, baseball, and other sports; meanwhile missing family events because you're on your cell or in the other room tracking all the college scores?
- Spending so much time just staying as busy as possible?
- Still caught in the loop of that eating disorder?
- Overdoing the fitness schedule?

- Ingesting crazy amounts of prescription medications, even though your physical health is good?
- Addicted to yoga, going to several classes per day, every day?
- Pushing as hard as you can on seemingly endless caffeine?
- Unable and unwilling to sit still for more than 15 minutes, incessantly in motion?
- Continuing to attract friends and lovers (and even family members) who hurt you?

The simple truth is, you're madly engaged in these neurotic paths, because

You're running!

Plain and simple. As hard as you can. You're doing everything in your power to run from that tidal wave of pain that has been chasing you your whole life. You're tired and running to keep that lifetime of feelings from rising up inside you, ringing in your ears, and knocking you down. You sell it as running 'to' so much in life, but in truth you're always running 'from' that great unseen force that you dare not talk about or even take a moment to think about, so terrifying is its nearness in your life.

You're either running from:
- You're incredibly, ridiculously painful past (and present?),
- The mind-numbing dissatisfaction and boredom of your life,
- All the voices in your life that have been telling you what to do and how to run your life, or
- All the voices in your life that are forever criticizing you.

The fear of that wave of pain overwhelming you is so great that you run as hard as you possibly can. You do everything in your power to keep those voices inside you from rising up and consuming you. You're certain they would kill you if they caught you. And so you run, in every direction, in no direction.

And yet, the real truth and tragedy of it all is there will be no joy until you have the courage to let that giant tidal wave

26

overwhelm you, let it knock you down, let it rise up from within you and finally pass out of you. Until you actually face that which terrifies you most, you will forever run. The wave is always there, until you face it.

Running Without Knowing You're Running

Hope, a Pacific-Northwest client in her mid-40s, recently told me she had the epiphany to end all epiphanies, while in the final moments of her Sunday morning yoga class. "Sven, for whatever reason, I was thinking about the birth of my first (of three) sons. 23 years ago, I had invited my older sister into my room for the whole birthing process. I wanted to honor her and make her feel loved by sharing my most special moment in my life. And it was the craziest thing, right after my son came out and was being weighed and cleaned by the nurses. My sister, who had birthed both of her children by C-section, in that sacred moment of my greatest joy and greatest vulnerability, said to me, "You're so weak! You complained through the whole thing.

"Sven," she continued, "It hit me on that yoga floor, Sunday, that I have been defending myself for 23 years. And I started to cry. What you have been telling me finally sunk in. There is this whole deep well of pain that I never even knew was there. I have been running from that pain without even realizing I was running from it. Because I've just always been defending myself, I never even knew there was pain behind it and under it. But I did what you told me to do whenever pain comes up. I just sat in it. I let myself cry the whole day. And it was scary, because I realized how big it was and that it went back with her, long before Tommy was born."

Hope never knew that her pain was there, because she was too busy protecting herself from an aggressive older sister and younger brother. 23 years! She never knew that going into that pain could yield such fruit. Defending oneself is the natural response to a perceived threat. But few of us are ever taught that there's a second step – to go past the defense and anger to allow oneself to feel the original pain that was inflicted. By seeing it, acknowledging it, and feeling it, we purge it. When it is out of us, it is no longer in us. We're no longer running. That is healing.

"Sven, by the end of the weekend, I felt better already. I knew there was a whole lot more that needed to come out, but I already felt lighter just from what that one day of mourning brought. It was amazing! I know my life is going to be different now. I get it, Sven. I finally get what you've been teaching me. I've finally experienced it. I'm actually excited to find more painful experiences in my past, because I want even more lightness."

"The cure for the pain is in the pain."
--Rumi, Sufi poet

Facing The Fears

Interestingly, whether it's a hardcore addiction, defensiveness, or a serious compulsion that you just can't seem to stop (even if you know it's killing you), your addiction and the facing of your fears are inversely proportional. The more you go into your deepest fears, the more your compulsive, defensive, and destructive behaviors decrease. See, the more you face your heaviest fears, the less power they have over you, because they release the burden on your heart. Looking at and sitting in the fears have the profound effect of near-completely eliminating their power over you.

Thus, not only does your confidence increase, which is a nice but less significant effect, but what also increases is the room in your head and heart. For, the grand effect of it all is the killing of the voices, fears, and sheer volume of the people you've been running from. Therefore, your need to run is radically reduced. The pot smoking, drinking, obsessive exercising, absorption into your kids' lives, and so forth all fade away. The soul no longer needs them as an escape mechanism. You're creating a life you no longer feel the need to run from. Life itself makes you happy.

On the flipside, the less you face your fears, the more your addictions and/or compulsions continue to increase. Also quite interesting in this equation is the fact that just reducing your addictions does not have the effect of reducing the fears driving them, which is a common mistake of those just treating behaviors. *Without addressing the underlying fears and core beliefs, nothing changes in the long term.* Worse still,

28

There is no external reality
That can make the internal reality permanently go away.

One of the great myths that keeps you stuck in unhappiness and fear is, "If I can just change my external circumstances or get more of everything (money, love, security, fame, respect, possessions), then my inside reality will change, the tidal wave will go away. That, really, is one of life's greatest disappointments and shocks. No amount of stuff or experiences can, in the long run, make that hole inside full or make soul pain disappear. Most people don't experience the truth of that until middle age. And it is a brutal, brutal teacher. You realize you've spent decades pursuing a myth, spent your life on a path that holds nothing at the end. Sure, it had some fun times along the way and perhaps even provided you a decent living. But that gaping hole inside you, or that gnawing truth you've been running from, is still there, waiting for you like an old foe waiting to be vanquished.

So, you can keep running, if you like, if you think the running will help – i.e. if you're still too scared to turn and look it all in the face. You can just be as stubborn as you want to be, perhaps even taking pride in your stubbornness, perhaps convinced you can solve it all yourself and that you don't need anyone's help. Go ahead, stubbornly run!

But, here's the real truth of the matter,

Your pain WILL get worse!

This stuff doesn't magically go away. This stuff doesn't magically heal itself. No, when the gods talk, they will be heard and heeded. You can try to quiet their voices with all your pursuits. You can attempt to quiet the voice of your very own soul, longing to be heard, so that you can be set free. You can keep running, or at least try, but the gods will exact their wrath on a life that they know to be less than you, a life they wish to extract you from.

The Universe – your own soul! – longs to lead you to higher ground and immensely greater joy. But we so cling to that which is secure. Security is safe. And the soul and Universe are not the least bit interested in safe. They exist to lead you to abundant life, fulfilled life, exhilarating life – that which you *know* you want but are terrified to pursue. And so, they whisper. That still, small voice in the bottom of your soul. That tiny pulse rising up from deep within, longing to be heard.

Everything else is fiction and ultimately a dead end. Until we have communion with and act on that whisper of the soul, there is nothing but unfulfillment, churning of the gut, spinning of the mind, and joylessness and anxiety.

Do you have the courage to find and heed your voice?

Song Recommendation

Buy these songs.

1) A great song that gets at our society's obsession with running from our problems, particularly in using drugs to run. I love this song, so intense! *Kevin* (Feat. Leon Bridges), by **Macklemore & Ryan Lewis.**
https://www.youtube.com/watch?v=rnL9kzxRtbIKevin
2) The singer and wordsmith, who provided the soundtrack for the most intense 10-15 years of my own spiritual journey was **Dan Fogelberg**. This song, *Ghosts*, nails the horrible and beautiful https://www.youtube.com/watch?v=Hn2-VLqAGpgGhosts memories dripping with high emotion that we run from. They sneak up like ghosts, when we're alone, when we're relaxed, and when we're tired. And so, we run. Solitude is too scary. Idling is terrifying. Nothing will do, except to run, until we simply tire of running.

Journaling Recommendation

1. What is your preferred means of running? Are you an addict? Do you like the ponies? Jack Daniels? Maybe your poison is good ol' American over-working or over-exercising? Smoke a lot of grass? Paste your butt to the couch and binge incessantly on this Golden Age of television they say we're in? Or maybe it's just sheer busyness – constant movement and commotion? Or is it Oreos, pizza, bread, and more food? HOW are you running?
2. And now the real whopper: WHEN did you start running? I know you're going to say 'I don't know' or 'It came

gradually'. And maybe both of those answers are true, but I want you to push harder. Give me an answer. Find it. When do you recall the balance being tipped? When did you really most start running?

3. And what triggered it, at that point? I mean, you didn't start running a year or five earlier. And you could've started five years later. Why did you start running from your feelings at that particular time in life? What happened?

4. From what are you running? What is the one message you can't bear to hear or look at?

5. What do you most fear in your life?

6. What feelings are you most hiding from? What is the one feeling you are LEAST likely to express in your life or most afraid to express?

7. Can you imagine not running? What are the five biggest ways your life would most be different if you were no longer running? And what's the single biggest thing that keeps you from stopping the running?

Book Recommendation

Buy a copy of the book, *The Dark Side of the Light Chasers*, by Debbie Ford. Great book for diving into the parts of your self that you have been hiding from and most need to express, in order to become full and alive.

CHAPTER 4

CHANGE WILL NOT OCCUR
'TIL THE PAIN GETS BAD ENOUGH

The single most frequent mantra my clients hear from me is simply this:

**Change will not occur,
until the pain gets bad enough.**

No matter how bad you think your life is now, it's still not as bad as some greater pain if you deviate from the path. And it's that potential pain that keeps you stuck in this present life you're in.

The simple fact of the matter is that unless you drill down to the real source of your pain, your pain will only get worse. Again, this stuff doesn't magically heal itself or magically go away. Either it gets solved through willful action to dive down to the core, or it expands.

That expansion – that increasing of your pain – is both tragic and glorious. It stinks when God or the Universe, or the machinations of your own soul increase life's pain, particularly just when you found yourself saying, "Well, this can't get any worse." (It always can. Don't tempt the gods.) The pain can go beyond insufferable, breaking us and breaking us further.

**The ego, like the egg,
if of no use, until it is broken.**

But, there's an amazing upside to it all, not while you're in it, but when it finally breaks your fear of the future you want to pursue. See, *eventually the pain of now gets so bad that it exceeds your fear of tomorrow*; it exceeds your fear of what people will think, say, and do if you become that which you really want to become.

Eventually, the pain gets so bad that you don't care anymore about potential future pain that might come from leaving the path you're on. You don't care anymore about the very fears that yesterday kept you hamstrung, locked in this life of misery. In effect, pain gives you strength. Pain even gives courage – beautiful, mad courage. That is the glorious part. The irony is that the strength and courage that come after being broken exceed the great strength that kept you hanging on to your lifeless path amid the many problems it wrought.

Pain burns off blockages. When the pain gets bad enough it energizes us to do the formerly unthinkable. You reach what I call 'The Screw-it Point' (at least that's what I call it in a book that I've committed to not swearing in). It's when you finally don't care anymore. Old fears finally, effortlessly fall away and you say with crystalline resolve, "Screw it! I'm doing it!" Great pain yields this odd, hybrid fruit. Pain – horrific as it can be – is an extremely powerful motivator.

It's yet one more life example of the simple truth that blessings are curses and curses are always blessings. Inside of pain, inside of hardship, inside of hard questions...inside the dark forest of the soul, inside whatever hell you are going through, there are always pearls of wisdom, new insights, and fountains of new power. Further,

The grand blessing of going through hell
is that it's not as scary the second time.

And it is near-completely defanged by the third or fourth time. You learn and know the earmarks and milestones, the critters and crags that rise up to meet you on the path to and through hell. Go to the very farthest reaches of your sorrow, stay there awhile, and all of a sudden you don't quite fear going there again, or going into fear, at all. It's tremendously empowering. It may not be on your Top 10 list of things to do, but it doesn't cripple you, either, if you know you gotta go there.

Further, because the second time of going through hell in life is not so scary, we tend to move on it earlier in the painful state, rather than hanging on and hanging on, until things get their absolute worst. But this is one of the real goals of the spiritual life – to hear

34

and heed the deep, quiet inner voice sooner and sooner each time. It's so easy to not heed the quiet inner vibe/pulse, to ignore it, hanging on to what-was, hanging on to what is safe. But when, in the past, we've seen life spin out of control enough times for not following that inner calling, when we've seen our problems metastasize because we didn't heed the whisper of the soul, we quite naturally begin to listen and act a bit sooner. Because the amount of pain necessary to move us off our inertia or present circumstances decreases. Previously, it was your very strength that was your downfall. It kept you holding on to a set of experiences or circumstances that were killing your spirit. You held on and held on and held on. But as we age and go through hell enough times, we stop trying to hold on when the winds of life are calling us, beckoning to a new and higher existence. The fruit of the spiritual life is determined by your willingness to sooner and sooner hear and heed that inner vibe...and to quit the path when it has run its course, when the voice of your soul is calling you away from the old path and to a new one.

And if we begin to treat that inner voice with deliberateness and meditation, trusting it becomes easier and more fluid. We must welcome flow, not just when it's calling you to something, but most especially when it's calling you away from something.

Change will not occur, until the pain gets bad enough. And if you're not changing, it's simply because your pain hasn't gotten bad enough – and it will get worse! You're staying right where you are – safe, not moving – because you don't have to yet. But once it does take you to your limit and you do act boldly, the fruit and growth after the pain are on such an exquisite level that you presently are incapable of imagining them. It really is that great! But it's just doggone scary, right up until that point where you do finally take that leap.

Song Recommendation
1) The first song recommendation I have for you is a classic that speaks right to the place in life I refer to as 'The Screw-It Point,' where you no longer care about pleasing others, no longer care

about all the things that have kept you locked in an unhappy life, and no longer care about wasting your life. It is **Phil Collins's *I Don't Care Anymore***. Buy it. Sit in it. Let it strengthen you for what is ahead.

https://www.youtube.com/watch?v=xLpfbcXTeo8IDontCareAnymore

2) The second song is about the spot of feeling like you're caught in a loop of hiccups, hardships and hurdles – longing to escape but feeling stuck in the never-ending cycle. Purchase **Eminem's *Lose Yourself***, and give it a good long listen. While we definitely get more than one chance in life, this song is still inspiring as heck!

https://www.youtube.com/watch?v=_Yhyp-_hX2sLoseYourself

CHAPTER 5

YOUR LOVE CUP

In my last book on relationship infidelity, I discussed a concept that has been a part of my pastoral work and spiritual counseling work, for decades. It springs out of the propensity and even pride that some people have for being 'brutally honest.' I am not a fan of brutal honesty. I am not a fan of brutal anything, unless as a last resort. Yet, so many people consider it some sort of virtue to be so with others, even if they can't be with themselves.

I have found through my mistakes in life that being brutally honest is never anything more than telling other people what is wrong with them. But that's easy. It's easy to go around callously pointing out everything that is wrong with everyone else and what they should do differently. Far more difficult is to find and focus on the good in others, even when others can only see the bad in themselves. But this chapter isn't for turning the brutally honest into the 'let's be positive' crowd (though I'm quite a fan of that crowd, much of the time).

Rather, what I've found is that, generally speaking, brutal honesty only fractures relationships and creates fissures, widening into impasses between people. Brutal honesty is condescending and hurtful. It is to see yourself as above someone else and to see others as in need of your infinite wisdom. It doesn't bring people together, but breeds underlying resentment and bitterness, and rightfully so. It is so incredibly easy to default to put downs and name-calling.

The most difficult act in relationships is to engage in what I call 'radical honesty.' Radical honesty means to reveal to someone you love (or care about) your fears, your dreams, the parts of yourself you are not proud of, and the parts you are certain you will be rejected for. And there ain't nothin' more terrifying than that. To reveal to another person – particularly someone you want to keep – your real truth is life's scariest venture. And it is that precise fear that is at the heart of nearly all depression and anxiety and why many people turn to brutal honesty, instead. For, it's far safer to villainize others and forever keep the focus off oneself. To show the world who you really are requires a lion's courage. It is, at its root, to stand humbly before another, rather than above them.

Brutal honesty
is telling someone else what's wrong with them.

Radical honesty
is telling someone else what's wrong with you
or what you're most afraid of them knowing about you.

Great relationships are built on the latter;
defective and destructive relationships are constructed on some
derivative of the former.

Yet, that's where the gold is. We can never truly love someone, until we know who they really are, warts and all. We can never be or truly feeeeel loved – truly believe it – until we have shown someone who we really are, warts and all, and been loved for it. And that is life's most courageous act (because, what if they don't love me for it!?!).

As my father, the old, country pastor said to me,
"Love is vulnerability."
It is a constant opening and opening to another person.

This incessant opening is more than just simple honesty ("Where were you, last Friday night?"). It is revelation – the revealing of your soul to another person:
- Who are you, really?
- What are your greatest fears in life?
- What are your greatest fears, in this moment, in this situation?
- What do you dream of?
- What are you wasting? Time? Energy? People's attention? Every opportunity that has ever confronted you?
- What are you most scared to reveal to me?

- What is the one thing you have never told anyone?
- What is the great sin that constantly pulls you down or sucks the life out of others?
- How do you most harm people?
- Who *are* you?

This! This is radical honesty. *This* is the stuff of the deepest and most powerful relationships. We've been taught that in work and business to be vulnerable is weakness and only leads to failure. But in relationships precisely the opposite is true. Relationship success demands vulnerability, demands the revealing of self. And nothing could be more terrifying.

I could not even begin to count the number of female clients who have said to me, "Sven, I just want to be loved for who I am." To which I invariably respond, "How the heck can anyone love you for who you really are, if you don't show them who you really are?" One requires the other. Radical honesty!

Of course, if you feel like you can't because you don't trust him (or her), you have to ask yourself the hard question: Is your fear of him (or her) hurting you based on his having hurt you in the past or is it based on your past, before him, and having been hurt by previous loves and your family and/or friends? If he has hurt you and you know he will likely hurt you again, then you have to ask yourself the question, Why the heck are you in the relationship, at all? If it is not him or anything he has done, but it is your own fear that keeps you from opening up, then a serious dose of radical honesty is precisely what you most need. For, you are holding yourself back and your relationship back. You. You are doing it, because of your terrifying fear of being seen for who you really are.

I have countless clients who have spent their entire lives flying below the radar, doing only the bare minimums, doing everything in their power to never stick out or never have their head above the crowd (for fear of it getting chopped off, so to speak), employing all their effort to not be seen. They grew up being taught, likely by their parents, that to be seen brings criticism, disappointment, pain, even death. "Far easier to be rejected or criticized for a fake version of myself than to be criticized or rejected for showing the real me. But it's better to fly below the radar, altogether." And so, they were mediocre in all things, never fully exerting themselves, never revealing what they truly wanted, never admitting to having aspirations, and never doing anything that might draw attention to themselves. (And so, they come to later in life with boatloads of regret and seem to be forever looking backwards.) Why? Attention brings pain. To be seen means to be criticized. And that just hurts too much.

It's far easier and far less painful to be brutally honest than radically honest, far easier to keep the focus on other people, and to always make them the bad guy or the inept one when things aren't going well or when you're unhappy. Or, in an odd twist on this theme of not wanting to reveal oneself, it's easy to keep the focus on others by always listening to others, always deferring, always giving attention. Always keeping the spotlight off yourself, counter-intuitive as it seems, and always focusing on another with positive attention is motivated by the same thing as when it's done with negative attention: "As long as I keep the attention off me, I'm safe. I don't like me. So why would they?"

As long as everything, good and bad, is outside you, you never have to take responsibility for who you really are; you never have to own your truth. You never have to become an honest and real member of the human race. Mostly, you never have to either look at your truth or reveal your truth and be seen for who you really are, admitting that you are good and admitting your flaws and warts, too, no matter what anyone else says. It's easier to be a bully in a relationship by keeping the focus on the other person's failings; easier to take advantage of someone else's openness and graciousness; easier to use people. And, it's easier to always give, again always keeping the light off yourself.

"Speak the truth in love," **(the Christian apostle Paul).**
It's easy to always speak truth and be harsh.
It's easy to always be cuddly and speak love.
It's far more difficult to speak truth and love, simultaneously –
to set occasional hard truths within a greater, ongoing context
of appreciation and positive attention.

The reason people spend their lives hiding – behind walls, behind others, behind facades, behind perfection, behind mediocrity, behind indifference – is because they have been taught to dislike themselves. They have been taught, either explicitly or – far worse – implicitly, that who they really are does not have worth or is bad or useless. And who wants to be seen for being bad or no good? No one, of course. So people stay hidden.

Even though the longing to be loved is palpable and insatiable, the thought of showing anyone who they really are is unthinkable. It's like they have this giant hole inside that is longing to be filled, by any means necessary. And, rather than seek to heal it and fill it, they seek instead only to hide it.

And this is where we get into the realm of spirituality, when we start talking about that hole deep inside; that pain; that longing; that seemingly incurable ache of the soul. It has been said by mystics and theologians past that we all have a God-sized hole inside of us that no amount of addictions or compulsions can fill. Yet we long to be filled. And so we spend our lives running – running away from the pain and running about feverishly, like a squirrel gathering nuts, to find love anywhere or to find temporary fixes to make that pain of emptiness go away, at least for a moment.

Yet, the filling of that hole is a task only for the spirit of the Universe, however you may define it. Only the true calling of the soul can fill that hole. And, truth be told, it was full before you were born. You were created whole. You were created with the coding of your wholeness written on the computer chip of your soul (see Chapter 22). Emptiness comes from deviation from your original coding. Wholeness returns simply by having the courage to re-become who the heck you were put on this earth to be. To fulfill God's purpose for your life you have only the task of becoming your truest self. You were made brilliant, original, on fire, and having incredible authenticity to bring to life. But you were taught, post-birth, to loathe who you are (or some significant aspect of who you are), to distrust your deepest inner voice, and to become some bastardized version of yourself that enables you to fly below the radar, not be seen and not be criticized.

And that is neither God's purpose nor is it any recipe, whatsoever, for happiness. Not lasting happiness. And certainly not any version of inner peace or clarity of purpose. As long as you ignore that God-voice in the depths of your soul – where the God-voice and your own voice fuse and are indistinguishable – you simply cannot have peace or joy, purpose or any true power. For you are an existence then rooted in and driven by fear, not self-love and God-love. Fear is, by definition, a state of weakness. Thus living in and being driven by fear is to attack life not from a position of strength but weakness. That never ends well. You are, by definition, at disunion with the spirit of the Universe and all life. For, you have rejected the one and only life most entrusted to your care. (Far easier to just tell everyone else how to live, run your children's lives, and dominate or be servant to those around you than to actually live your own doggone life authentically, isn't it?)

But radical honesty calls for something much different. It calls for revelation. It calls for opening. Great relationships – not the least of which is your relationship with your own self – are built on great acts of courage, great acts of revelation, great acts of trust.

Do you have the courage to finally acknowledge your truths, be/say/do/have/believe/become who you really were made to be, and radically reveal your truth to those whom you love?

The Love Cup

Truth is, every one of us is going through life trying to get our Love Cup filled. Regarding that hole inside. I prefer to think of it as an empty cup. A Love Cup. Because we have been taught that who we are is no good, not good enough, doesn't matter, isn't wanted, or what have you – i.e. because we never got the love we needed to feel like our Love Cup is full inside, while growing up – we are all forever trying to get love. I mean, isn't it really just pretty much that simple. We're all trying to get love, in one form or another.

We try to fill that lack of love, that emptiness, with Prozac, over-working, over-parenting, whiskey, cheating, gambling, weed, drugs, incessant busyness, and the old standby FOOD! Filling, filling, filling, running, running, running....and all because of that giant empty Love Cup inside.

We each have a Love Cup we're carrying around through life. And, we're each trying to get our Love Cup filled. It's that massive part of our existence that is underneath everything else we do.

Sadly, we contort ourselves in all manners and directions to get it filled. No matter who we are, every person is trying to get their Love Cup filled. The Love Cup is nothing more than a simple metaphor for understanding the needs of the soul, specifically the colossal human need to feel loved, and then meeting those needs. It's the grand spiritual endeavor of life.

We were created to feel full – to receive love, to be able to hold love inside, and also to be giving instruments of God's love in the world. Yet, empty is where we find ourselves, at some point in life or for a long stretch, perhaps for as long as you can remember. The Love Cup is bone dry.

We can't seem to get filled, because to get the Love Cup filled (love that lasts, rather than temporary splashes of love that evaporate as soon as they come) demands being loved for who you really are. Filling the Cup only comes from discovering and revealing to the world who you really are – radical honesty, both with yourself and with life. And that only comes from you actually loving who you are, believing in yourself enough to be seen. Ain't nobody gonna truly fall in love with you 'til you fall in love with you. Fact.

The Three Missing Love Languages

Filling the Love Cup can come in the form of hugs and kisses, which we all love, or many other forms. Back in 1995, Gary Chapman wrote the international bestselling book, *The 5 Love Languages*, which discusses the notion that love in relationships comes in 5 basic categories: Words, Touch, Quality Time, Acts of Service, and Gifts. For Chapman, each person in a relationship has a way, or ways, that he or she most likes to receive love, as well as ways he most naturally gives love or was taught to give love, growing up. Thus, what often happens in relationships, when there is a breakdown, is that couples discover that how one person is showing love, often quite emphatically, is not a way that the other person perceives being loved. One person can feel they're loving the crap outta the other person. But the other is thinking, "When are you gonna start loving me?" If the way you most like to receive love is through quality time together and words of love are hollow for you, but your your mate is forever showering you with loving words and gifts, then you might experience a great deficit – feeling unloved and feeling that your spouse genuinely doesn't care about your needs.

I have used Chapman's model in my work with couples and am a big believer in that basic set of love languages and his book. However, over time, my 89 year-old mother and I, who have both done a great deal of spiritual counseling, believe there are three more whoppers for showing love. *The first, and perhaps biggest, is showing someone else your real truth – telling them who you really are, including your truest fears, dreams, failures, and history.* Radical honesty. To reveal your true self is to shatter all illusions of perfection, goodness, having it all together, as well as badness, worthlessness, and nothingness. It is to show your full truth. It's the scariest thing on earth to do, but it is one of the highest forms of love. It is to risk the ultimate rejection of your truth, of you.

**The most powerful expression of love
is to show another person
who you really, really, really are
...to the point where it scares you to do so.
The sheer terror of doing so is testament to the sacredness of the act.**

Revelation of self is fundamentally rooted in trust – trust of the other and trust in self and fate or God – i.e. trust that no matter what happens, I'll be okay. To be able to trust is a higher state of existence – a life that is no longer intimidated by the monsters of fear. To share the scariest parts of yourself with someone, when we almost never share those parts with anyone else, is to say, "You are different. You are very special to me." And that is a very powerful statement of love, the most powerful.

The second form love that I cannot overstate the importance of in life, and which is so lacking in relationships, parenting, and work settings, is just plain listening. More specifically, it is the action of inaction, of being fully present to another human being. To simultaneously give the spotlight to someone else and make another person feel heard is potent hooch. It's far more than just quality time. It's for another person to feel you don't have one foot here and one elsewhere, but have both feet right here, right now. It's the action of giving attention when we forever long to be in the center of the universe, to keep the attention on ourselves. And this demands both a relinquishing of ego and the simple, yet difficult ability to be present.

Yet, it is listening, not as a form of self-abnegation or trying to hide (as mentioned earlier), but as a going against type, when type is the common human desire to take attention. (If type is to always listen and thereby stay hidden, then to go against type is to speak, to reveal.)

When my son was two or three, I recall, I was sitting on the floor of my house with him, doing a kid's puzzle. And, I found myself getting irritated with him for not doing it right or quickly enough...a three year-old!! WTH? It was ridiculously stupid on my part. But in that brief moment of stupidity I had a revelation. I was getting impatient and rude, not because of anything he had done to warrant such treatment, but because my mind was elsewhere – work, relationship, worries and interests. *I wasn't present.* I was unable to give love fully because I was unwilling to check out of my life, momentarily, to be in his life and world.

Love is presence. Presence is the necessary precursor for listening, for truly hearing the words, longing, and spirit of another's story.

As an aside, the Jewish and Christian faiths both assert that all sin starts from making yourself the god – i.e. the center of the Universe, from failing to put and keep God and neighbor at the center of the Universe. And we go through all sorts of permutations to keep ourselves at the center of the Universe and get all the attention that we hope comes with that. Every other sin grows out of this one, most basic sin – this belief that I am the center of the Universe.

Thus, it is extremely powerful to deliberately yield that spotlight to another human being, even if only for the three minutes you're in the checkout line at the grocer, or after a long day of work. Further, it is extremely powerful to know that someone is giving up the most treasured thing of life – attention/spotlight...love – to be present to you. To deliberately and graciously give the spotlight of positive attention and presence to another human being is rare and such high art that people pay top dollar to me and other clergy, therapists, psychologists, psychics, bartenders and even escorts/hookers to possess it. To have someone simply present and positively focused on you is gold.

The third form of love that I am particularly fond of, and believe in the grand power of, is questions. I am an absolute believer that questions are love. There are few things that more convey "You are now at the center of my world" and thereby give positive attention than asking a question of another person, and not just one question, but a second and third follow-up question. I, personally, gauge the degree I am going to let someone into ever-more-inner circles of my personal life largely based on how many questions they ask of others, not just me. I want to know not just if they are naturally curious, which is a big part of it (and reflects an open mind), but also if they are both capable of and eager to cede the spotlight. For, as with presence, to ask questions is to give energy and attention to another person. I like people who get joy from giving energy to others in the form of conversational attention, in part because it is a such a difficult thing for a great many people to give up. To be fully present to another human being is incredibly difficult and incredibly noble. In my life, I enjoy people who listen not just until they think of what they want to say next, but until they think of what they want to *ask* next. To speak in questions, rather than statements, is to focus on another, when the natural human inclination is to do the opposite.

But to couple that temporary removing of self from the center of the Universe with the actual ability to make someone else feel heard – genuinely listened to – is an experience we all seek and one missing from far too many childhoods. Children, especially teenagers, so want to feel heard and allowed to speak their budding truth without fear of judgment, and thus experience being tacitly approved of. And the lack of this love method, as well as the two prior, lead to more adult problems than anything else.

How The Love Cup Really Gets Filled

Whichever forms the love may take, we're all trying to get love from others. Yet, one of the grand goals of life – of the spiritual path – is to begin to get that love from yourself, to learn how to fill your own Love Cup. We get to this in later chapters.

However, for now, it is important to understand the simple concept that so much, if not all, of our lives is the mighty endeavor to get our Love Cup filled.

However, love is such an overused word and often becomes a bit fuzzy and complicated in its meanings and interpretations, much like the word 'God'. Therefore, staying with that notion of attention, I have found that *the easiest way to understand love, at least regarding the Love Cup, is to think of it simply as positive attention.*

Anything that is experienced as
positive attention
fills the Love Cup.

Again, positive attention can come in many forms. Chapman's five languages of love. My three love languages: listening/presence, radical honesty/revealing of self, and questions. There are also other ways of thinking about positive attention: validation, approval, security, comfort, kindness, hugs, actions of support and service, and so on.

The pouring of love into the Love Cup is a wonderful experience. It feels good to have the love from another coming into us. And it also feels great to pour the love from our own Cup into that of another. But the greatest peace and joy come from when you give that daily positive attention to your own real self and the needs of your soul. Nothing heals and fills the Love Cup faster and more enduringly than giving energy – in the form of positive attention – to your true self, which is the very thing you have been taught is unworthy of love, positive attention and energy.

Song Recommendation
1) Great song for you to buy and listen closely to: ***Secrets***, https://www.youtube.com/watch?v=qHm9MG9xw1oSecrets by **One Republic**.It is so perfect a song for this topic of opening your heart and revealing your real truth, not just to others but to your own self, opening the possibility of getting your Love Cup filled, both by yourself and others.
2) The second song I commend to your listening pleasure and personal growth is ***Come Talk To Me***, by **Peter Gabriel**. https://www.youtube.com/watch?v=a7ysopXvd1EComeTalkToMe

CHAPTER 6

AROUND THE DINNER TABLE

As noted in Chapter 5, everybody is going through life holding out their Love Cup, trying to get people to pour love into it, trying to get it filled. As children, we're particularly tuned into this, whether we're aware of it or not. And, the fewer sources of love a child (or adult) has pouring in love, the more frantic and neurotic the pursuit for love becomes, come adulthood, to the point of out-of-control in its worst states.

The way a child's personality develops is by basically responding to the primary adults or influences in his/her life. The child, quite innately, just tunes into what mom, dad, or the kindergarten teacher, uncles, aunts, grandparents, Sunday School teachers, etc like in a kid and then becomes that kid. The personality becomes this accumulation of fragments of what it takes to get positive attention, or love in the Love Cup, from this person or that person in the child's life.

The fewer sources pouring love into the child's Love Cup, or the less overall amount going into the Cup, the more of a chameleon the child becomes – forever changing personalities in an incessant quest to get love wherever and whenever he/she can. In contrast, the child who is consistently, significantly, and through multiple love methods given love realizes that he or she doesn't need to change his/her personality to get love, but instead experiences a constant flow of love, quite apart from his or her actions or personality changes. This child develops with less anxiety over not knowing who to be.

Yet, even in the best homes, the child is constantly reading the parents. At the deepest levels, quite apart from any conscious action, the child is becoming whomever he or she has to be to get love into the Cup, to some greater or lesser degree.

So, imagine a large family of four or five kids around the dinner table with mom and dad at each end. Each kid is, metaphorically speaking, holding out his or her Love Cup. It's like a bunch of baby robins in a nest with their mouths agape, begging for food. Except, in this case it's food for the soul; love, the most important building block of life.

Thus, each child develops particular personality traits, even dominant ones, based on what he/she believes is necessary to get love. So, around that table you have the good kid, the funny kid, the quiet kid, the rascal, the chatty/happy kid, the smart kid, the creative kid, etc, based on whatever is valued by the parents. (And those parental values can be conveyed both explicitly and wordlessly.)

Also, while actually giving love to one or another child, the good parent models for the other children the giving of love. The parent says, "Bethany, how did your big test go today? What was the hardest part?" "Gregory, how are things going with your new girlfriend?" "Tony, are you still protesting the playground rules to your teacher and principal?" "Will you teach us, Sophia, right now how to divide two fractions? We'd love to hear." By giving attention to one or another child, the parent pours love into that child's Love Cup and shows the other kids how to give love and, more simply, how to be a responsible human being. Yet, by deliberately moving focus and love around the table, the parent is tacitly conveying the extremely powerful message, "There's plenty of love to go around. There's no need to fight for it or compete. We'll just take our time making sure everyone gets their Cup filled." By implicitly conveying this abundance, the parent puts the child's soul at rest.

Again, every form of love is fundamentally nothing more than the transmission of positive attention, the transfer of energy, to be precise. So, it's not just the dinner table. It's the sports field, the garage, the bedtime bathtub, the kitchen, in the car, and on and on. The job of the good parent is to be consistently pouring love into the Love Cup of the child/children. That's what parenting is. It's the transferring of energy, the transferring of love to the child, so that, first, the child can have a happy childhood. And it is the transferring of love into the child's Love Cup, so that, second, the child walks into adulthood without a love deficit. A deficit of love in that Love Cup radically increases the odds that that now-adult-child will engage in destructive and self-destructive actions to steal love, to keep the spot in the center of the universe, or, worse, to give everything away in hopes of getting a little bit of love, in return.

So, the act of giving attention is a powerful one, both to be on the receiving end of it, but also to witness someone you love doing it to a brother or sister, friend or stranger. And the child learns, eventually becoming an instrument of this exact same act, wanting to win the parent's love for doing so, but also experiencing the sublime joy that comes from both receiving and giving love to others and himself.

Problems At The Dinner Table

But now, imagine if one of the parents at that dinner table never got his or her Love Cup filled, as a child or in life. I have known countless clients and families wherein one of the parents is still very much engaged in the act of getting her/his own Love Cup filled, because it never got filled when they were younger. And so, they effectively use their children to fill their own Love Cup. Ain't nothin' worse than this!

See, the job of the parent is to fill the child's Love Cup, not just feed and clothe the child. And, in theory, the parent got her/his Love Cup filled as a child and throughout life, and is therefore always able to engage in the act of pouring love into the child's Love Cup.

But, far too many parents go into parenthood with empty or half-empty cups, or cups forever hemorrhaging. And so, they begin to siphon love from the child as he/she ages – using the child to meet his/her own needs for love, acceptance, price, listening, guidance, or what have you, whether through affection, attention, or later through time and stolen decisions.

If, for example, the mother at the head of the table (or the father, single parent, grandparent, foster parent) of the big family, never got her Love Cup filled, she may use family dinner time, or any other time, as an opportunity to talk, on and on, about her life and her day and her never-ending stories or complaints. By constantly keeping the spotlight on herself, she is stealing the attention from her children and husband. Thereby, in effect, she's running around the table pouring love from her children's Love Cups into her own!

Or, the father who listens to the achievements of the children, only to cap each story with the proclamation of some achievement of his own in some petty game of one-upmanship with an 11 year-old. Stealing praise, the thinking goes, "I'm only good when everyone else is below me, even my own children." Yes, the mark of a small man. But, far worse, it has the effect of stealing love from the child. And the child begins life with the neurosis of never getting enough love, a state that starts far younger than most people realize and protracts well into adulthood. Resultingly, the empty Love Cup syndrome now gets passed on into yet one more generation, extending the family disease.

Basically, if you can't give positive attention, both regularly and significantly, you're not ready to be a parent, because you'll end up stealing it from your children. And that is the most hideous of diseases.

So, let's say the parent(s) never got their Love Cup filled. The real problem arises in this Love Cup equation when the parent is not pouring love into a child's Love Cup. When a child is not getting positive attention, he/she will resort to getting negative attention, for that is infinitely better than no attention. No attention means 'I don't see you. You don't matter.' It's a negation of one's very existence.

Children have a way of making their needs known. The louder the tantrum, the greater the love need. And the parent is forced to change, or the child becomes infinitely more rebellious and harder to handle. (As the saying goes, Adults don't make children; children make adults.) In effect, the child's soul is expressing the magnitude of its pain and longing. Tantrums are never just about what is happening in the moment. It's always, always deeper stuff. And the parent is forced out of the center of his/her Universe, forced to put the child there, at least long enough to transfer some amount of love into the Love Cup of the child.

If a child is not getting positive attention, not getting the Love Cup filled, the problem always tracks back to the same source: the parent(s) never got his own Love Cup filled, or somehow it got emptied. A problem child is always the result of a problem parent.

So, back to the mother (or father) at the dinner table. She might be a perfectly loving, hugging, kissing, serving, and saying-I-love-you-a-lot-type of parent. But she has this unyielding proclivity to talk incessantly. And talk and talk and talk, to the point of the kids rolling their eyes, a lot, having heard mom's same stories innumerable times.

The effect of this inability to give more attention than she takes is that Cups are going unfilled. In fact, they're being drained by her. This becomes highly problematic for the child, his spiritual development, and the positive growth of his personality. For, basically the child is now competing not just with three or four other siblings for love, but is competing with his own mother for the attention of the family, just as everyone else at the table is now in competition for the limited supply of love – a supply that is now also diminished by one parent, who has become a taker rather than a giver. A shortage of love ensues, no matter how full the father's Cup is.

In its worst forms, where the parent is forever using the child to get his/her own emotional and spiritual needs met, it's fundamentally a form of spiritual incest, or emotional incest. It is invading and stealing from the child to get your own needs met. The effects can be far more debilitating, long term, than anything else the parent could do. Perhaps the parent with the empty Love Cup manifests that shortage not in the form of incessant talking but in the form of incessant working, as an adult still trying to win the love of an ungiving and perhaps even now-deceased parent. Or, perhaps the siphoning of love from the children comes in the form of using the child to get the parent's affection needs met. I'm not talking about sexual abuse/incest. I'm citing the all-too-common occurrence of one parent basically falling in love with the children (while perhaps the other falls in love with his/her career) and using the child for lots and lots of affection, hugs, kisses, and hugs and kisses, all the while couching it in terms of doing it for the child, when it is about far more than that. Or, even worse, the parent who commits emotional incest, using the child as her therapist and emotional tampon, of sorts, dumping adult problems and gripes onto a young human being ill-equipped to handle adult problems.

All of these convey to the child, "Your needs aren't important. Mine are." Despite whatever actual words of love might be coming out of the parent's mouth, the actions of the parent convey something different. And the soul of the child picks up on it, "I'm not important. I don't matter. All that matters is mom or dad." And a child, at least when young, is generally very eager to oblige and give to the parent. That 'taking care of' nature then becomes part of the child's personality, dangerously so. Or if not 'taking care of,' the soul of the child takes on some negative or self-destructive form that is driven by the parent's failure to give sufficient love. The child's Love Cup reads 'Empty.'

That's when all sorts of goofy stuff starts to happen in a family. That's when kids really start acting out, parents fight harder for control, and ever-greater conflicts arise, both at home and at school.

Yet, if the parent routinely fails to pour love into the Love Cup of the child, bitterness grows, resentment grows, and depression grows. All that is bad and unhealthy grows in the heart of the child. It may get buried deeply or it may live on the surface, but it is there, always there.

The real tragedy is that this generally doesn't start in the child's teen years. That's when it reaches the level of serious conflict, because the child's spirit and strength have increased. The parent may be significantly losing control by then. And the conflict is just the symptom. But the problem, itself, started long before the teen years. The parent had been stealing love, or at least not giving it, long before that happened.

This problem of a parent whose Love Cup was never filled can have the effect of damaging the actual Love Cup of the child (addressed in later chapters), in addition to shorting the amount of love in the child's Cup. And a child with an empty Love Cup becomes an adult with an empty Love Cup, perpetuating the cycle and engaging in all manner of self-destructive actions to either fill the Cup or run from all the pain of feeling only empty inside.

But damaged or not, each one of us is forever trying to get more love into the Love Cup of our soul.

Energy Transfer

In the end, the giving of love in the form of positive attention is about the transfer of energy from one person to another. Whether it is understood by physics and the science community or not, we all feel something – some boost, some lift, some internal change – when someone has given us love, when someone has made us the receiver of their positive attention. There has been a movement of energy from the giver to the receiver. We've all felt it. Love is energy. Positive attention is energy.

Assuming all is well with the Love Cup, the body stores that energy, either to feed off of or to transfer to someone else. But it is energy, fuel, capable of giving warmth to the bearer.

In positive adult relationships, there is a back-and-forth flow of this life energy. In negative adult relationships, there is an imbalanced flow – one person taking more than they're giving. In a positive parent-child relationship, the flow of energy – of positive attention – is largely one-directional, from parent to child. It is neither the child's job nor in his ability to create any sort of equal balance of energy flow toward the parent. And any attempt by the parent to make it so results in a net loss for the child, simply because the child has less to begin with, less years from which to have it filled, less alternate sources from which to get love, and a less developed capacity to meter the flow of love outward. Thus, the child easily drains off what little love and life energy she has, because her inclination is to give it all away, which is humanity in its purest state. But it's only humanity's purest and wisest state when A) the Cup is whole and possessing of love, as opposed to having a hole in the bottom and thus hemorrhaging love as a spiritual disease; and B) the bearer of the Cup knows how to replenish its contents.

It is that flow of energy, both in and out, that drives the human animal. It is the desire for positive attention, for love energy. We are all driven by the desire to fill the Love Cup and give love to others.

Song Recommendation
Check out the song, *Time for me to Fly,* by **REO Speedwagon**. It refers to a love relationship, but can be also used to better understand parent-child relationships, too.
https://www.youtube.com/watch?v=tZr4XHlHP1cTimeForMeToFly

CHAPTER 7

A SHIP CROSSING THE OCEAN

The reason I call myself a 'spiritual counselor' is because, above all else, I believe in the power of core beliefs. I realized, early on, that if you really want to change someone, be it yourself or another – both what they do and what they feel – there is no hope if you simply try to change their actions. I saw it in the military, as a D1 athlete, and as an NCAA Head Coach for Strength and Conditioning, as well as in all my years as a spiritual counselor, pastor and Emergency Room chaplain.

Until the core beliefs driving the bad behaviors and crummy feelings are changed, nothing changes, at least not to any lasting degree.

Thus, I am in the business of drilling down to, identifying, and cutting out those core beliefs that are so obviously not working for my clients. Then, of course, new beliefs have to be inserted that actually serve my client. Before a person's external life can be life-giving, the root causes driving the system must be life-giving.

See, at the core of who a person is are core beliefs, generally the ones people are most aware of, even if they don't actually think about them very often. As you progress up through a person's self, you next encounter what most people consider their principles, and finally on top are the behaviors or actions.

It is in this realm of principles and actions that most people spend the bulk of their time. What they think, what their goals and wants are, what their values are, and how they shape their identity, at least to any conscious degree, all fall into this realm of principles, which they then see as the shapers of their actions.

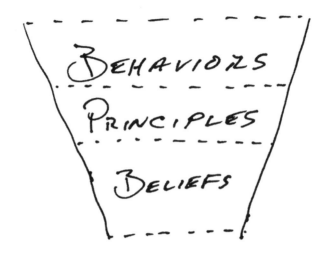

The problem is, most principles are just back-fill. That is, I no longer believe that principles matter for much, at least when it comes to the question of what really drives a person's actions and creates happiness and fulfillment. What is really driving actions is people's core beliefs – their deep beliefs about life, self, people, and the world, as well as their fears and dreams. But, because beliefs, by definition, can neither be proven or disproved (or can be both proven and disproved) – i.e. because they are not always tangible and logical – they become much more sketchy to defend and live by when a person is being criticized by the important people in his/her life.

Therefore, people create principles, based on some measure of logic, to justify the actions that are really springing out of core beliefs and fears. Principles are the pretty face we put on to sell our actions.

And the simplest way to understand the sheer power of the core beliefs is to imagine a ship traveling across an ocean or two. If that ship's navigation is off just 3-4 degrees at the start of the journey, the ship will get farther and farther off course, the greater distance it travels. A ship leaving from Los Angeles for Hawaii will end up somewhere in China or even Russia. Both are great countries, but you're going to be terrifically underdressed when you arrive.

Same with even the slightest changes in the deep beliefs of the soul. If those deepest beliefs are changed, by the time they pass up through principles and actions, the person's external life starts looking radically different from how it used to look. It diverges immensely from the life of even a close relative or sibling, who got a very similar set of original core beliefs.

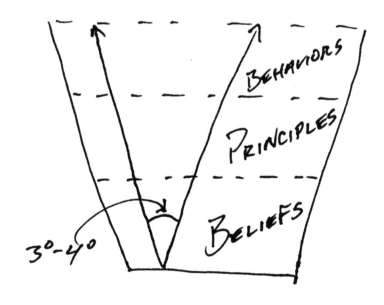

This is why going down to the deep beliefs, when you're trying to turn your life around, always has the greatest and most lasting effects. It's changing the input into the navigational system of your soul that was mis-programmed when you were growing up. And it's why changes only to behavior, such as when a spouse threatens to leave, never last. The core beliefs never changed. So, the person will pretty much always revert back to actions that reflect the core beliefs. This is also why change and growth can be so scary and so disruptive to relationships and families. People with new beliefs no longer fit. So, either the other surrounding people must change or the one who has changed must be forced back to what they were or expelled. All lasting change is completely contingent upon changing those core beliefs.

Journaling Recommendation

1. What are a few examples from your past where the slightest shift in your core beliefs resulted in a dramatic shift in your actions and, thus, the results and events in your life?
2. What are the areas of your life where you most need to make a shift of a few degrees in your beliefs? What is the single biggest core belief (to the degree any one person can be aware of their own core beliefs) harming your life?
3. What would those shifts in belief look like?
4. What's the single biggest thing holding you back from doing so? What is your biggest fear in considering doing so?

Song Recommendation

Give this one a listen; buy it. It's all about the drilling-down. It's all about your real, truest self down deep inside, yearning to come out. *I'm in Here*, by **Sia**.

https://www.youtube.com/watch?v=Owr4U55WpDsImInHere

CHAPTER 8

THE WET CEMENT OF YOUR SOUL

I have a recollection, a very vivid image, from when my daughter was young. I was looking out the front windows of my house in Minneapolis onto the giant boulevard of grass and trees in front. There, my daughter, Svea, was laughing with my son. He was chasing a ball, as was his wont. And she, my dear girl, was twirling in her white sun dress with floral print.

It was a sunny, summer day; a light breeze blowing through. Her bare feet were in the lush green grass. And there she was, simply twirling in the sun coming through the oaks. She couldn't have been more than two, maybe three, years old.

Twirling. Blissfully happy. Not a care in the world.

And it has occurred to me many, many times, over the years, that *that* is how we come out of the womb. Twirling!

No child comes out of the womb thinking they're no good or not good enough, or feeling unlovable or that their very existence doesn't matter. No kid is born believing they suck. That is not the natural human state. Our initial state is one of carefree bliss, love...one of twirling.

Thus, if I have a client darkening my door, unhappy, needing help, depressed, anxiety-ridden, dead inside, unfulfilled, numb, and/or longing for so much more in life, then something happened between twirling and now. Something happened to make the twirling stop.

Somewhere along the journey, usually very young, a lie got implanted into the child. The child was told, implicitly and/or explicitly, she's no good or doesn't matter. It was a lie. It was never true, then or now. And that lie got reinforced, again and again, as lies tend to be when inserted by the most powerful and influential people in our lives – usually parents, significant family members (uncles/aunts, siblings, grandparents), or teachers/clergy, as well as the incessant background noise of society. But again, usually it's the parents who implant the lie.

See, when we're children, we're wet cement. And, as every kid knows, what gets pressed or written into wet cement hardens. 'Tommy is a fink' or 'David Loves Amy' stays in the neighborhood sidewalk for years, even decades. Whatever images, words, and impressions are pressed into the wet cement of a child's soul stick. The messages of childhood harden, concretize, and calcify, becoming the bedrock of the person's identity and existence, quite unbeknownst to him/her.

**When we are children,
we're wet cement.
Whatever messages get pressed into the wet cement of the child's
soul,
whether deliberately or inadvertently,
harden and become the bedrock beliefs, even below the other
core beliefs,
quite hidden from view,
for the remainder of that child's life.
Never underestimate the power of hidden, calcified beliefs.**

Once hardened, there, down in the very depths of the child's soul – away from the peering eyes of even the most introspective soul later in life, yet fully present everyday – these core beliefs become, if I may mix metaphors, the primary operating system of the whole machine.

A person's entire life could consist of one haywire path after another; or, worse, it could be one massive success after another (quite counterintuitively, often the most ridiculously successful clients are the most unhappy and unfulfilled, and possess the most debilitating messages and impressions in their cement). And no matter their failures or their successes, no matter how many therapies they try or people they talk to, they just cannot seem to pull themselves out of their life funk.

Why? Neither they nor the people they're talking to have any clue what they're really looking for. They have no idea that what is most powerful is what is unseen. Always. Most therapists and clergy lack the ability to go deep enough – to expose what is written in a person's cement, and then create new, life-giving beliefs at the core of the person. Too often the focus is on the known and visible, simply because it's known and visible and therefore easier to work with, even though changes are never lasting. Too many clergy and therapists simply don't have the experience or useful understanding of that which is unseen inside a person.

**One of the grand truths of life
is that things are seldom as they appear.**

Yet, that is precisely what is needed – a destruction of the cement and it's ill-formed message that is robbing the bearer of life. Also needed is a creation and implementation of new beliefs. For it is the core beliefs written on the soul that control everything. It is not the will that drives a human life, but the beliefs of the soul. Change those beliefs, change the person, change the world.

Journaling And Meditation
Questions for your journaling, today:
1. When did you stop twirling? At what age do you remember life becoming not-pretty, heavy, unhappy, or laden with a distinct sense of being really self-conscious?

2. Why then? Why that age? What happened? What do you remember being said (or unsaid)?

3. Who perpetrated the action(s) or words that caused you to stop twirling?

4. Have you ever in your life said even word-one to that person?

5. Write a letter, today or this week, to that person. DO NOT send it; just write it out. Flush out the most powerful feelings you have about that event and all that followed in years afterward. Use the strongest, even most offensive language you possibly can. Express your anger, your rage, your hurt, your tears, your sorrow, your regret for not saying something sooner, perhaps. Say it all. What is the single biggest thing you want to say or have never said to this person? What is it you most want to ask this person?

6. I'm not saying you should, but would you ever speak to or confront this person? Why or why not? What is it you most fear most in doing so – their defense, their denial, or their indifference?

Meditate on this notion of smashing the hardened cement deep inside you that holds all of your negative self-beliefs. See yourself smashing it with a sledge hammer or dropping it into the most powerful acid and melting away forever. See yourself pouring gorgeous, fresh cement that you're going to press in or write in the most wonderful, powerful, life-giving beliefs (which we'll add throughout the book).

Now, journal a bit more:

1. What is the biggest, GOOD thing you can possibly imagine being written into the cement of your soul? What would feel the best? Is it, "I am wonderful," "My life matters; I MATTER," "I am good and good enough," "I LOVE who I am and who I am becoming," "I believe in you," "I am wanted," "I like me. Heck, I love me," or is it something completely different? Why that phrase?

2. What is the single most negative thing you can think of that was pressed into the former cement of your soul? Are you ready to smash that belief and let it go forever?

3. What are five sentences that explain what that would feel like?

4. Who would be most excited for you to become who you really

are? Who are the people who would be your biggest supporters? What is the one sentence each of those people would say in support of you (and make it different for each person)?

Song Recommendation

1) I have a beautiful, little ballad for you that speaks to how we stray from twirling, how life gets lost as we abandon our true selves amid the lies that get inserted into us: *The Sand and the Foam*, by **Dan Fogelberg**.
https://www.youtube.com/watch?v=Oh8H-SGoJ0ETheSandAndTheFoam

CHAPTER 9

THE 3 BINARY GATES

So, imagine it's your first week on the new job and, among your many duties that week, you're given a packet of information from the HR Department and the Finance Department. One of the pages in that packet indicates your company's 401k terms with employer matching. You pick up that form, read it over, take it home to talk over with your spouse, eventually sign it, and then send it back to the Finance Department. It's a good deal, one you decide you'd be crazy not to take.

Well, those **actions** of...

- picking up,
- reading,
- taking home,
- signing, and
- sending back, as well as the action of
- allowing the direct withdrawal from your paycheck

are all driven by **principles**, right? I mean, you're doing it because you have values or principles that guide your life, including your finances. Underneath the surface of all of your actions are all of your life principles, on everything from finances to food intake, from parenting to physical fitness. And it's reasonable to assume that those guiding principles in this case of your 401k might read something like:

- 'Always be socking money away for retirement'
- 'Always have money on hand for a rainy day'
- 'Don't live paycheck to paycheck'
- 'Save!'
- 'Take a good deal when you see one'
- 'Invest wisely'

Well, as mentioned previously, it's not really the principles that are guiding your life, not ultimately. For, below the **behaviors/actions** of your life and below the **principles** that drive them are the real drivers of your entire operating system: your **core beliefs**. Beliefs, by definition, can neither be proven or disproved. Or, they can be both proven and disproved. They are generally greatly infused with, (if not the outright direct result of) tremendous fear, as well as some aspiration...but mostly fear. They are something you believe, often quite apart from logic. And, they are much more powerful than principles, much more compelling.

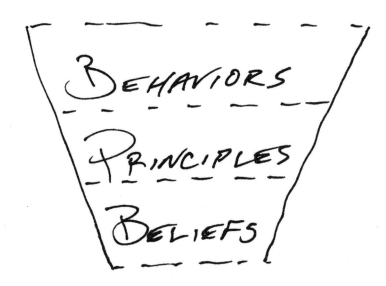

In the case of your 401k, the likely core beliefs driving both the principles and, eventually, the actions run something like:

- 'Life is uncertain'
- 'We lose the ability to make money as we age'
- 'Life is scary'
- 'Life is unpredictable'
- 'It would be horrible to be dependent on others'
- 'The WORST thing that can happen to me is to be destitute'
- 'I'm afraid of getting old'
- 'What if I lose my job?'

Every single one of those beliefs can be both proven and disproved. Life IS uncertain, but it's also quite predictable. Many DO lose the ability to make money as they age, yet a great many actually make more money, the older they get, if only by compounded interest, alone. Life IS (or can be) scary, but it's also quite routine and unintimidating. It COULD be bad to be dependent, but it also could be an unexpected delight, at least for a while. It COULD be the worst thing to be destitute, but it also is in no way life's scariest thing to be destitute; surely the death of a loved one, particularly a child, would be infinitely worse.

So, again, these are core beliefs, something you hold to be true, regardless of logic, reason, or provability. Yet, because they are driven by your greatest fears and most compelling aspirations, they are far more powerful than mere principles. It is your core beliefs that are truly driving your actions. Principles and values are about how you appear to others. Beliefs are the real reasons you're doing what you're doing up on the level of actions and behavior patterns.

As mentioned in the last chapter, change those beliefs, even slightly, and everything else changes, quite radically. By the time you get up through principles to the level of actions, even the tiniest adjustment of beliefs will bring about a radical change in behaviors, whether it's regarding investments and a 401k or something even more important.

The fundamental mistake many therapists and clergy make, not to mention well-intentioned friends, is the hyper-focus on actions, or behaviors. For it is on the surface of life that our problems manifest. So, it is quite natural to believe that that is where the solution lies, as well. It doesn't. Trying to change behaviors never changes behaviors, at least in the long term. It's in the business of beliefs that the exciting and lasting stuff really happens.

The 3 Binary Gates

Still, underneath all of the actions and principles is something even more powerful than the core beliefs, something that runs the whole machine, something even the core beliefs answer to. They are what I call the 3 Binary Gates. They rest on top of each other, above the soul, below the core beliefs.

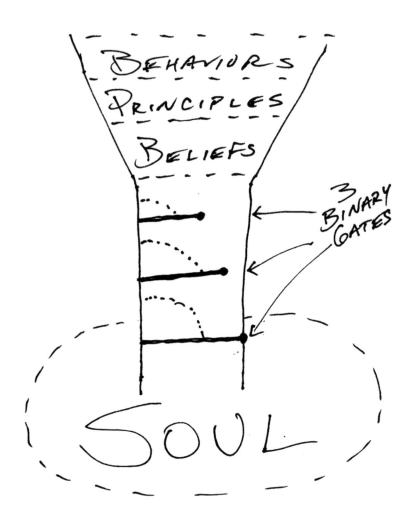

A person can have the most wonderful and fulfilling actions, the most detailed and logical principles, and the most positive and functional core beliefs, but if any of the 3 Binary Gates is closed, it blocks the upward flow of the voice of the soul. The whole system gets gummed up, runs dry, or simply stops working. This manifests in the forms of depression, anxiety, severe confusion, stops and starts, career frustration, emptiness, no sense of purpose, strong sense of unfulfillment in life, boredom, great negativity, and so many more ways.

While I've done decades of work with the poor and homeless, I have also made a fruitful and very exciting living working with tons of people who have it all – great house, great career, great spouse, great kids, great income. Everything seems great, but they are ridiculously unhappy, including great unrest in the soul and great anxiety in the head. All the actions, principles, and core beliefs seem to be just peachy, but something is so obviously amiss. It all tracks down to these 3 Binary Gates

The 3 Binary Gates are the most powerful beliefs driving your life in every way. Each is binary, either open or closed. On or off. Full or zero. Each is stacked on top of the next and they increase in intensity and importance, the deeper you go, closer to the soul.

Right below your core beliefs, is the **First Binary Gate**. It is simply:

"I am wanted" or "I am not wanted."

The message of this first Binary Gate was conveyed through the words and deeds of those who were primary in your early life and then confirmed, time and again, by people throughout your life. Thereby, they become cemented in the soul. Somewhere in life you got one of two overriding messages; either "I am wanted" or "I am not wanted." If you got the message 'I'm not wanted,' this message became an immovable, impenetrable source of core negativity and despair blocking the flow of your true self rising up from your soul, no matter how pretty life looked on the surface.

The child (or adult-child) whose first Binary Gate is flipped to the 'off' or 'closed' position of "I'm not wanted" is the one who was ignored, forgotten, or pushed away. This is the kid who had the overwhelming siblings that stole all the attention in the home. This is the kid who, no matter what he/she did, couldn't get a pat on the back or a kind word to save his/her life.

No matter where this child turned, he got no attention; he just could not find anyone to pour love into his Love Cup, contributing greatly to a feeling of being alone in the world. Where the average child is always trying to get his Love Cup filled, this child often becomes very desperate, very early. A massive contortion of the self begins, so as to become whatever he must become to get someone – anyone! – to pour love into his Love Cup.

NOT WANTED – NO LOVE SOURCES TO POUR LOVE IN

WANTED – AMPLE LOVE SOURCES

I have had clients who have distinct memories of feeling this way, as young as 3 or 4 years-old! To feel that no one loves you leads to great emptiness and great desperation. This child (and later this adult-child) will do anything to get love, positive attention, or even the slightest amount of niceness from another person, often engaging in risky or self-destructive behaviors to do so. This person will engage in the pattern of behavior of giving far more love than they ever get. This is because, at the core, they believe that's all they're worth. They're just happy to get any love and give up far too much love to get any small portion they ever receive. They'll spend their lives blaming mates or lovers, or claiming they have a 'bad picker' inside them that seems to always pick the wrong guys/women. But the real problem resides inside their own sense of unwantedness.

If/when this person does get love, it is never, ever enough. And this person will chase, unceasingly, the source of any such positive attention or niceness. Sadly, this person is easily manipulated by others, deliberately or not, who innately sense the desperation behind the pursuit. Eventually, this person simply begins attracting people who don't challenge this 'not wanted' belief but simply confirm it in word and deed.

You wonder why you have people in your life who don't give you love or only seem to take – energy, time, good will, emotional health – from you? It's because those people are the most familiar. They mirror precisely what you received by the most significant people in your life, growing-up. Interacting with them would be grating or annoying for many people, but for you they're hand-in-glove, even for as much as you hate them or they drive you crazy. Their way of treating you is familiar and, thus, oddly safe.

Your experience of people who are in your life but don't want you is that there is no love flowing toward you or into your life from them, except that they meet the most basic requirement: they're here with me. And that's all. But in an odd way that feels like enough, even though it in no way is. Maybe you're the giver – giving and giving and giving love, getting never enough in return. The way we feel wanted is that there is a positive balance of love and energy flowing back and forth. We feeeeeel someone giving love to us. One big effect of not feeling loved or wanted is that the child very easily translates this into an even more powerful negative belief. A child's mind very naturally converts 'I'm not wanted' into 'I'm no good' and 'I'm not worthy of love.' Unwanted becomes unworthy. What was formerly an external problem – no one around to pour love into me – has now sought a cause, a reason for the external problem. External goes internal: 'Something must be wrong with me,' 'I suck.'

The Second Binary Gate below the core beliefs is the simple, yet extremely powerful belief:

"I'm good" or "I'm not good enough"
or it can be:
"I'm a great person" or "I suck."

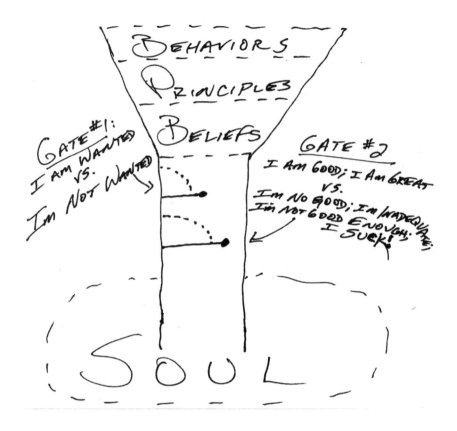

Again, it's binary: either off or on, one or the other, open or closed.

This is the really, really powerful place in which most people feel their struckness. Some can even see it clearly and articulate it. They know their own sense of self-loathing. It's the second-most powerful Binary Gate.

There are many ways the second Binary Gate gets closed. This gate is not just about someone not getting positive attention and love, and then converting that to self-suckery. As with the first Binary Gate, this is about getting very clear negative messages and criticism.

This is the girl who brought home their second grade report card with seven A's on it and mom's first response was, "Why'd you get the (lone) C?" Or, it's the boy who was told after scoring two goals yet fanning on the puck in front of the net in the 3rd, which would've given the win, "You're an embarrassment." No matter what, this kid was never good enough. And the kid who feels they're never good enough translates that message of 'not good enough' from mom or dad (or both) very easily into 'not good' or even to 'bad'.

Unless a distinction is made for a child between the action and the child's very identity when they're being scolded, the child – being a child – will quite naturally equate the parent's condemnation of the action (justified or not) with a condemnation of the child, himself. The child's identity becomes the messages conveyed consistently. And make no mistake, regardless of what you think your surface, or literal, message is, the child very much picks up on the underlying message that they're not good enough or no good, at all. That's just how a child's mind works. And *that* is the message that gets pressed into the wet cement.

This is especially true if the criticism comes many times, over the course of a childhood. And, it's quite reasonable to assume that if a kid got such messages once or twice, the kid got such messages a heckuva lot more times than that. For, a deliberate parent makes many mistakes, just like every other parent, but the type of mistake doesn't regularly repeat – i.e. the deliberate parent doesn't consistently make the same mistake, particularly when it holds the potential for impacting the child's very identity. So, if it happened twice, it likely happened more than twice. And so, the kid made the quite natural leap from judging action to judging identity, precisely as the parent did.

It's such an easy jump for a child from "I did bad" to "I am bad." The former is the judgment of a solitary action; the latter is the indictment of the child's entire character. Or, in worst case scenarios, the kid was flat out told by a critical, even abusive, parent, grandparent, or aunt/uncle that they were bad. No jump required.

The resulting effect on the child's Love Cup is that it distinctly and powerfully got something else put in it other than love: crud! Rocks, sludge, crap, and more rocks and crud. The child who was taught to believe that she was not good enough, no good, or just plain bad began to experience the Love Cup filling with negative messages. And those don't go away just because she is getting small amounts of love from other sources. It's possible to have an open first gate but closed second gate. But because the second gate is bigger and more powerful, it can do more damage by being closed, obstructing far more flow of soul up and outward to full expression.

Where the person with a closed first Binary Gate has few or no sources of love, at all, the person with a closed second Binary Gate experienced the insertion of powerful negative messages. Those messages usually started as judgments about her performance and behaviors in life, but quickly translated in the mind of the child into judgments about actual self-worth. Again, the parent (or significant power source) of the child may have inserted these rocks and crud messages deliberately or accidentally, in words or in actions (or inactions). But, the underlying message was always there. The negative messaging got in, stuck, stayed, and calcified. If these messages of 'no good', or 'not good enough' were repeated, they became the very messages imprinted in the wet cement of the child's soul. Permanent internal negative programming, undermining every success, caused two steps back for every one forward, increasing internal emptiness even if external greatness expanded.

This child, who received explicit or even implicit criticism of being 'not good enough' undergoes a radical change. She begins to fear any reminder of that message that was pressed into the cement of her soul: "You're not good enough." So, she created a life where there is no external hint of 'not good enough,' no potential for criticisms of inadequacy. Everything becomes the quest to hide the real self.

**This second Gate is the gate of high-achievers
and far too many women, nowadays.
These are the tenured professors, multi-billionaires/-
millionaires, CEOs, and extreme go-getters.**

Life for these folk often looks super great on the surface. This woman looks totally put together, on top of it all, succeeding, and up-and-coming. But she is chased by the dark demon of belief, deep inside, that nothing she does is ever good enough. She is forever proving herself, forever seeking higher praise, forever running, all the while thinking, "Maybe this will get me the praise that mom never gave me."

And let it be known, this message of "not good enough" or "you're inadequate" is being passed from one generation to the next just as prevalently by mothers as by fathers, nowadays. And it is always driven by a parent whose own Love Cup is filled with the exact same crud.

The crud in this child's (or adult-child's) Love Cup is basically manure and stones. This person is quite literally full of crap messages – spiritual poop and heavy negative spiritual rocks. And that's why the depression and heavy feelings kick in. The person feels just plain heavy inside. I'm of the belief that the damage done to a child by spiritual abuse exceeds that of physical abuse. Physical scars eventually fade. But the messages of spiritual abuse, which are what this chapter is about, haunt and run lives amok well into middle age, or later. These are inordinately powerful messages, particularly because they were implanted when just a child. The power of a parent over a child, as well as the extreme level of trust that a child has for a parent, combine to imbue any message with absolute certainty and the very power of the gods, themselves.

As he ages, this child can fit only the tiniest amounts of love or positive attention into her Love Cup, because it is so filled with negative messaging. He is, quite literally, full of sh-t. And until that crud is both identified and extracted someday, there can be no joy. This kid is simply incapable of believing they're good and lovable, because they're so full of precisely the opposite messaging. This is the kid who becomes a depressed adult, a neurotic and high-anxiety adult, an adult who just can't seem to figure out what the problem is with her life, how she can have it all and still be miserable inside.

This child or adult, at some point, begins trying to escape the reality of what's going on inside her. This is the manure pile and rocks from which eating disorders spring, as well as Xanax dependency, pot addiction, infidelity, bulimia, drug use, risky sexual behavior, and/or so much more. Life becomes two-faced: forever trying to be perfect on the surface and forever trying to escape her own head when not trying to be perfect.

This crud that fills the Love Cup – i.e. the soul – is that which blocks the flow of her true spirit and true voice rising up from within her. All of the fear-driven perfection and negative messages block her soul from expressing itself. Nothing of the true self is allowed to see the light of day, instead forced down into the darkest recesses of oneself. Showing the true self to the world would mean risking the most painful type of criticism. It is one thing to be criticized occasionally for the fake you you have become. But it is infinitely more terrifying to ever be criticized when showing the real you to the world, as you did when you were a child and first felt that deep sting of criticism.

The Most Powerful Part Of Your Life That You're Completely Unaware Of: The 3rd Binary Gate

Yet, for as treacherous to the soul as the first and second Binary Gates are, they pale in comparison to the power of the third and final Gate. This is the gate closest to the soul that often closes simultaneously with one of the upper gates. This bottom gate is the one that controls the whole system.

Everything – all of your life – boils down to this one gate. The third gate gets closed when a young girl or boy:

- gets that message that his grades weren't good enough, or
- when that child brings home an art project from preschool, only to have mother or father say with a scowl, "Why'd you use purple?" or
- has a mom who rarely leaves the bedroom, and is depressed and bed-ridden; and the kids go on about cooking, doing laundry, and fending for themselves, or
- when the boy asks dad to play catch, but dad regularly says he doesn't have time, or
- when mom is too busy with her business to not just be around for the child but to not even be fully present when she is around the child, or
- when dad is an alcoholic, whom everyone in the family is on eggshells around, fearful of when he will explode next, or
- when the grandparents or favorite uncle always seem to favor a sibling, or
- when there is a sibling that naturally gets a lot of attention, or
- when mom is gone most of the time to be at her boyfriend's house, leaving the kids to cook and clean for themselves, or
- when there is no mom or grandpa to tell a girl she ought not get into drugs in middle school, or
- when the six year-old puts on a theater production in the garage with neighborhood kids, only to be met with condescension or criticism from an insensitive parent
- when there's a 'golden child' in the family...and you ain't it

When any such events happen to a child, the message the child gets is "Who YOU really are is irrelevant. You need to become what I want you to be." The person with a closed third binary gate believes "the real me doesn't matter" or "the real me simply doesn't exist." **The Third Binary Gate is:**

"I matter/I don't matter."
More accurately,
"the real me matters" or "the real me doesn't matter."

The First Binary Gate is about the child's external world ('No one wants to give me love'). The Second Binary Gate is about the child's interior world ('I suck' or 'I'm not good enough'). The Third Binary Gate is existential ('The real me doesn't matter or even exist').

The 1ˢᵗ Binary Gate is an assessment of external reality. The 2ⁿᵈ Binary Gate is an assessment of internal reality, a value judgment. The 3ʳᵈ Binary Gate is not about good or bad, but whether the person's true self even matters, and that is a nuanced but significant difference.

What makes the Third Binary Gate so long-lastingly more powerful is that it is not merely about *value*, but about the very existence of the child – the real identity of the child, as opposed to that child's function in the parent's life. It is an *existential pronouncement*: "The real me doesn't matter; it just doesn't exist." To say someone/something doesn't exist is incredibly powerful. But that is what the parent is doing.

Or, for example, if the parent uses the child to dump the parent's problems onto, the child's significance and existence get minimized, even negated. This far-too-common occurrence instills in the child several messages, not the least of which is 'You exist to serve my (emotional) needs' and 'Your problems don't matter; mine do (or mine – and by natural extension me – matter more than yours/you'), such as is often also conveyed by the alcoholic or abusive parent.

This is a very easy message for a child to get. For example, it may start from a parent saying, "I'm sorry I'll miss your dinner/soccer game/school play/birthday party, but I have work and work is important." If it happens enough times, the child very easily and naturally translates this into, "Work is more important than me," which is just a small step from "I'm not important," eventually becoming, "I don't matter."

This may seem silly or even easily surmountable for an adult. But it's neither silly, nor easy for an adult, because it has become written in the cement of their soul. And it's inordinately powerful for a child. This is exactly how a child's mind thinks. Actions carry meanings. Carried out enough times, these actions become meanings that a child takes on as part of his or her identity, pressed into the wet cement of her soul. And this is never good.

What happens when a child gets any of these messages, but particularly the third one, is that she says, "Screw this pain" and without even knowing it, takes the 'real me' and sticks it in an imaginary cigar box, wraps that box in hardcore duct tape, and sticks that box waaaaaaaay down deep inside herself, under the bed next to the Christmas sweaters, never to be opened again.

This child then becomes whomever he, or she, has to be to win positive attention and avoid negative attention, or criticism. So painful is the message "The real you doesn't matter" that the single biggest fear of life becomes showing the world who you really are. The rest of his/her life is spent hiding, running from the pain, and living in some form or another of soul misery. Period. End of story. For, any sort of criticism from childhood forward becomes a highly charged reminder of that pain from childhood, when it was conveyed to her in no uncertain actions that who she really is just doesn't matter.

Why?

The effect of that 3rd Binary Gate
being closed
is that a hole gets punched
in the bottom of the Love Cup.

And, that hole is small enough to keep in any solid crud and rocks of negative messages that may come in, yet big enough to drain out all the liquid love of positive messages.

This is huge! A hole in the bottom of the Love Cup of the soul changes everything, effectively negating the ability to acquire and pool any feelings of love inside. A Love Cup with a hole in the bottom means the bearer will never feeeeel loved or feel good, except in fleeting moments of ecstasy from some sort of drug or experience.

Poke a hole in a styrofoam cup. Then pour water into it from a pitcher. Run your finger along the inside of a cup, after you've poured the water and it has drained out. The inside walls of the cup are moist. There is residue of the love poured through. But it is only residue, only a reminder. The love never pools inside. It just teases and is gone.

Believing in the very negation of his existence, this child (or adult-child) is simply incapable of containing love. It just drains out. There is never enough coming in. It may feel good passing through, but it never stays. The child-as-adult may have everything in life, all the successes and veneer of having it together, but deep inside – pressed into the very bedrock of his soul – is the belief that the real me doesn't matter. This person feeling loved is always dependent upon something/someone external. She can't feel loved, or even feel good, by herself, because 'herself' is empty, or maybe empty of love. Instead, she's full of crud messages. This person is forever dependent upon her exterior life to feed her interior life and thereby pour love into her. And, quite frankly, there is never enough love or love sources. (By the way, this person as a parent bleeds her children of their life energy, whether they're aware of it or not. She's a spiritual vampire.)

However, the worst part about the hole in the bottom of the Love Cup is that this person has a visceral feeling of hopelessness. When there is a hole in the bottom of the Love Cup there is literally no hope of ever being filled up with love. How could there be? Any love that flows in is gone just as soon as it came. The growing awareness of the unending emptiness of the Cup quite naturally is experienced as hopelessness.

**A hole in the Love Cup means
there's no hope of ever being filled with love.
And this produces anxiety. High anxiety.
A franticness.
And a powerful, deep depression that most people, therapists
and clergy
can never quite put their finger on.**

Like that damn squirrel frantically foraging for nuts, this person feels the coming winter and is certain of the instant depletion of anything good that comes. Certain of death, there is always a looming sorrow.

And so, the reason people engage in all manner of negative actions, 'bad' behaviors, or paths that hold the potential to greatly screw up their lives is because they live in fear of running out of love. So they frantically forage in all directions, no matter how dangerous those directions might be.

Driving it all is the fear of showing the world who they really are, because they've been told their real self just does not matter. They've been wounded at the very deepest level. So, they keep the surface clean and engage in all manner of escapism beneath the surface, out of sight from judging and criticizing eyes. They cannot find love in honest ways of standing up for their needs, because they do not believe that their own needs truly matter or even exist. They simply are incapable of believing that they even have worth enough to ask. They. Don't. Matter. At least not their real self. The only pseudo-mattering is the fake self – the persona – they've laboriously built, over decades. For, it is that persona that others feed off of, give approval to, and deem to matter. And it's all a lie.

Marital infidelity, for example – that hidden form of foraging for cheap and unfair positive attention and life energy – is always rooted in the fear of truly showing my real self to my spouse, not to mention the world, because such vulnerability is unthinkable. It's way too scary, in no small part because the relationship was built on my being this fake self. Rather than stand up and speak one's truth, rather than be strong and insist on what life would truly make him happy, this person hides his real self out of sheer terror. Cheating is always generated by fear. Always.

The power of the third Gate is that it keeps people locked in fake lives that are inherently unfulfilling, mind-numbing, and soul-crushing. It keeps the real you forever hidden. Everything, everything, everything is driven by fear. And this is weakness.

The imprinting of this message into the cement of a soul is so strong that the original source of the message could've long ago faded away, but it still rings in the head of the one who received it. This great lie that got imprinted in the soul is so powerful that it becomes the person's own identity. The voice of the parent becomes indistinguishable from the child's/adult's own voice. He thinks he hates himself, when really it was a lie that was implanted, someone else's hate or indifference. Worst of all, the voice or actions of the parent are no longer needed for the perpetuation of this completely debilitating message. The adult-child owns it now.

Look out if that parent, who was the original source of the message, dies. Don't think the message dies with the parent. Quite the opposite. Death often makes it ten times worse, because the parent and her message are then viewed with nostalgia and a certain gravitas we afford only the dead. It becomes much more difficult to extract the voice in this case.

And the message inside just runs on this infinite, never-ending loop: "I don't matter. The real me just doesn't matter." On and on, forever sucking the life out of your very soul. You no longer own yourself, but are owned by an external power source that has been internalized. And decades of pain ensue, no matter how good and perfect you may look on the outside.

The source of all your pain in life is the fear of becoming the real you. To be, say, do, and become on the outside that which you are in the deepest depths of your insides is unthinkable. The fear of speaking your truth and living your real self are at the root of it all. It is the fear of what others will think, say, and do if you show the world who you really are. Tragically, you will never be happy, until you do the one thing you're most afraid of: remove the fear and then be, say, do, have, look like, live wherever, and become that which your soul is calling you to.

Until you become the real you, *until you finally matter to you,* there will be no joy, no lasting peace, no fulfillment, and no cessation to the running and anxiety that grip your soul.

Song recommendation

Download and listen to *Let me be myself* by **3 Doors Down**.
https://www.youtube.com/watch?v=RmDYbiyMHvoLetMeBeMyself
Real spiritual stuff!

CHAPTER 10

GROWING RODS AND VIDEO SURVEILLANCE

Here's the trippy part. Granted, it's a bit of a dopey metaphor, but stay with me.

After stuffing the real self into the box, deep down inside, the kid then grows four steel rods out of the top of her head, say six feet long. Two of them arch out in front her at the 10 and 2 o'clock positions, and two hanging out over the back at the 4 and 8 positions. At the end of each of those metal rods is a video camera; two, actually; one pointing out and one pointing in.

Essentially, when this kid packs her real self away, deep inside, she begins monitoring every person around her. She becomes an expert at reading people, if she isn't already from reading her parents and significant influences. The outward-pointing video cameras are forever monitoring the sources of influence, reading what it is they want in order to be pleased, specifically in order to give positive attention, in return. Remember, it's all about love into the Love Cup.

"Mrs. Anderson, the teacher, likes attentive and smart girls; so I'll be attentive and work hard to be smart, or at least look smart." "Mommy likes it when I'm quiet and have perfect grades. So, I'm just always going to be quiet and makes sure there's nothing wrong with my report card or at school." ET terrace. On and on.

The child basically becomes this amalgam of whatever she has to be to, basically, purchase positive attention and avoid negative attention from those who have the power to give it. Life ceases to be about being real or even happy, really. It becomes about being perfect, or at least creating the illusion of perfection. Perfect grades. Perfect hair. Perfect clothes. Perfect manners. Perfect words. Perfect decisions. Nice to everyone. Many successes. No conflict. Lots of smiles and gratitude lists.

And that's the purpose of those other cameras at the end of the rods, the ones pointing in. The kid is forever monitoring herself, making doggone sure she is constantly perfect.

I have had clients who would lay in bed at night, as children, running through in their mind all they did in the past day, reviewing for slip-ups and areas to avoid in the future, things that caused pain, humiliation, embarrassment. As a child! Can't you just see the level of neurosis and self-loathing starting in a child possessed by such thinking and living, possessed by such an all-consuming, fear-driven belief system? Is it any wonder children become shy or terrified to speak? Is it any wonder some children spend their lives flying under the radar or just skating by, terrified to stick out or open themselves to criticism in any way? Is it any wonder why so many children and young adults become afraid to have dreams in life (and yes, I have had countless adult clients who have said to me, "Sven, I don't think I've ever had a dream," which is a statement so unfathomable and breathtakingly tragic), afraid of opening up their great desires and passions to the crippling criticality of those who claim to love them most?

Some became *so* obsessed with perfection and *so* terrified of that criticism that they added one more thing with the rods and cameras. They ran a microphone up inside their own brain, so to speak. I have had clients who confess to laying in bed at night monitoring and reviewing not only their actions from the past day but their own thoughts, looking for any hint of bad thinking, bad thoughts, or anything *dirty* inside them. The level of neurosis! As a child!

The level of self-consciousness and sheer terror necessary to drive a child to do this is unthinkable. As an adult, it can be easy to think of this as no big deal, to pass it off as childish nonsense. But that is to miss the child mind and spirit in all of this. It is to fail to see and feel it as a child would, where every offense is grievous and terribly painful. Without the liberty to cry it out and talk it out, and thereby extract the pain from the soul, it becomes implanted – a fully charged, embedded memory. And that ain't good. Further, that wounded and spiritually crippled child is forever alive inside the individual, no matter what sort of 'responsible' adult-ish veneer is used to paper over it.

It is precisely at this moment – at this moment necessitated by the survival of the soul of the child, when the rods, cameras, and microphones of self-scrutiny are unwittingly put into place – that the powerful voices and messages of the external power sources become internal. It is precisely at this moment that the incessant, infinite loop of the voice of the parent hits 'play'. So, when the day comes that this person finds herself in my office for counseling and I ask her something like, "Who is your biggest critic," or "You say you're most afraid of failure, but I want to know whose voice you most fear hearing if you do fail," or "What person is the biggest undermining force in your life," she answers, "Oh that's easy. It's myself. I'm my own worst critic."

Of course, that's never true. Well, it is on the surface. But what has really happened is that the critical voices that were never hers, to begin with, have become so tuned into, so obsessed over and fixated on, that they have become indistinguishable from her own voice. And therein is the crime, when she owns as her very own the very worst messages she ever possibly could. And, as shall be examined later, this is why the parent has to less and less express his or her wants and expectations for the child. *The child (or later the adult child) already knows!* The child has been tuned into the messages, spoken and unspoken, of the parent, since the very youngest age. The teenager or young adult knows EXACTLY what the parent wants, expects, or demands without the parent ever having to utter a word. This, of course, is why so many parents can get away with the throwaway line, "But I tell my kids they can do whatever they want in life" or "I never tell my kids what to do. They're free to be themselves," or "I never told my son where to go to college or told my daughter who to marry," or some such things. The messages and expectations of the parent(s) became so embedded and foundational in the child, running on infinite loop, that the parent is always present, always demanding, always critiquing.

And it is this mad infinite loop that becomes the voices in her head that she tries to escape in teen years or young adulthood. It is this cameras-and-criticism driven mind that makes her so susceptible to peer pressure in her teens. It's a longing for the calming of the mind, even for a moment, that drives her to drink, smoke pot, drop out of school, or become overly sexually promiscuous in college or after. It's the desire for escape from this incessant churning of the mind that drives the bulimia and anorexia, the depression and anxiety, the incessant busyness and desire for chaos and drama. It is in this moment, when the rods and cameras are put into place, that her fate as a runner is cemented – until the cement gets smashed, she will forever run from what is inside her, trying to create escapes and pseudo-solutions outside her, to no avail.

Adulthood

The really crazy part about this stuffing of the real self into a box down inside is that it doesn't magically stop, come back up, or go away when the child becomes an adult. Heck, it gets worse, actually, because more and more negatively charged memories accrue, only confirming the not-mattering. The soul becomes more and more numb, over time, from being ignored. The spirit becomes deadened. And the fear only increases.

Barring some major life event that jars the person, cracking open a giant fissure in the soul and spilling open the box inside, that box and the accrued pain demand more and more energy to keep them down. Suppression of true self – suppression of the soul – requires huge energy, sapping every other aspect of life. It can require just as much energy, or more, to deny or suppress something as it does to actually purge it. And life energy is finite. If you're using your life energy to keep down all the old stuff, it's energy you ain't got for new stuff and exuberant living. You're being bled dry by a soul that ain't truly living, that is blocked. You're being bled by a series of core beliefs that keep one foot on the brake, even as you attempt to put a harder foot to the accelerator.

And so, whether it's the teen years, college, or adulthood, life becomes more and more about getting high on the side, in one form or another, (whether cheating, boozing, over-working, binge-eating, or something else) while attempting to maintain the illusion of perfection in the eyes of everyone else. As you live the lie in your everyday life – perfect husband, perfect house, perfect career, greater and greater successes, perfect income, perfect kids, perfect clothes, and perfect hair still – your emptiness inside only increases. The numbness increases. The deadness increases. The pain increases. The misery increases. *The longing to escape increases.*

The child who grew rods and video cameras keeps it up, well into adulthood. Sadly, what he sees in all the self-surveillance footage becomes less and less pretty. He sees his lie in HD clarity.

He sees his own self-sabotage: all of his surreptitious efforts to get high in some self-destructive way. He sees the imperfection slowly eating through the veneer of perfection and success. (And all of this is the soul trying to explode the lie, so the soul's truth can finally be free.) This is the adult who, after some extended social interaction is self-consciously replaying the whole scene and sending out emails apologizing for this or that gaffe or slightest of social failures. It's the adult whose Love Cup fills more and more with the rocks and sh-t of self-loathing rooted, of course, in the judgmental voices from decades prior.

It feels hopeless and terrifically maddening, not the least of which is because you can't seem to slip the bonds it has on your life. People tell you to get over it. They say, "What's wrong with you? You have everything." Even you don't understand it. But there it is, a life that's a mess and completely unintelligible, an illogical misery. You live in complete unawareness of the core beliefs driving the system, the fear-driven ethos, and the real you in some cigar box deep inside...waiting, longing to be free.

Song Recommendation

As a brilliant and passionate expression of this loneliness and sense of hopelessness that come from living inside yourself and living with this never-ending sense of dread and failure, I commend to your listening pleasure **Don't Give Up**, by **Peter Gabriel**. Buy it and dive into the words and power. https://www.youtube.com/watch?v=uiCRZLr9oRwDontGiveUp

Bonus Track

Check out:

- Bonus Track 2: *Why Telling An Adult 'Just Get Over It And Move On' Is The Dumbest Thing Ever.*

CHAPTER 11

EMPTY LOVE CUPS PRODUCE RELATIONSHIP CAMELS

The effect of a rock-filled, crud-filled Love Cup with a hole in the bottom – that is, the effect of someone possessing the deepest beliefs that they aren't wanted, aren't good enough, and/or don't matter – is that all of life is impacted, most especially relationships. Life becomes much, much heavier and that bleeds everything. One of the most common problems I see in clients is massively bankrupt relationships and marriages.

Y'know how a camel can go a long time, across a desert, without water?

Well, many years ago, after a few eye-opening relationships, I realized that I had become what I now call a 'Relationship Camel.' A Relationship Camel does everything in his/her power to make the other person happy. Relationship Camel's excel at pleasing others, waiting on them, anticipating their needs, and giving, giving, giving.

The underlying thinking goes, "Oh, I'll give you everything you want. Here, let me get that for you. Let me do this for you. Don't worry about me. I can take it. Just let me do these things for you. Just give me a little bit of love, in return." Just as a camel can go a long distance without water, a Relationship Camel can go a long distance on a little bit of love or on almost no love at all.

See, what the Relationship Camel is doing is fundamentally purchasing love, and at a very high price. The Relationship Camel is so used to not getting love, or only used to getting small amounts, that when he/she finds someone who even gives a little, she gives up everything and all concerns to win a breadcrumb more. In fact, this type of person is often found with someone who, because of their upbringing and core beliefs, gives far less love. People who are big takers of love are often givers of very little; and big givers are often small takers; hence, a perfect, if ill-begotten, fit. Further, it is a situation quite familiar to the Relationship Camel, as old as his/her childhood, where all of this was learned in the first place.

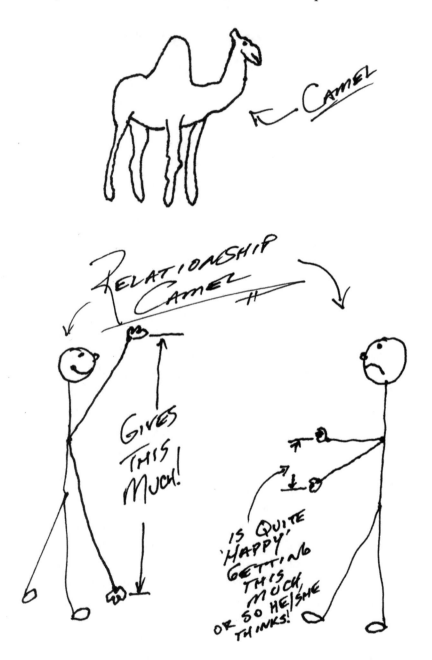

But here's the wacky part: a Relationship Camel also often falls in with a taker, simply because the Camel doesn't know what to do with someone who gives a lot of love. For as much as she may long for a giver, a Relationship Camel becomes discombobulated when she is not the main giver. She doesn't know what to do or how to act. She fears that if she stops, or even slows, she won't be loved.

Even more screwy, a Relationship Camel tends to not trust someone who gives too much, or what seems like too much, based on what she thinks she deserves. With people who believe, at their core, that they don't matter or aren't good enough, the more love their mate shows, the less she trusts him. In other words, if a Relationship Camel finds herself in a personal or professional relationship with someone who gives a lot, the Camel, male or female, tends to not believe the other person is telling the truth. Big givers are untrustworthy to the Camel, because they go against the Camel's inner self-belief.

Chew on that one, a minute! Even if the Camel – let's say it's a woman in this case – is thought to be wonderful by her mate, she (the Camel) not only won't believe his words, she won't believe him to be a credible person. For, the words coming out of his mouth go against the truth of her spirit, her own self-belief that she's no good or doesn't matter. He may be giving her the very salve she has been seeking her whole life – sincere words and actions +of love and adoration. But she won't trust him, not because he is not a credible person but because she perceives him to be non-credible, because he speaks a truth that goes against her deepest beliefs of self-loathing and self-abnegation.

Or, even still more odd, she'll see him as flawed, or look down on him, for loving her. Many women think, "What must be wrong with him if he likes me?"

Her own distrust of him – based on nothing about him – thus effectively undermines the relationship. When we don't trust, we don't open up. We hide behind walls, and don't reveal who we really are. She's convinced that if he knew the *real* her, he'd leave. So, her distrust of him causes her to pull back, which, again, insidiously chips away at the relationship, because he is not receiving the real her. If he is bonding with her, it is with a false version of her, or only a surface version of her. And no people can truly bond if they don't reveal their truest selves. So, eventually he does, in fact, pull back and/or leave. Her prophecy is fulfilled. She creates the very eventuality she sought so assiduously to avoid. The fear kept her behind her walls and the walls are what keep him from ever being able to truly know her and love her. And so, he quit, just as she predicted (and enacted). In other words, her own negative self-belief is the cause of the destruction of the relationship.

A female client will say she wants, more than anything, to be loved for who she really is.
To this her lover responds,
"How can I love you for who you really are if you don't show me who you really are?"

That's why Relationship Camels prefer people who are takers, who only give a little bit of love, because they, quite ironically, feel they can trust such a person more! The words and actions of a taker, and the underlying message on which they're based, are familiar and therefore easy and consistent with what she has always heard and believed. They're safe. And so, a Camel keeps picking takers, because the takers' messages are reflective of her own beliefs and what she has been taught, since young. She keeps allowing it. The big lie she was taught – 'You don't matter' and/or 'You're no good' and/or 'You're not wanted' – drives her life and manifests more pain, in the form of unhealthy relationships. And so, the Camel will go on purchasing love – giving a big chunk of themselves for a little bit of the prized love in return.

But, worse, the Camel is forever making her happiness commensurate upon someone else's happiness, if for no other reason than the fact than the taker generally only gives love to the Camel when he's happy. I mean, how many takers do you know that actually give love when they're unhappy? 'Taker' implicitly means 'not giver'. So, the Camel is forever looped into, susceptible to, and almost entirely driven by the feelings of others, especially those closest to her, who demand she keep pouring love into their hole-poked Love Cups. (And, those relationships only end when the Camel realizes she keeps pouring love into a person who never fills up with the love she gives. For, the love is gone as quickly as she gives it.)

So, the Relationship Camel basically lives in a world defined by 'happiness by proxy': If you're happy, then I'm happy; or, I'm only happy when the people around me are happy. In other words, there's only the loosest correlation between how much I invest in life and how much happiness I have (rather than, "I'm in control of my own happiness.") I have less control over my own happiness, because it is dependent upon an intermediary – my mate or boss or parent or son/daughter – who has to be made happy first, or whose happiness is the very definition of my own happiness. How messed up is that?!

Yet, you keep choosing that, keep choosing to live that. Granted, it's your choice, at this point, now that you see what the source is. But, you really gotta wonder about the logic of choosing to live this way. Forever strung-out on whatever the people around you are feeling, utterly incapable of even fantasizing about what it must be like to feel *your own* feelings, instead of being weighed down by everyone else's.

Rather than a much more direct correlation between my investment in life and my happiness, rather than invest directly of myself into myself by choosing the people, places, plans, and paths that make me happy – that give love, life and energy back to me in big helpings – if I'm a Relationship Camel, I invest in others with only the slightest hope that they will give me some love in return...because I can go a long distance on only a little bit of love. Rather than invest my love directly into the paths of my own happiness, I invest my love near-completely into others, hoping to get some of the run-off, at some point.

Among my Wall Street clients, this sort of relationship, stock or fund investment – high cost, low payoff – would be considered a terrifically bad investment, to be aborted, or shorted, immediately. And yet, a great many people in their personal relationships will continue to pour good money after bad, or good energy after bad, as it were – investing and investing and investing in people who have already established, through a long pattern of behavior, that they have zero interest in offering any sort of return on investment.

Yet, of course, the problem is not the other person. The problem is not that the taker is doing this to you. The real problem is that you're allowing it. What does it say about you that you'd allow someone to treat you this way? What are you saying about you by allowing this? The root is always found deep inside the Camel him-/herself, particularly in her belief that this is all she deserves, as well as her inability to both conceive and create a belief system and concomitant life that are anything different.

When A Relationship Camel Breaks Up

I'm getting ahead of myself, a bit, as I hit on more relationship and marriage stuff later in the book, specifically how to know if/when it's time to break up. However, it's salient, at this early stage in the book, to understand both who the Relationship Camel is and how she (or he) thinks, both in and out of a relationship. Doing so sets up a more complete understanding of the Love Cup and the 3 Binary Gates, providing something to ping off of.

So, for now, suffice it to say that the point does come when a Relationship Camel says she wants a divorce or a break up. It comes from pouring love, attention and energy into someone else's punctured Cup and from having no love pool inside of herself. But she experiences it as deadness, emptiness, numbness, exhaustion, depression, and lack. And eventually, the deadness and pain become so great that she has no choice but to leave.

But now, here's the really kooky part. At this point of pulling away from her spouse, things seemingly change very quickly in her partner, but the results are deceptive and therefore confusing to the Camel. This leads to bad decisions and more pain. Whether because she is simply exhausted from too much giving or because she has actually begun the process of changing her self-beliefs, if a Camel begins to end a relationship, the Relationship Camel's mate often becomes a prince, sends flowers, wants to be with her and, in short, becomes the person she always wanted him to be. This is the confusing part, because it can be powerfully intoxicating, at least for a while.

But it's a deception, whether intentional or unintentional. For, the Camel's mate hasn't solved the real problem driving his initial taking and indifference, the indifference that led the Camel to break up in the first place. There has been no change in the taker's core beliefs or 3 Binary Gates that drive behavior. He has only changed his surface behaviors. This is a glowing testament to the power of core beliefs, as well as the truism that trying to change behaviors never changes behaviors, long term. Core beliefs must change. Otherwise, the flowers, softness, kind words, and giving of attention peter out. Eventually, he *will* revert back to his old self, as sure as the sun rises in the east. More often than not, this reversion comes after only months, or sometimes weeks. Nothing has changed deep inside, so the behaviors simply cannot last. In the end, the pretty veneer rubs off and you realize that any last ditch efforts by your mate are simply too little, too late, and but a chimera. Out of fear, he whipped up some action. And it dissipates at the point he realizes that either she's not going back to her old giving ways or he's sick of giving soooo much.

I have a dear friend, whom I played violin with and was in orchestra with, from 1st through 8th grades. This friend, Hokan, has owned his own company with his now ex-wife, since his early 20s. He has factories in China and the US, splitting his time between the two, and eventually fell in love with a woman and started a family in China. After 25 years of doing business in China and particularly after getting to know his Chinese wife's peasant, rural family, Hokan says that the leaders of China have a fascinating understanding of their own peasant people, most of whom live a very poor existence, much like that of his in-laws.

Hokan explained it to me over a Skype session,

> *"In rural China, a great many peasants may get only one loaf of bread, per week, from the government. The communist leaders are savvy and realize that they don't have to promise these peasants a big house and a middle class existence in the suburbs to keep them happy in their squalor. There's no point in investing that much or even falsely offering that much. It's unnecessary. The peasant is incapable of even conceiving of such an existence. No, all the leaders have to promise is a second loaf of bread, per week, and those peasants will think they've hit the jackpot. They've just doubled their earnings!*

This peasant mentality is precisely the pitfall of the Relationship Camel, when it comes to breakups or time to divorce. Having lived in relationship poverty for so long, the Camel is susceptible to being sucked back in by a two-loaf mentality, by a mere double return on profits, as if that's some sort of victory. Whether the Camel's mate realizes it or not, precious little is required to lure the Camel back (highly unlikely the mate is consciously aware of it; more likely, the mate simply wants to continue to invest as little as possible to get immediate returns. Think about it, how long can the mate sustain such a high love output, when he too has an empty Love Cup?). So soothing is that balm of a second loaf – whether in the form of flowers, notes, touch, kind words, attention, or just plain time together ("Someone actually wants to be with ME!") – that it can lead to a massive distortion of reality. It engenders the false belief that life is tolerably better now and that this can actually last, not to mention the naive belief that this is actually even a distant relative of happiness.

Bad, bad, bad. Life is not markedly better now. And, it certainly won't last. It can't.

Yet, sometimes that is what it takes before we're fully, 100% ready to leave a relationship. Sometimes we have to get the strength and self-love to leave, see the effects of my change on my partner, get sucked in, and then get sucked back down before we have the real, lasting 'Aha!' moment that nothing has changed and ain't nothin' ever gonna change. Sometimes we have to get lured back by the attention and shiny things and grand lies of leaves seemingly turned. Sometimes our growth requires getting sucked back down, when in a position of growing inner strength, before we see things with keener eyes, see the changes as illusions, and make decisions more lastingly.

In the end, however, the plight of the Relationship Camel in a marriage, intimate relationship, or divorce is almost irrelevant compared to the Camel's relationship with his or her own self. The problem is never the Camel's mate. It's not even the Camel's actions. The problem driving the whole equation is the Camel's core beliefs and Binary Gates. Everything flows from these. The Relationship Camel only ceases to be a Camel when she has the courage to change her core beliefs and thereby begin the process of living deliberately and, in the end, much more happily.

100

Journaling Recommendation

1. In which relationships in your life are you investing way more than you're getting?

2. More importantly, are you beginning to understand the correlation between core beliefs and the shape of the world around you, the world you've created? Are you beginning to understand that even the slightest shift in core beliefs is a shift in the tectonic plates underneath your life, creating earthquakes of change in your life principles and eventually your actions?

3. Which relationships have you been sucked back into by shiny baubles and grand promises? How long did it take for these 'changes' to peter out? What do you think caused them to peter out?

4. From whom did you learn how to be a Relationship Camel – the person who taught you how to live with a taker and make a taker happy? And who was the taker in that Camel's life – the taker you, yourself, likely still fear critique from and long for praise from?

5. How bad does the pain of deadness have to get before you're finally ready to let go, become unwound from the emotions of others, and finally live not just freer but lighter? When do you finally realize the futility of 'happiness by proxy'?

6. 'How can I love you for you really are, if you won't show me who you really are?' Are you still hiding behind your walls? Has your pain gotten bad enough that you're willing to risk and open up?

CHAPTER 12

THE BAG OF ROCKS ON YOUR BACK

As mentioned in Chapter 2, every experience in life and every memory has an emotional charge, either positive or negative. Every negatively charged memory is like a rock that has been put in a giant burlap sack on your back. When we're young, it's nothing to have a few negative experiences and then to carry around some rocks on our back, because: A) We're young and have energy; B) For the most part, only so much can accrue in the short time of a young life.

But it does accrue. And accrue. And this is a problem.

The kid who has a crummy childhood is accumulating rocks in that burlap sack very, very quickly. Again, that kid has a ton of life energy, which is accompanied by the very naive belief of, 'I can take it. I'm fine', and which is sometimes drained by parents who use children for their own emotional needs (see 'Emotional Incest' article on the BadassCounseling.com website).

Of course, one thing we learn as we age (and with some folks it comes later than sooner, unfortunately) is that we can't take it, at least not without some grand price. And there is always a price for carrying around a gunny sack of negative energies – i.e. memories loaded with a (sometimes significant) negative charge. Internal pain and negative messages that were pressed into the cement of your soul, back when it was still wet and massively impressionable, slowly wear down your belief in yourself, wear down relationships, wear down dreams, and wear down physical health and *energy*. How can a person possibly maintain any energy when they're, metaphorically speaking, carrying around a 200, 300 or 500 bag of rocks on their back? Negative internal stuff is weight. Fact.

I mean, are you actually surprised you're depressed, when all of your life energy is spent carrying around a 500lb bag of negatively charged life experiences and memories? Just because you find ways to avoid thinking about these memories and feeeeling their emotional charges does not mean they are not in you, affecting you, pulling you down. Those negatively charged memories drain a person's life energy, no matter how much people try to conjure willpower to avoid them, be happy, get over it, or any other such nonsense.

Drained of so much life energy, you check out of life. Check out of relationships. Check out of greater responsibilities. Or even check out of day-to-day functioning. Why? You simply don't have energy. The internal stuff affects – greatly! – the external stuff.

And what's crazy is that people can't figure out why they can't get motivated to do what they know they want to do; can't figure out why they sabotage the very relationships they know they want; can't figure out why they just can't peel themselves up off the couch or can't put down the bong or the bottle. That bag of rocks leads to all manner of addiction. And what's worse is that people focus on trying to get rid of their addiction, as if the addiction itself is the problem. It's not. In fact, the addiction has been an odd friend – the only thing keeping you alive, by giving you occasional reprieves from the weight of life, time and again. It is the only thing that has enabled you to shut off the incessant running of your mind and the massive negative thoughts and beliefs coursing through your system. Fix the core beliefs and Gates driving you, root out the viruses infecting the operating system, de-charge the memories, and all of a sudden the burden of life is gone, energy returns, and the addiction becomes unnecessary and is much more easily moved past.

A gifted and experienced therapist is really in the business of pulling the rocks out of your bag and taking them from you. The book you're reading is my lovely rock garden in my back yard, metaphorically speaking, because all of my clients' rocks of negatively charged memories have no meaning or charge for me. So I can take and take someone's rocks, unburdening them of a lifetime of pain, lightening their load, enabling them to move forward, and turn them into something useful or beautiful.

What's quite ironic about this whole concept of carrying around life's negative energies is that this is one of those areas of life where it's no grand blessing to be 'stronger'. See, the stronger person will tough it out for a whole lot longer, years or decades even, rather than finally break down and begin the process of letting go of the negative energies. This is a situation where it's far better to be wise than strong. For, why carry around a lifetime of negative energy if you don't have to? It makes no sense, as it is only holding you down from being light and at peace, and only holding you back from being your true self.

Except that people fear the pain of bringing it all back up again. Fear feeling it again as the pain leaves the body. Fear feeling stupid. Fear being overwhelmed by the pain. Fear that the pain will never leave, once it is given oxygen and light of day. And so, people engage in all matter of neurotic and destructive behavior to run from the bag of rocks, at least to the degree anyone can run from a 500lb bag of rocks that is firmly affixed to their back or run with a 500lb bag of rocks firmly affixed to their back.

But it does pass. And there are mechanisms for doing it more quickly, which is why I strongly recommend learning the discipline of using the Sedona Method. For years, I also used journaling, which is highly effective, if a bit slower than Sedona, which I only found about 10 years ago. We start by asking the surface questions about what's hurting or bothering oneself, then ask deeper questions, like 'What's below that' or 'Why am I feeling that' or 'What triggered that?' A bit deeper and a bit deeper, eventually it is very possible to get down to the root of the matter, and that's when the real magic happens. I'm also a big fan of letter writing. Regularly, I have clients write out the most vehement, angry, hurt-filled letters they can possibly flush out to the people who have most affected them....and not mail the letters or hit the 'send' button.

I require all clients to write their life's story in a full autobiography to me, before I ever start working with them. Not only does the autobiography enable me to be fully versed in their life story ahead of our sessions, but it helps many a client to see his or her own life more clearly. Occasionally, clients even have their own epiphanies, upon writing their autobio, before they even meet with me. The catharsis of writing out one's story and afflictions is its own reward, but then having life-clarifying revelations, as well (again, before they ever even meet with me), is a jolting experience for those who experience it.

But without articulating the event or memory as well as the feeling, or negative charge – through effective counseling, Sedona

Method, autobiography-writing, or journaling – there can never be full release of the charge. Sorry, it's not possible to just exercise your problems away, or yoga them away, or pray them away. You can't busy them away, parent them away, massage them away, or work or smoke them away. These things release the physical anxiety or physical lethargy that grow out of the charged memory, but not the charged memory, itself, that is causing the energy problem. These physical things can trigger them to come *up*, but they only come *out* by codification (words – talking, writing, or some form of definition of the beast of a memory). There has to be articulation of the memory and the release of the feeling that goes with it. We never know what we really think and feel, until we're forced to codify our thinking and feelings – i.e. to put it all into words. But it also requires drilling down and down, until the true essence of the problem is articulated. And with that clarity of thought comes the capacity to release the charge that comes with it.

As those charges get released, it is possible to then have the memories of life without the knot in the stomach, the racing pulse, or the desire to run from the memories. They become simply memories; de-charged memories that require no effort to carry or run from, and that no longer have power to anger you, upset you, drag you down, or drain your life energy.

However, until you change your internal, the external will be always unfulfilling. You will never be happy or at peace. And that begins with first seeing your internal. You ain't what you've become. You're so much more!

Song Recommendation

The language is a bit coarse, but the message is so passionate, strong and beautiful. Please buy and listen to, over and again, *F**kin' Perfect*, by **Pink**. It's SUCH a great message!
https://www.youtube.com/watch?v=ocDlOD1Hw9kFuckinPerfect

CHAPTER 13

WHO OWNS YOU?

Fundamentally, what this whole conversation of stuff going on inside you boils down to is that you're in a proxy fight, a battle for ownership of your life.

The reason you have such unrest in your soul, the reason you lack clarity over your path, the reason you feel sapped, depressed, and/or anxiety-ridden, the reason the very life is being sucked out of you, day in and day out, is because deep down inside you actually believe that you do not own your own life. The source of conflict that is creating all this negative energy inside you is the grinding of two competing belief systems against each other.

One belief system begins with, "I own my life. I truly am free to be who I am, do what brings me joy, say what is in my heart, become whomever or whatever I wish, and follow whatever dreams light up my soul. I am good. I am lovable. The real me matters." Every action then flows from that core belief.

Yet, that belief system has been quashed for the better part of your 2, 3, or 6 decades on this earth. The competing, incumbent belief system fighting for ownership of your life and control of you is, "Mom (dad) really owns my life and I have to do what she (he) wants, or she'll undermine, mock, criticize, doubt, question, or in some other way tear down my idea and me;" or "Dad (mom) owns me and I want to make him (her) happy, because it hurts so much when he's unhappy with me. I'm terrified of failure and his disappointment in me. So, I'll just do what he wants. Or, I'll fight him a lot but generally cave in in the end. Or, I'll just do the exact opposite of whatever he wants," or "Mom and Dad have been so good to me in so many ways, so I feel horribly guilty even considering the possibility, not to mention speaking or writing it, that they screwed up or hurt me in any way." Or, "My wife owns me, because I'm afraid of her claws and wrath, or her disapproval and disappointment;" or "My kids own me, because I soooo want them to like me and love me (because no one really loves me and is nice to me, if I don't have them)."

The big question of life is simply this:

Who owns you?

You have been taught not only to defer to someone else, but you have been taught to distrust yourself and your own voice. Thus, it's not just a matter of winning the proxy battle and kicking the former owners out of your soul. It's also a matter of finally beginning to believe in your own inner voice. It's a matter of realizing they were wrong in certain things they said and did (or didn't do), no matter how well-intentioned they may or may not have been. It's a matter of realizing and acting on the simple truth: only you can fully know what is best for you, and your voice rising up from within you *can be trusted.*

When we're taught as children to take our life cues from someone other than our own self, what we're being taught at an even deeper level is that the true power source for your life is OUTSIDE of you, not inside you, and anything inside you is subordinate to external power sources and cannot be trusted. This is why it is still common practice in America for a man to ask the bride's father for permission to marry his daughter. Implied in the act is that she can't make decisions for herself and/or needs clearance from the primary power source in her life (daddy, or from daddy who is controlled by mommy). It doesn't stop there. In many wedding services, still today, the father of the bride walks her down the aisle and then hands her off to the husband. The symbolism is a passing of power. "I brought her this far. She's your responsibility now. I trust you. You're in charge...because we all know she can't take care of herself or be trusted with her own decisions and life."

And now, for the last decade(s), you have been struggling in life, because you are struggling inside. The exterior is just a reflection, or a gross expansion, of the interior. You have an integrated life: negative interior manifesting itself in a negative exterior. You have created on the outside what runs the inside: confusion, conflict, and great unrest. But in the end, what is driving the outside life is the same thing driving the inside life, mainly not-you. The goal, of course, is positive, authentic integration between outer and inner. Your authentic, true self is first *known* inside. Then it is created in physical form externally in the form of perimeters (boundaries), paths, pursuits, and purposes.

At the moment, though, you don't own you. You're in an ownership battle for your own life. And it's killing you, depleting you, wasting your life. You're trying to go after what you want and who you are, but you're held back by a powerful, competing impulse that wants to shut down any notion of living life your way. A part of you clings to that external power source of your past and its influence over you, because it is familiar and comforting. Resultingly, you're longing for an external power source to give you permission to live your life your way, as you've always done, both so you'll have more confidence in the path and so you'll forever be able to divert criticism from yourself if things go poorly, never having to truly own your life and its results. The thought of giving yourself permission and that being enough for you – i.e. the thought of living life without the comfort and security of someone else telling you what to do – is, quite frankly, scary for many reasons. The autonomy you crave is simultaneously the untethered feeling you fear and the openness to criticism you fear even more.

And until you actually believe that this IS your life – living in both the exhilaration and nervous fear, you will never be happy, never be free, never have peace in your soul, never feel fulfilled. Until the power source for your life shifts from being external to being internal, you'll forever be deferring your life to others, forever distrusting your own inner voice, forever looking to others to tell you what to do with your life – spouses, parents, siblings, bosses, friends, clergy, therapists, society, and even your own children (tragic as that can be; and I've counseled grown adults who ask their teen and even preteen children for life advice).

There will always be people quite happy to tell you how to run your life, whether in monumental or subtle ways. That can be a very easy, very safe way to live your life. There's never any conflict with anyone, because you just do what they say. Simple. The problem, of course, is that the conflict is inside you. You don't wrestle with others; you wrestle with yourself. And you engage in all manner of escape activities to numb you from the internal pain, or to make you feel alive from all your numbness.

As long as someone else runs your life, you're screwed. Because, they ain't you. No other person can possibly know what is written in the code of your soul. No person can possibly know to what you have been called. For as much as others, particularly parents and spouses, want to live your life for you, we each only get one life to live, not two. One. That's it. But you're abdicating your life and power over your life to someone else.

Yet, the sheer terror comes from the thought of standing up and shouting to the heavens, not to mention to the person with whom you're in the proxy fight, a clear and resounding, "NO!"

I have plenty of wives/spouses in my practice who tell me, "But Sven, I *have* said 'no'. I have stood up. I have made my voice heard. But nothing changes. My husband doesn't do anything, and my parents don't change when I stand up to them."

"No," I tell them. "You haven't. You've stood up, but then you've sat down. You've spoken your 'no' firmly, but then either immediately or later, you've turned your 'no' into an 'okay, you're right.' To truly stand up, to truly be sick of it, to finally tap the full voice of your soul's 'NO!' means to stand and not back down. It means to finally take full ownership of your life and not let anyone else tell you otherwise. You still believe he knows better than you do. You still believe, deep down, that he owns you or at least owns more of you than you do. You still don't trust your voice, above all else. And therein lies the problem."

There's that great, little scene from the classic movie, *Dances with Wolves*, wherein a Civil War Union soldier, John Dunbar, who has been developing a relationship with Sioux Indians near his plains outpost, comes into their encampment to have a conversation with the medicine man. However, because of the language barrier, the medicine man is forced to employ the aid of a white woman who was taken by the Sioux as a young child and has lived among them, as one of them, for decades since. She long ago lost the white language and in this scene struggles to rediscover it inside her. What we learn about her identity in the medicine man's tepee is fascinating.

In the scene, as the medicine man prods her to ask questions of Dunbar, yet before she can get the first questions out, Dunbar interrupts, "No wait. What's your name?" Pointing to himself, he says, "I'm John Dunbar. John...Dunbar. What's your name," looking at the woman.

She thinks deeply, trying to find the words. She then stands up and puts her hands on her hips. She gestures to him, like a player in a game of Charades trying to elicit a response. "Stand up? Standing? Your names is 'stands'? Stands?" She nods, confirming his guess.

She then sticks out a fist, the next word in her Charade. Seeing her fist, Dunbar says, "Fist? Your name is fist?" Imploring him with her eyes to put the two together, she replants her feet and shakes her fist again.

"Stands? Fist? Stands with a fist?" He says, to her head nodding, "Stands with a fist." He smiles at having broken through. Excited by their communication success, she nods affirmation. Stands with a fist. The name of her soul and spirit.

Therein is the lesson for us. Until you stand with a fist for who you are, for what moves your soul, for what you need to do for you and your life, you will never be fully alive, you will always have unrest, and you will forever be owned. Until you stand *and don't back down*, there will be no life, no joy, no fulfillment, no peace, no true love, no true sense of you, today or ever. To finally claim ownership of your life and soul demands standing with a fist, until the territory of your internal and external life is finally and fully yours.

Song Recommendation

On this notion of ownership there is no better song than the little-known one by my all-time favorite group, **Chicago**; download *Feel (w/ Horns)*.

https://www.youtube.com/watch?v=WnzlA1U7NQcFeelwithHorns

CHAPTER 14

Y'KNOW WHAT YOUR PROBLEM IS!?!?!?

We've all heard it before, that question always meant to be answered by the asker (not the asked) and loaded with a hail of buckshot behind it: "Do you know what your problem is?" Whether coming from a parent, a supposedly well-meaning friend, a frustrated teacher, a boyfriend or girlfriend at break-up time, or an ornery co-worker, we've all had to choke down those seven words, often never thinking to say, "Nope, and I really couldn't give a crap what YOU think it is." But, whether out of fear of saying 'no' or out of simply being caught off guard, we let someone lead us into it, and we listen. Ugh.

And it usually then screws us up for years, even decades, to follow. Because, of course, we passively think it's anyone's right to tell us what they think is wrong with us and to render commentary on our lives any ol' time they doggone well please. We think we're obligated to listen and heed. Worst of all, most of us believe that someone else, especially those close to us, have some hidden knowledge of us.

Of course, they don't. But because most of us enter adulthood still owned by someone else (read 'parents', usually), we thus allow ourselves to be further owned by spouses, friends, bosses and society. Resultingly, we are not used to trusting our own voice. Thus, we allow external forces, often random ones, to render commentary on our lives. Most of us don't realize this, at least not until much later in life, when it finally occurs to us how much of life we've wasted believing the negative crap people put into us, either willfully or accidentally, also realizing the terrible toll it has taken, in terms of not just time, but energy and opportunities lost.

Until that day, we keep letting people answer that question:

"Y'know what your problem is?"

113

We actually *let* people expound on our lives, however they please – as if it's their *right* to do so – allowing it to do whatever damage it will do.

But, do you want to know the only true answer to that question?

There really is only one answer, deep down. If you're reading this book, if you're at this point of life of never-ending malaise, lack of clarity, depression, unrest of the soul, and/or anxiety, then there is only one answer to the question of "Y'know what your problem is?" I'm going to tell you, right now, what your real problem is:

Your problem is that
You actually believe you have a problem.
You believe something is inherently wrong with you.
Or, rather, you believe you *are* the problem.
You've been taught to believe that *who you really are*
Is innately flawed, problematic, irrelevant, or to be hidden and
even destroyed.

And nothing could be further from the truth. Your problem is the rock-solid belief in your own flawed nature. That's the heart of it. You've been sold a grand lie. There never was anything wrong with you. No child comes out of the womb believing they are no good, not good enough, or just plain cruddy. No, that's a taught belief. That belief in your own unworthiness is the one grand lie of your life that was implanted in you by someone else. Somewhere between birth and now you got your ass handed to you by someone who implanted that lie, and it's been messing up your life, ever since. Your life got robbed from you by this great lie that continues to eat you up from inside, attracting more and more situations, people, relationships, and career stuff that all serve to perpetuate that lie.

You've spent your entire life believing the problem of your unhappiness, not to mention the unhappiness of those around you, was because of who you are, what you do, what you say, what you don't do, what you don't do right, what you don't do well enough, and all the crud that goes along with these false beliefs. It's garbage and it always was. All because someone else didn't have the tools for attacking life and addressing it properly, didn't have the tools to slow down and be a deliberate parent or deliberate significant influence.

Thus, until you truly acknowledge and change your core beliefs and Binary Gates – not about god or the usual beliefs-type stuff, but about your own self and life – you will never be happy, because you'll always be draining yourself, from the inside out. Your Love Cup will have a hole in the bottom, be full of crud and lacking love sources pouring into it. That ain't good.

Actually, it is somewhat about god-related stuff. See, the reason these core beliefs have stuck inside you is because your god was outside of you, as discussed in the chapter *Who Owns You?* The real God or spirit of the Universe speaks to us from within our own soul. But, because most children venerate their own parents as gods, whether they're aware of it or not, they see their parents as infallible, including in the parental assessment that there must be something wrong with the child. And the notion of crossing that god's opinion, not to mention cutting that parent down from his/her godlike status is unfathomable for even adult-children.

Everything is beliefs. Everything. All of life emanates from the expression of the soul or the repression of the soul. The very secret of life is that you aren't who you think you are and your problem is not what you think it is. It's far, far deeper than that.

When I was 30, I cared what people thought.
When I was 40, I stopped caring what people thought.
When I was 50, I realized no one gave a crap, to begin with.

Journaling Recommendation
1. List each person in your past or present who has contributed to or reinforced your belief that you have a problem or are the problem.
2. Next to each person's name, list the specific phrases or messages they spoke to you that conveyed this message.
3. Now list next to each of those names and statements how each one made you feel.
4. Now write down all of the feelings you are feeling, right now, as you think about these people, events, and concomitant feelings.
5. Write a letter or email to each of these people, expressing in the strongest terms possible precisely how you feel. Don't hit

'send' or attach a stamp and put in the mailbox. The purpose of the exercise is to flush out the feelings.

6. Which of these people are still in your life?
7. Is it time to start cutting them out of your life, or at least start radically cutting back their impact and influence in your life?
8. Are you ready? Do you have the courage to do so?
9. Can you see the need for doing so?

Song Recommendation

I just like this song and its message. It fits quite nicely at this juncture. *All In All*, by **Lifehouse**.

https://www.youtube.com/watch?v=x6lcz5QZkUQAllInAll

CHAPTER 15

"ARE YOU SURE?"
HIS MOTHER ASKED, ALL HIS LIFE

I had been counseling the coach of a #1-ranked, NCAA Division 1 team a few times, sitting outside the quaint little coffee shop where we first got to know each other. It was blocks from a major US university and the rickety outdoor tables sat in the morning sun.

The season wore on and Stefon's team held on to its #1 national ranking in the polls. That means that of all the thousands of teams at all levels of this sport, from peewees to top collegiate organizations across the country, this team and this coach were, quite literally, the very best. Only a couple dozen professional coaches had achieved greater heights, were held in higher esteem, and actually knew more about this sport than Stefon. Stefon was, unequivocally, the best of the best.

But, as the post-season playoffs came, his hopes for a national championship were devastatingly dashed, when in the later rounds the most critical player on the team made a shocking error that cost the team everything – an error that player never, ever made, prior to that. Not even one time. And so, as post-season gave way to off-season, Stefon and I were reflecting for several hours one morning on that key player's critical error and all of the implications and causes of it.

"It was a mental error, wasn't it?" I queried. "I mean, it was so far out of character for this player that it just made no sense. Was it that his head was not in that game or what? Because his muscle memory and body work were simply in no way capable of making a mistake like that."

"I know, brotha. You're totally right," he responded. "But I blame myself, not him."

"As every good coach would and does; always looking for how I, the coach, could have done better to avoid such critical errors," I shot back.

"No, but in this case it's true, Sven." He then went on to regale me with the story of mid-season when he brought this player back from preseason injury into the starting rotation. This player, appropriately named Rock, was easily the best at his position, the most important position on the team. But he still wasn't 100% when Stefon wanted to work him back in. Stefon had been coaching D1 for 15 years by this point (after years as a pro player), had reliable assistants and one particular assistant coach who had been with him since the beginning. And this one long-time assistant was Rock's position coach. This position coach pushed very hard to not bring Rock back into the rotation so soon, believing him not to be ready and bearing fondness for his backup. And he and Stefon tussled back and forth, for weeks, mid-season, on this issue, all the while Rock was still riding the bench, until one day Rock's early season replacement booted completely in a critical, must-win game.

Stefon said to me, "Sven, when that replacement completely blew it and cost us a critical win, I shouted, 'SEE!' at my assistant coach."

Smiling, I responded, "Ahh! That's it, right there, isn't it? That 'See!' was your 'Screw you!' to your assistant; your angry 'I told you so, you dick!' And you have just revealed to me that this assistant coach has power over you. You refused to override your long-time assistant and put Rock in, basically a month earlier, even when you knew in your gut it was the right thing to do and knew Rock needed it for his season-long success and the later playoff success of the team. In your own intuition Rock needed as many reps as he could get, long before the national playoffs came around. But you didn't want to offend your assistant coach?

"You had been the #1 ranked D1 team in the country for months. In other words, except for the pros, you yourself were the very best coach in your sport in the entire United States and arguably one of the 50, or so, best in the world. But despite your success, the years of experience, and the fact that nearly every single coach in your sport in the country would come to *you* for advice, you chose to go against your own instincts and instead defer to an assistant, *not* because you thought it to be a better decision but because he has some power over you. That snotty little 'See!' was not just an acknowledgment of a mistake but it carried an attitude, and anger. You were mad at him for having power over you. But the real anger should be at yourself for giving him the power to override you, right? You, now in your late-40s, as one of the top coaches in the country and the world in your sport, still don't trust yourself and your own instincts. And what I want to know is where the heck did this come from? What I wanna know is how, why, and when did the top coach in the country start distrusting his own intuition? And by what unfathomable logic does the best of the best distrust his own instincts? It makes no sense. One only becomes best of the best by, in fact, unwaveringly trusting his/her own instincts. Furthermore, I guarantee if you override your instincts *in your own field of expertise* – where you're quite literally the top authority in the country – you're doing it in all the other areas of life where you're NOT the expert and thus already have more self-doubt and distrust of your own intuition. That means you've been doing it long, long, long before you got into this sport, in the first place. Dude, this problem, this distrust of your own intuition and self, is encoded into your original programming. So, what I wanna know is, What's the earliest memory you have in life of distrusting your own instincts?"

He immediately started laughing out loud. "Wow, wow, wow! Holy crap! I'm trippin' hard, brother! Wow! God, Sven, it is soooo funny you say that. Man! Man! Man!" Stefon shot back. In fact, he started laughing almost uncontrollably. I had hit it. "Instantly, when you said that, Sven, a very recent event came to mind. I was on a ski trip to Vail with my wife and kids, having a great time – yes, I ski! hahaha. And I called my mother, just for my weekly call. And do you know what she said? It's unreal, Sven. She said, 'You're skiing? Are you sure that's a good idea?' Sven, I'm a grown-ass man. It so pissed me off. I can't even tell you. I'm in great shape, active, still in my 40s, and she asks *that*? I was so mad."

"Wow! Stefon, that's it, isn't it? You nailed it. That is the grand virus written into the coding of your soul. Those three words: 'Are. You. Sure?'" The pieces were now falling into place. Slam dunk. There was far more to the story he shared with me and far more I volleyed back to him. But there it was, the story of his life. The story of how he lost a national championship that was rightfully his for the taking was written four decades prior, and he knew it.

"Those three words are the story of your life, aren't they? Your mom's been saying that, in some form or another, both in words and in actions, since as young as you can remember, hasn't she?"

Stefon nodded, now fully deep in thought.

The core message of your life is 'Are you sure?'

I went on, "You have been taught from a very young age to question, and even distrust, your own inner voice. And it took a major, life-rattling event, like watching a national championship slip through your fingers, for you to realize how powerful and deeply embedded this core life message has been. That loss had nothing to do with Rock and really nothing to do with your assistant coach's power over you. You have been taught to distrust yourself, even when you are the very best in your field. It had to do with your distrust of your own knowledge and instincts. You've told me before that your coaching success is because of your killer preparation and excessive planning. And, you make 5,000 decisions in a season, but there was one decision that you doubted and deferred on, and it was that one key decision that cost you everything. Rock lost that playoff game for you, because you dropped your focus, months earlier, and didn't trust your own instincts. You let your fear of your assistant coach and your own innate self-doubt take over."

He nodded again, "You're right. God, you're right."

I could see a gargantuan weight lifted off his soul right in front of me. His entire countenance changed. He had already accepted the burden of the loss. But now he knew the real reason why, and it was painful yet oddly, powerfully liberating.

"Implicit in that message from your mom to constantly doubt yourself – constantly ask yourself, 'Are you sure?' – is not just the message that you can't trust yourself but that you and your inner instincts aren't good enough and/or don't matter. And that is one gargantuan negative self-belief to have embedded in your cement, at the depths of your soul, at a very young age. It's not something that can be overcome by just changing your coaching methods or working harder. There was an inherent design flaw when your parents were crafting your being, if they were even that deliberate. They may have been fine people, but they passed on to you, perhaps from their parents, a self-doubt that is absolutely antithetical to maximum success and you saw it happen, right in front of your eyes."

I continued, "And the real mistake people make at this juncture, when they've now named the beast that has been afflicting them, is to quickly exonerate the parent with, 'Well, she was just doing her best.' I know this isn't going to sound real spiritual, but it can be a giant mistake to forgive too soon. Hate to say it, but it's true. And that will possibly be the eventual resolution. But the soul of the child – which is still what each of us is inside, as long as we're driven by the cement hardened with their messages – has every right to be angry and say, 'Why did you embed in me such a powerful message of self-doubt?' You may not ever say that to her face; and doing so is not really the point. But you have to sit in the moment, at least for a while, and realize that a well-meaning parent royally screwed up by causing you to doubt yourself. Later, there will be time for letting mom off the hook. But, for the moment, you have to first see clearly and admit what has been afflicting your life and decisions, as we just did. For, on this one issue, deep inside, you're still a wounded kid, distrusting yourself and wanting to please others, even subordinates. That kid needs to be heard, in order for that wound of self-doubt and concomitant self-distrust and self-dislike to heal. You must then simply sit in it, for a while. It's such a major revelation; there's no way you can't! I mean, reflect on the power of that one core belief and its underlying implications. So great was your self-doubt that no amount of willpower and perfect planning could overcome it. That's powerful hooch."

And right then, I reached across the table and shook his hand, congratulating him.

"What are you congratulating me for," he asked with a quizzical smile.

"Today is the first day, after 15 years, that you finally became the head coach at the U. You've been the head coach, but the truth is, you haven't been. You've been this weak version of a head coach. Today is the day you finally became your fullest self as a coach, finally eradicating the internal self-doubt. It's the day you finally stopped trusting your assistants over your own intuition. Trust em if they're right, but not if they're wrong. Dude, that's huge! Today, you finally became the CEO. You will never go back to distrusting yourself, because now you're aware. Congratulations, Stefon."

Sitting back, deep in reflection, a Cheshire grin creeped across his face.

So, What's The Point?

The point of Stefon's story is very, very simple. Never underestimate the sheer power – the colossal power – of core messages placed in us by those who have been, or are, significant to us. In this case, a national championship was lost because of the childhood message from a parent, reinforced over time by that parent and by subsequent choices by the man, himself.

Core beliefs have extreme power. If you get nothing else from this book, you must understand this one fundamental point: Soul beliefs are everything. More, as with Stefon, the real beliefs driving the equation of your life are in all likelihood hidden from your view. Also, intuition is king. It's everything. Integration of your inner and your outer life, which is predicated on trust of intuition, is the lone source of joy, peace, aliveness, and unleashing your greatness.

Journaling Recommendation

1. So, what are the core beliefs causing you to question, dislike, and distrust yourself, your life decisions, and your own intuition?
2. What have you lost, as a result of not trusting your intuition in a key moment? What did that feel like?
3. What does that make you want to do, moving forward?

Bonus Tracks

To keep moving forward with the Core of the Badass Counseling Method go ahead to the next chapter. For those looking for more insights and deeper challenges, check out these Bonus Tracks:

- Bonus Track 3: People Shout Loudest When Feeling Heard Least
- Bonus Track 4: Naming The Beast Is Half The Problem
- Bonus Track 5: Pouring Out The Love Cup Onto The Ground
- Bonus Track 6: The Greatest Fears In Life

CHAPTER 16

WE ARE CONSTANTLY BEING LED
TO HIGHER GROUND

I am of the absolute belief that the Universe – the gods, God, Higher Power, the Force, our own soul – is always leading us to higher ground. I absolutely, absolutely believe that. I don't know the whys behind it, but I believe it. I believe the words Jesus spoke, when he said, "I have come that you might have life and have it abundantly." I really do. Whether you're an atheist or a total Bible-banger, the calling of the soul and the Universe, itself, is always leading us to greatness, exuberance, and abundance of life.

Now, of course, we all want to take that to mean that God wants us each to have a million dollars in the bank, a big house, nice car, and a hot girlfriend/boyfriend, on top of a long, healthy life filled with great whiskey and lots of Oreos. But, the nature of the spiritual journey is that the higher ground and greater vistas the gods are leading us to are, almost without exception, nothing we can comprehend, not to mention plan, in advance. They are of a flavor and vintage we never thought we would enjoy. Just as life changes us, as we age, so does it rock what we experience as fulfilling and life-bringing.

But, alas, this growth and change that we experience, en route to higher ground and greater happiness, never come easily or without pain. They never come without fear. They never come without being broken of our ideas of what we thought joy should look like.

See, we so cling to that which is safe. We so cling to security, to that which is familiar, even if it stinks horribly. Familiarity breeds clinging. Clinging breeds inertia.

But the soul will have its way. Your own soul will break you of this miserable, half-life you've been living, even if your soul has to blow it up. Something in your soul calls out with your greatness and your true happiness, and it will be heard. And never underestimate the fact that the soul is far more powerful than the will. To desperately hang on to that which is familiar is easy; to destroy the will's grip on an unhappy path is heavy, hard work, requiring sacrifice. The soul connects to the forces of the universe. I absolutely believe that. And the universe, or the gods, move heaven and earth to get you to let go, no matter how tight your grip, no matter what they must do. They long for your happiness.

Never underestimate the fact that the soul and its beliefs are more powerful than the will and its abilities.

The gods are like a great strength coach. Muscles are not built up by working out, per se. When working out, you're actually tearing down the muscles – suffocating them, cutting off their supply of oxygen, pumping in ammonia and lactic acid. Thus, the workout is actually a breakdown. Growth occurs in the period of rest after the workout. But the hard work – the very hard work, the act of tearing down the muscle – must be done in order to move the body to higher ground, greater strength. Growth is preceded by the breakdown.

As they break your grip, they are leading you up the side of the mountain to higher ground.

Ever driven up the side of a mountain or to a significantly higher elevation? I have made many such drives with friends, girlfriends, or my children, over the years. You start at sea level or a few thousand feet above sea level when entering the park or at the foot of the mountain. But as you drive your car up the mountain, as altitude increases, as you progress through the switchbacks, you occasionally see a sign that says "Scenic Overlook." So, you stop with the girlfriend, get out, say, "Wow! This view is great," and take a few selfies. Right?

You then pile back into the car and keep on driving. Up the switchbacks, farther and farther. Eventually, you notice the car getting a bit hot, when you see a sign that says, "Scenic Overlook with services." So, you stop, shut off the car to let it cool, use the bathroom, and go to the edge, only to proclaim, "Holy cow!!! This view is even better than the last one. It makes the last one look like crap. This is incredible!" Then you hop back in the cooled car and keep on driving.

Lo and behold, after another half-hour of driving, you finally reach the summit. After parking, getting out, stretching the legs, and eating a sandwich, you walk to the grand overlook and exclaim, "Unbelievable!!! This view is greater than anything I could have possibly imagined. This makes that lower view look like crap, and the one below that look like crap too!"

The gods are forever leading us to higher ground and greater vistas. But, alas, the inclination is to hold onto that which is safe, to forever tarry at an overlook that is swell but ultimately unfulfilling. The soul longs for more, even as the mind and body tremble at the thought of letting go of that which is secure to move onward and upward. Of course, the simple fact of the matter is that if it doesn't scare the holy heck out of you, it's not your path. You have to go up the switchbacks of the mountain to reach the greater vistas; and switchbacks at higher elevation are not for the faint of heart. If you're not scared, it's not real. It's not-you. It's fake, contrived, chosen by someone else's voice, someone else's influence in your life, whether you're aware of it or not. If it doesn't scare you and pull from you some difficult new level of trust, it ain't you.

And, forever, life boils down to this notion of trust. Can the gods, the universe – the calling and providence of the soul – be trusted? Can God truly be trusted? I mean, with your life. Really, everything else gets burned off in the grand distillation of life, in the search for the deepest truth. And the remaining distillate is trust. It's not love; it's trust. Life is trust. Death is trust. Movement is trust. Silence is trust. Everything boils down to trust. Can you truly live in trust? Because, the anxiety of your life is distrust. ("Things aren't working out and I have to force things to happen and stay in motion"); and the depression in your life is distrust ("Things will never work out," or "So many times things haven't worked out that it's all gotten so heavy, and I find it increasingly harder to believe things will turn.")

It's so easy to talk the Christiany or New Agey or Yoga-spirituality jargon of trusting God or the universe. "I believe in trusting God," "I have faith," or "I commune with Universal Spirit," or "I am open to the guidance of my own Higher Power." Easy talk. But to do it, to live it; well, that's a whole different matter.

To live in a state of trust – total trust – is incredibly freeing, insanely difficult (at times), demanding of great self-discipline, and gratifying beyond imagination. However, taken even in just small doses, the life of decreased fear-driven living, increased trust and movement toward higher vistas always yields wonderful fruit, sometimes immediately, sometimes in areas of life you were neither expecting nor even seeking. But the fruits do come. The greater the trust and movement in the direction of your authenticity and truth, the greater the fruits.

Knowing it and Living it are Two Different Things

It has been said that when we hear the truth, we know it. It resonates inside us. It's as if we've always known it, but someone is reminding us that we already know it. There is, at the same time, both a freshness and a "Yeah, I totally get that."

In that vein, the three words I hear most often in my spiritual counseling practice are, "I know that" or "I knew that." Often, what I'm saying to a client is quite new but it resonates. Or, in other cases, they actually did already know it, as in they had previously actually thought about it. Sometimes, a client will even wave off what I am saying with a, "Yeah, I know that, Sven," especially if they have a bit of the know-it-all thing going on in their personality or the smartest-guy-in-the-room syndrome.

Yet, a client can spout all of the standard self-help catchphrases, but still be in immense confusion, unrest and/or inner pain. My response is always the same,

**Knowing it
and
living it
are two radically different things,
requiring two completely different skill sets and ability levels.**

Let's be really honest, if you're reading this book, seeking guidance and healing for your life, there are likely a few, or many, things you don't know and many things you know but are not living. This 'knowing it but not living it' generally happens because you don't believe in the particular truths. It hasn't resonated deep inside you. For, when something does resonate, we can't help but follow it. It doesn't require some grand exertion of will power.

So, when I encounter a client who isn't feeling it, or one who is convinced they have it all figured it out (despite their obvious lack of having it all figured out), the necessary step is to help them both see and buy into the full import of a given truth. Sometimes, it requires rattling their cage a little bit to help them see their words are just words. And being confronted with our own inaction on something we claim to believe in often is the push necessary to get things going. It can bring a powerful shift in outlook and action.

More often than not, the reason they're not taking action is because they're afraid of doing so, even when they acknowledge the value and wisdom of the particular truth. And, that fear is almost always the fear of what someone who has power over them will say or think. It's further testament to the simple truth that fear is far more powerful than mere knowledge. Fear can halt all action, knowledge and good intentions. And the only thing that has power over fear is trust (in the calling of the soul) and the accumulated pain that comes from fear. The absolute requirement for moving to higher ground of greater happiness and fulfillment is trust. Knowing it and living it are two different things.

Journaling Recommendation
1. What is it you know but aren't living?
2. Who are you most afraid of? Whose words and influence are still controlling your life, keeping you clinging to lower ground and an unfulfilled life?
3. Who owns you?

Song Recommendation

Buy and take a listen to *Kyrie*, by **Mr. Mister**, while reading the lyrics. The sound is sweeping, high-spirit 80's rock. The message is strong: both a nod to the Christian sub-ritual of Confession and Forgiveness and, more importantly, testament to the calling of the soul to go down into yourself and the core of your experience and truth.

https://www.youtube.com/watch?v=9NDjt4FzFWYKyrie

CHAPTER 17

'WHEN DID YOU KNOW?'

I had a client: Beautiful woman, late-30s, successful, never married, two kids – a mid-teens daughter and a 20-something son. She had reached the Director level of a midsize, national company specializing in business consulting. She was on the marketing side and was very, very good at what she did. And, to her credit, she had reached that level of competence and success without a college degree. A real self-made woman.

Well, Louisa had been with this company for about 10 years when she got a new VP above her. And things began to go badly, very quickly. Early on, he pushed her in ways that were neither productive nor even necessary. He began taking credit for her work and undermining her in meetings. Before long, she went from working nine hour days to 15- and 16-hour days;. She went from a smoking habit she had whittled down to one cigarette a day up to a pack and then pack-and-a-half a day.

Louisa stopped having time for her boyfriend and was eventually leaving home before her daughter left for school and getting home after she was asleep. She started getting calls from her school informing her of discipline problems with her daughter, including smoking cigarettes and pot, and even liquor in her locker.

Yet, she couldn't bring herself to quit the job. She feared never again being able to reach the level of success she had. On only a high school diploma, surely she couldn't keep her big house, pool, and fancy car, she feared. She *had to* stay. *Had to* endure. If she couldn't get a job at that level, she'd have to make do with less. Or worse, she'd have to start eating into her 401k and investments. Ugh. On top of this, she was a proud woman. The thought of losing everything she had built was too much to bear. It scared the bejesus out of her.

But life didn't help her out. As time wore on, she ran out of time for her dear girlfriends, who had been her soulmates and biggest cheerleaders, and was even working on weekends. Over the course of the year after the new VP came, her weekends got chewed up with work. Her life had spun completely out of control. And, slowly but surely, her energy deteriorated, she grew more fretful than she ever had, and seemingly everything that could go wrong did, to the point where it all couldn't get any worse.

Then it did, in the form of medical news. Her doctor had discovered both a spot on Louisa's lung and a hole in her heart!

The unwanted became the inevitable. A year after the new VP's arrival, Louisa turned in her notice, completely spent.

And her worst fear came true. Not only did she have to start eating into her investments to live, she couldn't find a lateral job and, worse, had no energy to even begin to do so. Wiped out, depressed and full of fear, she spent her days largely in bed, relieved to be out of there, and slowly resting and hopefully recovering. But she was still scared.

About nine months later, she ended up on my doorstep, needing counsel. Turns out, she knew a client I had formerly worked with and helped out of a similar spot – extreme fatigue, extreme loss, extreme fear and hopelessness.

Louisa and I worked together for about 2-3 months. The turnaround was quick. Her pain had gotten bad enough that her hunger for change had gotten big enough and her resistance to new beliefs had gotten small enough that she was finally on the cusp, ready. Pain breeds hunger and courage. She was a gung-ho student, eager for change and growth.

And, as the Fates would have it, as a result of her hunger for change and willingness to go deep, within months, she was painting again (for the first time in twenty years). She began singing in a garage band (for the first time in never), and decided to deliberately take more time off to not just rest her soul but begin to more fully re-find her true self. Happiness began to come to her life in ways she had not experienced since childhood, though even greater than she had back then. Within months, while holding a garage sale with her daughter, she struck up a conversation with a man who would go on to become the great love of her life.

Today, she/they live on a ranch in the Southwest US. She is living a non-corporate life, constantly in nature, and among 'my type of people,' she reports. I don't know what she's doing for a living. But, hers is a life that makes her ridiculously happy and, odd as it may seem, would not have come without the transformative fires she went through. A lot of pain finally burned off a life of 'not-me', so that she could live her authentic 'me'.

But it was after that year of hell and during our time working together that I asked her the most critical question:

"When did you know?"

"When did I know what," Louisa responded, quizzically.

"When did you know it was time to go, time to leave your job as it got worse and worse?"

"Hmmm." A long, slow smile came over her eyes and face. "Sven, it's funny you ask that. I knew after the first month."

"Isn't that interesting," I responded.

"I was just so scared. I knew I couldn't stay, but couldn't go. Yet, I also knew it wouldn't change, no matter how hard I hoped. I guess I never realized, though, just how bad it would get. But heck yeah, I knew right away."

I let that one sink in with her a moment, then pressed, "So, even though you *knew* you had to go, you stayed. You chose to *not* listen to your own inner voice. And that's a rookie mistake. That's the mistake we make hopefully less and less as we get further down the spiritual path – the mistake of choosing fear over our own inner sense of knowing our own intuition."

I went on to explain that the Universe is forever whispering to us. It is sending the tiniest pulse of knowing, or calling, to our conscious mind. It's the proverbial 'still, small voice' thing. And yet, we don't listen. We ignore the voice, the vibe, the feeeel, that tiniest ping coming up from somewhere inside us.

God is forever trying to lead us to higher ground and greater abundance and happiness. But we so cling to what is safe and secure, even when we know it's not right. We hold on with all our might and all our fear to that which is behind us, still hoping it is our future, despite all the pain it is bringing.

But the gods will be heard. Your own soul will be heard. They will have their way. Your grip will be broken. As the old proverb goes,

We make plans. God laughs.

And so, the gods conspire to make things worse. We say such naive things as, "Well, it can't get any worse." And God giggles at being able to mess with you some more to get you to let go of that which you think is secure, even while God is simultaneously exasperated that you're still missing the lesson. The gods basically stop whispering in that 'still, small voice' and start speaking in their 'inside voice', insisting on being heard. What was formerly a few things going wrong grows into more aspects of life coming apart and getting worse. Relationships tank. Time becomes short and stressed. Bad habits flourish. Louisa went from near-completely kicking her habit to a pack-and-a-half per day, an ungodly number of work hours, and less time and energy for her kids and friends.

And yet, rather than letting go of the safe and secure, we cling even more tightly to that which is behind us, dragging us down. Rather than making the 180-degree turn and moving up the mountain to new vistas, we hold fast to that which is sucking the very life from our soul.

And so, quite amused, the gods do what gods do. They shout. They break you of your belief in the immortality of your knowledge. Your great strength becomes a weakness insofar as it leads to even greater pain and hardship being inflicted on you by life, by the Universe, by the calling of your own soul. If you won't come quietly, they will drag you. The soul will be heard and heeded. They use the levers at their disposal to move you to where they want you to go – to a better life. Quite all of a sudden, your health breaks down, and your worst fears start coming true. You are thrust into a reality you could only imagine in a nightmare.

This is precisely what happened to Louisa. Adamant about breaking her grip on a fear-driven life, her own soul, in conjunction with the Universe, conjured a reality so powerful as to break down all of her pre-existing fears and beliefs. The pain had to get so bad as to break this fiercely driven woman and simultaneously give her the courage to walk into the very reality she feared most.

"And the point of it all," I told her, "is not just to move you to higher ground and more abundant life. The point and goal of the spiritual life is:

- To teach you communion with your own soul. You had been living a life for so long that simply was not you. And so, your soul had to speak louder. It had to break you out of that prison of not-you. There is no life, until you have a relationship with your own self.

- To teach you that when you do not listen and trust that inner pulse – that still, small voice – things will get radically worse.

- To next time listen to and heed that inner voice perhaps just when it starts shouting, rather than when it's in its full-throated fury. Then perhaps a few times after that you will listen to your inner voice when it is merely using its inside voice, when things have been going awry outside you, but have not degenerated into full-blown madness. Then, eventually, you reach the point in the spiritual journey where you've experienced *so many times* the inner whisper not being listened to and your life getting whipped up into a tornado of hellish experiences that you begin to really listen for it and trust it.

The goal of the spiritual life, the goal of communing with your own spirit, the goal of relationship with your own self is to hear that quiet voice, that quiet feel on your skin and in your chest, that ping rising up from the soul, that sense of knowing, when it is soft and quiet. It is to have the courage to heed that quiet voice because you have too often experienced what happens when you don't – the louder and louder shouting of life, the breakdown of all that was, the stress, the anxiety, the pain, and the chaos.. You know where life's going if you don't trust that quiet voice.

You were raised to not trust your own voice. But the grand truth of the spiritual life and the grand truth of

*happiness is that there is no joy without the in-tune-ness
to listen to your own quiet inner voice without it ever
having to shout; then to have the courage to trustingly
follow it – to act on it.*

*That is what it means to live a spiritual life. It is to live in sacred
trust with your own soul – your own intuition, or instincts.* It has
nothing to do with beliefs in God or gods, nothing to do with
afterlife or previous lives, nothing even to do with others. All of
those questions are secondary, even tertiary, and between you and
your God. There is no room for or even ability to truly draw close
to the Divine, until you can draw close to your own self. This is
between you and you. To love God is to live in sacred trust in
God's voice speaking quietly within. That which is truly you
resonates deep inside you. You know it. It feeeels right. When
you hit the key on the piano, it lifts a hammer that strikes a string
deep inside the piano. That string resonates with sound, deep
inside, just as the truth of who you are resonates deep inside when
it is seen, heard, or felt.

Distrust your own voice at your own peril. The gods will kill
you, kill who you used to be, kill what you are so feverishly and
fearfully clinging to, kill what you've become: distrusting yourself
and from seeking the approval of others. There absolutely must be
spiritual death before there can be new life.

**Creation is invariably preceded by destruction.
Things must die for things to live.**

Furthermore, the greatest destruction necessary for happiness
and fulfillment is the destruction of the belief that the quiet voice of
your own soul cannot be trusted and leads to anywhere other than
your highest good and greatest joy.

How Did She Become This Way?
But where did it all come from? What caused Louisa, or any of us,
to stop listening to that inner voice, such that the Universe felt the
need to shout, at all?

Louisa grew up in a family of eight. She was the youngest of six children. As I had grown up in exactly the same size family and position among my siblings, I could identify with Louisa. Though, her problem was in no way only a last-kid or big-family problem. Her situation was the result of a core belief that can be implanted in any person in any type of situation. Hers was just more obvious because of her particular family construction.

Fundamentally, Louisa grew up never feeling heard, or even much seen. Mom and dad had only so much love – in the form of positive attention – to give. Every human only has so much to give. Try to divide that between six kids, as well as a spouse, work needs, etc, and it can become very taxing on any person. If that taxed person already has a depleted Love Cup of their own, coming into parenting, that makes for an even worse situation.

The short version is that Louisa grew up believing that the real her didn't matter. Her Love Cup was perennially empty. She barely existed. Like every kid, she so longed for praise and positive attention. But there was never enough to go around. She was somewhat raised by her siblings and by her parents. But she was on her own a lot, which she admits had upsides. But, by the time Louisa got into high school, she was staying out late at night, partying, and engaging in risky behaviors for a kid. She had given up on trying to be the perfect kid to get attention. Being perfect hadn't gotten her any extra portions of love. The situation had become so dire – mom and dad had become increasingly taxed and wrapped up in their own lives with little left to give to their kids – that she was not engaged in positive behaviors to get positive attention. Now, she was doing negative things, rebelling, and breaking all the rules.

See, if a person can't get positive attention, they will do and say things that on the surface just look like rebellion but are fundamentally attempts to get negative attention. Sound odd? It is, but it isn't. Why would anyone seek negative attention – put downs, getting yelled at, scolding? Simple: negative attention is never just directionless rebellion. In many (though not all) situations, negative attention is sought because negative attention is far, far better than no attention, at all. The kid ain't aware that's why they're doing it, but that's why they're doing it. Under the surface, the soul longs to, at the very, very least, be acknowledged. Someone getting no attention is fundamentally being told, "You don't exist," which is synonymous with "You don't matter."

The optimum is to be told, "You're great. You're good. You're important. You matter." The worst is to be told through someone's actions, "I don't even see you. You don't exist." Thus, if you're not getting the optimum and your soul fears the worst, you will at least go for that (bitter-)sweet spot of negative attention in the middle that seems to create great havoc for others and only scorn for you. For, negative attention is still attention. Existentially, it's a statement that you still exist. You matter.

This is what Louisa did, or tried to do. But, unfortunately, her parents never yelled at her, rarely corrected her actions, and all-around simply had nothing for her, except the occasional criticism of her decisions. Her mom, even well into Louisa's adulthood, had the unique gift of being able to know exactly what to say to deflate Louisa's balloon. No matter how good things were going, her mother could say something like "But that's not that big an accomplishment, is it?" or "Your boss probably didn't have anyone else to give that promotion to, did he?" or "But you're not really there for your kids." Or, her mother could ask just the right question to cause Louisa to go into constant permutations of second-guessing herself, "Do you really think that's such a good idea, Louisa" or "But you were never really good at this sort of thing, were you?"

It would be easy to say that Louisa's biggest problem was that she was put down and became self-critical. That was, indeed, part of the problem. But the worst part for Louisa was not that she thought ill of herself, but that she had been taught to distrust her own voice (which was trying to get her out of a life she hadn't even realized she was sick of) and that her own voice (and her very existence) didn't matter. Any kid who is not taught to hear and trust their own instincts will forever second-guess their decisions and rarely act on what they truly want, not to mention forever be self-critical and always seeking external advice. Add severe criticism and that kid becomes hyper-conscious of themselves, disinclined to take risks, and averse to authentic self-expression of any sort, not to mention deathly afraid of failure.

But again, the self-critical voice is not the most detrimental part. The worst part is not being able to hear one's own voice, and/or being strongly inclined to distrust it.

As with Stefon in a previous chapter (the #1 NCCA coach in his sport), Louisa was taught that her true self didn't matter or certainly was not good enough to be trusted. And it cost them both dearly, for decades in adulthood. And because they wouldn't listen to the voice of their own soul, it had to get louder, make life worse, and eventually shout at them to change. The coach had to see a national championship – a rare enough opportunity in its own right – slip away before he was finally, maddeningly so hungry for change that he was willing to look at his deepest truths. Louisa had to lose what seemed like her entire identity, life, and even her health before she was finally willing to listen.

And listen they did. Change came quickly. Lives changed quickly. Happiness began to flood in quickly. And life looked very, very different. All because they finally chose to listen to the voice of their own soul.

Book Recommendation

A few years back, I fell in love with a particular chapter in a particular book, because it so well explicates a concept I had been selling in my normal, rough-hewn way, for years. This author does such a brilliant job of explaining this concept of listening to your body – i.e. intuition – and how it reveals your truth. May I strongly, strongly recommend the book *The Intuitive Way: The Definitive Guide to Increasing Your Awareness*, by Penney Peirce, in particular Chapter 6: Hearing Your Body Talk, specifically the section titled *The Sensitivity Scale*. Here's a tiny snippet from the book:

> *"...by learning to absolutely trust your body's first response, you will find the guidance you get is high quality. Goethe said these deceptively simple words: "Just trust yourself. Then you will know how to live"* (p105).

CHAPTER 18

YOUR ADDICTION TO BUSYNESS
AND THE 3 STEPS OF THE SPIRITUAL LIFE

I have spent the entirety of my adult life on my own spiritual journey, since I was 19 and left the US Air Force Academy, after two years as a cadet. I loved the military; loved playing Division 1 football; loved the challenge of high-level academics, athletics, flying, and military responsibilities; and loved being surrounded by the best and brightest. And I was good at it. I was on the Superintendent's List for military and academic excellence; was 'PQ', or 'pilot qualified'; had gone through sailplane training, earned my wings, and soloed in a plane with no engine, which is terrifying, acrobatic, and exhilarating. I had made it through sophomore year cuts on the Academy's Division 1 football team (which had beaten the Texas Longhorns in a bowl game and ended my frosh year ranked 5th in the country), which meant I was on the team as an O-lineman for my final two years. I had every reason to stay, on top of the fact that it was gorgeous Colorado and I was drawing a great paycheck as a proud member of the US military.

But somewhere in that second year, I knew it was time for me to leave. I didn't know why, only that it was time to go. As I said, my performance was fine. But, despite the success, my enthusiasm dropped off when I began to feel a pull away from the Academy. I had no idea why or what was going on inside me. I just felt this pull and my attitude began to sour. That I was getting killed in an honors macro-economics class I had no business being in was not a cause for my dampened enthusiasm, but a result of my decreased interest in being there. Normally, I'd power through a class I hated, basically forcing myself to do well. But this time was different; the whole situation was different.

I kept telling people, "I don't even know why I'm leaving, only that it's time to go." I had no idea what was going on with me. I had fought and planned, for years, to get into the Academy (I got into

USAFA and West Point), play football, fly sailplanes and then light aircraft, and eventually fighter jets. And here I was, in the middle of it, doing it, kicking it in the ass, having already overcome the hardest parts (the first two years), and now I was leaving. It made no sense. Completely illogical, but I knew I had to do it.

It was also a terrific blow to my ego. For, I had bragged, for years, about all I was going to accomplish in life. I was basically an arrogant dick in high school. Yet, here I was, walking away from a monster opportunity. Incredibly dumb. It made no sense.

The folly was only compounded when, upon leaving, I got accepted into an Ivy League business school (Cornell), which at the time was one of the top in the country, and football program...and turned it down, because I just felt in my gut that I needed to return to Minnesota. It felt right, but made no sense.

I won't go into the subsequent, boring details. The point is simply that I walked away from a colossus of a career opportunity and then a second one. By age 19, I had said 'no' to more opportunities than many people get in a lifetime.

Back then, I also had no idea what it meant to be on the spiritual journey. Sure, I had grown up in the parsonage, and our whole world was spirituality and religion. So, I got it, but I hadn't truly experienced it. It was religious jargon. Again, knowing something and living it are two vastly different things. I knew religion but I had never experienced the madness, the feel, and the intensity of spirituality – true relationship with one's own self and the spirit of the Universe.

And then came the chaos of knowing I had to leave the Academy and everything I had planned. I knew these choices were a disappointment to some who were near to me. My closest brother, at the time, didn't talk to me for over a month, when he learned I had turned down that Ivy League business school, an opportunity he coveted and would have killed for when he was my age. Friends looked askance at this formerly cocky, big-mouthed classmate with utter confusion and no small amount of schadenfreude.

Prior to leaving, I pretty much knew all of that would happen. (In the Bonus Track entitled *The Greatest Fears in Life*, I discuss the 'Fear of the Known'.) Though, the internal stuff was worse than the external stuff. The level of disorientation and utter absence of clarity were far greater than I imagined, for far longer. I had no one to guide me, who had experienced such a thing or gone on such an adventure off the accepted paths in life. There was no map.

The writings of Richard Bach, Shakti Gawain, James Hillman, and Joseph Campbell would end up being very instructive, particularly in understanding what it meant to enter the dark forest of the spiritual journey, as I had just done. But I was on the journey alone. Because I had no one to guide me, it would last in its most intense forms for the next 12-15 years.

In retrospect, I would see that I was not only sorting out my own life – who I was and who I was to become – but was sorting out a map for those who would come after, so that they might have what I never had. I had to suffer pain and disorientation more than others, so I could eventually help others (and have my wisdom and insights come from experience and not just a book). I had to learn and know the journey intimately, every step of the way.

Later, I endeavored what felt like the next call for my life, entering the path for ordained ministry as a pastor. This would be a hilly, treacherous path that would come at great price, both personally and professionally. Simultaneously, I was rather unwittingly building my spiritual counseling practice, writing books that yearned to come out, and wrestling with marital and family issues. All the while, I was simply trusting the calling of my own soul, from one venture into the next.

Yet, I was also continually coming under great heat from those closest to me and from professional overseers, because my path was not clear and was not one of the tried and true paths that people often expect of those around them. Compound that with the voices of pressure from myself, as well as the drumbeat of society saying, "Succeed. Succeed. Succeed," and I was really struggling.

But eventually – eventually! – it all began to fall into place. More importantly, I began to grow comfortable with the uncertainty and strange paths I was being called to, such as being an NCAA Head Strength Coach, living in my car for years, off and on, as I wrote a few books, and much later giving away all of my life possessions to live on the street (sleeping on concrete for 2 ½ years) to work with the homeless, destitute, and drug-addled with not a penny to my name.

As the years and decades wore on, more and more people began to come to me for counsel. Even while living on the street tending the homeless, I had police, military, high-level academics, wealthy, influential, young and beautiful finding me (somehow) coming to me for insight, for help on their own journeys. I don't know why, but they came. I don't know how they found me, but they came. As the years went on, I began to realize that mine would not be a normal path; mine would be a path entirely of my own making, where there previously was no path, led only by the calling of the gods from the quiet of my soul.

Market Corrections
One of the things that happens on the spiritual journey is that we experience the calling from within or are jerked by life to make major or minor course adjustments. Things happen – whether externally or internally generated – to pull us off the path we've been on. It can feel like a coming-apart, or a loss, or a state of bereavement, or confusion. But, even at its worst, it is always a movement toward something better, if we allow it to go the course it must and do not resist.

There is a similar phenomenon that happens in the financial sector. It's called a *market correction*.

Investopedia defines it thusly:

> **A reverse movement, usually negative,**
> **of at least 10% in a stock, bond, commodity, or index**
> **to adjust for overvaluation.**
> **Corrections are generally temporary price declines**
> **interrupting an uptrend in the market or asset.**

This defines well what happens on the spiritual journey or what pulls people onto the spiritual journey of what I call 'living deliberately.'

Some people are pulled onto the spiritual journey by minor course corrections, only to feel later called to major adjustments,

after they have built up confidence or after the pain of the existi
path has gotten so bad as to motivate action. (And as we've seen,
never underestimate the power of pain to give strength to make a
previously unwanted and avoided decision.)

However, in my case, the major market correction came first. It
was a correction of 50% or more, or so it felt. Everything after that
was a smaller correction, or adjustment – like the coarse and fine
adjustments on a microscope (if I may mix metaphors). I had the
courage to defy the powerful voices in my life and the Universe
knew that. So it gave me a hearty yank off the path that was not
mine. The military and being a fighter pilot were simply not my
calling, nor was going to a prestigious business school, nor were
either of those to be longer stops on my journey. I was called to a
path that there was no possible way I could have ever foreseen.
And I experienced a reverse, negative movement that was far more
than 10%, that lasted for over a decade, and exacted a mighty toll
on my life, eventually giving way to a long, slow, wonderful
uptrend.

The time since that first major course correction has been spent
whittling the off-course ideas, paths, people, things, events, and
beliefs. We discover who we are by discovering who we are not. To
become you requires saying 'no' to all that is not-you. And that is
infinitely more difficult than it sounds. It also requires dogged
focus, because not-yous are forever intruding on life, distracting,
attempting to pull you off course. This is the nature of the spiritual
journey – constant market corrections, some big, some small.

Courage And The Spiritual Journey
What I have discovered, over the last 30 years, is that going down
the spiritual journey and *living in concert with your own inner voice
and in union with the spirit of the Universe demands three
fundamental, ongoing steps:*

1) Hearing the voice.
2) Heeding the voice.
&
3) Letting go of trying to control the results.

OR,
as I prefer to think of it:

1)FEEL
2)ATTACK
3)QUIT

This is the full summation of the spiritual journey – of the authentic, deliberate life. All of life is encapsulated in these three little steps. This is the road map I have found for finally allowing joy, peace, happiness, and clarity into your life. Everything good hinges upon your ability to feel, attack, and quit.

And yet, for as simple as this little formula sounds, there is really nothing in life that could be more difficult than to create the solitude necessary to hear, the fire necessary to heed, and the open hand of trust necessary to quit/let go

The precursor to,
and the ongoing most important element of, the spiritual life
– the absolute *sine qua non* –
is courage.

Be it courage innate to your being, situational courage, courage that flows from trust in the Universe/God and/or self, or courage born of pain, the spiritual journey is impossible without it. It absolutely requires courage to slow down (when society says to keep pushing and driving) and allow yourself to hear your voice and feel all the pain that accompanies it, all the pain you've been running from so long; it requires courage to stand up and speak your voice, living your truth, knowing there will be many trying to stop you; and it requires immense courage to let go of the call, once you've invested so much of yourself into it and done all you felt inspired to do. Courage fuels the spiritual engine.

Step One: Feel
A very large percentage of my clientele is comprised of extremely successful, high-functioning females. A great many of them, as well as those females who are not as success-driven or are everyday

moms or getting by each day, are simultaneously driven to simply not stop. That is, we've elevated busyness to the level of Virtue in this country. Non-stop motion is seen by a great many women as some sort of badge of pride. "Oh, I have to drop off one kid at soccer, then two at ballet. Then I have a dental appointment, two meetings at church, and a meeting with the realtor, and that's just by noon." And, of course, it never stops, from morning to night, from one day to the next, from one year into ten more. Women in our society are just insanely busy. Somehow that is seen as a good thing.

It's not.

They're running. You're running. And not running to it. You're running from it.

As mentioned earlier, the mad, Zoloft-driven busyness is the problem, not any sort of solution. You're running from that giant tidal wave of feelings inside you that you fear will overwhelm you, if you slow down. The neurotic pace of your life is quite deliberate, isn't it? You act like it's not your choice and outta your control. But the chaos is a choice, isn't it? It's intended to keep you a step ahead of having to think about all that you don't want to think about, not the least of which is how non-deliberate and inauthentic your life is.

For many, male or female, young and old, the hardest part of the spiritual journey is just starting it, slowing the heck down and allowing that wave to hit you. The hardest part is allowing yourself to feel again. That's why the anti-depressants are so nice, right? Not that they really work (and there's plenty of suppressed research solidly indicating they're no better than placebos), but they seem to keep you from feeling. It's not just the constant motion that keeps you from feeling. It's the morning coffee, cigarettes, anti-depressants (and God only knows what other meds), the action, the over-exercising and over-eating, the over-parenting and over-working, the Kendall Jackson or vodka at night and/or the gambling, cheating, and every other manner of distraction. Anything to avoid the truth that your soul keeps trying to force up into your consciousness, so that you'll look at it, feel it, and let it pass through you and out of you, once and for all.

The notions of stopping and solitude are terrifying. It's just too much to comprehend, not to mention actually do. You fear it will bore you or overwhelm you. And it will. It will knock you down, perhaps many times. But it will pass. Eventually, this too shall pass, all of it. But first you have to go into it.

The person who most runs from hearing the inner voice, who most runs from slowing down and listening, who most runs from the FEEL rising up from the soul is the person who most craves security. It is the security of numbness, the security of pseudo-happy feelings, and the security of a supposedly safe and secure life that keep this person from going into their own soul and hearing their own voice. Why? Because they know already that their own soul is calling them to something a whole lot different than this miserable life they're living. That desire for security is a powerful driver. It is rooted, of course, in the fear of insecurity, specifically the fear of change, and the fear of what people will say if I do change. "Here, in this miserable present reality, I am safe from criticism and ridicule, safe from the pain I knew so well as a kid and since."

And yet, that plunging into the self and that purging of the soul are precisely what is required to begin a relationship with your own true self. That is precisely what is required if you are to begin to live authentically, if you are to begin to unpack that box that contains the real you, the box you wrapped tightly with duct tape and packed away deep inside you, decades ago. That is precisely what is required, if you desire to finally have peace in your soul and lasting happiness in your life. There's no two ways about it. Spiritual stuff ain't pretty.

The longer you run from your pain, the longer you run from your happiness. In that vein, I am not a believer in this whole culture of incessant focus on gratitude. Or, more accurately, I am not a believer in the notion that gratitude for all the good things is the spiritual way. I believe in purging. I believe that the pain yearns to come out, and that no amount of happy thinking can paper over the pain lodged deep in your soul. It has to come out. Heck, I even include on my gratitude list, every day, all of the negative feelings I'm feeling, from hate to anger, from pain to jealousy, and the full gamut. I picked up this tip in the book *Making Miracles in 40 Days*. I believe in it as a great addition to the spiritual discipline of journaling, because I am a great believer in the power of releasing negative energy stored in the body and in the soul, not to mention in the memory. So, I'm grateful for the pain, rage, fire, intensity, sorrow, and the like. For, I know it always yields greater wisdom, depth, peace and joy.

In solitude, in quiet is where we finally begin to hear our own voice. But what must happen first is that all of the fears, negative and not-you messages we've swallowed, and self-destructive core beliefs that have been pressed into us must be removed. They must be allowed to come up and out, precisely as your soul has been trying to do, day in and day out, all of your life.

And it hurts coming out. Just as those messages hurt going in, when they were first inflicted on you, they hurt coming out. But come out they do. And there are mechanisms for getting them out quicker and somewhat painlessly.

But once we begin to clear out the obstructions, our own voice begins to be heard, quite clearly. It can finally rise up from within our viscera. There's no longer anything blocking its rise. The occlusions are gone. Once we remove what no longer feels good, we allow what does feel good to rise up. You begin to know what really feels good to you and what directions you really want to go with your life.

Of course, this alone – this knowing – can be quite terrifying, in and of itself. Articulating your truth – i.e. putting into words that which you really are – is a higher order of creating. Feeling the impulse of something new rising up from within us is one thing. But then dwelling on and feeling it further is the next step of creation. However, to go from merely ruminating on something to actually speaking it is a radically big step and a much higher and more powerful order of creation. This is why people are so terrified of putting thoughts into words. A certain measure of responsibility and ownership happens when we speak our truth, as opposed to just kicking it around inside. To speak something means to be held accountable for it, more often than not. And so, most people wait for resolution to come in the head before ever giving words to a truth, an idea, or an impulse. Unfortunately, resolution often doesn't comes in the head.

But also, giving words to the pulse rising up from within usually means going against the wishes of all those people who want you to stay precisely the way you are and think precisely the way you always have, and of course act the way that is predictable and quite convenient for them. And because the thought of crossing them is so scary in its own right, it is far easier to just keep running. It is far easier, it seems, to never put into words the calling of your own soul. It is better, it seems, to never express or let out your discontent, your frustration, hurt, and anger. It is seemingly easier to never even begin to even consider it all, because you have fears of where it will lead. It takes so much courage to just stop and actually begin to listen to the calling of your own soul. Few things in life are scarier than this.

And this is what it means to live an intuitive and deliberate life. It is to begin to tune into your own intuition, your own sense of inner knowing. It is, start to finish, a relationship with your own inner voice. In that place, we are fully fused to the message and guidance of the Universe. And to live from that place of trusting one's own intuition and feelings is to unleash a power in your life that you have never known and simply cannot fathom, prior to doing so.

The fullness of the spiritual path and its many blessings demand your tuning into the voice of feel of your soul. If you are too scared of solitude, too afraid of no motion, unwilling to hear your own feelings, you are severely limiting the amount of joy possible in your life, if not eliminating it completely.

Step Two: Attack
Once we feel the call, once we know the direction(s) our own soul is beckoning us to, once we have taken the time and space to listen and feel, once we hear our own truth rising up from within the very depths of our being, once we allow that truth to be known...*to ourselves*...we are then confronted with the call to action. We're confronted with the monster decision to actually do it!

And that comes with its own set of fears, because you know exactly how those around you will respond. You know exactly what your brother will say, exactly what your mom or your BFF will say, exactly what society will say. You know exactly the resistance you will face. You know exactly how hard your knees will be knocking and how hard your heart will be pounding. The movement from speaking your truth to acting on it is another mammoth step to a much higher order of creation.

What keeps people from attacking life now with the voice of their own soul pulsing within them is the fear of what others will think. They fear the criticism AND how that new criticism will only tear off the scab of the wound from when they were criticized as a kid, when they tried to be real and authentic.

The source of all depression and anxiety, the greatest fear of all people, the one thing that kills more dreams is the fear of what others will think and say. I am an absolute believer in this truth. What is really killing you, right now, if you're really honest, is your fear of the voice and words – i.e. the disapproval and criticism – of someone who has power over you, living or dead.

But, the call is there, pulsing ever-loudly inside, waiting for you to finally begin. The call of your own soul begs for action. At its core, whatever the specifics of the calling might be, the message rising up from your soul is a mighty "NO!" It is a "NO!" to the life you have been living and to the life and belief system you had forced on you, at a very young age. It is fundamentally a loud and resounding "NO!" to the belief that the real you doesn't matter. In that "NO!" is the bold declaration to life, "I MATTER! DAMMIT, I MATTER!!!!"

Life begins at "NO!" Until you finally believe in you enough to act on it, no amount of anyone else believing in you will ever matter. Until you love who you really are, ain't nobody else gonna.

The person who most runs from heeding the inner voice, who most runs from amping up and attacking the vision that has been put in their soul, who most runs from the acting on their inner voice is the person who most craves approval. Sure, that's all of us. But for some people, the desire to be liked and approved of exceeds that same desire in others. It's an extremely compelling motivator to inaction. This person will engage in every manner of over-thinking, so as to clutter the mind deliberately, thereby undermining the call they know is there....and thereby not have to act. The over-thinker wants the path that offends no one and steps on no one's toes. That path doesn't exist.

The second step of the spiritual journey, is to dive in. It is to attack with full vigor that which you know you have to do. Or, more accurately, it is to attack that which you know you most want to do, even though it scares the heck out of you. It is to attack that which you simply know your soul needs to do for itself.

To live in full relationship with yourself and the spirit of the Universe is to take action when called. And it is to do it more and more with less and less hesitation. It is to simply trust the call, not always knowing exactly where it will lead and definitely not over-thinking it. If it doesn't scare the Berbers out of you, it isn't your path. It isn't your call. It's someone else's. People don't go to amusement parks for the safe click-click-click of the 'up' part of the roller coaster ride. They go for the insane ride down and around. If your life doesn't feel like the down side of a roller coaster – simultaneously terrifying and exhilarating – you're living what someone else wants you to do. You're choosing safety, which is really the need for approval over authenticity.

Step Three: Quit

Really, the sketchiest and often most frustrating part of the spiritual journey is the quitting of one path for another, and for so many reasons.

See, no call lasts forever. The call of your soul morphs, in small and large ways, as you go further down the road. Often, we are called to open and pass through this door not because the next room is the one we are to reside in, but because we must pass through that room, a stairway, two ante-rooms, a slide, and three time warps before we get to the door to the next room we are to be in for a while....at least til the trap door opens in that room and lands us in something even better.

But, the capacity to quit is paramount in the ongoing spiritual life. For, it is far too easy to get stuck in a past call when the Universe, or your own soul, is making it abundantly clear that this relationship, this career path, this location, this habit, or what have you is simply no longer your calling and must be walked away from. Much spiritual *sturm und drang* in life is because someone is holding on to a path or relationship that once was the call, but is no longer. For, it is just doggone scary to leave one path when every last issue with the next one isn't resolved. It's even scarier to leave one path when you can't see the next path clearly, or even in the distance. However, if you can't quit, you can't truly live.

150

We are called in life to quit things, just as surely as we are called to start things. Creation is invariably preceded by destruction. Things must die for things to live. We are called to quit things on the micro level, on the day-to-day level, constantly. And we are called to quit things on the macro level – big dreams, established relationships, big ideas and beliefs, career paths, and so on – more often than people realize. For the spiritual journey requires fluidity and malleability, not rigidity and force.

Vince Lombardi Was Wrong

Back when I was an NCAA Head Coach for Strength for all sports at what happens to be one of the top wrestling schools in the country (and thus is simultaneously part of a city/area that produces a lot of MMA/UFC fighters), I was often asked to speak to teams, coaching groups, campus groups, and auditoriums full of recruits and their parents. It was often in this last setting that I would reference one of the great mistakes by one of the greatest coaches in American history.

I would begin by pulling out a $20 bill and offering up to the crowd of parents and high school recruits this enticement, "I'll give 20 bucks to the first person who can shout out why this college is really here."

Instantly, kids shouted out things like "To give us an education" and "To help us get a degree." But as they were shouting, I would quietly fold up the 20 and announce that none of them were right. "You'll get an education, no matter where you go or what you do. And this school has a far higher purpose than getting you a degree or even giving you knowledge," I would tell them.

Continuing, "The real purpose of this school is to line up a buffet in front of you; this giant buffet of experiences – from studying organic chemistry to playing sports, from working at a homeless shelter to studying overseas, from playing wiffleball with your friends on the weekend to going to church or synagogue, from writing papers to going to cultural events, from dating to learning Tai Chi, and on and on. And your job is to step up to that buffet and to quit as many things as possible."

[pause]

Silence.

I had their attention now. I had used the one word athletes aren't supposed to speak and certainly aren't allowed to advocate. "Your job, especially now at this age, is to step up to the buffet of life and try as many things and quit as many things as possible, until you find those one or two or three things that you have no desire to quit; until you find that handful of things I could pay you money to get you to quit and you still wouldn't quit. See, as athletes we're taught that great Lombardi maxim, 'Winners never quit and quitters never win.' Well, that's just garbage. Winners quit all the time; quit training techniques for better ones; quit one sport for another; quit one career for one that looks more interesting or enticing; quit friendships that no longer are life-giving; quit places, persons, paths, and things that have become draining or debilitating. Winners are actually *constantly* quitting, forever refining what *is* their path by eliminating that which *isn't* their path.

Vince Lombardi was wrong when he said,
"Winners never quit and quitters never win."

"Your job for the next four or five or ten years is to throw that quote out the window, and to quit as many things as possible. Until you give yourself permission to quit that which is not you, you will forever be engaging in a life that simply cannot make you happy. And the truth is, when we're on the path that really lights us up, we work harder, we work smarter, we are more diligent, and we are more committed.

Every man must carefully examine which way his heart calls him,
then pursue that path with all his strength.
--Hasidic proverb

"Or worse, you'll find yourself juggling all these things that you started but have ceased to be fun. And now they're just sucking the life out of you. Or, worse still, you'll stop trying new things, unless you're certain you can succeed at them. In other words, you'll start living in fear, in hesitation, and in an ever-shrinking and supposedly safe life.

"If you don't give yourself permission to quit now, when you're young, you'll be 45 years old, like your parents are now, and you'll be knocking on the door of my counseling office, because you realize how unhappy you are. And parents, your job is to give your children permission to stop and start, permission to quit, permission to 'not know' what they're going to do with their lives. You need to stop asking your kid what their future plans are, because that short-circuits the process of discernment by putting so much pressure on the end result, rather than finding the right fit."

What's true in career choices of college kids is true in relationships with lovers and the relationship with your own self. Until you give yourself permission to quit the large, medium, and small things that are not-you, you will forever be stuck in a life of things that are not-you. And what do you think the odds are of you being happy when you're doing things and living a life that are not-you? What do you think the odds are of you becoming happy when you're forever bleeding yourself of life energy, refusing to quit and refusing to build a life of joy and aliveness?

Great athletes, musicians, businesspeople, and so forth quit many times: positions and paths that aren't quite right, personal and professional relationships that don't work; and habits and disciplines that no longer bear fruit. In July of 1965, at the Newport Folk Festival, Bob Dylan, whom *Rolling Stone* magazine lists as the greatest rock artist of all time and whose signature sound is unequivocally linked to the acoustic guitar, plugged in and played an electric guitar, effectively quitting exclusive devotion to the acoustic guitar, all while a giant cultural cacophony raged against that change. He was dubbed a Judas by his fans and the folk music community, while simultaneously fusing it with the rock community. Michael Jordan quit baseball, after earlier quitting basketball when he was still better than most players in the game. Jackson Pollock largely quit figurative representation, not to mention easel and brush, when he stumbled upon splatter painting, or paint pouring. Howard Schultz quit selling and marketing coffee makers when he stumbled upon the Italian coffee shop experience in Milan and realized that quality of coffee and the coffee shop experience were what was missing in the U.S. I have had some very accomplished professional gamblers as clients, who stoutly attest that the hardest part of winning at their craft is laying down a hand, and the biggest mistake is forcing one when something is off or doesn't feel right. Wayne Gretzky, arguably the greatest hockey player of all time, quit playing when he was no longer at his prime and also later quit coaching when he realized he wasn't nearly the coach that he was the player. As a deliberate parent, one must constantly adjust and quit old parenting techniques and philosophies that aren't working. People constantly quit schools, jobs, relationships, diets, workout plans, life paths and the like that just no longer feel right. Allowing one's call to rise up from within, and then following that call, absolutely require the courage to quit that which is not-you.

The third step in daily and yearly spiritual, deliberate living is really a master-level step. It is the capacity to let go of trying to control the results. And this is key, not to mention incredibly difficult. See, once we hear the calling of our soul, we see a vision of what the future is to look like. And it is the compelling force of that vision that drives us to speak and take action amid seemingly insurmountable odds and certain blowback from those who want us kept where we've always been.

But we are called to actions, not results. You are not called to conduct the whole orchestra; you are called to play the doggone cello to the utmost of your ability and only for as long as you feel inspired to do so, until the Universe asks you to start playing the timpani. We simply are not called to produce results. We cannot control results, only actions. If there's one thing my most successful business, artist, military, and sports clients have confirmed, over the decades, it's how elusive results are. Control is an illusion. This is where a lot of people go off course.

See, this is where it is necessary to stay tuned in to the calling and whispering of your soul. For, it is so easy to slip into forcing action and forcing the results we have envisioned in our head and want so badly, rather than taking only inspired action. To live in concert with your own soul means to attack life when inspired, but also to throttle back when not inspired and walk away when the call feels done.

And ceasing to act when not inspired is no easy feat. In fact, in our culture to not act, to not be in constant motion and frenetic activity, is to be considered a fool, at least if you wish to be seen as driven and actually living a life of purpose.

We are called to actions,
not results.

The person who most runs from letting go of the results, who most runs from quitting, who most runs from the inner voice when it stops inspiring this course of action is the person who most craves <u>control</u>. And letting go of control is monstrously difficult for many. This person fears the insecurity of not knowing what's next, as well as the agitation of not having something to do, do, do. But sometimes life calls us from 'doing' to just 'being'. And when you're a doer, just being is hard as heck. "When things outside of me aren't in control and just-so, I feel out of control and highly anxious inside." This person fears what people will say when they see she has not finished it the way she said she was going to. This person made a resolution, decades ago, that they would keep everything under control (read 'just perfect'), so that there is no room for anyone to criticize her on anything, which is her greatest fear, as is the anxiety when things aren't perfect. To not control every last detail and every last result is to put herself in the crosshairs for someone she believes will take aim at her and hurt her, just as they did when she was a child.

And so, this person forces all manner of actions, even when they are not inspired actions. This person tries to force the vision, and we just don't have the ability to force something that is not in the cards, written by the gods, luck, the Universe, God, or just one's own soul. Further, forcing action when not inspired not only rarely yields greater results, it often screws everything up more.

Salespeople, businesspeople, handymen, athletes, musicians, military tacticians, artists all know what I mean when I bring up the notion of forcing action. We've all tried to make something happen when it just wasn't flowing.

But we don't trust that feel, do we? We force our way through it. And that's the mistake. That's where the greatest room for spiritual growth is for a great many people.

155

It's predicated on the notion that the Universe, or God, can't be trusted. And that's a bold statement to make. Either you trust that God is speaking through that inner voice, or you don't. Either you fully go on your intuition or your claims of 'trusting my gut' are BS. But if you do trust it, that means always being in tune to it, even when it's telling you to pull back when you so want to keep surging forward, attacking. It can be tremendously frustrating to have to pull up when you're in mid-attack. But, as with Louisa in an earlier chapter, we learn to trust that inner voice, more and more, after going down paths of not listening to it, after not trusting it.

Incessant attacking comes from being married to results, rather than simply being married to actions, or callings. As much as you want particular results, you'll seldom get them exactly the way you've imagined them. No, the Universe has a way of getting the best out of us by getting us off the path we had envisioned, the path that initially drew us to action. And that breeds results that are better – albeit very different – than those we imagined.

This is one of the ironies of the spiritual journey. The vision and dream that get you going are seldom the vision and dream that you are called to for the long haul. I saw this in my years of work in the field of marital infidelity. The person we cheat on our spouse with is often the person put in our path to compel us to leave an already-dead relationship, but it is almost never the person you later end up with for any long period of time. Or, the dream you have for your new career – the one that initially strengthens you to leave what has become a dead-end, lifeless job – is not always the one you end up in, because you discover that as you grow and change more, your tastes, influences, passions and callings change too. And, as I said, this can be tremendously frustrating if you're not expecting it, or if you're overly clinging to the initial dream.

There's that great line from the rock group, *.38 Special*, that goes:

> *"Hold on loosely*
> *But don't let go.*
> *If you cling to tightly,*
> *You're gonna lose control."*

That really sums up the third stage of the spiritual journey so well. Hold on to the vision that animates you and gets you out of bed in the morning ready to attack. But simultaneously let it go each day, too. Be prepared to walk away from it, when the action is no longer inspired. For you are called to actions, not results. The gods have plans that we cannot know. And when we fail to give them room to work their magic, we come up with results far less than what they could have been.

There is a spirit and energy to life that we cannot control, that exceeds us. And the nature of the spiritual life is both acknowledging and giving room to, not to mention trusting, that spirit of life that is unseen and uncontrollable.

The highest order of creation
and the true master level step of co-creators and those on the
spiritual journey
is to let go of that to which we feel called.
The final order of creation is:

pulse>thought>word>deed>release>pulse>thought>word>deed
>release>pulse...

To simultaneously hold on and let go is no small feat. It is this notion of releasing control (and the need for specific outcomes) that is a stumbling block for a great many people who desire to live freer and more alive. It is so hard to let go of control of life. Further, it's so hard to set your vision on one thing and also tell others this is your vision, and then let go of that vision when it is not accomplished. We so fear looking stupid and we define unpredictability, or even just change, as stupid. So people cleave to security and consistency, even as they engender increasing boredom.

We all soooo fear looking stupid and being criticized for it that we'll continue all manner of garbage just to avoid it. To move on to a new call, or to walk away from a course of action absolutely demands the willingness to look foolish. And most control freaks – which is a whole lotta folk, at least when it comes to their image, in one way or another – loathe the idea of looking foolish, because the scorn and ridicule are too much. They remind us of the when we were ridiculed or criticized as children when we tried something new or gave expression to our real self-rising up from within. And that's just a pain too great to bear, for most.

The simple truth of the spiritual path is that one call morphs into a new calling. Back in my late 20s, while simultaneously working my way through seminary, I possessed a powerful desire to have a speaking career. The greatest joy I could imagine was to be a paid traveling public speaker. I was good at it, loved it, and believed I packed a good punch. I had even created opportunities for this to happen and certain opportunities fell in my lap. I lectured at the graduate level, university level, and to several small and large spiritual groups and organizations, not to mention sports teams.

Then I met a guy at a picnic, who spoke for a living in the real estate field. One off-hand comment by him forever changed the arc of my life and career, introducing me to my next life calling, one that would run concurrent with the speaking, counseling, and pursuit of ministry. He said that if I want a speaking career, I had to have 'multipliers' – tapes and books to sell that enabled me to be in more than one place at a time.

The light bulb went on. His recommendation was more than that. It resonated deep inside me as my own truth, my own next calling, and for far greater reasons than just making 'multipliers'. It felt bigger than that. So I started writing (for publication. I had been journaling since I was 13 and knew how to express myself. But I had never even considered 'real' writing). Articles got published, two books got started. Five years later, the book that put me on the map, naming and presaging the rise of the Spiritual But Not Religious movement, was published. And my writing took off. The breadth of my impact expanded greatly.

Interestingly, I had more speaking gigs: more lecturing at colleges in more fields (from sports psychology to spirituality, from general fitness to the sociology of religion in America), as well as speaking to police departments, youth groups, churches, and companies. I got fired from or lost ministry positions three times for supporting gay rights (long before it became fashionable to do so) and multiple times for radical theology mixed with what was seen as a personality that was too intense. Thus, while the original calls inside me were to ordained ministry as a Lutheran pastor and Emergency Room Chaplain, and an additional career as a traveling speaker, they morphed into a very strong calling to write and counsel, which is the bulk of my work today, 25 years later. Even though I still speak and all of my work is spiritual leadership, it's just not within organized religion, anymore.

The point? One call leads to the next, sometimes faster than we might like. In fact, I used to tell people, when I was a pastor, that we so often feel we're waiting, waiting, waiting on God to give us our next calling, or mission (the old kairos/chronos sermon). But the problem is seldom that God's not speaking the next call fast enough but that the call is too scary or not what we imagined or wanted. Or, God is calling for action over there in that area of your life when you want answers and action in this part of your life, over here. So, we hold out for another one. God's calls are usually pretty obvious, clear and quick, oh and fear-inducing, not slow and comfortable. But, we miss or avoid 'em, because they ain't what we want or the fallout, or price, is too high. We claim to want a high and noble calling, but chafe when we get one that means walking counter to the path that is expected of us.

On the spiritual journey, you will be called in new directions. And if the new direction does not simultaneously excite you and scare the daylights out of you, it's not your call. If it's safe, it's not your call; it's you doing what you think you 'should' do, what someone else wants you to do, or what's safe and within your comfort zone. The call from God, or the Universe, or your own soul is scary and invigorating. It gives energy. It inspires. It does not take your energy or drain you. Sure, there are bad days. But even on its worst day, even though there are occasional drops in the stock, the stock of your true calling always trends forward and up. All of this requires the courage to quit that which feels forced or is simply no longer you.

Looping Back

The three steps of the spiritual journey are a constant loop. We are constantly overlaying one step onto the next. I may be in step three, career-wise, but I'm in step one when it comes to discerning if we should have another child. Or, perhaps I'm in step two regarding standing up to my parents, but I'm in step three regarding trying to sell the house.

We are constantly FEELING, ATTACKING, and QUITTING in different areas of life. This is what it means to live in communion with the soul. This is what it means to live an inspired life. It means trusting that inspiration. It means trusting that no matter what happens, *I'll be okay*. No matter what. To live an inspired, authentic, and ultimately an invigorating life of true aliveness means to live in trust of your own deepest intuition and fully acting on it when called, *and not acting when not called or truly inspired to do so*. To have that great relationship with your own self means to no longer care what others think, especially those who have been the most powerful voices in your life, and it means letting go of trying to control results.

You are called. You must act. You must let go of the results. You must quit. You must quiet yourself and wait for the next call. You will be called to something new. You must act. You must let go...

The challenge and joy is in, literally moment to moment, hearing and following the energy from deep within. Trusting that intuition. Trusting the very whisper and pulse of the Universe in you. There simply is no other life.

Song Recommendation

Purchase, listen to, and dive into the song *Hold On Loosely*, by **.38 Special**. The band is singing of love of a woman, but the words are so easily converted into the love of something you consider your baby. Perhaps it's a dream, a business, a career, a passion, your art, your child, your family, or something else that is massively important to you. One of the grand challenges of life is to simultaneously hold on to and let go of that which we most want. It is so easy to kill that which we most want by holding on too tightly. It is easy to spin ourselves in circles and tie our stomach up in knots by trying to seek control and force results, always limited to just one vision of what the ending must look like.

https://www.youtube.com/watch?v=vJtf7R_oVawHoldOnLoosely

The master of the spiritual life lives something different. It is to live in a state of trust, a state of letting go, a state of not needing exact, particular results in order to be happy. It's a monster challenge, but so gratifying when it is mastered or even endeavored.

Bonus Tracks
Core readers: Move on to the next chapter. Advanced readers: check out these Bonus Tracks:
- Bonus Track 7: The Dog And The Electric Fence
- Bonus Track 8: The Purpose Of The 'Why'

CHAPTER 19

EVERY MORNING, LIFE IS WHISPERING TWO QUESTIONS IN YOUR EAR

The simple fact of the matter is:,

**Every morning, when you wake up, while you're laying there in that moment
before your day begins with your short walk to the bathroom,
life is whispering two questions in your ear:
Who the heck are you, really? And
Do you have the courage to be who you really are?**

The bottom line truth is, You ain't bein' who you is. You're living this mass of built up values that are not yours, paths that you never wanted, beliefs that just don't jibe with your soul, and words coming out of your mouth that feel foreign to you.

You're living someone else's life, or some accretion of the lives of others. But you sure as heck ain't living your life. Too scared. Too safe in the non-deliberate, over-thinking, ever-suffering life you're in.

And the Universe/God/the gods call, "No joy!" to anyone who claims that non-path as the false prescription for their own life. To those who would choose safety, the gods grant misery. To those who would risk originality, the gods grant exhilarating uncertainty and that coveted *aliveness.*

This is why all human existence rises and falls on courage and courage alone, specifically the courage to be original, not just to rebel against something or someone but to author one's own life, to stand up to the voices that would tell you how to run your own life, and to choose your own authenticity. This deliberateness demands the resounding and courageous 'yes' to the truth of who you are and that which is your calling. I have counseled those who have taken life and fought to stay alive, those on the edge of death and those

163

who've been dying since childhood. Continually, time and again, it has been shown to me that the greatest fear in life is being who you are. An authentic life. Nothing scarier than that.

Hence, courage.

Journaling Recommendation
1. Who are you?
2. What is the longest and most complete identification and definition you can give of yourself?
3. Do you have the courage to finally be who you really are?
4. Lastly, what, or who, is the biggest obstacle to you being, saying, doing and becoming that which you most fully are?

CHAPTER 20

HOW DO I BECOME ME WHEN I DON'T EVEN KNOW WHO I AM?

"**B**ut Sven, how do I become the 'real me' when I have no idea who the real me is? I mean, if the real me was stuffed inside some box deep inside me, decades ago, as you say, how do I ever figure out who I am? How do I open and unpack the box? What you say about the core beliefs and 3 Binary Gates makes total sense. I get it. What scares me about all of this is I have no idea who I really am and no idea how to find out."

This is a question I hear every week. Now we're getting somewhere.

Ah, now we're getting somewhere.

My first response to this question is always, "Don't get down. For the simple truth is that part of becoming the real you is discovering that which is not-you. All the missteps and unfulfilling paths are wonderful, though painful, research. They're all things you can cross off the list. But also, every not-you is talking to you, trying to teach you. You must ask the questions: What is this not-me trying to teach me about life and about me, specifically? This is what it means to learn from failure and setback. This is part of what it means to live deliberately. No relationship, career, or life *cul de sac* is a waste if you learn what it is trying to teach you. So, don't despair."

> ***The grand mistake of life***
> ***is to have the experience but miss the meaning.***
> --TS Eliot, paraphrase from *Dry Salvages*

But my second response is that it's very important to understand a significant point.

Finding Yourself vs. Allowing Yourself

As mentioned previously, one of the grand problems of life, at least at the spirit/core level, is that we tend to posit control of our life *outside* of ourselves. It starts, obviously enough, in childhood when the parent basically controls every last element of the child's life. The child trusts the parent, is dependent upon the parent, and for the most part is completely subject to the power of the parent.

Then, in theory, as the child reaches 10-12 years old (or roughly puberty) and begins the very natural movement away from the parent as the primary power source and knowledge source in life, the parent encourages the child to not depend on the parent so much in decision-making and in defining of self. But, of course, that's when it gets harder for the parent to let go. Just when the parent most needs to step back, the parent most wants to step in. The parent has already invested so much time, energy, and love. Every chauffeuring to a band concert or baseball game, every school event, every meal together is one more cord binding the parent's identity to that child. It becomes a tall order to change how that love for the child then gets expressed. Worse, the parent now knows that the decisions have greater consequences as the child ages. And so, wanting to spare the child the loss that comes with bad decisions, the parent – either explicitly or insidiously – controls the teen's decisions. That seems to save headaches now, but is always a setup for failure later, when Billy moves into adulthood. For, Billy then lacks the capacity to make decisions and accept or recover from failures, fall downs, and screw-ups. He has never stood on his own two feet and learned the confidence and clarity that come with making his own decisions *and* his own mistakes, free of judgment.

Worse still, however, is the fact that by removing Billy's ability to make his own decisions, the parent teaches the child to not trust himself, not trust his/her own inner voice. And it could be argued that a 13 or 16 year old ought not trust his/her own voice. But that is precisely when the child must begin to develop a relationship with his own self, there in the safe laboratory of small consequences (compared to adulthood) and being surrounded by non-judgmental, encouraging love, words, and actions. For if that transfer of power over the child from parent back to the child never happens, the kid becomes an adult who is forever looking for someone to tell him/her what to do, how to act, and what decisions to make. That is an extremely vulnerable and dangerous position for any adult to be operating from.

Yet, there's still an even worse factor playing in the equation of parental hold on control over the teen and his/her decisions. It's called pride. Embarrassment. Putting on a good face.

Few people are more vain than me. Yet, I have siblings, friends, clients and acquaintances who are quite devoid of my vanity, who nonetheless confess they struggle constantly with the desire to control, or at least influence, their child's decisions, because of how it will reflect on him/her, the parent.

This longing to control our kids, for reasons both protective and tragically selfish, sets up a child who becomes an adult, who is always looking outside himself for definition. The trail goes something like, "Since who I am was always defined by someone (or something) outside of me, now, as an adult, I seek my identity and meaning outside of me."

And this cuts to the quick of what the real quest for self is about. Fundamentally, it is never a quest outside of oneself. Far too often, it is mistakenly endeavored outside oneself. Heck, even I still do this, at times. Because you've been taught that your own instincts and thoughts/feelings shouldn't be listened to and thus can't be trusted, it only makes sense that you'd try to find yourself outside yourself.

But that is never where the solution lies. That is why we're never really in the business of *discovering* or *finding* ourselves, as if it's somewhere, out there. Point of fact, the real mystery of life is the quest to *allow* ourselves. It's about removing that which blocks the flow of your one, true voice rising up *from within you*. And, make no mistake, blockage is always, always, always fear. Always. In one form or another. That which stands between you and yourself, you and your true voice, you and your aliveness is fear.

The grand task of life is not finding yourself, but allowing yourself. But because you have forever posited the power source for your life *outside* yourself – parent, teacher, boss, girlfriend/boyfriend, spouse, society – you are forever looking for some new truth *outside* yourself, as if it is something we 'find'. You are caught not just in looking for the wrong thing but looking in the wrong place, caught in the belief that the power source need be outside yourself.

Fundamentally, you've not given yourself permission to be your own power source. Heck, it's possible the thought of doing so never even crossed your mind. That's how entrenched you are in external thinking. This happens in no small part because you were taught to not trust yourself, your own decisions, your own ability to know, and your own capacity to navigate life, not to mention be your own power source.

For example, if you believe that you must have a better job, a mate, a new mate, a bigger house, more money, more prestige, etc in order to be happy, you are caught in the never-ending belief in the external power source. And, as a result, you will never, in fact, be happy...in no small part because you are using what others say will make you happy to make you happy. And until you've identified and are living that which moves *your* soul, you cannot, by definition, be happy.

For another example, on a parenting note, I encouraged my own daughter and son, at roughly age 12-13, to begin dating a bit, to experience holding hands and a first kiss, etc. I wanted them to experience love, infatuation, heartbreak, hopelessness of love lost, recovery, new love, getting broken up from, and having to break up from someone you care about but cannot be with anymore. I wanted them to experience all of this, when young, so they're not getting bowled over by these experiences for the first time or two in college, when the stakes are higher, or when they're in their mid-twenties and need all of their energy and attention on building their career. If a kid is experiencing massive heartbreak for the first time when she's also trying to kick butt in her career, it'll kill her and potentially massively sidetrack her career; or, worse, it'll cause her to start stuffing down her feelings and just powering through, which is never a happy solution, long term. Most importantly, I encouraged my kids, when young, to dive into relationships and all that comes with 'em so that they'd get used to hearing and acting on *their own inner voice* in relationships, get some reps, and feel confidence and trust in that inner voice. When you haven't been given permission to trust your own voice, it becomes so easy to give away your power and life direction in a relationship. It becomes so easy to lose yourself, forever tuned into making your mate and others happy, completely forgetting about your true self. And I can happily report, today, that my kids are in their mid-twenties, happy, and building their careers. They're still getting their reps in relationships, and enjoying it. But, the setbacks and heartbreaks aren't devastating them or throwing their lives off course, and they're far more in-tune to their own inner voice.

To become your real self, to live your truth, to become happy demands living your own voice, which is inside you. Thus, it demands allowing your truth to rise up from within, scary as that may be. And to allow your truth to rise up means to remove all blockages, all negative messages, and all fears, both externally and internally. And THAT is the scariest part – to actually confront, actually wade into the stuff you're most afraid of. To quote the great 20th Century mythologist, Joseph Campbell,

"The cave you fear to enter holds the treasure you seek."

The truth is, your path will find you. There is no wrong step. The path of allowing who we are means discovering who we're not. The path to authentic you goes through many not-yous. Hence, there is no such thing as wasted time. Everything today is an element of your tomorrow, no matter how hideous or shameful it feels. Everything of your past is part of today's wisdom. You just refuse to look at it, see it for what it really is, and mine it for all the massive gems of wisdom it holds.

You may worry that you won't, or can't seem to, find your path – the path of your greatness, the path of your joy, the path of really feeling ALIVE and on fire. But the only thing you need to do is accept and release the fear, trusting that the greatness will come, trusting that the path will find you. And it will. It already has. You're already on it. It's ALL working for your good, even the hard, confusing, or seemingly fruitless parts.

My own failures, setbacks, and years of immense struggle were the very fodder of my present success. If I had not failed and fought my life so hard, I would have little comprehension of the pain of others also in the fight, which is critical to my work. More importantly, I would have no concept of how to lead others out of the misery, because I would have never had to figure out my own way out of my misery. I would have never found the answers if I had not so intensely wrestled with the questions.

Everything on the path of life is fodder and fuel for what is next.

Song Recommendation

By the time the late-90s rolled around, I had two young children. As a result, Disney movies were a staple in my life. And, I gotta say, I'm a fan. Pretty much love 'em all. Love the stories, the characters, and especially the music, because they're loaded with great messages, far more than just advancing the particular story line of the particular movie. Recognizing that, purchase the song *A Star is Born*, from *Hercules*. It's an upbeat song with a fitting message that speaks to the frustration of not knowing the way but discovering that the map is inside you; your heart knows the way. And while that's a giant cliché, it's also a giant truth. Give it a listen.

https://www.youtube.com/watch?v=KBm_-kW4W-UAStarIsBorn

Journaling Recommendation

1. What have been the 3 primary paths you've gone down that were not-you or no longer are you?
2. Okay, now the telling part. What were each of the three paths sent to teach you, both about life and about you? What would you not know about you, or what would you not presently be, if you had never gone those directions?
3. In a previous chapter you assessed the difference between your parents' values and yours. Can you see now more clearly how identifying your own voice and values is critical to living your own path? In what ways?

CHAPTER 21

DIAMONDS AND RAW SEWAGE

O nce my clients understand the need to become themselves and *allow* their true selves to come up and out, and after they express the frustration of not knowing who their true selves really are, I tell them:

The single biggest mistake people make in trying to get happy is that they do more things that make them happy.

[paaaaauuuuuse]

[paaaaaauuuuuse]

[breathe]

Now, yes, read that again.

Doing more of what you love, or, worse, *having* more of what you love (and the constant possession, acquisition and consumption, as if cluttering your outer world will somehow fix your inner world) is not the answer!!! Or, more accurately, doing and having more of what you love is only half the answer, at best. I'm not against doing, having, being, believing, saying, and becoming who you really are. In fact, that is part of the true essence of the spiritual life. But, again, it's only a partial fix, one easily mistaken for the full solution.

Imagine that everything in your life that makes you happy, everything that breathes life into you – every person, place, path, plan, and purpose that either energizes you or brings peace – is a diamond you're holding in your cupped hands in front of you. You gaze at them, happily delighting in how great it makes you feel to have them.

However, there's a problem. And the problem is that you can't really appreciate, much less see, your diamonds, because you have giant pipes above your head disgorging raw sewage onto you. It's pouring over your head, onto your body, and it's getting into your eyes, even though you try to keep them shut; it gets up your nose and even into your sealed mouth, because you have to breathe. It's all over your body, down your crack, and splattering all over the ground around you. And by 'raw sewage' I mean sludge, cigarette butts, rat feces, big guy pubic hairs, half-eaten cans of cat food, coffee grounds, urine, and, well, you can imagine the rest.

Truth is, it doesn't matter one bit how many diamonds you have in your hands. If you have raw sewage pouring over you and getting into every orifice of your body, you ain't ever going to be able to appreciate those diamonds, no matter how high their count or how grand and glorious they might be under other circumstances.

Well, just as those diamonds are every positive, life-giving energy source in your life, the raw sewage is every negative energy source in your life; every person, place, thing, purpose, plan, path, climate, geography, inner beliefs and thoughts, or whatever else that sucks the life out of you, numbs you, bores you, or for which you have to conjure energy just to go to, go into, or engage in any way. The raw sewage is every last thing that pulls you from you, drags you down, tries to control you, depresses you, bleeds you, heightens your anxiety, or in any way takes you from your happiness and peace.

And because it pours down in such copious amounts and gets in every orifice, eventually all you can see, smell, taste, hear, and touch is raw sewage; all you experience is the negative, for the most part. And that ain't no way to live!

But here's the crazy thing about raw sewage, about negative energy sources: it doesn't take some grand amount in order for it to obscure everything you see, taste, touch, hear, and smell. You could have just one garden hose above your head going drip, drip, drip with raw sewage onto you. Eventually, it will still get into your eyes, nose, mouth, etc. Eventually, everything you see, taste, touch, smell and hear will be clouded with the negativity of raw sewage. Eventually, even small amounts have the capacity to ruin your experience of the diamonds. Negative energy sources are that powerful!

To draw a parallel, a quarter million gallons of drinking water can be contaminated by a mere one quart of oil. That's power! Negative energy sources in our lives have that enormous power. It is indisputable that a drip, drip amount of raw sewage is certainly better than vast amounts pouring into your life. So, yes, it does behoove you to begin to close, reduce, or cut off the negative energy sources in your life, even if you can't fully eliminate them all, right now.

So, here's what I want you to do. I recommend that you pour yourself a glass of wine or cup of coffee, relax, and pull out a piece of paper and pen. Then draw a vertical line from top to bottom in the center of the page. Now write at the top of the left half the word 'Diamonds' and on the top right write the words 'Raw Sewage.' Underneath 'Diamonds' write 'Positive Energy Sources' and underneath 'Raw Sewage' write 'Negative Energy Sources.' Draw a horizontal line under those headings. Now the fun begins.

In the left column, under Diamonds, simply make a giant list of every positive energy source in your life. Everything that gives you energy, inspires you, excites you, or gives you peace, relaxes you, pleases you, or brings relief and calm. List every person, thing, place, path, geography, culture, food, purpose, clothing, activity...*everything,* large, medium, small, or even tiny that brings you even the smallest measure of joy or peace. Nothing is insignificant or unimportant, if it brings you joy, peace, invigoration, enthusiasm, aspiration, calm, relief, or even a simple smile.

This isn't just a gratitude list. Similar but different. This is a list for the purpose of *identifying* that which you love, that which feeeeeels good, great, inspiring, or peace-bringing, not to give thanks for it, but to begin it or do more of it. So, list everything you *could* do or become, or *dream* of doing or saying, or *already* do, say, have, wear, think about, become, etc. My own list is very long and always getting longer and shorter and longer and shorter, from the seemingly mundane to the profound, and well into the ridiculous. Here's my list, as a way to help you get started.

Sven's Diamonds/Positive Energy Sources
- white elephant gifts, the stupider the better, and generally giving them even more than getting them
- piping hot mocha latte and sitting by my fire pit outside, while doing my morning journaling
- in the summer, wearing white tank undershirts, only, with shorts and sneakers, no socks
- biking in the extreme traffic of the Financial District of Manhattan, NYC, at midday
- changing lives!
- the perfect climate of my former city/home, Berkeley, CA
- waking up at 3am to write
- going to bed early
- laying in bed in the morning with Karen listening to *The Writers' Almanac* with Garrison Keillor
- hitting the weights only once a week for five hours
- watching Yutaka Sado conduct on *YouTube* (as a child, I would nightly live out my fantasy of conducting an orchestra

and choir by standing in front of the dark windows in our living room, blare the stereo to some concerto, and air-conduct the Boston Pops or the Academy of St. Martin in the Fields)

- living on a diet largely comprised of chips & salsa, McDonald's Sausage Burritos, and Oreos
- scotch, non-peaty, or straight whiskey
- reliving entire conversations, while I'm biking, and re-arguing them so that I win this time
- holding an audience in rapt attention, bending their minds, challenging them
- beer pong with Colbjorn and the LSU mutts he calls friends
- counseling for hours with a client, taking them deeper and deeper
- going into a state of deep relaxation and seeing the brilliant ideas and insights that come from this powerfully deep state (and I do it just by laying on my back; sometimes drifting into sleep, sometimes not)
- being challenged to let go of more (more wants, more feelings, more people, more things I want to have) by the Universe
- text messages from my daughter
- bright orange and kelly green
- badass guys, who are really friendly and kind, because they know they don't have to act all hardcore
- period movies
- my wisdom, clever stories, quotes, and nuggets I pull up from stuff I've experienced or learned
- camping
- my vanity, particularly regarding my body
- the smell of coffee
- trusting my own instincts over all influences, great and small
- masturbating
- laughing at myself or about my life, particularly when I'm alone
- when my siblings and I decided to suck it up, shut up, and play nice for my parents' 60th anniversary. It felt great and

was a great gift for mom and dad, whether they were aware of the animus haunting our relationships or not

- breakfast with my parents, enjoying the ritual of their morning devotions and prayer, which they've been doing every day of my life
- serving my gf, her sisters, her daughters, her company, and her darn dogs
- swearing, loudly and with flair
- aggressive, intense, fiercely passionate people
- Mozart!! in all forms, at all times, but especially at Lincoln Center with the NY Philharmonic
- doing physical labor for my brother, John, while he creates some big home project
- time with Todd, Lisa, and Jay – my fav friends
- the challenge to be still, relax, and trust the next calling will come
- wearing jeans, dress shoes, and a tight t-shirt to work as a spiritual counselor, each day
- old *Chicago*, before Terry Kath died
- excessively fat people who workout at the gym (I so respect that, because I know the extreme mental energy they have to draw up from their soul each day to do it! And they inspire me.)
- *Living in the Light* (Gawain), *The Power of Myth* (Campbell/Moyers), and *Illusions* (Bach)
- telling people (mainly my gf) when anything is from, or even remotely related to, Minnesota, such as Prince, Bob Dylan, Judy Garland, Charles Schulz (*Peanuts*), Dairy Queen and the Vikings/Twins/Wild/Wolves
- God's two greatest gifts to humanity: the beauty of a woman and the capacity to create music; I possess neither, but the admiration and love I have for both inspires me
- exposing my real self to you in this list (I'm literally laughing, right now.)

A ridiculous list, right? Oh, it totally is, and I acknowledge that!!! And most people would never be so dumb as to share it with others, nor would there be need to. (In fact, I recommend not sharing yours with others. It should be very personal, and thus private in the beginning stages.) But I am deliberately revealing a lot to show you the extent of what you must do in being honest with yourself.

See, it's MY list. I love it! Everything on that list is so important to me in some way, great or small, presently or possibly in the future. Further, that list is a small fraction of all the things that bring me joy in life or might bring me joy or peace in the future. Note also, the list reflects things outside me and inside me, things I feel, things I believe, paths I press toward, and things of the past. (I'm not a believer in just living in the present. I live wherever there is joy and calm, ecstasy and sublime.) The list is constantly growing, too. Constantly. I am ever adding new items, deleting (or reducing) things that have faded or no longer bring me joy. It's a fluid list.

Additionally, nearly every single thing on that list is something I do or think about or spend time on every week. Or if it's more of an occasional thing, I do it at least a couple of times a year, such as visiting my parents or going camping. Fundamentally, *everything on that list is*, in some form or another, what I consider *a spiritual discipline for me*. Each is something *I have to do* to feed my own soul. I have to.....because I want to. The less I do of them, the more my soul starts to run dry. They don't require effort to do, because I enjoy them and/or my commitment to them is not a burden but a joy; in that sense, they are truly effortless. But, they do require a life that stays focused on ever increasing them and doing them, when it is so easy to get swept up, distracted, and swept away from my true life by all the things others want me to do or all the things I think I'm 'supposed to' or 'should' do.

Okay, now go over to that right side of the page. And now is when it gets interesting. Really interesting. Now is when the greatest candor and honesty are required of you. This is where the proverbial rubber hits the road.

Begin to list every person, place, thing, belief, climate, clothing style, sexual act, societal expectation, family demand, self-image, daily activity, career path, or what have you that drains you, bores you, sucks the life out of you, bleeds you, numbs you, aggravates you, frustrates you, angers you, hurts you, drives you nuts, or that you have to conjure massive energy just to start. Internal and external. Big, medium, small, even tiny. List every 'should', 'supposed to', obligation, duty, responsibility, drag, drain, implicit requirement, and on and on that is just not you, not what you're about, not what you want to be about; anything that's in your life that doesn't feel good, or never has felt good, or used to feel good but doesn't, or just grates at the very essence of your soul.

Your items in this list may not matter one bit to anyone else, but they bug or bleed YOU. Just as the stuff that inspires me wouldn't inspire you or most people, so also the things that suck the life out of you might not do so to someone else, but they drain *your life energy*! They keep you from ALIVENESS! And for that reason, they are very significant and need to be on this list. There are no rules here. If you hate it, dislike it, loathe it, or don't want it, put it on the Raw Sewage list.

To give you a bit of an idea of what a Raw Sewage list looks like, here is one from me. However, please understand that my entire life's work in my own spiritual life is about cutting out the negative energy sources. So, I'm including items that were on this list for me, in the past, but no longer are, as well as a few present elements.

Sven's Raw Sewage/Negative Energy Sources
- cloudy days; I could handle the fierce cold of Minnesota winters, and even the snow, but not the gray skies of Nov, Dec, late-Feb, March, and April
- ties
- know-it-alls, guys with 'smartest guy in the room' syndrome, people who won't simply say 'I don't know'
- abusive women
- the belief that I'll never succeed at what I love
- the taste of coffee and the smell of coffee beans roasting
- the belief my penis was not big enough
- classical music on a Sunday afternoon. Hate it! (I love classical, but often had orchestra concerts on Sundays, as a kid, when I wanted to be home watching the Vikings or playing football outside with the neighborhood boys.)
- my sore thumb from the football league I played in two years ago
- clients who don't pay

- my jeans always falling down and making my butt look saggy
- my own desire to have more money and fame – i.e. security and approval – and how that sometimes cripples my creativity and relaxation
- flavorless cantaloupe
- stupid stuff my family expects me to do, but I'm not interested in
- the challenge to be still, relax, and trust the next calling will come
- the time wasted and negative energy drafted from being on Facebook
- all the career closed doors I've encountered in life, which when mixed with external criticism, made me suicidal for years, decades ago (which brought so many powerful insights, not the least of which were regarding the teachings and blessings from closed doors)
- always wanting more clients, more stuff to write, and more speaking gigs
- when I put negative energy out there in the universe, toward others
- having to shave my head each day, but having a bald spot and receding hairline, such that I feel I have no choice
- my vanity, regarding my career, in particular
- apologizing when I know the person won't reciprocate with their share of the fault
- witnessing non-deliberate parenting
- thoughts that who I am isn't good enough, and that I need to do and have more in order to feel good (which is asinine because I love me, most of the time; I'm generally a reasonably interesting fellow, and I excel at good-naturedly poking fun at myself)
- being in a years-long fight with my formerly closest brother
- working at jobs I hated or that simply bled my energy, or where I was just a cog in someone else's machine, giving my best energy, work ethic and great creativity to someone else's ideas, pursuits, and dreams

- for a very long time in my life, mental confusion, not knowing which way to go or what to do with my life, which was really me not yet knowing who I really was and NOT HAVING THE COURAGE TO BE THE REAL ME. But it was also my frustration with not having a system, back then, for knowing what to do and who I was.
- horror movies – HATE, HATE, HATE, HATE, HATE them! (They stick in my head for months and bring so much negative bodily energy.)
- cardio
- when women fart in public (call me old-fashioned)
- trash and homelessness as societal problems; both really disturb me

This list could go on and on, if I were to include all the things that have been on the list. But you get a good feel for the depth of the Raw Sewage, as well as the triviality of many things on the list. But they're important to me, or were at one time. And so, my task is and always has been to remove or reduce the presence of these things in my life.

The real challenge of life – the task of getting happy and becoming fully alive – now becomes and forever remains making the list on the left longer and the list on the right shorter. It's that simple! It really is. And, the Raw Sewage list requires constant diligence. It's little different from weekly waxing your car. In fact, I imagine myself constantly scraping the crud off the grates of my BBQ grill. Great food requires clean grates. That's what it is to be regularly removing the inevitable build-up of Raw Sewage in one's soul. It's not a once-and-for-all doing. Why? Because it's so doggone easy to get sucked into living on the agendas of those people we love or those who have power or influence in our lives. Keeping the grand artery up from your soul clean, so that your truest self may rise up from within and be lived in your external life – i.e. so that you may live a life where external life and internal life are fully integrated – requires constant vigilance against the fear of doing so. It requires ongoing monitoring of the Raw Sewage list.

And for most people, the real challenge is on the right list – making and keeping that list of Raw Sewage shorter and shorter, which begins and ends with something very scary.

The Single Scariest Word In The English Language
When we're children, the single scariest word in the English language is hearing the word 'No.'
- No, you can't have that candy bar in the checkout line at the grocery store.
- No, you can't have a go-kart.
- No, you can't go to band camp.
- No, you can't pierce your septum.
- No, you can't take karate lessons.
- No, you can't stay home from school.
- No, this isn't good enough. You need to do a better job.
- No, I don't want to play catch.
- ...and on and on, right?

But when we're adults, the single scariest word in the language is not hearing the word 'no'. Nah, when we're adults, the single scariest word in the English language is, in fact, *saying* the word 'No!'
- No, I don't want to serve on the PTA.
- No, I don't want to come to dinner.
- No, I don't want this marriage anymore.
- No, you can't go to band camp.
- No, you can't have the candy bar.
- No, you can't go to private school, because we can't afford it.
- No, this isn't good enough.
- No, you can't keep telling me how to live my life, anymore.
- ...and on and on, right?

The sheer terror of speaking a real 'No!' is something every adult knows, even the most self-actualized. It's just plain hard to speak one's truth, particularly when it means disappointing or hurting someone we love.

The fear people have of speaking their truth and doing what they love or really want to do is, at its core, the exact same fear that is stirred up at the thought of saying 'No!' to that which they don't want to do or be. It is, fundamentally, the fear of showing you who I really am. For, it is showing you who I am not.

'No' is a boundary, a fence. "No, you cannot come any closer." "No, I won't go and do that." "No, I won't go past this point." And by showing you where my fences are, I am showing you part of who I am.

And the fear in showing you who I really am is that you will not like me, if you know who I really am. The fear is that you will reject me, be disappointed in me, or in some way hurt me, if I show you my truth and my real identity. Saying 'No' is just scary as heck.

And, it's particularly scary when spoken to someone who has formerly had power over you, your actions, your words, or, worst, your identity. The potential loss and potential pain are far greater when a 'No!' is spoken to power or spoken to a love source.

But, the simple fact of the matter is that life begins at the word 'No!' It begins when you have the courage to begin shutting off the sources of Raw Sewage in your life. Or, at the very least, it means to begin cutting back the sources of Raw Sewage. Perhaps you cannot, in good conscience, cut a parent out of your life (though many do and wish they had done so sooner), but you can stop answering the phone every last time they call or text because they only call to deliver criticism or drama. Or, you can stop going to family functions, or you can erect whatever fence is necessary for you to finally have a modicum of peace in your life, or at least a significant reduction in Raw Sewage from that source.

One of the craziest things happens when we begin to cut the Raw Sewage out of our lives. It's hard to even imagine if you've never experienced it before, but life begins to get lighter. It really does. You literally feeeel lighter. It's an actual ongoing experience of lightness. The example I give is, imagine a hot air balloon that has been inflated while still on the ground. The pilot has ropes that he ties from the balloon to the ground. All of these tethers keep the balloon on the ground. Every time you cut another Raw Sewage source out of your life, it is like cutting another tether keeping the balloon on the ground. Once the ropes are all cut, the hot air balloon effortlessly rises up into the air. The key word is 'effortlessly.' That feeling of effortless lightness is indescribable, yet inevitable when we have the courage to live deliberately, cutting out of our lives the small, medium and large negative energy sources – things tying us down, bleeding the life out of us.

The Single Greatest Fear In Life: *Fear Of The Known*

Through our young years, into early adulthood, and the years we are just beginning the spiritual journey, we often still subscribe to the common notion that the greatest fear in life is the Fear of Death. And there is always a great deal to be said for the fear of death. Further, it's difficult to argue against the notion that the fear of death is the Mack Daddy of them all. It is always there, lurking, haunting our steps.

But as a great many warriors, poets, and terminal illness survivors can attest, fear of death is not the greatest of them all. Once you have truly looked death in the face, you realize that the greater fear is that of a life unlived. Death is not to be feared, but to be made friends with, or come to terms with. Death is what makes us feel fully alive; for it is offered to inspire authentic life and action today.

And based on how many people fritter away their lives in the daily miserableness of cubicle living, saving for ticky tack houses and manifold forms of consumption, and tiny victories over lethargy and the depressing life, it's hard to argue that they actually fear death. They have already chosen inner death, rather than aliveness. In those over, say, 40, those who've smelled the first wafts of death, if they really feared death would they not engage real living and a greater sense of aliveness. Nah, they fear something else, even more, something that keeps them from action.

Further still, how many people under the age of, say, 40 actually live in fear of death? Isn't it our common refrain about young people that they think they're going to live forever? Of course, because they live with no fear of death. They live, often, with abandon and risk-taking. That hardly indicates a fear of death. In the young, it indicates an obliviousness to death.

No, death is not the great fear.

The other grand fear we are all taught to quiver in the face of is the Fear of the Unknown. A great many big dreams and bold actions have been subverted by:

- The fear of simply not knowing if success will come,
- Fear of failure, and
- Fear of the hardships, hiccups, and hurdles that cannot be seen in advance.

All of these are derivatives of the fear of the unknown. If you ask most people, all that cubicle, small living is chosen because people fear stepping out. They fear not knowing what will happen. And so they remain in the safety of the familiar. Never, ever discount the power of the familiar in keeping people stuck in lives of security. The unknown is a seemingly giant beast.

However, it is far from being life's greatest fear. The unknown is what adds flavor and spice to relationships, business ventures, and new experiences. People don't go to the amusement park and ride the rollercoaster for the up; they ride it for the down.

Yeah, we cling to security in life, but eventually it bores the heck out of us. The soul longs for adventure, longs for the unknown, the original, the rush of the new. So no, the greatest fear in life is not the fear of the unknown. Sure, the unknown can be darn, darn scary, but it doesn't belong in the upper echelons of life's truly greatest fears.

As I regularly tell clients, the greatest fear in life is not what you think it is. What keeps people stuck isn't the unknown of whether they'll succeed or fail. It's not the unknown hiccups, hurdles, and hardships. And it's not all the multiple variables they simply cannot control, in advance.

Nah, what really keeps people stuck is the **Fear of the Known**.

The simple and absolute fact of the matter is that if you attempt this bold, new venture,
whatever it might be, you know
EXACTLY what your father will say;
EXACTLY what your best friend or co-workers will say;
EXACTLY what your dead mother will say in your head if you even consider doing it;

EXACTLY what society will say to you;
EXACTLY what your aggressive older siblings will say; and
EXACTLY what those bullies, from back whenever, would say.

The voices of them all still run your life. Until you own you, they own you. Rather, your fear of them owns you. It's so blatantly obvious and blatantly terrifying. And that's why you quit before you even begin or can never sustain the effort. It's not about willpower; it's about very specific fears of very known, obvious, imminent criticisms.

The greatest fear in life is not the fear of the unknown or of death. It is the fear of showing the world who you really are. The reason you've never really pursued your Diamonds is because you know EXACTLY what the world is going to say to you. Specifically, *you know EXACTLY what the most powerful people in your life are going to say.* And that scares the living heck out of you! Nothing scares you more than to pull the real you up from within you, then reveal it and have it criticized, once again, just as it was when you were a kid.

It's far easier to be criticized for a fake version of yourself, because it's not as real and raw. To show the real you and then eat their negativity is a pill too poisonous to the soul to even imagine swallowing.

And you may even think that it's not the fear of what someone else will say, but what you will say about your own self. This, of course, is nonsense, because no baby comes out of the womb self-critical. No, that critical, condemning voice got put into you, at some point, by the most powerful person or persons in your life. And so great was their influence that you now own that voice *as if it's your own.* It ain't, even though you now defend it and its limitations as if it were. You actually believe that you're your own worst critic. You aren't and never were. That voice that now runs your life was the big lie that got put inside you. It has always been the voice of someone else, likely the most powerful person in your life. (And perhaps that voice got transferred from the parent to your spouse or someone else new in your life. But the origin of the lie, the origin of the whole problem, goes back to the very beginnings of your life.

In my experience of changing lives, I have seen no greater fear than the Fear of the Known. It is the known (and what has been proven, again and again, by the power sources in our lives) that keeps us from authentic living, aliveness, effortless existence and flow.

The biggest fear that keeps people from the joy of an integrated life – where there is no chafing seam between the life dreamed in the soul and the life pursued in actions and words; the fear that keeps people in misery, turning them into walking corpses, already experiencing the death they claim to most fear; the fear that accepts ticky-tack, cubicle living; the fear that suffocates life most effectively is the fear of the words (and wrath-filled silence) of those people whom you already know do not understand you, never did, and are more afraid of your action's impact on their own anxieties than any supposed fate that might befall you.

And while that external criticism does indeed sting, at least for a moment, it is dwarfed by a greater fear. The sting of their criticism today is a painful reminder of all those underlying messages you got as a kid: You're stupid, you're not good enough, you're fat/ugly/skinny/weird, you're not really wanted, and the real you either sucks or just doesn't matter. Every one of the seemingly minor stings today is fundamentally a further negation of your existence. And when that process began in childhood (as it is invariably started by even the best-intentioned parents), it was so debilitating that it bred lifelong fear and the beginnings of a full, yet utterly empty life.

It is far easier (read 'less painful') to live with the fears than to walk into and thereby explode the most destructive lie implanted inside your core belief system. For, what if it's true that I'm no good and don't matter? In the end, your longing for approval of your own life from your former owners is what keeps you dreadfully unhappy and soul-drowningly unfulfilled.

This is what's at the core of the great fight for ownership in your soul. Until you can first identify/name them and then relegate those hyper-critical voices to a spot of insignificance, or even nothingness, you will forever be controlled by them, no matter how autonomous and tough you pretend to be. You will forever remain hidden, because you fear them. The real you will never blossom, much less see the light of day. And you will die a little more each day. And the worst part is that you *know* it's happening. You *see* it!

Regarding Raw Sewage

Of course, it's easier said than done. And either you're going to be vexed by saying 'No' to the negative energy sources or vexed by standing up for the diamonds you want to add to your life, giving yourself permission to say 'Yes' and not back down.

I do have clients whose greatest struggle is giving themselves permission to pursue that which breathes life into them. They feel guilty or selfish. But mostly, they fear the criticism they know will come. These are the folks that generally require more sessions of counseling for encouragement, strokes, approval, and more encouragement to keep building the things and paths that make them feel good.

What's interesting is that when I first explain this exercise to people, I barely get into explaining Raw Sewage when I see a flicker go across their face. Already they know one thing, usually a biggy (or two) that goes at the top of their Raw Sewage list. People *know* what their Raw Sewage is, or at least they know some of it or what/who is vexing them in the moment. More often than not, it's the precise reason they're in counseling, in the first place. Of course, removing it is something else, altogether, as is digging down to get at the deeper negative stuff really driving it all.

Right now, you already know a few of the things you'll put on your Raw Sewage list, don't you? But the thought of turning off those pipes of Raw Sewage, or even just turning them down, intimidates you, doesn't it? Scares you a bit, maybe even excites you a bit. But you know you gotta do it. Somewhere in you, you *know* you have to address it. It's not a 'have to' for anyone else, but 'have to' for your relationship with your own self.

You'll notice that there are certain items that are on both of my lists, or related things occupying both lists. This happens to everyone. For example, it's particularly visible in the job that you stay at because you're kept there by golden handcuffs – great pay, but sucky manager, work, or setting. But it can be true in relationships, family, or even parenting situations. In such situations where something straddles both lists, always the goal is awareness – to keep an eye on when some item tips, more and more, toward the Sewage side and shows no sign of relenting. It's when you know in your gut that this thing, this relationship, or this path isn't you anymore. Or, it's when you know that even though this particular thing might be on an occasional upswing, it's long term trajectory is that of a declining stock. It's trending downward...and you know it. It's reading patterns, knowing when a pattern is only getting worse and highly unlikely to change.

If you think it might be in the Sewage column, it probably is but you're afraid to admit it, afraid to talk about it. Because, of course, acknowledging that something is Sewage demands then acting on it. Ugh! Doesn't that mere thought bring a groan to your spirit?

But that's what life is. That's what makes the Diamonds and Raw Sewage exercise so doggone difficult. Cutting the dead weight from our lives is just plain hard, and it's scary. Saying 'No' to that which is not-you is monster terrifying. Yet, it is precisely that which is most necessary. The sewage either has to be completely eliminated or radically cut back.

Spiritual Life Imperatives
The spiritual life – and happiness, peace, and aliveness, which are it's sought after by-products – is first commenced and only successfully endeavored when the quest for more of what you love to do/say/have/be/believe/wear/live-in/become (your Diamonds) is PRECEDED by and ever-infused by the word 'No', specifically the discipline of and commitment to:

1. STOP **DOING** that which you don't want to do (and don't ever do again that which you don't want to do). Stop answering the phone when it's a person(s) you don't want to talk to or who is often negative. Stop saying 'yes' when you long to say 'no'. ;

2. STOP **WEARING** clothes, styles, or even hair styles or body styles that are not you. This may seem trivial when backed up against the other weighty matters in this list. But clothing, hair, and body construction are significant statements we make to the world about who we are, quite regardless of even how they are perceived. What you wear is a bold statement, even if it is a statement of your non-authenticity and desire only to fit in;

3. STOP **LIVING IN** places, cities, towns, geographies and climates that are not consistent with who you are. I have

been surprised, over the years, how many lives are radically changed, simply by a change to a climate that is more suited to who the person is. Certainly, location does not solve all problems or even a majority of them. But living where you feel you're supposed to be can make a huge difference in a person's level of joy;

4. STOP **SAYING** that which is not your truth. And definitely start becoming aware of the words that come out of your mouth that disparage you, particularly tapes you've been playing for decades about yourself, such as

- Oh, I'm not a good learner
- I can't win
- I always get colds/sick
- I never like new things
- People don't like me
- I'm always overweight
- I just can't catch a break, and so on.

Thought, word, and deed are the orders of creation. So, as long as you continue to perpetuate beliefs and words that reinforce a negative self-view, you will most definitely continue to create and attract negativity.

5. STOP **POSSESSING** that which you do not want to have and/or that which actually possesses you – i.e. that which costs you your being, saying, and becoming. It's incredibly life-sucking ground when your 'having' supersedes your 'being', when you have to sacrifice your soul and who you really are in order to have some pieces of wood (furniture), lumps of metal (car), or brick and plaster (house). A person can do whatever they want, but to me sacrificing my 'being' for 'having' is an ill-begotten path based on an ill-begotten belief: that things have greater power to bring happiness than does just being who the heck you really are.

6. STOP **BEING/BECOMING** and STOP **BELIEVING** that which you are not. And this is the whopper, because it means cleansing yourself, over time, of concepts about life, the

world, people, and anything external that does not resonate inside you as truth. More importantly, it means to stop believing things about yourself that drag you down from the inside – the lies and hurts that were put inside of you by others long ago, or even yesterday.

The Worst Sewage

As you might already guess, the worst of all types of Raw Sewage in your life is not the stuff outside you, but the stuff inside you. It's not your bf/gf, your BFF, your mom, your boss, or your jerk older sister or brother. The stuff that'll really kill you are the lies, beliefs, and disbelief that have been eating you up inside for decades. And this is the really scary stuff.

I have had a lot of clients, over the decades, who have seriously frayed relationships with their family or parents, who have spun out of control with all manner of self-destructive habits, who live in geographies or climates they hate, or are completely fried from careers they long ago stopped enjoying. Yet, despite all these things torn asunder outside them, always the core problem and most debilitating Sewage are values and core beliefs inside them – that which they believe about themselves.

And what makes this inner stuff really tricky is that most people can't identify the most debilitating stuff on their own, which is of course why I've written this book. Or, worse, they think they know what their inner problem is, but usually it's nowhere near the depth of the real truth. What's killing you is way down deep inside, hiding from view, yet driving the whole machine. It's at the root of your ever-spinning mind, your unceasing busyness, your killer depression, or your unrelenting anxiety.

'He Has Demons'

It could be argued that the whole endeavor of listing and increasing or reducing your Diamonds/Raw Sewage lists constitutes an attempt to create long term change in your life by changing your actions and behaviors first, when this entire book has been based on the notion that solely trying to change behaviors (or even starting with behaviors) never changes behaviors, long term; change must occur at the level of beliefs first.

However, the discipline of increasing the things that breathe life into you and decreasing those that bleed life from you is not, fundamentally, rooted in action but in the awareness of deleterious core beliefs and the destructive negative self-beliefs of the closed 3 Binary Gates. Even the slightest shift in those beliefs – which can come in the seemingly minuscule and innocuous form of doubting those beliefs or no longer seeing them as absolute, bedrock truths of human existence – is still a shift in beliefs (which precede action). And, as we saw in the chapter about a ship crossing the ocean, even the slightest shift in Binary Gates or core beliefs enacts radical changes by the time it reaches the level of actions.

And what's really interesting is that this is one more place where the Love Cup theories dovetail with the common language and ideas of popular culture. Most of us have, at some time or another, spoken disparagingly of someone, perhaps ourselves, by saying something along the lines of, "Well, she has a lot of demons," or "He needs to face his demons and deal with them." But what are our 'demons'?

Simply put, our demons are the core beliefs and Binary Gates that are working against us from the inside. The real demons that keep pulling you (or your boyfriend/girlfriend) down are not outside of you. They're inside. And they're always – yes, ALWAYS! – way down at the level of your deepest beliefs about yourself, which means they're always beyond your sight. 99% of people have zero clue what their real self-beliefs are. And those demons keep devouring you, infusing your life with negative energy, day in day out, year in year out, pulling you down, until life has ended and there's just this long string of monster disappointments. By the time demon beliefs rise up through the level of principles, up to the level of actions, the destruction they wreak on the life of the individual is immeasurable. Demons are the viruses affecting our lives, which we simply cannot see or seem to ever shake.

But the slightest awareness of or change in those demons, even the smallest diminishment, enacts significant changes by the time it rises up to the level of words and actions. Naming the demon and its origin defangs it, removing its power to undermine a life that should be happy and exuberant.

The Net Effect Of The Diamonds/Raw Sewage Exercise

The whole point and purpose of the Diamonds/Raw Sewage exercise is to help you begin to make decisions consistent with the belief, "I matter! The real me matters." It is to help you begin to make that Diamonds list longer – i.e. more and more identify and live that which breathes life into your very soul, rather than gain identity from a life cluttered with not-you detritus.

By taking action consistent with your new belief of mattering, you begin to patch that hole in the bottom of your Love Cup, the one that has been draining your hope for happiness. It is only by living as if you matter (which itself is predicated on, at least, the tiniest of breadcrumb of belief that you really do matter) that you eventually do matter to you and eventually to others and to life, itself. This is how the old cement gets crushed and new cement gets poured and written in.

To do so absolutely requires making that Raw Sewage list shorter, but not just because all of that Raw Sewage is negative energy you're carrying through life and its dragging you down, bleeding your life energy. No, the other reason for getting rid of the Raw Sewage is that it creates safe space to unpack the real you.

Do you remember that version of you – the real you of your truest soul – that got packed into a box and stuffed deep inside you, decades ago, when you were taught you don't matter? Perhaps you only remember a sliver of it.

To feel safe unpacking that which you truly are demands eliminating all the things and people that created the box, in the first place. It requires removing all the crud that accrued on top of it, over the years, while you lived in the faulty, untrue belief system. Safe space to become the real you is only created by pushing back the voices that created your fear and self-loathing to begin with.

To feel safe hearing your own voice,
you gotta get rid of all the other voices,
the ones that say your voice and the real you just don't matter,
the ones that created your self-loathing, in the first place.

Journaling and Meditation

1. Find a relaxing place and begin to sketch out, in great detail, your lists of Diamonds and Raw Sewage.

2. At the top of your journaling pages write the question, "Who or what are all of the people or things that have power over me? What are the internal demons and external power sources that I have not yet named but still have influence over my life?" And, "Why do I keep giving them power over my life?" and "Am I ready to take that power back and start running my own life, more and more? If so, in what ways, specifically?"

3. Go back to the list of 'Stops' in the *Spiritual Life Imperatives* section. For each section, list as many things as you can that you need to stop.

4. In a relaxed position and mental state, visualize bright, white, sparkling, healing streams of light and energy flowing into your body, driving out all impurities and wounds, and exploding the grip of demons, negative energy sources, and power imbalances in your life. Breathe in and visualize all those 'stops' leaving your body and leaving your life, floating away forever.

5. Now visualize the new life of the real you bursting up and out of you from deep within, cascading through and over your life with joy, happiness, and peace.

6. Whisper your mantra to yourself, this week, "I am free, happy and alive. Negative energy is shrinking. Positive and beautiful energy is expanding from within me."

Bonus Tracks

Core Readers: Press on to the next chapter. Advanced readers:

- Bonus Track 9: Non-Negotiables, I-Don't-Give-A-Craps, And The Power Of Percentages
- Bonus Track 10: When Positive Energy Sources Turn Negative

CHAPTER 22

THE COMPUTER CHIP OF YOUR SOUL

One of the greatest challenges on the spiritual journey is determining who you are and who you are not, and that which is and is not your path. It can be tremendously frustrating to have both the courage and eagerness to stand up and pursue an authentic life but not know which way to go. Heeding the voice inside, for some people, is much easier than hearing the voice. For, the price of hearing the voice (or feeling it, to be accurate) is the willingness to still your life, to calm yourself enough to begin to feel your truth inside. And that is just a scary as heck spot to be in. As mentioned previously, so many people keep running, in so many ways (addictions, busyness, relationships, distractions), so as to avoid the tidal wave of feelings, thoughts, uncertainty, fears and memories that would seemingly overwhelm them, if they slowed down, not to mention stopped and stood still.

But that's where the answer is. It's in the willingness to just calm yourself for a moment, for an hour, for some regular amount of time, so that the endless voices and thoughts may begin to pass and your own authentic voice might rise up from within. You cannot feel and hear your own inner voice – your own intuition – until you quiet your life and go into a state of relaxation.

A few tips for quieting life and quieting the mind:

- Some people like to meditate. Meditation is a powerful means for quieting the mind and thereby unlocking creativity and intuition.
- Some find their creative energy is tapped into through yoga.
- I have found journaling to be powerfully effective for me when I am simply laying in bed at 3am in the morning, when I often awaken. I keep two pads of paper next to me; one on which I'm flushing out all the thoughts and feelings inside me. On the other, I jot to-do notes as they arise ("Be sure to drop off dry cleaning today" and "Call that client before his

meeting Tuesday"), so that they are out of me and on paper for me to deal with later in the day. That allows me to focus on releasing all the feelings, fears, anxieties, etc that are coming up from my day and week, or from my past, through my journaling. When that stuff is out of me, I sink into a naturally deeper state of relaxation. Sometimes I drift off to sleep. Sometimes I lay there at peace and the most brilliant ideas, feelings, or new epiphanies come to me.

- I also recommend breathing exercises.
- Eliminating stimulants from your life for a brief time, or reducing reducing them, can help this. I went from an evening tiddly every day to eliminating all alcohol for four evenings/week. My sleep has improved dramatically and my creativity shot back up.

And then, in addition to the willingness to be still and listen must be the willingness to go a new direction, fail, fall down, mess up, and even quit when it no longer feels right. If your highest drive is the security of a certain, permanent path, best not to even get started on the spiritual journey, because you'll never get the security you seek, even as surely as you will get the aliveness you've always sought.

I like to think of this act of allowing your true self to rise up from within as a sort of 'reading the chip.' It's a simple metaphor, one that requires an ounce of belief in your pre-ordained originality. When you were born, the Universe inserted into you a computer chip, metaphorically speaking, onto which was written the code for every last thing about you – for your past, present, and future:

- what you're good at when you're 25
- what you stink at
- what you're good at when you're 45 or 65
- what flowers you like
- eye color
- Beatles, Stones , Dylan, or Zeppelin?
- your life values
- how you like your morning eggs
- height/weight

- type of girls/boys you'll like when you're 15
- type of women/men you'll like when you're 30 or 55
- what energizes you
- back-sleeper, side-sleeper, stomach-sleeper, or non-sleeper/insomniac?
- what depletes you
- movies you hate
- foods you love
- what you're allergic to
- Mac or PC?
- your love of old people
- your mild displeasure for cigar smoke
- your love of coffee
- your true thoughts on money and family
- your love of hockey
- on and on, *ad infinitum*

Everything. It's all there, written on that chip, deep inside you. To begin to know your over-arching dreams and paths, as well as answers to your day-to-day decisions, you must tune in to the chip written on your soul. This is only done by learning to feeeeel. Your body speaks the truth of your chip.

So many people want to know God's will for their life. "Love God and love neighbor" seems to be a pretty good formula for that. But what does it mean to 'love God'? Does it mean to pray to the sky? Go to church/synagogue? To love God and know God's will for your life is to be who God *already made you to be*. To love God is to read the chip that was implanted in you when you were made, then live it. Your GPS is already programmed. But you gotta be in the moment, tuned into your intuition, to feel it, not on auto-pilot. This is what it means to live deliberately, to be fully honest in each moment.

No One Else Can Read Your Computer Chip
And no one else can possibly know what is written on your chip. Only you. (This can be tremendously frustrating for you when you have parents, friends, and lovers who want to tell you how to run

your life or tell you "What's best for you." It can also be tremendously frustrating for them when you start realizing they can't know your chip.) And, in fact, your life's work is to find out....ALLOW....what is written on your chip. It is to begin to feeeeel that inner pulse of your own self. That is how we identify who we are. What is written on your own individual chip just feels good, feels right, feels exciting, brings relief, and/or flows effortlessly. To become who you really are, to begin to unpack that box from deep inside requires experiencing new ideas, new paths, new words and so forth to see how they feeeeel on your skin and in your body. It is to allow the voice of your soul to rise up, fill you, and be felt.

This is what it means to live in a deep and powerful relationship with your own self. This is what it means to live in communion with the spirit of the Universe rising up from inside you. This is what it means to hear and trust your own intuition.

Your body stores your truth. It stores your memories that have been charged with a particular emotion. Also, it reads to you the feel of some event, person, idea, or circumstance that is standing in front of you. Despite everything you have been taught, the answers to *your* life are not outside you; they are inside you and can be easily read, once you clear away the blockages, fears, pain, and debris of past experiences and untruths that have been forced upon your soul. You can actually feel what your next step is.

As mentioned, this also requires a willingness to start and stop, to quit that which is not your next step or next path. In the Hindi language there is a word, 'neti', which simply means 'not this.' At times in life, we do not know what the path is, only what it isn't. At times in life, all we can say is "neti, neti, neti." Not this. Not that either. And definitely not that. Oh, and for a while it was this, but it is not this anymore. The path to discovering – or allowing – who we are often requires discovering who we are not. That happens over time, with self-permission to quit or fall down, and a zone free of judgment.

Recognizing that your soul is constantly trying to communicate with you through your body and its feel, anytime you feel a loss of energy, lethargy, deadness inside or even an extreme anxiety it is your soul communicating to you that this is not your path. To know the path of the Universe for you is to trust and follow the energy.

When I was a young man, I attempted to discern my next path by trying to envision which path was the path of light and the path of dark. But that, I began to realize, was more just a mental exercise. I had an epiphany when I realized that in the Judeo-Christian stories, particularly in creation (whether you take those stories as fact, metaphor, or total fiction), the God is always breathing life into something to give it life. In the Jewish-Christian book of Genesis, the clay that God formed into a man did not actually have life until he breathed into its nostrils. The teacher, Jesus, breathed on his disciples in the upper room after his resurrection, and in so doing gave them his Holy Spirit. In other words, The way to know God's path for me is simply to find that path that 'breathes life into me'!! Once I realized that, everything changed.

The goal of life is that supreme feeling of aliveness that comes from living 100mph with your hair on fire. And that only, only, only comes from knowing who the heck you really are, which necessarily requires knowing who you are not. It's about having the courage to be who you really are, and having slowed your life waaaaay down, even stopped it regularly, to feel the pulse of the Universe rising up in its fully original manifestation in your own soul.

Your intuition is the GPS of your individual, authentic life. To "live in the moment" doesn't mean just to stop and smell the roses more or to notice the pretty trees. Living in the moment, in a spiritual sense, means to be tuned into your own vibe – that quiet voice of the Universe inside – in each moment, listening, feeeeeling, tuning into its calling and direction for what is next.

De-wiring The Child From The Parent's Chip

But the source of the problem of so many people being disconnected from their own sense of self – from their own chip – is that when we raise children we wire them into our own chips, as parents. We teach them our values, our wants, our loves, our dislikes, our everything. From ages 0-10, roughly, the child's life is near-completely an expression of my chip as the parent: Be nice to old people; look both ways before crossing; work hard in school; mind your p's and q's; be nice to your sister; etc.

The problem we run into as parents is that we never de-wire the child from our own chip, after, or even during, those early years. It's so doggone hard, as a parent, to let go of that level of control and influence. To see someone become you is mightily intoxicating. Further, precisely when the child most needs to begin wiring into and listening to his own chip, roughly around the tween or puberty years, is when the stakes become higher and the chance for heartbreak and loss increases. In the teens, the child naturally wishes to differentiate herself from mom and dad, to begin to express her own truth written on the chip in her soul, or at least begin to experiment to see what might be on her chip. She naturally wants to experience 'netis'. She wants to find and express what feeeels right to her and what doesn't. But the parent becomes afraid, not only of the child getting hurt, which of course is an absolute prerequisite of an autonomous life, but also of losing influence and in fact losing parental identity.

I mean, think about it, you've been driving this kid around, influencing this kid, teaching this kid, for years. Whether you ever intended to or not, your identity began to be wrapped up in this kid. Inch by inch, mile by mile, you became more of who they are. (Just as interestingly, *they became more of who you are,* which is why it's a specious claim to antagonize a late-teen/early-20s kid for being this or that, doing or not doing this or that, or overall disappointing the parent. The kid is just this extension of you; he is very little of anything he has created himself. You haven't let him. So how can you now blame him/her?) And to detach from that massive piece of your identity is terrifying for the parent. Of course the parent will claim, on the surface, that they fear for the child's safety and 'only want what's best for the kid.' But, deep down, the fear is also that I have no idea who I am, once this kid is gone; I *can't* let go. This is neither good nor even tenable, long term, for the parent or the child. It's just doggone hard to let go of a large chunk of one's identity.

But, alas, we each only get one life to live, not two. It's darn fun to live two, or more, lives. Yet, that's not how the story is written. You get yours and Junior gets his. You don't get his, too. Most of my clients, particularly the uber-successful ones, are hollow inside, because they have, or had, parents who are living two lives – their own and that of my client.

To contain a child, to steer a child, to box a child because of my own fears of not knowing who I am or not being confident about who I am is the worst crime imaginable. It is to steal another life because of my own insecurities. And we couch it in those utterly specious, ugly terms of it being in the child's best interests, terrified of the truth. Of course, this is the parent who never de-wired from the chip of his mom and dad, from the chip of society, and from the chip of those powerful influences in his life. And so, now the problem gets passed onto the next generation, unless someone breaks the cycle. It is actually easier to live and direct your child's life than it is to live and direct your own, as the latter makes one more subject to the criticisms of others. You've been terrified of your authentic voice and now Junior is terrified of his, because for Junior to not be so would mean simultaneously:

- Standing up to the most powerful person in his life: You!
- Disappointing you and/or angering you;
- Robbing you of a big part of your identity.

But this generational, dysfunctional hand-me-down has to be short-circuited. If not, your pain and frustration with life will become Junior's pain.

To begin to live your truth, whether at age 13 or 43, is to begin to hear and heed the voice of your soul. It is to begin to read your own chip and encourage others to read theirs. It is to begin to truly feeeeel again, for the first time. You have been stuffing your feelings down. You have been denying them credence by saying, "It's no big deal" or "I'll be alright" or "I'm fine" when asked what's going on inside you or when someone reads a vibe of unrest coming off you. By neglecting or even lying about your true feelings you fundamentally convey to life that your feelings, your life, your existence don't matter.

Gee, is it any wonder, then, that you continue to attract people and situations that confirm that belief? You are so comfortable and familiar with things that confirm your worthlessness that you keep choosing them.

Until your feelings matter enough to be expressed *by you*, you will not be happy and you will not matter. Until you matter enough to you to express your truth, you won't matter much to anyone else, no matter how much you keep begging them to love you, approve of you, or throw you some scrap from the table of love and life. Until you de-wire yourself from the chips of others – saying 'no' to their influence and power in your life – and begin to wire into your own chip, you will not be happy. You will continue living a fake life, a life that was never you, from the beginning.

Song Recommendation

This song, more than almost any other, has been so elemental to my own spiritual life. When I was in the deepest part of the dark forest, this song spoke to me. That was a very long time ago. Yet, this absolute poetry of **Dan Fogelberg's** verse still moves my soul. Download *Nexus* and pull up the lyrics, as well, so that you can dive into them as he sings. It's a beautifully powerful song. It speaks to the frustrations of the spiritual path, as well as the belief that there are forces guiding our steps, speaking to us, moving us. https://www.youtube.com/watch?v=XUZT8rl0BIoNexus

Bonus Tracks

Core Readers: Keep moving, right on to the next chapter. Advanced Readers:

- Bonus Track 11: Effortlessness And Flow

CHAPTER 23

YOUR LIFE MESSAGES, PART 1

S o, let me ask you a question. Actually, I'll ask it, then give you a few examples from my own life, then let you answer it. It's a simple question but it requires a bit of digging on your part, perhaps even ruminating over it, for awhile.

So the question is this:

What were the one or two biggest messages you got,
during childhood,
about the world and life, but especially about *you*?

I got three main messages, growing up. One, at home I consistently heard this message from my parents and siblings: "Sven is special. But don't compliment Sven; he'll get a big head." They likely had gotten sick of my bragging and didn't want to fan the flame. But, of course, the kid who is least hearing how good he is, is the one whose soul most needs to proclaim to the world his goodness and greatness. A death spiral ensues: the more he brags, the more he pushes away the people who bear the message he most needs to hear.

The second message I got, at school but not at home, was, "Sven, you're different. Be normal." A few great teachers and principals encouraged my originality: Mr. Byzewski, Mr. Schmaus, Miss Kelly, Miss Brown and later Mr. Loo, Mr. Stanton, and Joe Frank. But many teachers and principals didn't know what to do with it and so forced normality onto my soul.

The third message I got hammered into me was in my early twenties, from my wife, closest brother, and father: "Get a job. Get a job. Get a job. Get a job. Get a job. Get a job. Get a job. Get a job." Nothing seemingly mattered outside of this.

What's really fascinating, however, about the messages we get is that, even when the intent of the message is well-intentioned and not always malicious, there's almost invariably an insidious underlying message that does real, long term damage. These messages get pressed into the wet cement of our soul.

So, in those three messages I got there were also three underlying messages. In the first one ("Don't compliment Sven..."), the message is that our (the family) comfort is more important than the feeding of a child's soul with the necessary affirmations of his value and importance. So, the kid (in this case, me) grows up hungry – spiritually without food, taught that he doesn't matter enough to be given what he needs, what every kid needs: Praise. That's often a commodity in short supply in large families. The kid, deep down, then easily translates this implicit message into "The family matters, but I don't matter." And there is no message more deleterious to the soul than this one. This is the bottom and most lethal Binary Gate.

In the second message is the implicit message, "Different is bad; normal is good. You're bad. Be good." And it's that "You're bad" (or no good or not good enough) that really does lasting damage. It disinclines a person to show the world who they really are, to be real, to follow their own happiness. It tunes a child into others/adults to tell them who to be in order to get approval, in order to be told, "You're good." This is the very powerful middle Binary Gate. Yet, it's also a statement that the real you is ultimately irrelevant – i.e. the real you doesn't matter – which is also the 3rd or bottom Binary Gate.

In the third message ("Get a job...") is not just good, if ridiculously obvious, advice, but also an underlying message, "What your soul really longs to do, if it deviates from or somehow impedes having a job, is essentially irrelevant, or at least greatly subordinate to your capacity to earn money" and "Your identity and purpose are defined, above all else, by your ability to earn money." The underlying message is that who you really are doesn't matter; what matters is what we and society say you should do. Again, another example of closing that Third Binary Gate ("The real you doesn't matter").

So, you see, we are constantly, in both childhood and adulthood, receiving messages about the value and even the existence of our own self and soul. Every message is loaded. Every one of us has had the experience of knowing 'what someone was *really* saying' beneath their words or between the lines, whether that message was intended or not (often the message is very intentional, even if the speaker of it denies it; often its unintentional; and, as will be discussed later, often it runs directly and insidiously counter to more explicit, pretty messages). We are each constantly being battered by these underlying messages. And hearing and heeding your own true voice demands both identifying and rooting out these messages.

Unless you are deliberate about your core beliefs, creating boundaries around them and creating a life that reinforces them, you will forever be buffeted by the messages and influences of others, particularly those strong influences and power sources from your past. And that never leads to happiness, love and greater aliveness.

Journaling Recommendation

1. So, what were the most powerful messages you received, growing up?

2. And, as you consider those messages you received, begin to poke around and consider what the real underlying messages were. Remember, a child's mind converts all messages, even the most benign, into some judgment of his or her existence. Do you remember the NCAA coach in Chapter 15 ('Are you sure?'), and how that message of his childhood undermined his successes as an adult?

3. So, what were the underlying messages? Usually the underlying messages are some derivative of:

    ° You're not wanted.

    ° You're no good, or not good enough.

    ° You don't matter.

4. What does it feel like to see these conveyed to you in your past? How have those core messages undermined your life?

5. Do you desire to have those messages removed from your life and replaced with new, life-giving ones?

CHAPTER 24

YOUR LIFE MESSAGES, PART 2: THE GOLDEN CHILD, THE SIBLING, AND THE SPECIAL-NEEDS KID

"So, what would happen, Steve, if we were to run the movie of your life on my wall here, but turn down the volume or hit the 'mute' button?"

Steve responded, "What do you mean?"

"Well," I went on, "quite apart from any explicit messages you were given, what messages were conveyed to you, about you and about life, by the simple actions of the most important people in your life, particularly mom and pop, or your siblings and grandparents, if they were influential in your life?"

"Hmmmmm. So, like what would we see?"

"Yes, exactly. What actions would I see in the film of your life, if I weren't distracted by the sounds."

He paused and thought. Then you could see him shift from thinking to feeling. "Geeez!" Steve started to cry, softly. "Do you want to know what I see, Sven? My older sister couldn't fail. She succeeded at everything. She got everything." He stopped talking to grab a Kleenex of the coffee table.

"So, let me take a shot at it, Steve," I said, sensing that his tears not only surprised him but would embarrass him slightly to try to talk through, even though he fully knew I couldn't give a crap and was the very last person who could judge anyone for anything, as I had done more stuff to embarrass those around me, screwed up way worse, and had far more to be embarrassed by than anyone.

"Yeah, go."

"So, in this film of your life, we see the forgotten kid. You're always off to the side, aren't you? You grew up in the shadow of the Golden Child. The sun shone constantly on your older sister and you lived forever in that shadow, if not outright forgotten. That's what we'd see, isn't it?"

"Exactly," he confirmed.

"But it doesn't stop there. You wrote in the autobiography you sent to me that your grandparents were around a lot, but they just doted on your kid sister. So, you got the double whammy! And you were, well, not special. Right? In effect, you were sandwiched between two Golden Children. You were the vanilla kid. You were plain, couldn't stick out to save your life. Your younger sister took all the positive attention from your grandparents. And your older sister was the apple of mom and dad's eye. So, you, my little friend, were the forgotten kid, right? The film of your life is of you off by yourself, entertaining yourself; you fighting for attention; you trying to do things to have them put the spotlight on you, even a little bit; you even acting out and being bad, later smoking weed, boozing, or skipping school. You either did the perfect kid thing or the rebel kid thing, or both. And the fact that we're here today says neither worked."

Now Steve oscillated between the nodding and sobs.

"The message we see in the film of your life is two-fold. First, you don't exist. You simply don't matter. But also, we see that you felt unwanted. And those messages were not just delivered by mom and dad but further hammered home by their surrogates, grandma and grandpa. Serious one-two punch. There was no one pouring love into your Love Cup, was there? So, that film of your life reveals pretty quickly the status of your Love Cup. Ah the curse of being the Golden Child's sibling. Abuse of the soul comes in many forms, man. Many forms."

Some Ironic Family Happenings

Unless there has been a serious dose of deliberate parenting on the part of mom and dad to avoid it, one very common occurrence in a great many families is that one child is perceived by the children of the family to be the family 'Golden Child'. This is the kid who can, seemingly, do no wrong in the eyes of mom and/or dad, who is perceived by the other kids as being favored, and who is seen as receiving the lion's share of positive attention in the family. The Golden Child knows it, the siblings know it, and, perhaps, even the parent is aware that there is an unfair distribution of wealth, in the form of positive attention, in the family.

Of course, the challenge in being the sibling of the Golden Child is that there is no room to breathe. The Golden Child sucks all of the oxygen out of the room. The sibling of the Golden Child (GC) forever lives in the GC's shadow and forever experiences a shortage of love in the ol' Love Cup. There is just never enough for the sibling, because mom and dad are generally not deliberate in ensuring a wise distribution of their energy and attention.

The sibling of the Golden Child is the one who then grows up feeling they are not wanted, no good or not good enough, and, often, that their real self just doesn't matter. It's not a matter of just feeling deficient or unwanted by the parent. It's not just the harshness of the explicit messages but also the underlying or implicit messages, if we turn the sound back up on the film.

I've had siblings of Golden Children report that they were told such things as:

- Your sister is the pretty one (implicit message: you're not)
- You were conceived so that your brother wouldn't grow up spoiled (Yes, I've actually heard this from a few clients. Implicit message: your brother is the important one and your existence is, fundamentally, to meet his developmental needs – i.e. completely subordinate to his)
- Your sister is the important one (implicit: you aren't) and you need to serve her (Yes, I have clients whose parents actually said this)
- Your brother needs the extra attention, because he has a bright future (implicit: you don't)
- Your sister is the smart one and we need to do all we can for her (implicit: you're not smart and you won't be getting as much attention)
- Your brother can be the first to graduate from college (implicit: you can't; you aren't good enough)
- You're a scumbag (Yes, I actually had a father regularly say this to and about his son, while heaping nothing but praise on his daughter.)

A lot of really ugly stuff gets said and done in families, both in intentional and unintentional ways, where there is non-deliberate parenting. Remember, positive attention is love. Whether it arrives in the form of hugs, words of praise, pats on the back, extra time together, gifts, bragging about the child, extra opportunities, more listening and more questions, or that glow that comes over a parent's face when they are looking at an offspring they are fond of.

Negative attention is harsh words or actions. It is messages conveyed explicitly or implicitly. It is anything that does damage to the soul of a child.

What can be the most tragic part of this equation is when the parent is not even aware he or she is doing this (non-deliberate parenting). Thus, a parent will deny, deny, deny. Yet, every kid in the family knows it's true. Every kid sees the distribution of wealth. What matters is not what the parent is convinced is happening, but what is perceived by the children as happening. For a parent to see it requires a level of awareness that only comes deliberately – with both effort and humility, not to mention willingness to change.

So powerful can be the affection for a Golden Child that a parent will even redistribute attention they normally have for a spouse onto the special child. This is a level of familial breakdown that is in no way easily solved, much less identified, particularly in a culture that breeds the naive belief 'Children are the most important thing.' And as if this isn't bad enough for the spouse, it is rock solid, impenetrably clear to the siblings of the GC that they have no hope of getting the love they want. One person in the family is doing all the inhaling, and everyone else is forever out of breath.

This problem is only exacerbated when the family moves to a special school or city for the GC, or when there's an inordinate allotment of money toward the Golden Child's life. This just drills the siblings even further with the "You don't matter" and "You're unwanted" messages

The 'Ouch' Of A Special Needs Child

What's most fascinating, however, is that this disproportionate distribution of wealth doesn't just happen with Golden Children. I have seen the same phenomenon in families where there is a disabled or Special Needs Child (SNC). Meaning no intentional harm, at all, to the siblings of the disabled one and driven by sheer necessity, the lion's allotment of positive attention often falls on the disabled one. The oxygen, once again, gets sucked out of the room.

But what makes this situation sometimes worse than with a GC is the other children can sometimes be called into service of the special needs of the special child. I have seen this more times than I can even begin to count. I get why it's happening. I'm sympathetic to the great, unexpected responsibilities of the parents. Nonetheless, it's tragic, at least from the soul perspective. The underlying message is similar to when the sibling of a Golden Child is uprooted to a new school or city for the benefit of the GC. But what makes it worse is that the sibling of the SNC is fundamentally being required or expected to give up her own life energy, as a child, to another person, precisely when she should be getting her own Love Cup filled. In families where a sibling is expected to live in some measure of service to a SNC, that sibling is then daily pouring love out of her Love Cup to a more important sibling. For any human being to be forced (either explicitly or by dangling carrots) to give love to another is never a good thing. But compound that injustice with the fact that it's a child who is being expected to pour love out of his or her Love Cup and you have nothing but an absolute spiritual tragedy, one that will resound through the corridors of that sibling's life, long, long, long into adulthood.

Wanna give a child the clear message that who they really are and what they really want for their lives doesn't matter? Just require them to be an ongoing servant to the needs of a special sibling. I've also had clients with a drug-addled sibling, who were forever expected to subordinate their own needs to the Problem Child, in some cases even becoming the *de facto* parent to the child and spouse to the parent. That'll empty and mar a Love Cup good and quick. Remember, the job of adults is to give love. The primary job of children is to receive it, to be filled with it.

And, just when you thought it couldn't get any worse, add on the compounded guilt a sibling of a disabled kid feels because, well, "He's disabled. So who am I to want my needs met? He's disabled. I'm not as important and shouldn't be so selfish. I'm a dick for even thinking about my needs. Plus, mom and dad are stressed and tired, a lot. I should just keep quiet." The guilt over wanting more can be oppressive.

Whether the sibling of a Golden Child, Special Needs Child, or Problem Child, it is very easy and very common to grow up in the belief that you aren't wanted and/or don't matter, not the real you, just the you that is pliant and subservient to the needs and demands of the important child. Whether unintentional or intentional on the part of the parent, the long-lasting effects on the other children in the family are indisputable. A Love Cup or two gets a hole poked in the bottom and forever runs a love deficit.

The Plight Of The Golden Child
Now here's the crazy, upside-down part that can be the most difficult for the siblings of a Golden Child, the parent of a Golden Child, and, in fact, the Golden Child, himself, to get their heads around. Very often, the Love Cup of the Golden Child:

- Gets a hole poked in the bottom, as well
- Gets filled with crud and manure from being told, repeatedly, that they aren't good enough, and
- Is only sporadically filled with the types of love that make the Golden Child actually feel loved.

Almost without exception, Golden Children eventually feel like performing monkeys or that the parent is living vicariously through them, or that who they really are is irrelevant. Yes, that's right; the GC is often getting the exact same message the sibling is, just in different forms.

The grand irony of the Golden Child phenomenon is that in the entire family calculus the GC is experiencing just as much, or more, minimization or death of the soul as anyone else. The oppression of spirit committed by a parent against a Golden Child cannot be overstated. This parent will often tie the showing of love (not to be confused with the feeling of love) to the Golden Child with the GC's *performance*. By pushing the child, either explicitly or implicitly, to do what the parent wants, the Golden Child is taught to distrust his or her own instincts and negate his or her own wants. The Golden Child is taught, amid it all, that who he or she really is doesn't matter; his role is to be the role mom/dad chose and/or continue to choose without concern for the passions of the child. Life for the Golden Child is about performance, not authenticity. The GC is caught in the same soul-depleting trap as anyone in the profession of commission sales: Life is forever about quotas, hitting your numbers – i.e. producing results. Life is forever about meeting someone else's expectations for your life, forever about 'doing', not 'being' or 'becoming'.

And the really hideous part of parenting, particularly parenting a Golden Child, is that children are easily manipulated to meet the whims and wishes of the parent (which are, despite all protestations to the contrary, nearly always driven by that same parent's own ego frailties). Particularly effective in teaching a GC to 'hit their numbers,' so to speak, is withholding love. GC's are so keyed in to receiving the next reward that they'll endure long droughts of love withheld to get one. Thus, ironically and almost-unfathomably to her siblings, the GC's Love Cup remains close to empty; hungry, always hungry...and, for all of childhood, easily manipulated to serve mommy's and/or daddy's wishes, unable to distinguish between mommy's wants and her own. In all of this, the whole family algebra of love shifts to being all about mom's and dad's plan and ego – i.e. to filling mom's and dad's Love Cups. It isn't, and never was, about the GC. At its core, it's about bad parenting, specifically parents using children to get their own Love Cup needs met, or at least temporarily assuaged.

I have seen a great many Golden Children become very depressed or unmotivated adults. The pressure, the expectation to succeed, and the desire to win nuggets of love (or at the very least avoid criticism) are so great that this now-adult will not even try something new, unless there is reasonable certainty of success. (And when is that ever the case?) Worse, this now-adult often has no idea of what he/she wants to do or paths he/she wants to go down, because his inner voice has been squelched for so long, packed into a box long ago stuffed deep down inside. This is the now-adult who has an inordinate orientation to success and accomplishment, as opposed to enjoyment of the path or happiness. For this person, nothing can be enjoyed, unless it has some form of success attached to it. In other words, more often than not, the Golden Child's very life purpose, identity and worth are directly tied to performance rather than simply existence. And the GC is quite incapable of distinguishing his own inner voice from that of the sales managers – mom and dad.

Where the sibling of the Golden Child gets the 1st and 3rd Binary Gates closed – i.e. that he is not wanted and that the real self doesn't matter; the Golden Child, herself, gets the 2nd and 3rd Binary Gates closed. The Golden Child forever gets the message that they are good enough only when meeting the expectations of the parent – i.e. a performance-driven worth. And that's a nasty life to live, even worse because it conveys the not-mattering message, too.

Whether regarding a Golden Child, Problem Child, the sibling of a Golden Child or a Special Needs Child, this inequitable distribution of positive attention in a family is never a good thing. The greater the imbalance, the worse the outcomes, be they immediate or long term (read 'both').

What does the film of your life show? Are you the forgotten kid? The sibling of a Special Needs Child? The Golden Child? The Special Needs Child? What were the messages conveyed through the actions of those most important to you?

The Real Kicker

Here's the ugly part; or the even uglier part. Complicity. This is where it gets really nasty.

At this point, it's necessary to hearken back to the beginning of the chapter where we looked at many of the cold, often brutally calloused, and flat out abusive messages conveyed by parents to children, both implicitly and explicitly, in word and deed.

As we consider the messages conveyed to you in the film of your life by your parents or primary influences – whether you had a GC or SNC sibling, both or neither – it's generally very easy to isolate which parent was the one guilty of the most soul neglect, withholding of love, or even soul abuse, in a family. It's easy to see the one that was roughest, harshest, most critical, most demeaning, most unkind, most absent, most exacting, most impatient, most selfish. But, the really nasty part of the equation – the part that is far too often, easily, and willingly overlooked – is that, in most cases, *someone else let it happen.* Someone else was complicit, usually the other parent.

Who commits the greater crime –
the parent engaged in soul abuse or the one allowing it?

And see, this is where the family equation gets really sticky. Often, the negligent, abusive, hyper-critical, cruel, or rough parent is so bad that it's hard to believe anything else truly matters or has any significance. But that abuser exists within a power structure wherein the other primary power source – the other person commissioned with protecting the child – has abdicated his/her power to the other person. (Yes, it's done out of fear, but let's not be too quick to jump to explanation and forgiveness, as this robs the child of his soul's need for growth.)

I had one client, Tabitha, who articulated the terrible effect of complicity. She had been molested by her very successful father, as a child, and now was in her late-twenties admitting it for the very first time in her life in my office. Here we were, as we fleshed out the whole equation, discussing her mother. Tabitha thought long and hard when I asked her the rhetorical question of which parent commits the greater crime. She responded with this,

> "Sven, the parent letting the abuse happen is guilty of a different crime. My mom was guilty of betrayal. It was her job to protect me. Every time she let him touch me or pretended in her own mind that it wasn't really happening (and what does it say that I didn't feel safe telling her all about it? What does it say that I never trusted her with the truth, except that I knew she would either deny it or not do anything about it?). Every time she let him abuse my brothers with his brutal words; every time she let him even be around when he was drunk or on drugs; every time....*every time she didn't get us the hell out of there*, she was turning her back on us. She was choosing her financial security and her insane southern religious views that say "stay in a relationship, no matter what" over the safety of her own children. And if that's not textbook betrayal, what is?
>
> "But, y'know what, Sven," she said, as she dug deep and really took her time on this giant boulder now falling

off her shoulders, "the betrayal isn't even the worst crime, horrible as it was and horrible as the resulting distrust of her still is. The super (expletive) part of my mother's inaction amid all of that was that by not standing up, shutting him down, or getting us the hell out of there, she was normalizing his behavior. *My mom was normalizing this (expletive) as a working definition of a family. And it wasn't!* That was not a family. She was not a mother. He was not a father. And it has taken 29 years of knowing a few great souls who actually had good families, as well as heavy work with you for me to finally realize that mom was wrong! She normalized a situation that was neither good nor normal. Dad was a pig; that's obvious, even though a sick part of me still loves him. But it's not until now that I realize mom was wrong and just as treacherous in her weakness. And I am so scared that I'll never get past that definition of normal to create a good normal. I'm scared to even have kids, as much as I want them, because I haven't the faintest clue what normal really is or if it's really possible. And y'know what? By teaching me, back then, that that was normal, she taught me that any feelings inside me that said this wasn't right should be ignored. She completely corrupted any notion I had of right and wrong. For, if THIS – this violation of a little girl and her brothers – wasn't wrong, then what is? How can I possibly know what's wrong, or have any internal moral compass, if this giant thing isn't wrong? By normalizing it, she caused me to distrust my own inner voice, as you call it, and threw off my internal moral gyroscope."

Boom! With that colossal realization, so incredibly well-articulated, a calm came over Tabitha. In that moment, her life changed. Admitting her father's abuse had been the most powerful words she had ever spoken. But this ran a close second, and was possibly more important to her future family and relationships, as it meant deconstructing her old world and beginning the slow path of building a new one. It meant that her mother was, just as much as her father, strongly conveying the implicit message to her, "You don't matter. I do. My fears, my security, my religion matter. Your safety doesn't." And by doing so, the mother was engaging in soul abuse of her daughter, punching yet another hole in the bottom of Tabitha's Love Cup. And it meant she would not, also, have to find soul-nurturers on her own. She was not given any at birth. She would have to learn trust life. And she would have to be introduced to her own soul's voice and learn to trust it.

Whether in cases of abuse, GC's, SNC's or siblings of them, when parents are not parenting deliberately and courageously everyone suffers.

Song Recommendation

Download the great 70s classic song (and lyrics), **Lonely Boy**, by **Andrew Gold**. It speaks so perfectly to the lament of the sibling of the Golden Child.

https://www.youtube.com/watch?v=boAv-Bu4MrILonelyBoy

Journaling Recommendation

1. Which parent committed the greater crimes in your life? And what were the crimes?
2. Were you a Golden Child, Problem Child, the sibling of one, a disabled child, or the sibling of one?
3. What was the role of the 'other parent' in your life?
4. What got normalized in your life that never should have?
5. Is your Love Cup full of rocks and sludge? Or does it have holes in the bottom? Both? Or was there never anyone who wanted to pour love into your Love Cup?
6. What, or who, has kept you alive this long, despite the empty Love Cup?

CHAPTER 25

YOUR LIFE MESSAGES, PART 3: 'THE WORLD IS YOUR OYSTER'

"**S**ven, I never really got any negative messages from my parents, when I was a kid. In fact, I distinctly remember my parents saying to me, time and again, 'The world is your oyster,' and 'You can do anything you want to do in life," Johnson said to me.

I started to laugh. He was perplexed, not the least of which was because he thought therapists aren't supposed to laugh at anything a client ever says. And, while I'm rarely judgmental of my clients, this time the laugh just popped out. "Sorry, man. Wasn't laughing at you. I just hear that line a lot, particularly among my peers and old friends, who are parents. They all tell their kids they can do whatever they want. They can pursue whatever oysters they want, in order to claim the pearls they hold. Whatever makes you happy, they say. And while that may be the overt message, there are always those other times, those subtler, insidious times, when a completely different message gets conveyed."

"What do you mean," he asked, again perplexed.

"Well, for instance, I had a client who was told pretty much the exact same message. Armed with that, in his early-20s, he went from the Midwest to the west coast to go to music school. There, one way or another, he got wrapped up in a bit of a cult, or at least that's how it appeared to his parents. And so, they flew across the country, yanked him out, brought him home, then put him in counseling to de-program all the messages they didn't want him to have. Quite obviously, despite all their magnanimous words of the world being his oyster and him having full liberty to do whatever he wants, he could *not* do whatever he wanted in life."

"A bit extreme, don't you think, Sven?" he kidded me.

I went on, "Indeed. Extreme, but a true story. Further, far more common and far less dramatic are the million little conversations and million questions (and never underestimate the power of a well-

219

placed question to manipulate a child, teen, or adult-child) that get asked when the kid is considering college, tech school, majors, people to date, careers, places to live, people to be friends with, car to buy, who to marry, investments to make, parenting methods to employ, and on and on. And they're so subtle, but so many of them carry the underlying message 'You can do whatever you want in life.....*as long as it fits inside the parameters of what's acceptable to me, your parent.*'

"And that, my friend, is a categorically different message from 'You can do whatever you want.' I understand and have lived the parental instinct to protect my child. But that same instinct generally increases at the very time – the child's puberty and following years – when it should be most decreasing. And the underlying message in all those insidious questions or nudges, when the kid is considering his or her next step or steps, is 'you don't know what's best for you' or 'what you really want doesn't matter' or 'you should do what I, your parent, want'.

"So, despite all the 'Go conquer the world your way' nonsense emanating from even the most loving parent's piehole, there are usually significant negative, undermining messages implicit in the grand, seemingly positive exhortations."

"And so, whaddya do," Johnson asked. "I mean, my dad did something almost identical, not by telling me what I couldn't do but by passively insisting I turn down a Harvard full ride to study poetry, which I really wanted. He said it was my choice but he made it abundantly clear what he really, really wanted and all but insisted upon. He wanted me to go to the Naval Academy to play football and fly jets. My oyster meant nothing compared to the oyster he wanted vicariously through me. And I caved. I was 17. What was I supposed to do?"

"Johnson, you see it, first. Just seeing it, seeing the messages that have been shaping your soul and your entire existence has the massive power of reducing their impact, because now you're aware. Just admitting truth is huge. Seeing the truth deflates the truth. The Buddhists are always hammering on the notion of simple awareness. For, once you're aware of what is going on inside you or why you're doing what you're doing, and once you take it outside of you, it becomes much more difficult to keep doing that course of action.

Now that we have had this simple discussion and identified the core beliefs embedded in the cement of your soul, you won't be able to shake it. It'll stare you in the face every time you try to, again, make a decision from that old set of beliefs. And the unhappiness you've experienced from those flawed beliefs will cause you to begin to choose differently. And that's when everything changes."

Don't be misled by rosy appearances. Remember, things are seldom as they appear. Often, the most powerful negative message of your life lies right below that rosy surface.

Journaling Recommendation
1. What were the explicit positive messages told to you by the primary power sources and love sources in your life?
2. What subtler messages or events came at other times that either completely undermined those explicit messages or chipped away at their truth?
3. What are the parameters your parents have set in place for your life that you can't transgress, no matter what oyster you're pursuing?

CHAPTER 26

THE TRUTH IS OBVIOUS

I get a great many clients coming to me, who are stuck career-wise. Either they're in a job/career they have no passion for or, perhaps, they're between careers, taking some time off, or just uncertain what to do next. Often, there is joy and stability in other areas of life, such as relationships and finances. But there is great unease in the whole area of their life's work. Often, they long for more, long for less, or long for different, but they just can't put their finger on what it is. They just can't get past themselves. There's something they just can't see and it's blocking their path.

Of course, I go deep into the usual work with their autobiography (which I require from all clients) and explaining the Love Cup, core beliefs, 3 Binary Gates, and identifying the true power sources and negative energy sources in their life and in their core beliefs. For, each aspect of life influences the others. I help them see how these very powerful negative influences have been pressed into the cement of their soul and have been steering them well off course for decades. Very quickly, after seeing the massive influence of these other voices and desiring to finally be free, clients commence the words and actions necessary for full life ownership.

Nonetheless, the problem often persists of being unable to pinpointedly identify what is missing in their career or what direction they want to go next. Identifying and removing obstacles – usually inside, in their self-belief system – is only half the problem. Without a vision, there's no place to go, no matter how efficiently the machine may be running, now.

But the added benefit of removing negative energy sources and negative beliefs is that clients now allow themselves to think about what they really love without fear of backlash, criticism, or questions and doubts from others, past or present, that undermine dreams. In other words, they finally have safe space to allow the real 'me' to come up and out without being hurt or put down. In the past, they've not wanted to admit, or even look at, what their truth or dream is, because the price of speaking that dream or acting on that vision meant showing it to others, who might put it down or hurt it or hurt them. But, now with those negative energy sources radically deflated of their power to control and oppress the dreams of the individual, real truth can come up and out.

And do you know what I find? For as much as they stew, worry, and wrangle over what may or may not be next, no matter how much hand-wringing is frustrating them trying to figure it all out, no matter how foggy and terrifically unclear they feel about what to do with life, and no matter how hard they've already been searching, invariably:

The truth is obvious.
– Zen Proverb

More often than not, the real dream and passion for my client's life is right in front of his/her face. It's generally something they've always known or dreamed about. They've been denying or avoiding it so long, or making excuses (out of fear) for why it couldn't work, that they've lost their ability to see it. Yet, it's often so clear and so easy to see that the transition into it and pursuing it is almost effortless.

Who you really are and what you are called to pursue – i.e. that which makes your heart sing – is not out there somewhere. The real path that calls to your heart rises up from within. It is not found; it is allowed. And it's usually right in front of you, just as it has always been.

Once it is seen for the obvious truth that it is and how perfectly it fits with who you are, clarity follows. And clarity is a mighty powerful thing. Clarity brings motivation. Clarity brings strength. Clarity brings inner calm. Clarity brings massive energy in its wake. But there can be no clarity without the courage to remove all the negative energy blocking its flow up from deep within you. And that's the dirty work, the really hard, challenging, scary work.

Yet, what is true regarding your vocational calling is true regarding the calling of your soul in relationships, parenting, avocations, and more. The truth is obvious. Giving words to it is the challenge.

The Power Of 'When'
For the naturally curious soul, this notion of obvious truth raises the simple question, 'Why now?' It's a question I regularly hear from clients and audiences. 'If the truth is and always has been so obvious, why am I only seeing it or 'getting' it now?' And this brings us to one of the more ticklish aspects of the spiritual journey: The Power of When.

I have found on my own spiritual path and in the patterns I've seen in the paths of others that the most revealing question is often not where, what, how, or even why (though, 'why' is usually king of the hill in the Badass Counseling Method). The power question is 'when'? 'Why now'? 'When' is so revealing; often a back door to 'why'. Think about some of the great 'when' moments of history and life:

- Politics: Apart from the identity of Deep Throat, the two biggest questions of the entire Nixon-Watergate scandal (and the phrase most closely related to the scandal, ever since) were uttered by Senator Howard Baker, "What did [President Nixon] know; and when did he know it?"
- Religion: My pastor father, who had majored in Ancient Greek in college and studied Koine (Biblical) Greek in seminary, taught me, a full decade before I too would study both Ancient Greek and Koine Greek for my college and graduate studies, a very fascinating 'when' question, one that impacts billions of people, over the last two millennia. Mind you, I'm ten or so years old and my old man is giving me a lesson in Greek etymology and the difficulty of interpreting texts from one language (or two), particularly an ancient one (or two) to one's own language. But, it was so interesting that it stuck. "Remember," he chided, "in Biblical Greek there was no punctuation. So, in reading and interpreting the texts in their original language, meanings are not as clear as many a preacher like to make them. Consider when Jesus is on the

225

cross with a robber hanging on a cross on either side of him. One of them asked for Jesus' mercy, and Jesus then proclaims, 'Truly I tell you today you will be with me in paradise.' Now, Sven, where do you put the comma in that sentence? Remember, there's no punctuation in the text, so the interpreter has to insert it. So, do you place it before the word 'today' or after it? If you place the comma *before* 'today' (*Truly I tell you, today you will be with me in Paradise.*), the proclamation carries the meaning that the robber will be with Jesus in paradise TODAY, as if to say, 'Let's get on with dying, so you and I can get the heck out of here and go to heaven.' But, if you place that non-existent comma *after* 'today', the whole meaning changes. (*Truly I tell you today, you will be with me in Paradise.*) Rather than 'You and I are going to heaven today, buddy' the meaning is much less exciting, 'I'm telling you right now today, pal, that you will be with me in paradise, *someday*, whenever it is that paradise actually happens.' The placement of a mere comma, Sven, determines something as monumental as when heaven happens."

On the surface, this may sound like a trivial point, but it's not. For it raises the rather grave, far-reaching question of not where is heaven or how do I get in, as most Sunday School kids and even adults spend much time worrying about, but *when does heaven happen?* For, by putting the comma before 'today' it implies that the robber gets to go to heaven immediately upon death. Yet, nearly the whole corpus of Christian theology states that there is some grand and glorious Judgment Day in the future when it will be parsed out who goes up and who goes down. The entire Christian Biblical Book of Revelation is about how the end times will come and how potential ascent to Heaven/Paradise will follow. How is that theological point – eschatology – reconciled with Jesus's possible proclamation that heaven happens immediately after death? Most Christian theology asserts that heaven happens later, after the Judgment Day, but, quite ironically, most Biblical translations put the comma *before* 'today', implying that both Jesus and the robber (who was not Divine and thus have a back door to heaven) would be entering the pearly gates that day. The obvious present-day ramifications are such that, What does a pastor tell a couple who lost a child? Do they say, "Your child is in heaven" or "Your child will be in heaven some day"? Or, even more difficult, what does the pastor or well-meaning relative say to the child whose father or mother died – "Mommy is in heaven, right now" or "Mommy will be in heaven some day"?

- Sports. The question of when is one of the most central. Every timed sports record is answering the question of when. In football, nearly every game is marked by the question, 'When did his knee touch the ground?'

- Music. 'When' is perhaps the most important element of music. Tempo. Rhythm. Timing of entrances, alone, is huge. One little known fact is that many orchestras actually start playing after the conductor's downbeat or instruction to start playing. It's called 'playing behind the beat.' The Orchestra, rather than the conductor, is actually controlling its own timing, its own when. By waiting a tick before hitting their first note (and subsequently staying a tick or half-tick behind the conductor for the entire piece) an orchestra can interpret the speed, style and arc of what a conductor is seeking to accomplish. (It really is quite similar to that hundredth of a second that the batter in professional baseball has to 'interpret' what is happening in the pitcher's windup and release, as well as what kind of ball is coming out of his hand.) This enables them to increase their ability to express the sound.

'When' is an incredibly powerful question. And so, when I feel it is the most salient question to ask in counseling, I'll simply lay it before the client and let him or her tinker with it, a bit, "It's so fascinating that this specific even happened, right now, in your life. So why now and not two years ago or two months from now?" or, for example, "My question is not 'why did your wife cheat on you 8 years ago' but 'why not 12 years ago or 4 years ago'? What was going on in your lives then? *Why then?*" Furthermore, if she's cheating at eight years ago, it's reasonable to assume she was feeling ever-increasing discontent 9, 10, and perhaps 12 years ago. In other words, your marital problems didn't start at the time of the infidelity but long before it. So, when did the problems *really* start?" The answer to the when question gives birth to the question/answer I'm really hunting for: So, if the problems really started long before the infidelity, what *really* triggered the problems in your marriage? All of a sudden, the client is looking for answers in places they never realized there was a problem. Changing the when changes the problem and thereby changes the solution set.

Whether regarding cheating, or a major life catastrophe, or particular decisions that impacted many or powerfully impacted a few, here are the responses that tend to repeat themselves when people are confronted with the 'when' question:

- I wasn't ready, before. I was too _____. Or, I was not enough _____.
- I needed this event now, more than ever, to jolt me out of my comfort zone.
- That big thing happened in our relationship, at that time, because things had been building up for some time and then this one other thing happened, and it all went south from there. I hadn't even linked those two things together before, but yeah, things had been bad for a while, not overnight.
- I just had sooooo much fear from my past before, but not now.
- I was trying to please everyone before.
- I was too afraid to say (and show) what I really wanted.
- I've grown.
- I'm finally ready to hear it and grasp it.

There is something incredibly liberating and empowering for my clients when they realize it had to be now, not months later or years earlier, or when they realize why a particular event (such as cheating) happened precisely when it did. There was no other perfect time. The timing tells the real story.

And this gets to one of the most critical elements of the spiritual journey, whether you're an avowed atheist, rabidly religious, or more likely somewhere in between. It's the notion of communion with and trust in the spirit of the Universe. Recognizing the voice of the

Universe speaks to us from within and is indistinguishable from our own deepest soul voice, to have true communion means to trust the answers will come when the time is right. The when, is always perfect.

The truth is not only obvious, but it's almost always available, now. The only thing blocking you from knowing it now is your anxiety, your fear, and the fact that you're looking in the wrong place. There's that old saying, "Infinite patience yield immediate results." And that has a nice ring to it – it sounds clever – but it's like some doggone koan when you try to unpack it and figure out what the heck it actually means. By committing to infinite patience on a particular issue – ie by letting go of needing to know RIGHT NOW – the anxiety drops away. And once anxiety is gone, as well as the fear that is always the precursor to anxiety, the answer unfolds and reveals itself. And yes, that can be immediate. I'm not lying. I'm not just making this (expletive) up just to sound all clever and spiritual. It's true. Once you have the capacity to relax your mind AND let go of results (and the fear that drives the need for particular results) you will have nearly instant clarity. That's why meditation, journaling, the Sedona Method (mentioned earlier), and even therapy (at least with an excellent therapist) have such power. They release the anxiety and fear that are blocking you from seeing the obvious truth.

One More Thought On 'When' In Religion And Spirituality

Every preacher has, at one time or another, preached on the difference in Greek between 'kairos' and 'chronos'. Chronos is linear time – watches, clocks, your 4pm doctor's appointment on Thursday. Kairos is known as 'God's time' – 'in due time', 'when God is ready,' always, and much more circular and unpredictable time. And here's the real kicker you ain't gonna get in church: kairos ain't about patience; it's about now. See, most clergy, when preaching on the notion of trust in God's time, exhort people to be patient, trusting that your calling will come when it is time for it to come. But I don't believe that there is ever a time when God/Universe/Soul *isn't* speaking and speaking your next calling. If we're truly in tune to intuition – the speaking of our own body and skin – and the voice of the soul, it is always telling us what is next, specifically what is now. It may be a big message or big calling, or it may be a medium or

229

small calling. But what's next is always being conveyed, right now, even if it's a message calling you down into your deepest self.

And kairos is not only an issue of size of the calling. Often, we want to know what to do in our career life, but our soul, or God/Universe, gives us a tiny calling in, let's say, our fitness life, seemingly completely unrelated. Or perhaps in our family life. And in the end, it always weaves together. Or, perhaps you're desiring a calling or clarity in your relationship, but God gives you a giant calling in your financial life that completely resets the table of your life. All aspects of life play together, each dependent upon the other; all in concert.

But, most folk have no interest in the small and medium callings because they sooooooo have their hearts set on some big calling they want and want in a particular area. It may be a specific calling or it may be that they simply are not satisfied with anything other than something big. So, they reject the callings they are getting, because they want something better or different. In other words, the problem isn't that God ain't talkin'. The problem is that you ain't listening. Or, worse, you're rejecting the call, because your plans are, it appears, bigger or better than God's plan for your life. Or, more often than not, the calling or the obvious truth you are being called to is right in front of your face but you don't want it because the price is too high. The fear is too great. And that fear is often what keeps us second-guessing the calling, hoping for something different. So you keep asking God to speak and show you what's next, when God speaking ain't the problem. Execution is the problem, because you're just scared. So, don't try to make this God's problem or some kairos thing.

> **"If it doesn't scare the holy hell out of you,**
> **it's not God's call for your life.**
> **If it's safe, comfortable, or easy,**
> **it's not God's call. Fact."**
> --Sven Erlandson

And therein is the flaw. We only truly find our greatest purpose and joy when we let go of trying to control the results, when we trust the spirit of the Universe, trust it speaking through intuition, and trust that it knows (or our own deepest soul knows) better than we do. And once that turn happens, everything changes. Everything.

When we are truly in tune to the voice of the Universe, moment to moment, rising up from within, we discover that what vexes us isn't the frustration of moving too slow but the fear that comes from everything moving seemingly too fast. When we complain that God is not speaking, the real, underlying problem is that God is usually already shouting, but you are terrified of the price of what you're being asked to do or terrified by the sheer velocity of change that it will bring. When we are truly tuned in, no longer afraid, and fully trusting the calling of the soul, life is this exciting roller coaster of adventure and constant new tasks and endeavors. And even the medium and small callings are loaded with excitement, risk, challenge, and enthusiasm.

The truth is always obvious and always available, right now.

THE TURN

CHAPTER 27

THE PILOT LIGHT OF GREATNESS
BURNING DEEP INSIDE YOU

So, here's the other side having been taught, from a very young age that you are no good, don't matter, and/or aren't wanted. There's been a quiet counter-message running on infinite loop deep inside you. Its existence pre-dates the closing of your Binary Gates, the pressing of negative beliefs into your formerly wet cement, and the puncturing of your Love Cup. There's a quiet, little pilot light that has been burning, since you were born. Like the pilot light in your water heater that is always burning, waiting to be stoked by gas to full flame to heat cold water pumped into your house.

It is that pilot light that has been keeping you alive. It goes out, you go out. Without that deep belief, however faint, there would be no hope, no belief, no possibility. And you'd either be a corpse or a walking corpse en route to imminent death.

That pilot light is the message that was born the day you were. It is the eternal flame of the gods. It's the message that runs counter to the ill-begotten lie that was pressed into the cement of your soul that says you stink and who you really are doesn't matter. *The pilot message – this tiny sliver of light and heat inside you – is this quiet pulse of belief in your own greatness and goodness.*

Yes, somewhere in you, you honestly and fully believe that the critics are so fricking wrong! Somewhere deep inside you is this tiny voice screaming, 'NO!' No to all the critics. No to the negative messages. No to the control, the fear, and the negative energy sources in your life.

Even a person possessing the Dirty Trifecta of three completely closed Binary Gates (see Bonus Track 9) possesses a deeply registered belief that they are good. Somewhere deep in the soul is the Divine Spark.

That longing that you actually feel – that longing to be free and happy, the longing for ALIVENESS – is the heat of that Divine spark. You are alive because you still believe! You believe in you, even if it's only this tiny light, tiny pulse, tiny message, tiny voice, tiny feel, tiny vibe deep inside you. You do. And you long for it to consume your soul and life with happiness, purpose, and fulfillment.

See, you don't want to die. I know it. I've been exactly where you are, right now.

I've been at what I call 'the suicide point' before. I was there for roughly 12 years, off and on, to greater or lesser degrees at different times; ready, willing, at times even eager to kill myself, sick of it all, seeing no way out. In the end, I committed suicide. (And yes, I use 'committed' and not 'attempted', because my old self and old negative beliefs pressed into the cement of my soul died that day, even if the rebirth came slowly over the subsequent years. And, I know how everything begins to change after that.) April 17, 2001. I slit my wrists – 9mm deep on the left, 13mm deep on the right, I was later told; and that was all it took. I have the eight-inch scars running up my forearms to prove it. I bled for nearly an hour, as I looked out onto the San Francisco Bay. But I just didn't die. And I finally admitted I didn't want to do; but if I was going to choose to live, (expletive) had to change. A lot of it. So you see, I know this pain of which I speak. And I know the monumental change that is possible.

You just see no way out. Trapped. Forlorn. Frustrated. Perhaps even pulled to suicide (or maybe you've just considered it a few times).

But, I have news for you: the pilot light is still burning. It hasn't been snuffed out. Somewhere in you, you believe in your own goodness and greatness. Fact. Absolute fact. It may be faint as heck, but the pilot is burning.

And the grand goal of life, the goal of my life's work with others, even you now in this book, is to stoke that pilot light to full flame. Roaring. Unquenchable. Consuming your soul and life with happiness, purpose, flow, and fulfillment. Every day and year after my suicide was spent opening the 3 Binary Gates, seizing ownership, and pushing back or cutting out the negative energy sources and negative voices in both my inner and outer lives. With that daily work, happiness and peace grew...and grew.

The task of life is to fan to giant roar your belief in your own innate – *INNATE*, not earned, performance-based or success-driven – goodness and worth. And here's the kicker:

> **Until you believe you're good and great,**
> **Until you believe you truly have worth,**
> **Until you really start to buy into it with your own decisions, risk,**
> **trust, and boldness,**
> **Until you fall in love with you,**
> **Ain't nobody else gonna.**
> **The problem, in the end, ain't them;**
> **It's your perception of your own self.**
> **It's the lie that was pressed into the wet cement of your soul.**

Until you believe in your greatness and brilliant, wonderful goodness, it doesn't matter what anyone else says or does, because it'll all drain through you, like a Love Cup with a hole in the bottom. It'll splash out of you, unable to ever get in, in the first place, like a Love Cup that is so already full of crud, sh-t and rocks. Until you believe in you and fix the damn Cup, ain't nobody else gonna be able to fill you or even get through to you.

It is time to begin to truly believe in your own beauty, soul, goodness, affability, attractiveness, greatness, spirit, sexiness, worth, value, smarts, creativity, success, lovability, and so on.

Song Recommendation

1) Buy, listen to, and meditate on the lyrics to *Take Me to the Pilot*, https://www.youtube.com/watch?v=kTvsHSTJ2EATakeMeToThePilot by **Elton John**. I'm quite fond of the extended version, 'Live at the Greek Theatre (1994)'. **Ray Cooper** is monster on percussion. In fact, I'm writing this chapter (and others in this book) with that video playing in the corner of my computer. Terribly inspiring!

2) Also, a great song from **Queen**: Download *A Kind of Magic*. https://www.youtube.com/watch?v=0p_1QSUsbsMAKindOfMagic It really speaks to this notion of the flame of greatness burning inside each one of us.

CHAPTER 28

THREE THINGS HAPPEN AS YOU MORE BECOME YOUR TRUEST SELF

The simple truth is that the notion of being, saying, doing, and becoming more and more your truest self is scary as heck. It's scary because it means – finally, once again and for the first time, since perhaps childhood – showing your truest self to the world. It maybe only in bits and pieces, inch by inch, bit by bit, but it's still scary. Nothing more terrifies you than showing the world who you really are.

And *three things happen, as you more and more push through the fear and become your truest self*, showing the real you to the rest of the world (often right as you're discovering it for yourself):

1) You begin to lose people. It is a point of absolute fact – 100% guaranteed! – that if you have the courage to hear and heed your inner voice, if you begin to be, say, do, believe, and become who you really are, You. Will. Lose. People. Period! This is the really scary part. It's the part you KNEW.....before you even started....would, or might, happen. And this is what kept you from ever expressing and living your true self in the past. You simply feared the living heck out of losing people, some of whom have been with you forever, or for a long time, and whom you foresaw yourself having in your life forever. You know who it is. You know already what they'll say.

Part of what has kept you trapped in your past life is the fear of losing those who are married to the idea of who you used to be, those who like the security of who you've always been. You feared their criticism, feared their wrath, feared disappointing them, feared losing them, feared hurting them (as if you giving up your life happiness is more important than any short term sting they might experience by you changing, growing and getting happier) and so feared showing them your true self. Yes, there are important people in your life who, basically, want to keep you miserable and as you are, because it benefits them. Obviously, they'd never cop to it, but if you have these type of folk in your life, you likely already know who they are.

And the simple truth is that you WILL lose some of them. Fact. Period. End of story. And loss stinks. It's painful. Though, to be clear, that pain is almost entirely on the front side of the loss. That is, you'll fret far more over the *possibility* of having to kick people out of your life and people leaving you than you will ever mourn losing them *after* their departure. Beforehand, you see that you need them gone (or radically pushed back from such predominance in your life), but the vision is muddied by fear of how it will go down, what they'll say, the reluctance to hurt their feelings, and, to a smaller degree, what it'll be like to have that gap in your life where they formerly stood. And, if we're honest, it's also a bit hard to imagine living without whatever good it was they brought that caused you to keep them in your life, at all. But, but, but a funny thing happens after the leap of faith is taken and the deed is done – after you've excised them from your life, or from a place of such significance. All the fears of actually doing it – hurting them, the fall out, and their reaction – are gone, for the work is done. When those fears are gone, you have the greatly magnified clarity of your original vision for doing so. You have nothing but the startling vividness that this was absolutely the decision that needed to be made. And you wonder why you didn't do this, years earlier.

Additionally, the period of losing people is short. Once you commence the biggest life adjustments of shifting your course, that is when the most losses of personnel happen. Pretty much right at the beginning. Why? The people most roped into and, in fact, facilitating this existence that is sucking the life out of you are almost exclusively those closest to you. They are the most vested and thus have the most to lose. Those further away from your daily life and drama have little or nothing to lose by you becoming someone new. So, those closest to you will see changes immediately and resist immediately. And you will be faced with a decision, forced by life itself to decide who you really are and what price you're willing to pay to become who you really are.

But that is the price of authenticity. The price of saying, doing, becoming, having, and being who you really are – i.e. living originally and authentically – is losing some people who have no interest in who you *really* are, deep down, and who want nothing more than to keep you locked into that being of who you used to be but no longer are, who want the security of that which you always were but no longer are. They want the familiarity of who you always were, even if they simultaneously criticized who you always were.

There is no joy without loss, no self without purging, no truth without a cutting away of not-self and the people whose security is hardwired into the false version of you.

2) You begin to gain people. The grand triumph of the courage to show the world who you really are is that you begin to attract people you didn't even know existed. Fact. Fact. Fact. Room is created for great good to flow in. And flow it does. Effortlessly, people begin to walk into your life and rain blessings, joy, love, support, and encouragement – not to mention a new sense of genuine ALIVENESS – on you and in ways and amounts you never even knew existed. That's no hyperbole; it's fact!

People who say, "I LOVE who you are" walk into your life, to your amazement and utter delight. There will be people who say, "I love who you're becoming" or "Heck, I just adore that you don't even know, for sure, who you're becoming, but that you have the courage to risk and venture forth and just make the hard decisions to become who you really are. I just stand in awe of your courage!"

And that is a marvelous feeling! To risk and have it pay off is amazing! To trust in life, the Universe, and in the belief that no matter what happens you'll be okay (...and then to have that risk and courage rewarded with genuine love, approval, and appreciation) is just glorious, outstripping the losses of former people. We have all met people who have a certain glow, and energy, something that causes others to naturally gravitate to them. This is what they have. This hard-won authenticity. It causes the massive energy of the Universe to flow up from within them no longer blocked by closed gates, no longer blocked by the fear, negative self-beliefs and more fear that formerly kept their truest self down and kept the natural font of energy from flowing through them.

**The more you have the courage to become your truest self, the more you will begin to effortlessly, even shockingly, attract people.
It is a fact of advancement on the spiritual journey.**

Those fears that keep the real self down are strong. Of course, one of the biggest of them is the fear of criticism – ultimately, the fear of looking stupid, feeling foolish, making a mistake, and having someone cite you for such foolishness. The Greek philosopher Epictetus said, "He who wishes to improve must be content to be thought foolish and stupid." The great American innovator, Steve Jobs, specifically stated in the culmination to his commencement address at Stanford University (2005), now viewed in its many cuts nearly 100 million times on YouTube, "Stay hungry. Stay foolish." There is a direct link between greatness, happiness, and the willingness to look foolish, particularly when that willingness is pointed in the direction of becoming your truest self. As they say in athletics, it's the 'playing loose vs playing tight'; playing loose (sometimes even playing sick) leads to great performances. For, that willingness reflects <u>openness</u>, <u>courage</u>, and a <u>shedding of the bonds of fear</u>. And it is nestled inside those three things that we find the real magic happens.

3) Amazing things start to fall out of the sky. I know this may sound like ridiculous hokum to some people, but it is predictably so common. I have had clients see all new opportunities happen in unexpected ways in unexpected areas of their lives, once they started cutting loose the Raw Sewage and started having the courage to pursue the Diamonds of who they really are, live where and how they truly want, and pursue the paths that breathe life into their soul.

I had one client ride the elevator down from my office, after our second session together, only to call me from the lobby to say that she just got a call for a huge opportunity for her business, completely out of the blue, an opportunity that wasn't even on the map prior to getting into the elevator! Granted, that shocking immediacy doesn't happen every time, but stuff does begin to happen and quickly, all the time. No lie. And what made it so odd in this case is that she wasn't even seeing me for career-related issues.

She was pushing growth in her personal life, but the energy and breaking-open of her life spilled into her vocation, because it's all woven together. She was ecstatic!

I had 45 year-old client fulfill a lifelong dream to live in Hawaii. She had been considering it, for a good long time. However, the possibility of finally making this dream happen always butted up against the reality that she had a bulldog that was her best friend in life and she simply could not afford anyplace in Hawaii that would allow her to own a dog, not even close. A month after our 6-hour session together, after she had done some really hardcore Diamonds/Raw Sewage work on her own, she emailed to say that, completely unexpectedly, she had received an email from a woman she had known back in college, who heard at a party that she was wanting to move to Hawaii. Turns out, the old college friend owned an apartment building there, which (you guessed it!) allowed dogs; oh, and would she be willing to be the onsite caretaker for 5-10 hours/week in exchange for reduced rent? It was beyond great, well more than she was hoping for.

I had a client who hired me to work with her two teen stepkids. After a month of working with the son and daughter, particularly helping the kids to express more fully their truths of who they really were (as well as helping the parents to hear, acknowledge and encourage these revelations) and begin to make decisions that spoke their truth, a most unexpected thing happened. One evening, the 15 year-old son came into the kitchen and did something he had never done in their 15 years of parenting him. Without being solicited in any way, whatsoever, he apologized TWICE for a couple of very serious problems he had created, not just in breaking the family rules but breaking the law and in mistreating his parents. It was a gift (and a turning point) the parents could not have fantasized about in even their wildest dreams. The genuine contrition was so out of character, so new. For them, it powerfully signaled the possibility of a whole new reality.

The point is that things happen when we radically change our soul's belief system and begin making decisions consistent with those new beliefs, most specifically the absolutely elemental belief 'Who I really am matters and is good.' When that one turn begins to happen, people and the very Universe, itself, respond differently and in the most glorious and unexpected ways. Blessings fall out of the sky. Fact!

Journaling Recommendation

1. Who are the people you are most likely to get blowback from if you were to, more and more, be, say, do, believe, and become who you really are?
2. In this list, circle the people you are most afraid to lose.
3. Write out the three main reasons for each person why you are afraid to lose that person.
4. Who on your list do you not fear losing? Do you not fear losing them because A) they would not leave you, if you were to more and more become yourself; or because B) you simply are not afraid of living without them (or without their diminished presence in your life)?
5. Write about what it would feel like to lose these people.
6. This is a very simple question: Could you live without the people you've circled? I'm sure it would be hard to lose them, but, in the end, could you live without them (or with their diminished presence)?
7. Does it change your perspective on more fully becoming your truest self to know that, in the end, you can accept, live with, and move on from the loss of any of those people? How?
8. Does it change your perspective on living your truth to know you'll begin to attract new people, who are better suited to who you're becoming?
9. What type of person – what characteristics – would you most love to attract? What would make your heart sing?

Bonus Tracks

Core Readers: I recommend you check out Bonus Track 12 with the Advanced Readers. I think you'll like it. Then come back and move on to the next chapter.

- Bonus Track 12: Words Speak Louder Than Actions, Not Vice Versa (This is a really great read that I strongly recommend. It's about the broken heart of a cop, named Speedy.)

CHAPTER 29

JUMPING SHIP

I want you to do a visualization with me. First, what's that part of life that isn't working for you? Perhaps it's your whole doggone life. Now, think of this life you've been living, the relationship you've been in, or the career path that's not working as a big ol' schooner ship with sails and masts. See that ship falling apart, rotting, on fire, or perhaps even sinking. Instinct says to get off a sinking ship.

The simple fact of life is that it's easy to jump from this ship when you can see the next ship in the distance. Making big life changes is doable when we know what's next, when there's something better to swim to.

But what if you can't see the next ship on the horizon? What if you can't see the next relationship, next career move, next step you need to take with a troubled son or daughter, or next anything in life? What if all you can see on your horizon is the pseudo-security of the slowly sinking ship you're on?

Truth is, you gotta learn to swim. You gotta learn to tread water.

It's no coincidence that in dream interpretation, as well as the texts and histories of the world's religions and myth systems, water is often seen as symbolic of or as a metaphor for the soul or the deepest, scariest parts within a person. Thus, to dive into the water – to jump from security into the insecurity of following soul – is to swim amid your own scariest inner parts. To swim, to tread water, is to essentially, finally sit in that which you have spent your life running from – the lies and stories that have been dogging you, your whole life.

The reason we cling to that which is secure, the reason we stay on a ship that is sinking – or at least terribly uncomfortable, painful, just crummy, or no fun anymore – is not because of the insecurity of not knowing what ship is next, per se, but because being in that insecure state demands energy, lots of it, energy which now can no longer be directed toward running from or stuffing down all the crap you've been running from. Further, treading water, or not being in motion swimming toward whatever is next, means that you are ripe breeding ground for all that stuff to finally invade every pore of your body. Again, more anxiety.

In my final year of seminary, decades ago, I took a class simply titled, "Weddings and Funerals." The professor made a fascinating point quite specific to the topic at hand – the liturgies of weddings and funerals – yet relevant to this discussion of the fear of jumping ship. He simply offered the query, "Why do people, even those who are devoutly non-religious, come to the church and religion in times of weddings and funerals? Why then? What is it that's unique to those two situations that draws people to something they otherwise avoid?" He then went on to answer his own question. "On top of the sheer gravity that religion brings to certain situations, there is something very powerful about ritual and ritualized behaviors," he said. The power of ritual. There is something uniquely soothing about familiar and repetitive behavior, as well as familiar settings faces. Collegiate and NHL hockey goalies are notorious for their elaborate pre-game and in-game rituals, from elaborate visualizations to dressing the exact same way before every game, from counting the number of times they tap their stick on the goalposts at a face-off to counting the number of water sips they take from their bottle. The high stress of being completely in the spotlight for three hours while 30+ high velocity hockey pucks are shot at your face demands implementing actions that calm the nerves and, if lucky, invoke the favor of the hockey gods. But it's true of all positions in all sports. Every baseball player has a ritual, great or small, before stepping into the batter's box. Musicians and artists too; my ex-wife was a Broadway-level dancer who had a series of rituals on performance day from exactly what type, when, and how much coffee to drink to her series of stretches. Truth is, we all have highly ritualized behaviors, whether we're cognizant of them or not. Familiarity is an incredibly comforting and strengthening element of life as we face the anxieties and fears of both daily life and big decisions.

However, ritual and familiarity also have a tremendously debilitating power. Often, we cling to them because the thought of new action, new paths, and new faces and settings instill fear in us. It is so easy to hold tightly to that which is familiar – patterns, environs, faces – even when we know it is simultaneously sucking the very life out of us.

But the simple truth is, sometimes we just have to get off a ship that stinks. Sometimes things are so bad we just have to leave. Sometimes the universe is screaming to us so loudly – our external world has completely fallen apart and our internal world won't stop churning – that there's nowhere to run, and no way to deny the destruction. And that is a scary proposition. The notion of trusting that if I jump ship, I'll be okay, no matter what, is an anathema to most folks. It's inconceivable.

Yet, that is the calling of the gods. Your soul is calling you down, into the dark waters of your soul, into yourself, into the dark forest. You're not just being called to the next ship, the next path, or the next distraction. You're being called to the solution, if you have the courage. You're being called into the thing you've been running from, and also to the pilot light of your soul, down to that which is driving everything. You're being called down so that you can finally see and smash the cement – the very bedrock of your being – that has been imprinted with the messages that are corrupting the entire system of your life.

Jumping ship is terrifically scary stuff, especially if there is no new ship to swim to, instead only the knowledge that this present ship ain't where I'm supposed to be. But, often in life, the only way out is in, the only way to new life is into the thing you fear most.

Song Recommendation

Download *Place in this World*, by **Michael W. Smith**. Beautiful power ballad that is so apropos to this notion of the Divine Spark burning deep inside each one of us, particularly when we consider that at our deepest depths our own truest voice is indistinguishable from the voice of God, himself. And it is that true Divine voice that gives us direction, gives us hope, and gives us solace when our heart most longs for reprieve from the pain and longs for the possibility of true and lasting joy.

https://www.youtube.com/watch?v=LpXMnY_t03MAPlaceInThisWorld

CHAPTER 30

EVERY DECISION IN LIFE
BOILS DOWN TO TWO THINGS

As we more and more consider this turn from a life of not-you to greater deliberateness, authenticity, and aliveness, the pressure to make life-affirming decisions increases. This means fear increases, too. The power of fear to short-circuit life and aliveness cannot be overstated.

Ultimately, in some form or another, every single decision of life, large or small, can be distilled down to a choice between trust and fear. It's not always immediately visible, but it's there. Everything, every decision – large, small or medium – somehow boils down to:

A) **Choosing fear** and thereby walking away from that which truly stirs your soul and calls to you from the future; or maybe it's not choosing a 180° opposite path of what you want, but a lessening of boldness, or going for something 20° safer than the direction you feel called, just slightly watered-down; or

B) **Choosing trust** and thereby walking into your fear; choosing what feels good and right to you, even though it makes your knees knock and your palms sweat.

What the trust really is is the belief (even the knowing) that your feelings will survive – i.e. that you'll survive on the inside. Once you can see, believe, and trust that, even in the worst case scenario, your inner life won't blow up, everything changes. It is trusting,

"I'll be okay. I'll recover.
Life goes on.
No matter what happens, **I'll be alright."**

And for as ridiculously trivial as that may sound, it is an incredibly powerful statement to really say and believe. For, people's greatest fears are never what will happen to them on the outside, but how it will feel on the inside, after that external stuff happens. THAT is the debilitating part of fear. THAT is what keeps people from pursuing what they know will make them happy.

In the end, the only path through fear and toward that which moves your soul is trust. The path of happiness is 100% contingent upon trust.

Happiness and a fear-driven life are inversely correlated.
The more fear drives a person's decisions, the less happy they will be.
The more a person has worked fear out of their life, the greater their happiness.

Oh, and as an aside, on this notion of trust, many people in relationships hide behind their walls and hold back from revealing their true self, until their mate reveals his/herself to be fully trustworthy. So, in other words, Paul may be a terrific guy, who has never wronged me. But I'm going to hide behind my walls of distrust, because Peter, Steven, and Ryan hurt me, in the past. In other words, I'm not even fully present to Paul. I'm judging him based on other people, not on his merits. I'm still in the past. He may be the greatest guy in the world, but I cannot see it, because I'm still living in fear.

In the end, there's only one absolutely certain way to fully know if someone can be trusted or not. Trust 'em. Then see what they do. Granted, it's a painful route, but it's the only route of absolute clarity.

Truth is, you'll never fully see who a person is until you fully reveal who you are. Because, until you do that, it's impossible to know if they are reacting to the real part of yourself or the fake part. To speak in relationship algebra, you fail to isolate the variable as long as you are continuing to infuse new (false) variables into the equation. If you are 100% honest and authentic, then any reaction you get will be a clear response to your real truth, indicating where they are at and who they are. But obviously, in order to do that, you have gotta so believe in the value of who you are that you are not put off if they don't respond the way you want them to. And the simple truth is that you wouldn't be reading this book unless you, at least to some degree, believed you are not fully worthy.

But that's where the gold is: fully authentic living. You see people much more clearly, not just because you're not clouded by your own fears but because you're getting responses that are pure, insofar as they're not stimulated by false projections from you.

So, do you have the courage to trust the calling of your soul by trusting that, no matter what happens, you'll be okay? Are you ready to finally begin living? Are you ready to learn to swim?

Journaling Recommendation
1. What are the five scariest things you would have the most trouble letting go of in your life?
2. What is the scariest part about trusting that, no matter what happens, you'll be okay? Why?
3. What are the ten parts of who you are that you most fear revealing to others and to life?

CHAPTER 31

THE POWER OF THE THIRD PATH

We are led to believe that at every crossroads in life there are two paths, and your job is to decide which one to take. The crossroads may be on some major life decision, such as, 'Should I take the job in San Diego or stay in Boston, now that I've begun to build up a base of friends and cool things I like to do?' Or 'Have a third child or buy that vacation cabin?' Or, 'The University near home or that intriguing college 1000 miles away?'

Or, the crossroads might be on something smaller, such as, "Your parents' or my parents' house for Thanksgiving?" or even "Train for the marathon that I've always wanted to run or really become more deliberate about slowing life down and getting more rest at night?"

Or the crossroads can be even minuscule, yet significantly important nonetheless, such as, "Do I really need to be drinking coffee everyday or is it just a habit" or "Should I tell Susan that I just can't be her friend anymore?"

Bottom line, we are constantly, even daily or hourly, meeting crossroads. And, while it might be tempting to think I'm over-writing the scene a bit, every crossroads really is a reflection of your values, your beliefs, and your fears. It's little different from a corporation constantly re-assessing if each decision is consistent with its mission statement and core values. If the choice at each crossroads (even or especially the small decisions) is not consistent with who you really are in your soul, negative energy begins to build up inside, even slightly, bit by bit. Of course, making decisions consistent with one's own soul naturally demands being first in tune to the rumblings of one's own soul. Everything is predicated on that. And if you're still running from the voice of your own soul, still refusing to slow down, still refusing solitude, then the decisions at each crossroads are not consistent with your truest self. Thus, negative energy is building upon the very negative energy you're already running from.

The Choices At Every Crossroads

In both the big and small, as well as the medium, things in life, we are forever (even daily) at crossroads, forced by life to make a decision, this way or that. And classically, this crossroads, this fork in the road, holds two paths, which we are forced to choose between. Each path then determines what comes next, each building on the last crossroads.

But the most important aspect to crossroads that many people are quite unaware of is the simple fact that there are never just two choices at a crossroads. In fact, when distilled to their essence, there are always three. This is a critical point to understand.

For so many people, the crossroads and decisions of life start at a young age and are defined by two paths: the path that is expected of me by others and the exact opposite path that is basically my rebellion against those who are trying to tell me what to do with my life. The first is the path of 'shoulds'. The second I call 'The Screw You Path' or 'The Path of the Middle Finger'.

The first path is the path of acquiescence, being a good boy/girl, and fulfilling obligations to others. It is the path of fear. It is the path of no originality, no authenticity, and no liveliness, no spirit. It is the life ruled by an external power source. Ironically, this is a very exciting path, simply because it's easy: Just do what the important people in your life tell you to do. No thought required. Granted, it gets very hard later, because it'll suck the very life outta your soul. But it's almost always a clear path, assuming there is no dissonance between the important voices in your life.

I counseled a 20-something gay man who had been in a serious relationship for several years, since college. Interestingly, he had almost never in his entire life fought with his father, who had largely been a single parent. He respected his father and his father totally encouraged his being gay. The son came to me because he was, for the first time in his life, arguing and fighting with his father. He was at an almost complete loss for why. There were many nuances to the equation, but one of the most obvious whoppers to me was that the young man now had more than one primary power source in his life.

So now the two primary power sources were not in harmony. It's not that the two power sources – his father and his lover – disliked each other, per se. But the young man's partner had very different ideas about life, about my client's past, and even about his father. And my client embraced a great many of those new ways of looking at life. Of course, the father saw this as a loss of loyalty and love. He was greatly threatened. As a result of all of this, my young client, who had made a life out of doing what he was told, now had massive inner turmoil. So, what does a person, who normally does what is expected of him, do when he's told two different things by two roughly equal external power sources? This is where my client came to me – smack dab in the middle of this angst and confusion. He couldn't make a decision to save his life. For, no longer was the path of 'shoulds' a clear out.

The second path is the one of rebellion. What this path lacks in originality (as it is rarely little more than going in the opposite direction of whatever is the first path – the path of 'shoulds', of explicit expectations) it makes up for in spirit. This path will feel like an original path to the person traversing it, and it will look like it to others, simply because it is out in the forbidden land prohibited by whomever is still the real power source in this person's life. However, just because it is forbidden by the external, other person does not mean it is authentic, or the true path for the person traversing it. It is nothing more than a big 'Screw you!' to the person(s) seeking to control this person's life. It is full of hubris and gusto, but it is, in the end, a *reaction*. It is not a self-generated action.

Now, this Path of the Middle Finger requires carving it yourself – going it alone – but you can already see the path because it is made visible simply by the fact that your external power source doesn't want you to take it. It is defined by the negation of something else, something expected. Further, The Path of the Middle Finger is also far more easily endeavored because it is cooked up and kept boiling by the hurt and anger rising up from the depths of your soul. But that doesn't mean it's your path, your *authentic* path, reflective of your deepest inner truths. It's just a path of defiance, still dependent upon an external power source for that initial pulse and push.

Go too far down the Path of the Middle Finger, become too deeply ensconced in your rebellion against your external power source, and it becomes a willingness to take yourself down as a mighty "SCREW YOU!!!!" to your father, your mother, or whomever is trying to control your life, whomever has been trying to tell you that who you really are doesn't matter. The person driven by the most violent and angry 'Screw you' will self-sabotage, self-flagellate, and self-destruct in a sort of, "You think I'm no good and don't matter? Fine! I'll really show you how bad and worthless I am." This person is in no way driven by authenticity and inner truth, only by the pain of negation of his external power sources.

Again, the Path of the Middle Finger takes strength and spirit. It is worthy of respect for that strength it demands. But it must not be confused with a soul-driven path.

The Madly Successful Women Who Are Forever Stuck On The Path Of The Middle Finger

One of the exercises I regularly engage in with my clients is to explore the notion of 'trigger words.' I explain that I have certain words or phrases in my own personal life that are indicators of foul things afoot inside me. These 'trigger words' are indicators of when I am inadvertently going down a path that is not in my best interests. For example, the words 'should' and 'figure out' are huge trigger words for me. When I find myself thinking, 'Man, I need to figure out what I'm going to about...' or when I realize I am saying to myself, 'I should go and...' or 'I should tell him...'. Anytime I find myself using the word 'should' to myself, I know I am about to do something not because I want to do it, but because I am doing it for some external power source – family, girlfriend, society. Anytime I find myself using the words 'I need to figure out...' it is a spot-on perfectly clear indicator I'm trying to force an analysis or force an end result. I'm not letting go, trusting flow, and living in the full knowledge that inspired answers will come at precisely the right moment.

Well, Badass Counseling seems to attract an inordinately high number of extremely driven women. As a result, I have seen a distinct pattern in the trigger words of off-the-charts successful women. There are two phrases intimately tied into each other that have kept these uber-achievers locked in a somewhat gratifying, yet painful and draining life course of supreme accomplishments.

The trigger words that started the whole mad quest in their lives, decades ago, were 'You can't,' 'You'll never...' or some derivative thereof. These words incited them to violence on their own souls in the form of seeking to prove themselves in the eyes of either a mother or father who spoke those fateful words:

- You'll never amount to much
- You can't do...
- You're not good enough to...
- You'll never be worth your weight in salt
- You're not smart enough to...
- You can't become...
- You're not pretty enough to...

These colossally insulting words triggered a whole lot of women to become world-beaters. Further, they gave birth to the three (or four) most glaring and forceful triggers words in the successful woman's head:

I'LL. SHOW. YOU, (expletive)!

If I've got a very driven young or middle-aged woman or a very tired, yet successful middle-aged woman coming to me for counseling, I know for almost absolute certainty that she is stuck on the Path of the Middle Finger. She is a very successful rebel, or rebel-good girl, unwittingly trying to not only prove herself to a parent who never believed in her but break the soul's cement into which are written the powerful words, "I'm not good enough."

Thus, one of my tasks is to help her see that those triggers words – *I'll show you!* – are reflexively, compulsively driving her to do things that I do not believe her soul actually longs to do. And the fatigue she is experiencing is a direct result of spending a life on a path that was never hers, to begin with. Seeking a life of greater peace and happiness, she must move into greater deliberateness. Specifically, she must first become aware. She must look for and see, or hear, which words or phrases are ringing in her head whenever she is about to take an action, great or small. Is this next action driven by the words, 'I'll show you'? Or, perhaps it is driven by 'I should' or 'Screw you, I'm gonna...'.

These trigger words, and more, are immediate indicators that the action you are about to engage in is driven by an external power source, not your own, authentic voice. And really, the point of this book is that there is no lasting joy on any path chosen by an external power source.

The Third Path
The very real and not-so-obvious truth about crossroads is that there is always The Third Path. It's there, but you can't see it. And the reason it's not visible is because it has not been made by anyone else, yet. It doesn't exist yet as a path. It's original, to be defined by you. You have to make it yourself. You have to cut away the brush and carve your own path, which is the very definition of an authentic life. You are authoring it.

The Third Path is the path that is neither determined by or even instigated by any exterior influence. Instead, it rises up from the depths of your soul as little more than a pulse, a vibe, a feeeeeel of "I know I have to do this. I know I have to go this route where there is no route." The Third Path is born of your unique, individual authorship; born of the very voice of the Universe speaking its very specific and unusual message to your individual existence. It is to make a path where there is no path.

In Arthurian Legend, when the knights would begin their grail quest, leaving Camelot, they would walk their horse along the edge of the great forest, looking and waiting for the place where there was no path, the starting point that just felt right. For the quest or journey to be original it had to be where no one had trod before. It had to be an outgrowth of the knight's own instincts and calling. The knight's task was to engage original experience and offer interpretation of it for others to experience. If there is no originality, it is merely a repetition of someone else's path (someone else's interpretation of life), and therefore not requiring courage, and therefore not noble or worthy of his life.

No one else can know what the Universe, or God or your soul, speaks to you. NO ONE can tell you what your Third Path is. That's part of what makes it so scary. And that fear is what makes it so much easier to just keep on listening to all the other voices in your life, all the external power sources that want to tell you what to do. The risk in listening to others, rather than yourself, is almost non-existent. They keep liking you and you get to keep residing in the safety of no-risk.

But, the Third Path requires the sheer silence necessary to feel one's own inner voice. And this is only accomplished by first weeding out, or at least severely pushing back, all the voices in your head that want to run your life and tell you which paths to take. Yet it also requires letting go of your own urge to say, "Screw you." And that's no small feat. Standing up to, standing against, and ultimately removing or reducing the voices of others in your life is one of life's scariest endeavors. Perhaps even more difficult is the task of ridding yourself of your lifelong reflex to stubbornly resist external influences. It is to cease being so tuned into the influence of others and cease to be so controlled by them, always doing their opposite. Yet, it is also the precursor to peace. And it is from that peace, within that peace, that your own true voice finds life and bubbles right up to the surface, yearning to be felt and lived. It is in that peace that your own first step and next steps become visible. And that is the compass for the Third Path, requiring neither shoulds nor rebellion.

On my left forearm is tattooed an excerpt from a quote by the great author and mythologist of the 20th Century, Joseph Campbell. In his *Power of Myth* interviews with Bill Moyers for PBS, he discusses precisely this notion of authoring one's own path and the price it exacts:

> MOYERS: But aren't many visionaries and even leaders and heroes close to the edge of neuroticism?
> CAMPBELL: Yes, they are.
> MOYERS: How do you explain that?
> CAMPBELL: They've moved out of the society that would have protected them, and into the dark forest, into the world of fire, of original experience. Original experience has not been interpreted for you, and so you've got to work out your life for yourself. Either you can take it or you can't. You don't have to go far

off the interpreted path to find yourself in very difficult situations. The courage to face the trials and to bring a whole new body of possibilities into the field of interpreted experience for other people to experience – that is the hero's deed.

The hero's deed – that is, to be the hero of your own life – is to feel and live the voice of the Third Path at every crossroads as it rises up from within, sometimes as a thunderous knowing what is what, and where one is going, but often as little more than a quiet pulse, or ping. And that ping requires having the spiritual ability to engage solitude, still one's life and mind, and feeeel it rising up from within.

Journaling Recommendation
1. Which path have you spent most of your life on, the first or the second – shoulds or 'Screw You'? Which are you on now? Is your greater instinct to conform and do what's expected of you or to rebel and take the 'Path of the Middle Finger'?
2. Do you have the courage to begin to cut a new, third path?
3. What would the third path look like, for you? What's the first scary step?
4. What's the scariest part about carving your own path where there presently isn't one?

Song Recommendation
I'm a big fan of this song, by **Queen**. It both inspires and well-defines clarity of purpose, which is precisely what comes when you have the courage to go your Third Path, when you have the courage to be original and follow the calling of greatness from the pilot light of your soul. Buy and savor the tune and message of *One Vision*.
https://www.youtube.com/watch?v=kvpsEKSNkkAOneVision

CHAPTER 32

'YOU'LL KNOW'

My father tells the story of when he was a student in his mid-20s still working his way through college and seminary, before eventually entering the ministry and spending over 60 years as a Lutheran pastor in North Dakota, Texas, and Minnesota. He had, one day in a back stairway coming up from the laundry room of the dormitory, met a beautiful young woman who, in his words, 'made my heart go pitter-patter' – the same criterion he would offer to his five sons and daughter as a means for knowing when someone was in the ballpark.

Then, over the course of a few years, as he got to the know girl better and better, he felt his love for this woman grow and deepen, until one day, back on the large family farm in Northern Minnesota, he asked his mother a fateful question. She was working in the traditional blue and white Swedish kitchen, preparing one of an incessant string of big meals for the men at work in the fields. As he sat at the table and talked about the latest goings-on in his busy life, his mother, Walborg, listened. Paring knife in hand, she chopped, sliced, and skinned – apron around her waist, summer sun coming in the window over the sink.

But the conversation and flurry of meal prep stopped cold when LeRoy, whether in Swedish or English, asked what would be a fateful question, "Mother, how do you know when the girl is the right one?"

Walborg, neither shocked nor caught off guard, as if she had seen it coming in her second of four sons, quietly stopped, set down her paring knife on the counter and slowly, wiping her hands on her apron, turned to the eager young man. Resting one hand on that same counter to steady her powerful, farm-built frame, she paused to look into young LeRoy's eyes. She had met the girl precipitating this question and was impressed by her rather severe work ethic and full fluency in her own role in making a farm work. Walborg liked her very much, but it was not in her belief system or her idea of motherhood to force the hand of any of her five children, especially on the very largest of life questions.

Pausing, staring her son in the eye, in the most serious of voices, she almost inaudibly transferred words that would never leave my father and forever frame every one of his life decisions, well beyond this major one. Pulled back to her native tongue by the gravity of the moment, she firmly, quietly stated, in Swedish,

"Du vet."

And with that, she silently turned, picked up the knife, and returned to the work of the day, knowing the conversation was done and the decision was now out of her hands, firmly planted where it belonged: in the boy, plunging him deep into thought.

Her wisdom? Seemingly contrary to the words of pastors and parents alike, she delivered the most powerful words she had in her to pass on to her son:

"You'll know."

No longer content to tell her adult children what to do, but insisting they commune with their own inner voice at that deep spot where it meets the spirit of the Universe, she pushed her son into that leap-of-faith realm. She insisted he learn life's greatest lesson: you must trust your own inner voice, your own intuition. It will tell you when the path is right, if you have the ears to hear.

The words of that old Swedish woman resound down through the decades, speaking even now to you and me. The fretting and stewing we engage in, day in and day out, are quite unnecessary. For the absolute fact of the matter is:

When you're in tune to your inner voice,
When you have quieted the voices of fear and anxiety,
there is no stewing required.
You'll simply know.

And if you don't know, it means you either have not stilled your life well enough to feel the creative pulse of the Universe succinctly sending its message to what should be a receptive soul, quiet and ready; or, quite frankly, it is just not yet your time to know. It's not time and it's not right. You're being called to action in other areas. And no amount of trying to force the equation or force the resolution, will bring any amount of clarity or the power that clarity brings. If it is your path, you'll know...when it is time to know.

If you don't truly know with the resolution of a clanging bell that this is your path, it is not your path, no matter how much you want it to be your path, want the girl to be the one, or want to have whatever the path seems to offer.

Some call it 'intuition', some 'the voice of God', some call it 'gut instinct', some 'the voice of your own soul'. But what is consistent in them all is the experience of *knowing*, the experience of clarity.

This is the formula for all of life, great and small: You'll know. Your sole job is to day in and day out, moment to moment, tune in with a quiet soul. It is to be so present, so rested, so at peace in your soul, even in the most harried of times, that you can feel the pulse of the Universe in that moment speaking to you.

Of course, to have the self-control and self-in-tuneness necessary to oscillate between dead-stop, calm meditation and 100mph attacking life with your hair on fire when called to act requires focusing on self-knowledge, self-trust, and self-discipline. It means spending this life you've been given on more than just the acquisition of more crap, the longing for greater leisure and adventures, and the clinging and mad clinging to security.

I know all of this sounds cockamamie to a whole lot of people. But it is the most profound and very, very real truth I am capable of speaking in my 50 years of mining life for its deepest truths and 25 years of teaching and strengthening others to do likewise. The whole truth of the Universe, particularly that which you need to know right now, is in that place of peace and receptiveness. Until you can throttle back to that place and sit in it without agitation, fear, or any overwhelming emotion, you're not ready, not there, and not likely to experience peace or lasting happiness anytime soon. There is no way 'you'll know' what is you, your path, and the perfect decision for you, *until you shut your piehole and start listening.* We listen by first clearing out the voices that are not native to who we are, the voices that conflict and cloud our vessel, the voices that depress and drain our energy or push us to mad anxiety.

You'll know, but only when you have the courage to stop listening to all that causes you to not know. That is the day life begins. That is the day you commence your relationship with your own self.

Journaling Recommendation
1. This may sound like an incredibly dumb question. However, if you were to be totally honest with yourself, right now, in your journaling, write out the answer to this question: what is the god's-honest truth when I ask you, What do you know; I mean truly know? Not, what are you willing to admit, but what is your truth? Can you feel it, yet? Let me put it this way: what is the truth that has been there, all along, that you have been avoiding, constantly second-guessing, or simply not seeing because it was hiding in plain sight?
2. What is the great unanswered question of your life or your future? What is it that you do *not* have resolution to?
3. Is it possible that you know exactly what your truth is? Is it possible that you already know the answer to what you claim is the great unanswered question of your life? Is it possible that your problem is *not* that you don't know what your path or truth is but that you're terrified to act on it?
4. Living a truth or a new dream demands being judicious in to whom you reveal it, much as a tiny shoot coming out of the ground needs to be protected from too much sun, too much rain, not enough of both, and the constant threat of rabbits or a human shoe. In what ways do you need to be judicious in what you share about what you're being, saying, doing, having, wanting, believing and becoming? Who might do your dream/shoot harm? Can you be judicious in what you reveal to that person(s)?
5. What's going on inside you, as you consider what you really know about your life and path? What do you feel as you consider those who might undermine your new paths and purposes?

CHAPTER 33

CLOSED DOORS ARE GREATER BLESSINGS THAN OPEN DOORS

One of the most difficult concepts to get one's head around can be that everything is gift – every negative experience, every depression, every sorrow, every loss, every frustration, every disappointment. We are so programmed into thinking good things are good and bad things are bad. But, what if the 'bad things' weren't inherently bad? In fact, what if the supposedly bad stuff in your life were, in fact, the single greatest blessing of your life, upside-down as that may sound? In fact, what if the greater the feeling of negativity to something, the more powerful a blessing it is?

On the spiritual journey to intimate relationship with your own self, you will learn more about yourself and about life from the supposedly negative stuff than any of the positive stuff, but only if you open your eyes and your heart and mind to mine the experience for the gems of wisdom it is holding in its hand. It is to ask the question, "How is this seemingly negative, painful thing the single greatest blessing of my life? More pointedly, what is this horrible experience trying to teach me that I have just not been learning?" Think about it, teams make more changes, adjustments, and growth from losses and mistakes than wins. When you're winning, you don't change significantly. Why would you? That can quickly lead to stagnancy. Losses reveal weaknesses. Thus, losses and setbacks are the soil of greatness, if they are mined for the insights they bear.

Everything – and I mean everything – has the power to radically change your life for the better. Yes, even death sentences, terminal illness, loss of a child, death of a dream, divorce, and more. You name it and I've probably encountered it either in my own life or in my 25 years of doing this stuff – working with cops and convicts, war vets and veterinarians, hedge-fund CEOs and hog farmers, professional actors and Olympic athletes, world-class musicians and faculty of the top universities, the destitute and the most drug-addled success stories.

I know that this one shift in your core beliefs – from believing bad experiences and suffering are 'bad' and should be run from, at all costs, to seeing pain and suffering as holding life-changing insights and wisdom – changes everything. More than almost anything in your life, this shift and the openness it requires completely change the game; or, they change how you attack the game. Accompanied by the journaling necessary to accompany such questions and really mine them (so it's not just something you're doing in your head but are actually getting out of you), this shift in core beliefs enacts transformation of a life. After the pruning, growth begins. Real growth, like you've never seen.

Add a hearty dose of courage on top of that mix – courage to face the hard truths and the real sources of raw sewage in your life – and transformation comes rapidly.

One 40-something client had a father, growing up, who was quite critical of her weight. As with a great many women, each of her days brought obsessive thoughts about her body and weight, though to a rather unusual degree. "The result, Sven," she remarked, "is that I've stayed in shape, have kept a great figure even after childbirth, and now I actually make a living teaching others fitness and martial arts. It's bizarre and I kinda hate to say it, on one hand, but in some ways Dad's obsession with weight was one of the best things that ever happened to me, even though it caused a lot of pain, before."

On a somewhat smaller level, I regularly remind my clients that closed doors are a far greater blessing than open ones. Discovering who we really are requires discovering who we are not. Closed doors are the biggest sign of the Universe talking to you. I spent decades trying to beat down doors that I wanted to enter. And, as usual, the Universe won, refusing to open the relationship and career doors I wanted, unless I radically contorted who I was, which was something I was unwilling to do and in the long run incapable of doing. The Universe, in other words, was doing me a favor.

A closed door is the Universe giving you a message: either keep trying to get in, or walk away and go to what is next. And, truth is, only you will know which to do, only you will know which feels right. The knowing can only come from being still. And eventually, if that door does come down – boom! – you are moving boldly in the direction you feel called to go. But if you keep trying and the Universe (which is far stronger than you) keeps it shut, then you gotta ask yourself, "Hey, is this a clue? Maybe this isn't my path." And it's hard as heck to let go of a path we really want or feel called to, especially when we've invested great time and effort into it. But a message is a message. In the words of the literary critic, Neil Forsythe:

> *"If the path is bad,*
> *an obstruction is good."*

Closed doors are always a blessing. They not only test resolve, but more often they guide us. And, what we find as we age – assuming we're tuned into the small voice of the Universe, rather than just always waiting for the big wallops – is that we can do far less beating down of the doors, yet still get startling results. We just sense things earlier. We are more receptive to the subtle nudges. We sense sooner that it's time to let go of this door, and the lust for what's behind it no longer has the power to fully consume you and enflame you. We do far less trying to bend the Universe to our own will, and instead attune ourselves to the will of the Universe communing with our own soul. For there is a peace and a power, a sense of purpose and a path that just feeeeel soooo right. Life becomes more fluid. You still attack life, when inspired, but only when inspired. The days of beating down doors like a full-tantrum three year-old kicking, screaming and rolling about on the carpet are long gone.

But all of this demands letting go of the very American notion that I must – absolutely must! – impose my will on the world and force my wants to happen. And it's just doggone tough to let go of the brute force method. It's hard to trust that things happen when I don't try to make things happen. That's a really tricky concept to both understand and, more, to actually live out. That action of, daily, letting go of forced action demands tuning into when an action is forced and when it's flowing or inspired, which of course requires the self-discipline of stillness to know the difference. Then it must be followed by the capacity to actually let go of the desired action and results.

This is where meditation, releasing/accepting, journaling, therapy (either self-therapy or with a gifted counselor), and all of the spiritual disciplines become so critical. They are what facilitate the letting go, the throttling back, and the trusting that all is flowing, even if I'm not working at it. The essence of the spiritual path and all it brings are the spiritual disciplines of rest, calm, journaling, physical vigor, inspired and intense action, meditation and so forth.

Journaling Recommendation
1. List the top five things, events, situations, or people that you have considered the biggest curses of your life, that would be almost impossible to find good in.
2. Now, under each one, write the questions: How was/is this event or person the single greatest blessing of my life? What was this thing sent to teach me about myself? About life? In what way is this learning I received precisely what I need for life, moving forward?
3. What have been the 3-5 biggest closed doors, disappointments or frustrations of your life?
4. How was each one perfect? What would you have missed out on, quite possibly, if you had gotten what you wanted?
5. Even if you never say it aloud or forgive the person who did it, what if the most wretched, horrible thing of your life was sent for your pruning – a gift from the gods? What if you simply can't see and don't want to admit the gems of wisdom it holds in its hand?

Bonus Tracks
Core Readers: Move to the next chapter. Advanced Readers, here you go:
- Bonus Track 13: When The Soul Burps Gold

CHAPTER 34

DUMBEST EXERCISE EVER....BUT IT WORKS!

For those who are struggling greatly with any sense at all of self-worth, I offer what I concede to be the dumbest exercise ever. And it is so because we've all seen some version of it already, whether on late night TV or elsewhere.

Yet, for as simple and laughable as it is, you'd be shocked how monstrously terrifying it is for a great many of my clients, to the point where they simply cannot bring themselves to do it, no way, no how. I had one client who abjectly refused, for weeks, to even consider doing it, until I said I'd have to consider stopping my work with her.

Simply this, I want you to stand in front of a full-length mirror, if you have one, buck naked, both physically and spiritually – seeing yourself inside and out – and state six or seven sentences several times. And I want you to do it twice a day for thirty days. It'll take you five minutes a day. Heck, do it for a week and tell me it doesn't move the needle, even a small amount in that small time.

Stand in front of that mirror, buck naked, and say with vigor:
- I actually (expletive) like me!
- I'm a sexy mother (expletive)!
- I'm beautiful!
- I'm smart as (expletive)!
- I (expletive) love how creative I am!
- People (expletive) love me; heck, I love me!
- I'm (expletive) brilliant!

Sounds stupid, doesn't it? You're laughing right now at how dumb it is.

Yet, as I said, you'd be shocked how powerful it is. And do you know how I know, because no sooner do I say it than you wince from doing so. You can't do it. Or you resist it, because somewhere in you, A) you don't believe it can work; but also B) you don't believe the words. And so, a full frontal assault on what you've previously believed your truths to be is one more mechanism for breaking the hardened cement of your core, false beliefs.

Granted, this must be done in conjunction with the other concepts and exercises of this book, specifically identifying your core beliefs and fears, and your 3 Binary Gates under them, and then diving into and changing them. But it is a powerful and scary tool, nonetheless.

I have had numerous clients so full of self-loathing, both physically and spiritually, that they had removed all mirrors from their house, only worn long-sleeve shirts and full-length pants in public, or simply avoided going out into public, altogether.

And, of course, that hiding of oneself physically is but a metaphor for the hiding of what a person (wrongly) perceives to be their own dirty, hideous soul. So deeply and vigorously has the great lie been implanted in them that their life is fully consumed by misery, self-loathing, even hatred, and ultimately longing for escapes. That's why this is such a powerful exercise. It is the breaking of old metaphors and old beliefs. It is part of a greater process of going directly to the pain, rather than continuing to run from it, and allowing that same pain to wash over you and pass out of you.

Moths And The Necessity Of Sitting In The Pain

There was a young boy who, while playing in his back yard one day, found a cocoon attached to the leaf of a low-lying branch. Very excited, he stood staring at the little white cloud puff. Then, as a million little boys had done before him, he snapped the small branch. brought it inside, and inserted into a Mason jar he retrieved from his mother's cold storage room. He added a few extra leaves, screwed on the gold lid, then used a screwdriver to puncture the lid with a few air holes. Ever so gently, he then carried his glass treasure into his bedroom and slid it onto the dresser, proud of his mini-home construction and eager to watch the drama unfold.

Well, one day evolved into the next. Each day, he came home after school and scampered into his room to see if there was movement. Each day, nothing, until one day he noticed the tiniest of cracks in the little white pillow. Giddy with fulfilled anticipation, he was struck with an idea – a wonderful, helpful idea.

He gently pulled the jar from the dresser, grabbed his brother's mini-toolkit, took jar and kit out into the warm sun of the back step, and plopped himself down for his first foray into micro-surgery. Possessed by the brilliant idea of exhuming the butterfly from the billowy casket of his past life, he extracted the small X-ACTO knife from his brother's toolkit, then made the smallest and most delicate of incisions down the length of the cocoon. As expected, this gave the moth inside the perfect opportunity to slip out and begin her new life.

By this time, the boy's mother and father had come out of the house and were standing at the door admiring their boy's handiwork and the gorgeously colored moth that emerged. As it stood and fluttered it wings, the boy squealed with delight. "Watch, Daddy! Are you watching?" The three of them were riveted by the beginning movements of this new life. The beautiful little creature, as if aware of her audience, extended her wings and flew off a few feet to a nearby blade of grass where it alighted. Then to the petal of a lily close by. Then back in the direction of the boy. Little hops here and there, a foot or two off the ground. Again and again, she more jumped than flew from blade to branch, until the boy queried, "Mommy, why isn't she flying away?" Mom and Dad were wondering the same thing as concern creeped over their faces. And it wasn't long before the gorgeous new life settled on the concrete of the back step and stood there, for what seemed the longest time, 'til eventually she lay down, dead. Unable to fly, she was unable to live, much to the shock and sadness of the boy and his parents.

A quick internet search later, the young family discovered that the small boy's attempt to help had actually produced the opposite result. As it turned out, the moth needed to fight her way out of her own cocoon. For, the struggle is what gives her wings strength. The struggle is necessary. To be confronted with, sit in, and be required to fight her own way out of her pain and prison is precisely what gives power and flight to the new life. There is no shortcut or end-around. The pain is the cure; the struggle is the strength.

Journaling Recommendation

1. What is the pain you continue to avoid? What is the part of you that you most loathe? Do you have the courage to finally sit in it and allow it to wash over you and pass out of you? Do you have the courage to change your language about that one aspect (and others) of yourself?

2. What is the single most difficult, positive thing you could possibly say about yourself to yourself? What is the one affirmation you could almost never believe? Why? What power source implanted that belief into you? I challenge you to make that affirmation the one at the very top of your list, the one you do most repeatedly.

Song Recommendation

I'm recommending *Helplessly Hoping* here, https://www.youtube.com/watch?v=v0RC21L2xq8HelplesslyHoping by **Crosby, Stills and Nash**. It's a love song, of sorts, but the crossover to the relationship between you and your own soul is not hard to recognize. For those who are a bit saltier (and like rap), try the song by Minneapolis group, **Atmosphere**, *GodLovesUgly*. https://www.youtube.com/watch?v=RS_3pED-wJoGodLovesUgly

PARENTING

CHAPTER 35

EVEN GOOD PARENTS CAN SERIOUSLY HARM A CHILD'S SOUL

There is a quote that I can never remember or find the author of (which bothers me, because it's such a pithy, brilliant insight) that so powerfully sums up the necessary path to lasting joy and authentic living:

> *"No man is truly free,*
> *until he can live as though his father is dead."*
> --Unknown

It would be very easy to pass this off as derivative of the old saw every-man-is-forever-trying-to-win-his-father's-approval. And while there is a measure of that in this quote, there is a far deeper reason for the necessity of the parent-killing, or living 'as though' the parent is dead, as it were. (It should go without saying, but the quote can be read for any gender and either parent, not necessarily same-gender parent.)

It's the negative messages of the father (or mother) that got pressed into the cement of your soul. It is the disapproving, critical, dehumanizing voice of your parent that is ringing in your head, on an endless loop. It is the very real presence of your parent (or primary power source) that is killing you.

Heck, that parent may be long dead, but the voice is still there, isn't it? The actual death of a parent is often far worse. For, death can bring a sort of romance for only the good of the past, a sense of nostalgia for things they said or did. Or, it can bring a sense of greater power, wisdom, or truth to what they said, even when precisely the opposite is, in actuality, true. The deceased parent may have been completely full of hateful, demeaning, or simply meaningless crud. But their death and the wistfulness that can accompany it, not to mention filial loyalty, often lead to a substantiation of words that never had value to begin with.

Or, in many cases, it's actually easier for the child (whatever age she might be) to separate herself from the parent's messages when she hates the parents or has a crummy relationship with the parents, today. But, in another vexing conundrum, the parent lives and the adult child actually has a decent, or improving, relationship with the now-aging parent. Thus, the adult child must kill the parent of his/her childhood – rage against it, call it out for being wrong, delinquent, and utterly inept, even if never actually saying it *to* the parent, himself – while simultaneously engaging in a somewhat loving, new relationship with a parent that is either too old, too frail, or past it to own the crimes of a childhood marred. And that tightrope is no small thing, even while it's a perfect example of the fact that the answer, the retribution, the validation, the change that is really needed is not outside you, but inside you, cliché as that my sound.

In yet another oddity, *the most difficult* parent to kill is not the parent who is alive, dead, or greatly loathed or a better person, since they got older. The most wrenching situation of parental control or domination (or significant influence) to extract yourself from is when the parent is, and pretty much always has been, loved and admired. Because the parent did some things (or many things) right and the adult-child has mixed feelings – genuine fondness and (perhaps deeply buried) anger or loathing. When you love and respect them, first off, it can be very hard to differentiate their values from your values, their truths from your truths. It can actually feel like an unloving act to be something other than what the parents are. As such, it brings guilt. Or it can feel like a disappointment to oneself or to the parent for not measuring up by going the same path as the parent, even if the parent him- or herself doesn't see your path as lesser (which is part of what causes you to love and admire them, in the first place).

For example, in my own life, it took me well into my third or fourth decade of life to admit that I am basically an atheist, at least in relation to the religion of my parents, my upbringing and all that I loved, growing up. (To be clear, I'm an intellectual atheist, rejecting over time most of the strata of nonsense contrived by systematic theologians and followers, be they of the

20th or the 1st Century. However, on the experiential level I'm very much a believer in something I, a words guy, really cannot articulate. I've just seen and experienced way too much of the inexplicable – stuff that neither science nor I have any answers for – to not believe in some great Unknown.) Also, I had to admit that I am simply not as giving of myself as my parents are. I have profound admiration for my parents and I know that no matter who I am, they have only love for me. They may not always understand me, and perhaps they never really have, but they never stop loving me, in thought, word and deed. And my fear in coming out as an atheist and more selfish person was that I feared letting down, hurting, and worrying two people I madly love, especially now in their 90th year. But I had to do it. I had to, in my own self, kill the parent and parental influence (that was causing me to parent non-deliberately – ie against my own values and also my own inner nature), and kill my inclination to kill myself to save the parent or not do the parent harm.

Over the decades, I have had numerous clients and even some friends discontinue counseling with me at the point I required them to write a letter to their (living or dead) parents (or a dominating/influential sibling or extended family member), a letter I never require a client to send, only to write. Tough cops and military folk, successful people in all industries, even a few psychologists and clergy. So many balk when I hold their feet to the fire to express in writing the ways their parent/parents let them down, hurt them, frustrated them, and disappointed them; and when I require my client to then in the same letter express the fullness of their feelings of hurt, anger, sorrow, and even rage. Even when I will help them see and admit in the counseling session many of these things (often through what they inadvertently reveal or leave clues to in the autobiography I require of them), they will turn tail, deny, avoid, resist offering any greater expression in written form of the truths that rock their soul, or even stop counseling. Or, interestingly, some will even, later, flat out deny admissions they made in our counseling sessions or wrote in their autobiography about parents, when I push them to write it out and write out their real feelings again, but in the form of a letter.

That's how terrifying the truth can be, particularly as related to a beloved parent. They see anything but love and respect for the parent as a betrayal, even when the facts clearly point to great disappointments and the insertion of treacherous self-beliefs into the now-adult child, when a parent did some things right and it's painful to look at what they did wrong. With seeming betrayal comes further self-loathing by the client. The thought of what they saw as turning on a parent (even a dead one) – not to mention fear of realizing and admitting maybe the parent didn't love them as much as previously thought or that the parent did some really messed up things, even amid the love – was unbearable and they bolted. Parenthetically, I've seen people exhibit the same behavior pattern when the person in need of killing was not a parent but a lover (usually unrequited, to some degree). They so idolized and longed for the lover that they couldn't bear to look at the truth of what the lover did and how the lover made them feel.

And these same clients and friends then cannot figure out why, why, why their lives never seem to change and why they can't figure out their own inertia or incessant inner wrangling. To fully admit the truths of their life would turn everything on its head; villains become heroes and heroes villains. And, for some people, that's just too much to bear. So, sadly, they will continue to suffer and lose more time, until the pain gets bad enough.

Until you can kill that parent of your childhood (or at least begin by radically pushing back their influence in your life and their presence in your head and imprints of your soul), until you can admit that (despite their best efforts) they blew it as parents in one or two key ways, despite other successes, you'll never get out of your crud, never be free. It will always be in you. You can pretend to be the together adult, but the real wound and negative core beliefs are still eating you up inside. Guaranteed.

Your parents may be wonderful people now. I have no idea. But they screwed up as parents, at least in one or two critical ways. They may have had a world of great intentions. They may have done plenty of stuff right. But in the end, even pretty good parents can implant very powerful negative messages in their children. And until the parent and the core beliefs they wrought are put to death inside you, you will never know peace. Never. Simply, never.

Premature Or Foolish Forgiveness

Further, it can be so easy, upon seeing the messages the parent conveyed to you and admitting what untruths the parent implanted in you, to immediately follow with, "But I understand why they did it, because they had x, y, or z going on" or "They had pressures and lies in them from their own parents."

Every bit of that may be true. In fact, it most certainly is true.

But, to jump to forgiveness or even excusing the parent too quickly is the giant mistake. It's the adult talking, rather than the child in this situation being given his due. As a child, you were saddled with oppressive, negative messages that you've had to bear your whole life, messages that were in complete, or near-complete, denial of your true value. You've had to carry that your whole life. And now it's time to hand it back, whether the parent is living or dead, even if only to take it from inside yourself and move it outside yourself. It's time to see it fully and to admit the breadth and depth of its impact and to *make the parent of your childhood own it, so that you no longer will.*

I mentioned premature forgiveness briefly in an earlier chapter, but it is so loaded that it bears repeating. Forgive too soon and you, the adult-child, keep owning and carrying the burden that was never yours, to begin with. For, to excuse it or 'understand' them too early is to fundamentally place the parent's needs over your own. It is to say to life, "I don't matter" or "It's not that big of a deal" when, in fact, it is a giant deal. It is to move too quickly past something that needs to be sat in and soaked in. Until you fully weigh and accept the gravity of what they did to you, and that you were just a child, and that it was wrong, and that you've been carrying this doggone colossally heavy burden your whole life, you will never, ever be able to let the full weight of it go. Your forgiveness will have been tragically misplaced, premature.

You must realize, you got screwed, kid.

Until you can fully admit that *and* see the impact of that screwage in the many aspects of your life – all stemming from your core beliefs – you will never have full healing. It simply can't happen.

Until your father's (or mother's) negative beliefs about you are out of you, they are still in you. And the real you is basically dead.

279

You are a walking corpse. And you simply cannot, by definition, ever be happy, at peace, of a clear mind, and of a clean heart if you're dead inside.

Questioning The Theory

A dear friend of mine, who is very quiet, Ivy League-educated, a deep thinker and whom I've counseled occasionally and have profound respect for, recently remarked over Mexican food, "Yeah Sven, I don't buy the 3 Binary Gates theory you've been telling me for the last 15 years. People get all sorts of messages, as kids. It's never just one message of 'Oh, you don't matter' or 'You're just not good enough.'"

"Great point," I replied. "But when you're a child, it's not the full breadth of messages received that matters; it's the effect. The effect on the child, particularly as the message is repeated a handful of times, over time, is that the child really starts to believe the negative message, especially when the negative is backed up by the actions of the parent, quite regardless of concomitant positive messaging."

Think about this: When you have your end of the year review, at work, and your boss tells you ten things you're doing great and the two things you need to work on and improve, which are you going to be thinking about as you walk out the door, even over the next few days, and as you celebrate New Years? You're thinking about those doggone two things that your boss nailed you on.

As adults, you and I tend to do that when we get any sort of feedback on just about anything? We tend to hear the negative far more loudly than the positives, right? Right! So, how much more prone to focusing on the negative feedback is a child? How much more vulnerable is a child, who by his nature just believes what adults say, particularly the ones he/she most loves and respects? It doesn't even take repetition for the child to begin to own it. But add that repetition and even the mild negative message becomes deeply pressed into the cement of the child's soul. It quickly becomes concretized as the very bedrock of the individual's identity, even if such an outcome was never, ever intended by the parent.

But a parent will defend herself, up and down, to the adult-child with, 'But you're not seeing all the *good* I did.' Irrelevant. The bad is more powerful than the good.

Recognizing this extreme susceptibility to negative influences that children have, is it really any grand stretch to understand how even generally good parents can do some serious damage? Working my way through college and graduate school, I worked in many restaurants, getting to know many chefs. I was taught by these masters of ingredients, chemistry, heat/cold, and recipes that there are certain recipes and certain ingredients that are so sensitive – so requiring of a gentle touch and extreme care – that even the most brilliant master chef can easily mess them up on any given night. Ask a pianist about *Rach 3* or Bach's *Well-Tempered Clavier.* Ask a coach, personal trainer, or serious (natural) bodybuilder about the tightrope of the Holy Grail of simultaneously growing serious muscle and staying trim. Ask a trader or investor about the extreme volatility of dealing in derivatives. Ask even a command pilot with thousands of hours of flight time about flying aircraft in wind shears and unpredictable air. Heck, one of my clients was a former drug dealer intimately familiar with the production side of marijuana, who informed me that even the tiniest fraction of lighting errors in growing marijuana can result in the loss of an entire crop, or at the very least a radical reduction in quality and, hence, profitability. In a great many professions, arts, and sciences there are certain elements and situations so tenuous, so fickle, or so unsteady, or so temperamental that even the most accomplished in the field can screw them up. In Formula One racing, the cars are such insanely finely tuned, handcrafted works of art, really, that even the world's most experienced and gifted drivers routinely overtax, misuse, and mess them up.

Children are the same way, times 1000. Their spiritual development is so fragile in those earliest years that even a very deliberate parent can do damage. An adult, even a very well-meaning one, can say something just once, or never meaning harm, or in complete jest to a child, but the soul of a child has no filter or capacity to differentiate kidding from reality, large message from small. Thus, if it's heard, it gets in; if it's repeated, it sticks.

Sometimes, it doesn't even require repetition. One of the 3 Binary Gates gets closed. Like the most difficult recipes, the soul of a child is so sensitive, so volatile, so utterly brittle that even a master can screw it up. Even the most loving parent can screw up. Even a rather good parent can simultaneously and unwittingly deliver two exact opposite messages to a child – simultaneously pouring love into the child's Love Cup and poking a hole in the child's Love Cup. Chew on that one for a minute. Thus, part of the damage that can happen to a child's soul is not just that negative messages get pressed into the soul (closing the Gates) and the Cup gets damaged, but that positive ones do, as well, such that confusion is bred inside the child. A neurotic pinging between 'I am no good' and 'I am loved', between 'I don't matter' and 'the real me *does* matter' ensues, often lasting decades into adulthood. The Binary Gates stay closed, but other, less-powerful messages of love and mattering pop around inside the child and adult-child. The child never possesses a certainty of self, which is a necessary precursor to peace.

As we've seen, so powerful is a closed Binary Gate in the soul of a person that it can completely undermine (and, in fact, be the ironic cause of) an otherwise massively successful life, later on. Make no mistake, any external successes that adult goes on to achieve are no indicator of soul health or genuine happiness.

I do somewhat agree with my old friend. We do each have a pilot light inside that burns quietly with belief of greatness in one's soul. The positive belief, whatever its original source, is there. But the power of the 3 Binary Gates is so great that it can squelch the power of the pilot light of the soul, completely undermining a life that should be happy.

Journaling Recommendation

1. List the top 10 things you love and adore your parents for? What does it feel like to think about each of those things?
2. Now the toughie: What are the 3-4 things for which you have the strongest negative feelings toward your parents (or the one parent you venerate most)? Describe those things, events, or memories in complete detail.
3. And slightly tougher: Let it all flow; describe in the strongest language the truest, realest, and most powerful feelings you

have toward your parents for each of the memories in #2. If you were to be completely honest, what is it you really feel?

4. If you have no strong negative feelings toward a parent(s), is it possible you're lying to yourself? Is it possible you're denying the truth? Is it possible your instinct to protect your parent, or the memory of your parent (and the guilt of betrayal from doing the opposite), is so great that you'd rather deny and avoid than face it?

5. What are you honestly feeling, right this moment? What does that particular feeling tell us about the weight of this particular conversation to you?

Song Recommendation

I remember this song so vividly from my childhood. I remember it striking me, even as a kid, as perhaps the single most depressing song ever, with such an incredibly powerful message. Yes, it's a song about regrets. But it is so fitting for this discussion of even great parents – well-meaning parents – making colossal mistakes *and* the reality that bad habits get transferred, quite unthinkingly from one generation to the next. Daughters raise their daughters often in the same mistaken system of beliefs and actions in which they themselves were raised, despite their efforts to do just the opposite of how they were raised; same with sons and their sons. Download the song and give a good long meditation on its words and meaning. *Cat's in the Cradle*, https://www.youtube.com/watch?v=bSwL9deXNW8CatsInTheCradle by **Harry Chapin**.

CHAPTER 36

CHILDREN LOVE PARENTS MORE
THAN PARENTS LOVE CHILDREN

I spend a lot of time, outside of the office, thinking about and meditating on the lives and stories of my clients. I see their micro-patterns. I feel the pain of their hardships. And, in the nicest treat for me, I get to be taught by their lives and decisions about human nature. New theories coalesce in me, over time; new ways to attack problems; new meta-patterns become visible; new insights come that might help future clients, friends, or even my own life.

In that vein, over the years, I've seen any number of unusual juxtapositions. Two seemingly unrelated concepts come together to inform and deepen the other, one often turning the other on its head. Here are two unusual concepts, or sets of questions, I've wrestled with, over the decades, that relate to our discussion.

Concept One

One of the distinct phenomena I have seen over the years is the strong willingness of children and adult-children to endure far more at the hands of a parent than a parent would ever endure at the hands of the child, even when that child becomes an adult. I have come to see that there is an odd thing that exists in the relationship between parent and child. A child's loving actions toward a parent are unconditional, even when they shouldn't be; and a parent's actions toward a child are conditional, even when they shouldn't be. It's as if children love parents more than parents love children.

I regularly hear parents proclaim how much their children are the center of their world and the most important thing in their lives, but then go on in the child's teen and adult years to engage in actions that can only be characterized as far less than loving, not the least of which is subtle, or overt, manipulation of the child to meet the parent's needs and wants. Teen and young-adult children will sometimes engage in manipulation, in return, but I'm of the belief that that is conditioned behavior, already taught and given acceptability by the parents.

I have simply seen incredible amounts of damage done to the vast majority of adult-children I work with by the parents who claim to love them. The parent easily makes her feelings of love for the child a justification for *doing* anything she wants to the child at any time, where those actions are clearly not loving and/or definitely conditional. The parent engages in actions the child would never engage in, in return. And I'm not even talking about something as grievous as blatant abuse. I'm talking about that giant gray area where actions can be somewhat defended as loving, but really aren't. Justifiable actions of conditional love for the child easily slip into manipulation of the child; the parent cannot distinguish (or chooses not to distinguish) between the child's best interests from the parent's wants. And those are two very different things.

And, if actions speak louder than words, is it not reasonable to assume that the parents do not love the children; or, more accurately, is it not reasonable to assume that parents do not love children as much as children love parents?

Because of the initial power imbalance in the parent-child relationship – with the parent holding all the power and the newborn none, and the dependency, love, and trust that relationship naturally engenders – a child generally far more loves a parent, particularly when it comes to actions than a parent does a child. Also, because of that same trust, love, and admiration, a child is far more inclined to be vulnerable to the parent than the parent will almost ever be to the child, until the natural decline of age and life energy happens, when the roles of dependency often invert. Repeatedly and ongoingly, a child will submit, even well into adulthood, to the whims, fancies, expectations and power of the parent, very often to the significant detriment of the adult-child. And, if you're reading this book and have a broken or crud-filled Love Cup, I can all but guarantee this is part of the problem you're suffering from. There is a gross imbalance of the love the equation between you and your living or dead parents. Guaranteed. It ain't unconditional both ways, no matter what is being said to the contrary.

The downside of this is that, even into adulthood, a child will feel:

- Guilty for crossing the parent or considering crossing the parent;
- Afraid to stand up to the power of the parent;
- Fearful of disappointing the parent;
- Fearful of losing the parent's love and support;
- Afraid of hurting the parent's feelings, even when the parent might have engaged in some seriously hurtful things toward the child in past or even present years;
- It's not her place to demand that her voice be heard by the parent, even in adulthood;
- Most unwilling to speak the truth of the past, or speak of the child's need to distance him-/herself from the parent (or at least the parent's influence).

So, an adult-child will keep silent, keep his/her truth in, and refrain from standing up to the parent, even the parent of his childhood that still lives strong in his own head. So powerful is the influence, even still, and so great is the love, even if the love is buried deep, that a child will hate/fear few things in life more than the mere thought of truly standing up to the parent. Or, more accurately, the adult-child will hate/fear few things more than the mere thought of simply standing up *and not backing down*, whether the parent actually hears or not. The wobbly-kneed fear is of standing up, finally, in life and not sitting or backing down.

Yet, until you shift in your core beliefs to the notion that your voice, feelings, and truth matter more than the voice, feelings, and truth of your parents, you're screwed. You will never be fully happy. Happiness naturally demands communion with your own voice, giving it the respect and guiding presence in your life that you formerly gave to the voice of your parents.

That doesn't mean you have to be mean to your parents, cut them completely out of your life, or even stand up to them, in-person, at all. Or maybe it does, depending on what feels right in you. What it does mean is that there must absolutely be a shift within in you to you actually mattering enough to squeeze their voice out of your life, banished from your head forever, or at least radically cut back.

There must also be a shift from "love equals obedience" to "it is okay (and good) to love someone and not do what they say." This last shift is a radical one, particularly if the family and parents do not define love that way. If love is seen as obedience, then the 'No!' rising up in the adult-child must be stronger and louder.

For, saying "No!" is when life truly begins, when the showing of loving actions becomes deliberate and appropriate to a situation. That is when you finally begin to claim ownership of your life. Slowly but surely, life changes; happiness comes. The Love Cup begins to fill.

Concept Two

Years ago, I found myself wrestling with the very common notion of unconditional love as the ideal in relationships and parenting. I came to believe that in discussing unconditional love it's very important to separate two things: feelings of unconditional love and unconditional actions of love. For, I have seen so many lives ruined for decades, because someone kept giving loving actions to a person who repeatedly, over time, gave them quite unloving actions, in return. Whether they felt obligated, felt strong feelings of love, or felt afraid to do otherwise, they gave at great personal price to an ungracious receiver.

It left me thinking: Is unconditional love the ideal?

When my children played together, in their younger years, if my daughter was mean to or hit my son (almost never happened), her mother or I would send her to her room for a timeout, accompanied by brief remarks, "We don't hit in this house, young lady. If you are upset with your brother, you need to talk it out with him." My daughter's unloving actions were not rewarded with flowers, cotton candy and pink bows. Nor were they given a generally neutral response or non-response. She had engaged in negative action and received negative action from her parents, appropriate to her age. Called out but not demeaned, she felt what she had done wrong. Her contrition was apparent. Now, through it all, my feelings of love for my daughter are unwavering. I loved and love her immensely. But warm feelings do not translate into soft, lovey-dovey actions in such a moment. No, they are tempered by metered, deliberate actions that are in the best interests of the family, her brother, and her own future development.

If my son were to, later in life, go to jail for hurting another person (hypothetically speaking, because it'd never happen, as he's a very kind soul) I would not show up to visit him in jail with a cake and warm and loving words. My showing actions of love to my son is conditional upon his being a decent human being. There's no doubt I have massive feelings of love for my son, no matter what he does, but he wouldn't get handfuls of cash and big warm hugs.

Or, in a relationship, if someone is repetitively treating me poorly, such that there is a clear and obvious pattern, I do not reward that behavior with loving action. I respond to negative actions with clear, strong boundaries and firm words. My feelings of love are still there, but the loving actions are radically curtailed.

Without the ability to differentiate between and separate loving feelings and loving actions, we allow people to run all over each other and ourselves. Unconditional *feelings* of love are great! Actions of love that are not conditional are a form of slow suicide.

One Last Note

This leaves one question largely unanswered and, in fact, unasked. I've discussed the notion of unconditional love from parent to child, but how does unconditional love look flowing from child to parent. You might be able to guess the answer, based on everything that has led up to this point in the book. However, let me be clear: In the first 25-35 years of the child's life, it is not the child's responsibility to love the parent.

A child will naturally pour love onto a parent, or anyone else, unless the child has been stuffed with fears, anxieties, and expectations to meet the parent's needs. And make no mistake, a child does need to be taught basic standards of respect, decorum, manners, and the like. But it's a giant step from teaching a child how to channel their love to instilling in a child an expectation that they must be a love source for a parent. In fact, this is one area where deliberateness is critical. The child, at any age prior to the decline of the parent, must be taught explicitly that the parent is stronger than the child, and strong enough to take care of herself, which therefore means the child is in no way responsible for showing love or tending to the needs of the parent. What a child, teen, or 20-30-something shows in love to the parent is strictly optional (again, assuming standards of basic respect and kindness are observed).

See, the simple fact of the matter is that a child feeeeels incredibly overwhelming love and admiration for a parent, and it is far too easy for that giant feeling of love to spill into loving actions of responsibility for the parent. That is misplaced love that too easily metastasizes into a child pouring love into the adult Love Cup, rather than always the opposite.

I was close to a young woman who specifically stated that she wanted to have kids, so that "I'll always have someone who loves me." This is pretty much the exact wrong mentality by which to go into parenting, for it implies that the child(-ren) is being created to meet the needs of the parent, who feels inadequate – ie short on love – and unable to get her own love needs met by appropriate adult means. This is the parent who will be forever siphoning love from the child's Love Cup, rather than forever making it her responsibility to, in fact, fill the child/adult-child's Love Cup. Recipe for total disaster. For, it means that a child, rather than filling with love (poured from parents and other adults), will be constantly feeling drained of love (read 'depression and anxiety', not to mention 'just plain tired'), which leads to all manner of self-destroying behaviors to try to frantically get that Cup filled (and to feel alive, at all), behaviors that only get more intense and more hidden, yet more difficult to keep under wraps with age.

Really, the point of this entire book is:

Children do not exist for parents;
parents exist for children.

Nothing screws up cement and Love Cups like that equation becoming inverted. And it requires immense discipline on the part of a parent to not steal loving words and physical affection from a young child to get the parent's own Cup filled. It requires a deliberate, disciplined parent to not get his/her own pride fix met through the actions and achievements of a teen or twenty-something. It demands both self-awareness and great forbearance for the parent of a 20-30-something to not vicariously live the parent's own broken dreams and missed opportunities through the young, fresh, and easily malleable life of a still-tethered adult-child, particularly as the parent sees his own vigor and opportunities blowing away. And, at the last breath, it is a profound act of letting go to place no burden or expectation to fulfill a promise in the lap of a child.

CHAPTER 37

GRANDMA CHARLOTTE'S WISDOM
ON PARENTING THE SOUL

Part of the solution necessary to either counteract negative messages that have been placed inside kids – i.e. the closing of the Three Binary Gates – or to short-circuit the gates ever being closed in the first place is that a divorce must occur. It must be repetitively placed in the child's head that his/her actions are, to a very, very large degree not his/her identity.

One of the single greatest gifts I was given as a child
was from my mother, who was extremely deliberate and disciplined
in conveying the message (when I screwed up):

"You're not a bad person; you just did a bad thing"
and
"You're not a dumb person; you just did a dumb thing."
(I heard this one, a lot.)

For, it is far too easy for a child's spirit to believe that the criticisms about a particular action indicate the inherent nature of the child's character and worth, "Mommy said I did a bad thing *again*. I must be a bad person" or "Dad keeps saying I'm lazy. I must be lazy. I'm no good." The child isn't doing this consciously. Instead, organically, the child equates commentary on his actions with commentary on his worth and existence, unless there is a deliberate, repeated effort by the primary power sources and love sources to divorce action from identity. The greatest damage is done to the soul when individual actions are linked to identity. A child may screw up a million times in a multitude of different ways over the course of a childhood. All of us did, as kids. (Heck, I screw up a million times over a multitude of different ways, before noon each day, and they call me an adult.)

So, if each of those very natural screw-ups is never de-linked from the child's identity, or sense of self, that child WILL believe he or she is a total screw-up. And it won't take 10 or 15 years for that to happen. It'll happen by age three or four. As long as behaviors in a child are linked to identity, the spiritual development of this child is toast. The Binary Gates will close early and close hard.

And, the really tricky part – stick with me here – is that into adulthood a person's actions DO, in fact, more greatly indicate the nature of their character and worth. But, the notion that children, say, under age 12, are engaging in anything that is truly generated from their own self – *causa sui* – and not some direct or derivative result of their parental programming is, more or less, nonsense. A child's actions are almost exclusively an indicator of the parent's character and personality, not the innate nature of the child. For, from 0-11 years old (and too often far longer), the child is little more than an extension of the parents and their values. So, to punish or criticize the child for actions is iffy business, at best, because it is hardly an exhibition of their own character and more a manifestation of what they've been taught.

Thus, while the children are young and still in the business of determining right and wrong action, and who they really are, it's quite unfair to allow for even the remote possibility that they might start to believe something is wrong with who they really are, rather than just how they're acting. That's why it demands deliberate effort to specifically convey to the child that this criticism is not a reflection of who they are but merely how they're acting in the moment, "You're not a bad person. You just did a crummy thing."

The child has no autonomous sense of self yet. Thus, the criticism of the action must be divorced from criticism of the person, which is far more powerful and permanent. Conversely, the core identity must be affirmed. And, even more importantly, with that affirmation there must be an ongoing recognition in the head of the parent from the beginning of the child's life that he or she IS an autonomous being that must one day be let go of; and that letting-go must start sooner than later.

She once told me that it wasn't until her late-30s that she began to both live and parent deliberately, "and everything changed," she said. My mother was adamant in saying, "You're not a bad/dumb/irresponsible/lazy person, you just did a bad/dumb/irresponsible/lazy thing."

The long term effect in my family-of-origin is that six kids (and now our own adult children) grew up and now live without the hyper-critical self-judgment of every mistake. In families where action is divorced from identity in a child the fear of failure is radically reduced. The capacity to shrug off mistakes and move on is increased. More, the innate sense of self-worth is never undermined from inside, or even questioned, because it was deliberately and repeatedly affirmed. A base reservoir of love is firmly established in the Love Cup. Thus, possessing self-love and self-respect, as is a child's nature, the child (and later adult) goes out into the world already imbued with a moral imperative to treat others as he or she has been treated, which is only with love and respect.

Journaling Recommendation

1. Are you parenting deliberately, or are you simply doing that which your parents did? Or just the opposite of what they did? (Neither of the latter two are true deliberate parenting. Neither is parenting's Third Path.)
2. What is it you know you're screwing up on in your parenting? What do you know you need to change to begin to parent more deliberately? From what to what?
3. Do you have the courage to change?
4. Do you have the wherewithal and presence of mind, in the moment, to convey to your child that he/she isn't a bad person but just did a not-so-good thing? Or, are you undisciplined in the heat of the moment, such that you lash out or say something potentially hurtful to the soul of your child? Do you need to widen the amount of time between stimulus and response?
5. Are you careless with your words in your parenting?

CHAPTER 38

MOTIVATION AND YOUR 22 YEAR-OLD SON
(OR YOUR 35 YEAR-OLD SELF)

I get a lot of kids coming to me, sometimes quite by accident, wondering what makes me tick or sometimes simply overwhelmed by the unhappiness of their own lives. And, for me, there is a very special excitement that comes from working with teens and kids in their early-20s, because there's a malleability, an openness, a receptivity to my message. And every teacher loves an eager student.

More importantly, if I can change the self-perception and core beliefs of a young person, they have the chance of not wasting 10, 20, or more years living in deference to an external power source and external primary orientation point. In other words, the effect of changing the core beliefs of someone when they're young is that they begin living authentically sooner, thus enjoying far more happiness longer.

Of course, to receive my message at a later age (rather than teens/twenties) often means that it's more likely to take root, because an older person has tried many other paths in life and seen them come up empty. When older, our pain has gotten so bad that our hunger for a solution has also increased. Whereas a kid may see my message as one among many and may not rely as heavily on it, often slipping into Last Man Syndrome – simply taking the advice of the last person they talked to, particularly when it's an influential adult. Or, the kid will resist me and what I bring to the table, simply because they are convinced they know better, as we all did when we were 22.

But, more often than not, I end up working with teens and 20-somethings because it's their parent(s) who brings 'em to me, wanting me to fix 'em. In other words, in the mind of the parent, the kid has a problem or, to be fully accurate, is the problem. Therefore, in the mind of the parent, the solution requires changing the kid.

(NB. What follows is precisely the same concepts I use very often with 35 and 45 year-olds struggling, in particular, with career lethargy and unfulfillment. Interestingly, the 22 year-old who cannot get started and the 36 year-old who has accomplished much but is feeling dead in his career and life are suffering from almost exactly the same spiritual malady.)

Your 22 Year-old Son

One of the patterns I have seen a great deal of, in the last ten years in particular, is the lack of life motivation among males. It afflicts all ages, but particularly a great many under the age of 25 or 30. It's quite prevalent. Often they are college-educated or in some other way successful, or at least appear to be on the surface. But their lives are drudgery.

It's the drudgery and lack of motivation that vex both parent and child, and not just because they are living in mom/dad's basement, as there is no inherent crime in that or indicator of lack of motivation in that. Rather, it's that getting out of the house, or scraping themselves up off the couch and starting life that requires a massive conjuring of energy, every time. That is what perplexes both parties. To the external observer (read 'mom and dad') it's depression, lack of motivation, or laziness, not to mention the growing rebelliousness that usually accompanies it, as the young man feels judged and misunderstood.

And so, moms and dads bring the kids to me, as if I'm some sort of boot camp that will tough love them into shape and get their lazy butts off the couch. But my work ends up being not at all what they expected, and in fact ends up being pretty much the opposite of what mom and dad want.

The Root Matter

What I've found in my decades of spiritual work is that lack of motivation invariably boils down to three things, each of which is present to varying degrees in the unmotivated person:

- **Fear.** Always fear blocking the path, blocking the spirit. More often than not, the unmotivated person, regardless of age, knows exactly what they want (beyond just some form of escape), but they are terrified. Terrified of failing. Terrified of disappointing all of the critical voices. Terrified of doing life on their own, without support of others, such as mom and dad. Terrified of showing the world who they really are and what really makes their heart sing. One foot on the accelerator and one foot on the brake – revved up but utterly incapable of movement or sustained movement; or they're simply herky-jerky in their movements.

- **What you say you want ain't what you really want.** Some clients become so contorted by the primary power sources in their life that they can't hear their own voice. Or, they still so desire to win the praise of the critical voices in their life (again, read 'mom and dad' or 'family') that what they are doing is not authentic – i.e. originating in their truest inner voice – but is some derivative reaction to what others want, or don't want, from them. It is one of the first two paths (what is expected of me; the opposite of what is expected of me), but not the third path (what is uniquely me, quite apart from the praise or criticism of others). They make stops and starts, or can never really seem to get going. The pressure to succeed keeps them from ever really starting or fully engaging, because they're often choosing paths for the success, not for the love of the work of that particular path. And that, 99 times out of 100, is the result of parental expectations and criticisms, parents who don't realize that the only path a kid will ever get on and stay on is one on which he simply really enjoys the work or organization, quite apart from the successes or failures. Bottom line, they're not going after what they most wanna be going after.

- **The sheer weight of life**. In one form or another, all lack of motivation comes down to this. That 500lb bag of rocks they're carrying around on their backs, full of memories charged with highly negative emotions, keeps them from sustaining an effort or often even beginning one, even if they know exactly what they want to do, say, be, have, look like, feel like, or become. Sometimes life is just so heavy as to preclude any movement, whatsoever. And the real tragedy of this particular situation is the lack of hope, particularly when the client is a mere 22. It's tragic. These are the clients who are so beaten down by life that they are ever on the lookout for both escapes and miracle cures. But again, the heaviness of the past plays in conjunction with the fear of hearing and dealing with the critical voices of the present. Taken together, they are simply too much to bear.

As a result, many people become stuck in life, engaging in every manner of escape, each day losing belief that aliveness is ever possible.

**If you're unmotivated to go after what you want
and you can't seem to figure out why,
the reason for your lack of motivation is unequivocally one of two things.
Either there are fears blocking the pursuit of what you want,
or you don't really want what you say you want.**

The ugly part of this equation, at least for the anxious parent trying to 'fix' their kid, is that the parent is often the very cause of the present situation, creating a Love Cup full of crud and/or a gaping hole in the bottom. I am not a believer that any person can just get over their problems without assessing responsibility where it belongs – on those who pressed soul-killing messages into the cement of the then-child beliefs.

Thus, when I volley the ball into the parent's court, they are often caught off-balance and refuse to concede fault or accept responsibility. Wanting to merely 'fix' the kid rather than solve the real problem, some parents simply pull out and pull their kid out. It's far too easy for the parent to keep the problem outside of themselves – i.e. on the kid – rather than even consider that they are part of the very problem they are trying to solve. Better to villainize someone else, even your own child, than to begin to look at the 'Holy Crap!' experience of realizing this was my own doing.

Just as importantly, few parents realize that, after about age 13, kids don't want to be fixed; they want to be heard. Those are two very different things. So, the 22 year-old resists to ever-increasing degrees. The unmotivated 22 (or later 35 or 45) year-old is so because his voice has not been allowed to be heard. The kid's soul has no voice. He has been taught that his voice, his truth, and who he really is simply don't matter. He's terrified to speak and live his truth. Therefore, it's not that he lacks motivation, per se. Instead, it's that he can't bear the thought of the parental and familial criticism, particularly when paired with the heaviness of the past.

Yet, the solution, at this age, isn't just about changing the kid. Well, it is, but it isn't. Yes, I have to sell the kid on a message he is usually quite eager to hear spoken by someone other than himself – i.e. that his voice matters. The equally important solution, at least if the kid is still a minor or still dependent upon the parent, is that the parent needs to begin to realize he/she is both part of the problem and part of the solution. Whatever serious depression or anxiety or screwed-up behaviors are occurring in the kid's life are the direct result of the parent's actions. Period. Parent and child both have responsibility, but the parent created this situation.

This comes as a very rude and unwanted awakening for many parents. The parent's inner fears keep saying, "As long as I keep focusing on the kid as the problem, I'm safe. As long as I keep resisting any possibility of me being at fault, my own spirit won't get hurt." So, they keep the focus and blame on the young adult, in no small part because that 22 year-old is an easy target. The parent still has sway over the young guy. He's still living under a powerful external power source, particularly if that external power source is housing and feeding him, and not afraid to remind him of that fact.

You can thus understand that the reason I sometimes dislike working with kids is because I'm not a fan of having to confront unsuspecting parents with the often severe reality that, even if they were great parents in many ways, they screwed up, as all parents do. They made mistakes. They sent destructive messages.

The biggest challenge to the growth and happiness of a dependent kid is a parent unwilling to concede fault, accept responsibility for it, and acknowledge the validity of the kid's voice and autonomous aspirations.

And, while it'd be great to follow his truth with the approval and encouragement of the parents, the kid has to, in the end, learn and decide to believe in his own voice, believe in its value, and believe in its absolute necessity for that experience of aliveness and happiness. In the end, if the parent will not concede fault and grant permission to the adult-child to live his own path, the 22 (or 37) year-old must find and speak the resounding "NO!" rising up from his soul, longing for a voice. Absent that, he will forever live under that oppressive weight of fear and heavy rocks on his back.

Are Your Values Different?
In this situation where a client has particular fondness for his parents, yet needs to find his 'NO!', I ask what is a rather dumb, yet difficult question:

**Is it possible that
your parents values are different from your values?**

Dumb, obvious question, right? Surely, no two people on earth have the exact same values in everything, all the time. But it's so clear that a great many people have never thought of it or thought of *how* their values differ from those of their parents – what specific values are different and why. And far more difficult, in the case of an adult-child who really loves or digs his/her parents, is the simple act of admitting 'I am not my parents. I am not identical to them.' For, this forces the adult-child to give himself room to be different from his parents, and that's okay. Again, when we love our parents or hold them up as the epitome of good, the notion of differing from them is almost unthinkable.

It's so obvious, but also not so obvious. So, it's terribly obvious that you and your parents will have at least some different values. But it's not so obvious, because even in loving homes there can be a spoken or unspoken belief that there is only one good way, one acceptable set of values, or there may be a range of values but they have to be in the ballpark of acceptability, as determined by the primary power source in the home.

For, once you concede that it is even possible that your parents' values are not, in fact, your values, is it not then incumbent upon you to determine which are and which are not? Would not the quest for self-discovery pass directly through the section of the dark forest marked "The maze of values mine and not mine"?

Once you concede that your parents' values may, in fact, not be yours, you then have to sit down and begin the task of writing out what you believe your parents' values are, based on your 25-year or

55-year history with them. You must then begin to really ponder and answer which of those are you, which of those you choose, which of those you reject, and which are cornerstones of your existence.

Yet, the act of articulating how I am different from my parents, even in some obvious ways, has the effect of cracking me open to the possibility that there might be bigger ways I'm different from them. More, it has the effect of giving myself permission to be different from them, whether in small or big ways. It gives my own inner voice permission to exist, be heard, and be followed, when all my life I've been waiting for them – my external power sources – to give me permission.

And once that hurdle is crossed with a client, it only then becomes an issue of digging down into the client and discerning what his or her real, own values are; and then living out those values. But, for many, the mere suggestion that they can have a voice that is different from their parents, in any significant way, is something that has never even really been considered. Or, worse, the much more unthinkable notion is that he no longer needs their permission to live his life. He needs his own permission. Validating his own voice means that he can then extract mom and dad's voice and values from inside him. And extracting the voice of mom and dad never comes without consequences.

This brings us right back to where we started the chapter. For, those consequences are the real fears that inhibit most coveted action. It is the fear of criticism – the voices of the power sources – that is at the root of depression, anxiety, and inaction.

The grand challenge to pushing through your lack of motivation is to:

1. Acknowledge that your values are different from mom and dad's and the other significant people in your life;
2. Delineate what their values are and where you deviate from them – i.e. what your values are;
3. Summon the courage to stand up and say, "NO!" to theirs and "YES!" to your (fighting back at all fallout that you know will come from doing so, or simply walking away from the fallout, because you are under no obligation to stay and endure the criticisms anymore);

4. Boldly begin a life built on your values. It's gonna be hard, at least at first, but it will also be exhilarating, because it is the path of your liberation and your greatness.

Journaling Recommendation

1. Many motivational writers and speakers as the question, "What would you do if you knew you could not fail?" So, write that at the top of your page, and take some time to flesh out all of your answers in your career and personal life.

2. However, I think the far more illuminating question is, "What would you do even if you knew you would likely fail, or if there were a very high probably of not succeeding?" In other words, what life path would you engage in if it weren't about the success but about the love of the work? See, this is the real question. This is the path that is going to hold your attention. No matter what path you take, you're going to have many failures, fall-downs, and screw-ups. And if you're only in it to have success, in the end, these failures will eventually blow out the flame of excitement. But if you love or believe in the work, the inevitable failures of life won't extinguish your zeal for the path. You might some day become even more interested in something else, but you'll not abandon your path simply because of hardships.

3. What are the paths you know, with relative certainty, that you do not want? What are you done with, or over? What paths, tasks, work, settings, or what-have-you are not you? Do you have the courage to no longer be them and pursue them?

Song Recommendation

I'm a big fan of this song. It's even on my workout mix. So inspiring. And it's a good swift kick in the butt for kids and parents, alike. Download the song and lyrics, ***Something to Believe in***, by **Parachute**.

https://www.youtube.com/watch?v=zyVZ4uVHYRwSomethingToBelieveIn

RELATIONSHIPS

EVERY SHARED EXPERIENCE IS A CORD BINDING TWO PEOPLE TOGETHER, MAKING UNBINDING TRICKY

One of the reasons that break-ups are so doggone hard is that every shared experience that two people have is one more cord that wraps around the two of them. The more difficult, challenging, or delightful the experience, the stronger the cord that goes round. The more emotionally charged the experience, the stronger the cord. Again and again, round and round, the cords go.

So, when it comes time to break-up, when the mountain of manure between the two people becomes so large and so acrid that they simply cannot stand it any longer, the break-up demands the breaking or unbinding of the cords. The more the cords, the harder it is to unbind. An extreme amount of energy or negative experiences is required to undo the cords. Or, done rightly and least painfully, a massive amount of energy and deliberate positive effort is required to talk out, listen, forgive, and step their way through a break-up.

The Shift in Beliefs Necessary to End a Relationship
The reason a person will blow up a relationship before they will actually exit it gracefully and by deliberately talking out their desire to leave is because deep-down, in their core beliefs, they still believe that their desires are not warranted. They believe that what they want – specifically, in this case, to leave a relationship that no longer feeds their soul – is irrelevant. They believe, essentially, that the needs of others are, ever and always, more important than their own needs, wants, and feelings.

**I don't want to hurt those I love...
by doing what I most want to do.**

This lack of belief in my own value manifests as not wanting to disappoint those people around me who might be sad about the ending of the relationship, such as the kids, parents, in-laws, and friends. It also manifests as not wanting to hurt my spouse by leaving him/her. For, even though I may no longer be 'in love', I do still love them.

However, what's underneath this fear of hurting those I love is that persistent fear that drives all others: What will they say? More specifically, if I hurt or disappoint those I love, or those who love me, they will think less of me and criticize me.

And it is that fear of criticism that is causing you to stay stuck in this dead or dying relationship. It's not really the fear of hurting and disappointing them that keeps you stuck. It's the fear of what they'll say to you and about you when you hurt them. Your fear of disappointing them is really driven by what they'll think or say about you *after* you disappoint them. *That* is what you fear – those words.

But there's one more, even deeper piece that makes ending a relationship so vexing for some. It goes right down to those core beliefs and 3 Binary Gates. The fear of hurting those I love is driven by the belief that doing so would be selfish and I have to always be selfless; selfish is bad.

**Do I really matter enough to hurt someone else,
particularly my own children residually, to serve my own needs?
Surely I don't matter enough to justify hurting someone else.**

This is one of life's heavy questions. And the simple fact of the matter is that, of course, you have to matter to yourself to do this. More, it's impossible to go through life without hurting others. Further, how much damage is being done, both to yourself and others, by *not* taking this action? How much harm is being done by this ugly status quo you're in.

There are those times in life where we simply have to take a seemingly 'selfish' action to engage a market correction, or course correction. And yes, there is pain, particularly in the short term. But when greater truth is seized and moved toward, it leads to greater peace, purpose, and joy for all parties. It just usually takes a while.

This fear of what seems to be a 'selfish' action is a great mistake. I think we have a profound misunderstanding of selfishness. It's far too black and white, far too either/or. When working with a client, I like to take a blank piece of paper, turn it sideways, and draw a line from left to right in the middle of the paper. At the far left of this continuum I write the words 'Totally Selfless.' At the far right end I write 'Totally Selfish.' And I place a little 'x' in the dead center of the continuum.

I then go on to explain that any supposedly selfish or selfless act exists within the greater context of who a person is. If you have a person who is generally a very selfless person, or even a totally selfless person (not that that's fully possible, but you get the point), and they then do something very selfish, it moves them only slightly toward the middle of the continuum. Within the greater context of a long time of selflessness, one or two big supposedly selfish acts do little to move the needle anywhere near being totally selfish, even if they feel totally selfish by doing these one or two acts. They're acting so out of character that it feels inside them like a violation of humanity.

But the totally selfless person *needs* to move more toward the center of the continuum – yes, needs to be more 'selfish.' And it's never a static position in the dead-center. It's always this oscillation between selfishness and selflessness, one side feeding the other side of one's character and spirit.

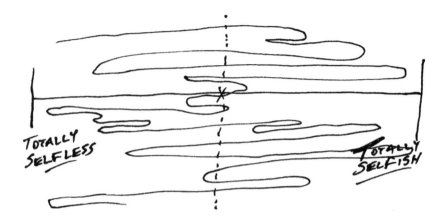

The person who is too selfless is unhappy and depressed precisely because they are so selfless, precisely because their core beliefs and 3 Binary Gates hold the belief that they don't matter enough, if it all, to act in their own interests, at times.

And the craziest thing happens when an extremely selfless person does something supposedly selfish. Everyone around her (especially the person feeling most hurt or with the most to lose) shouts, "You're being SO selfish!"...even though the person is nowhere near being even halfway selfish. And, on the opposite end of the spectrum, when the person who is generally extremely selfish does the slightest selfless thing and he proclaims to the heavens and all who will listen, "SEE HOW SELFLESS I AM!!!"...even though that lone selfless act sits in a giant context of selfishness. If that selfish person acts true to character, any remotely selfless lone act will be followed by many times of reminding the receiver of how selfless he is.

The very selfish person hoards love and protects the Love Cup from anyone who might presume to steal even the tiniest ounce from his or her Cup. They have known the effect of the hole in the bottom and know that every dash of love can quickly vanish. So they steal it wherever they can. The very selfless person, on the other hand, too loosely pours it out to others, hoping to get some love in return for their selflessness. The selfless person never experiences the Love Cup filling up, only lack. Both the selfish and selfless suffer from broken and crud-encrusted Love Cups.

And so, the simple truth is that if you have spent your life making others more important than you, constantly serving them at great price to yourself and you only seem to be getting more and more unhappy, you need to do more for yourself. It's not selfishness, as we generally tend to think of it; it's necessary tending of the soul. And it all starts with changing your core beliefs and 3 Binary Gates to reflect the simple truth that who you really are actually matters. You need to be bold enough to stand up and say, "I matter. The real me matters. I am good. And the real me is wanted....most especially, *by me!*" From there, it is necessary to start making decisions and choosing actions consistent with that belief. Do this one thing of finally mattering to yourself and everything changes. Change the core belief and nothing is ever the same.

Song Recommendation

Another intense **Peter Gabriel** song, *Blood of Eden*. Buy it and get the lyrics, too. Really great stuff, particularly the duet in the middle. https://www.youtube.com/watch?v=bySvsbl2ZooBloodOfEden

CHAPTER 40

UNHEALTHY PEOPLE COME IN TWOS

Before I ever begin working with any couple, I have two things that I tell them. The first is before I even accept them as a client, set an appointment, or ask them for an autobiography. It is simply this:

I am not in the business of fixing relationships.
I'm in the business of helping two individuals become their fullest selves.
Then, and only then, they can turn and look at each other in their fullest glory and decide if this is the person each wants to spend a really long time with.

See, all relationship problems flow out of individual problems that predated the relationship, long before they ever even knew each other. Until those real, deeper problems are fixed, ain't no amount of relationship counseling gonna put a dent in the problems between these two people.

Of course, when I tell people that, they have no clue of what I'm talking about. It's sounds good to them, but they have no idea what is in store for them. Usually, the person most angry or most pushing for separation/divorce is the one who claps loudest when hearing that I'll be going into each person's individual crud. For the angry or most disenchanted one is the one most convinced that the other person is the problem. Thus, it's a bit of a disappointment and eye-opener when the other shoe drops.

The second thing I tell them is saved for once each of them is finally in my office. (I almost never meet with a couple together in the first meeting, because it's usually just a mess of finger-pointing and soul-sucking nonsense, and it's difficult to dive into each individual's life story when the other is present) It generally runs something like what I'm about to tell you, the reader, right now:

I've got bad news for you, it's not just your husband's fault. Not just your boyfriend's fault. Not your girlfriend's fault (for the men reading this book). It ain't the missus. Yeah, they're a pain in the butt, but, alas, so are you. But it's worse than that. And no, I'm not about to throw out to you the tired cliché, "It takes two to tango."

Nah, it's far worse than that. Because, a person can say "two to tango" about a relationship, and then in the very next breath state that their mate is really unhealthy and needs to get help. In other words, "Sure, I left the cap off the toothpaste, but he's borderline, bipolar, and narcissistic." It's the old, "Sure, I do little things, but he does BIG things wrong." Or, my favorite, "She's bi-polar (or some other disease). I looked it up on Wikipedia and she has all the symptoms!" (Never mind that people get bachelor's degrees, then master's degrees and PhD's in psychology, and go through medical school and residency, and still bi-polarity is the most misdiagnosed psychological disease in all of medicine. But somehow, magically, you and WebMD managed to nail all her problems. Yeah, right!)

In short, what they love to tell their family, tell every friend and anyone else who will listen (namely me, the counselor) is, "I'm healthy. He's not."

Let's see, how can I put this??? Hmmmmm. How about: hahahahahahahahaahahahahahahahahahahaha.

Yes, that's me laughing at you, or at least your incredibly naive belief that you're healthy and he's not (or she's not). Sorry, but pretty much as a rule:

Healthy people don't get into relationships with unhealthy people.

Just ruminate on that one for a minute. Further, healthy people, as a rule, don't stay in relationships with unhealthy people. So, if you're in a relationship and your mate is supposedly unhealthy, you are too.

"Think about it," I tell clients. "Why would a healthy person – someone who has a clean spirit, a life cleansed of fear, sorrow, depression, and anxiety – get into a relationship with a person who does not? It makes no sense. You might work with unhealthy people in your vocation as a therapist, nurse, pastor, social worker, teacher, or really any type of work. But you're not going to let an unhealthy person into the most intimate of your inner *personal* circles as your lover and life companion. No truly healthy person would ever do that, because it would cost her *her* very spiritual health. Now, a person on the path to becoming healthy might still be in a relationship with an unhealthy person. But the difference between your healthiness and their unhealthiness is not as great as you like to think, simply because such a great disparity would've already blown you two apart as intimates. In order to stay healthy, a healthy person protects his/her borders and won't let an unhealthy person stay too close. It's too disruptive. Healthy people aren't without problems or issues, but they've made their spiritual life a priority for a long time and know how to move through failings and difficulties. Thus, selling yourself as healthy while pointing the finger at your mate, saying he/she is unhealthy, is a ridiculous notion, and not the mark of a spiritually healthy person."

Such a position reflects a deficiency of understanding what, in physics, is known as the Heisenberg Uncertainty Principle, which, to paraphrase, simply asserts that

I must constantly remind myself that
I am part of the problem I am trying to solve.

To assert that my mate is the problem and I am not, or not as much, is an attempt to villainize him/her and lionize myself. It is a scrappy effort to keep the problem outside myself, keep the attention focused on you, so that no one will see how screwed up I am. "If I can just fix him, then I'll be happy," the thinking goes, implicitly stating your happiness lies outside of you. It is an attempt to skirt the stuff that is really at the core of both why I have had problems in my past and why I still presently do.

It is also an attempt to control. To control the narrative. And by trying to control the relationship story you are fundamentally showing weakness, which is, of course, a sign of un-health. For, it is essentially saying that I am willing to harm this other person, even if only their reputation or how they are perceived, so that how I am perceived will not be diminished or will be exalted. That need to be perceived well is a mark of deficiency, or weakness. To do it at the expense of another person radically compounds the offense, unjustifiably, and thereby radically increases the profundity of your own weakness.

If a person can't control you, they'll attempt to control the story about you.

In other words, to the insightful observer, your heated attempts to look good only reveal your insecurity and selfishness, powerfully underscoring how unhealthy you truly are. For example, I get a lot of clients attempting to capitalize on the cultural misbelief that men are bad at expressing feelings and emotionally closed off. They will point the finger at their male partner or husband (or son) and recite how his lack of emotion is killing the relationship. That keeps the focus off themselves, at the expense of the person they claim to love. Insecurity compounded by hypocrisy.

So, unhealthy people always come in twos. Where there is one, there is most definitely another. And it's likely you! A healthy person simply can't be 'tricked' by appearances, but trusts underlying energy. And if the energy, the vibe, ain't right, he or she ain't getting in.

So, if you're in a relationship with someone you believe to be unhealthy, you have some work to do, because you're toting some luggage too, even if your evolution out of unhealthiness came after you got together. The fact that you're still in says you ain't as healthy as you proclaim. And even if you're getting out, I'd be willing to bet there's plenty of residual stuff that needs to be extracted before you're fully healthy and flying high again. Guaranteed.

Journaling Recommendation
1. What are you hiding?
2. In what ways do you keep the focus off yourself?
3. Why are you demonizing your mate? What are you afraid of? What are you hiding?
4. What's the biggest accusation you use to keep your partner/spouse looking bad and you looking good? Are you a hypocrite?

5. Are you ready to start being honest? Are you ready for radical honesty? Or, are you going to keep using people you claim to love?

6. Now, I'm not denying that your mate has done stuff wrong. I'm objecting to your claiming you haven't. Even more pointedly, why have you continued to *allow* it? What does that say about you? And here's the whopper: What fears in you have perpetuated you staying in a relationship you claim is awful and unfulfilling?

7. What's really going on inside of you that you are not admitting?

CHAPTER 41

THE IMPASSE BETWEEN TWO PEOPLE

Do you feel you and your spouse/bf/gf growing apart? Do you feel like one of you has one foot in and one foot out? Or, perhaps you feel like one of you is often putting a toe in the waters outside the relationship, in some way or another? Has the relationship been deteriorating, for a long time?

I'm of the very adamant belief that any time there is a persisting and expanding impasse between two people in a relationship – any relationship but especially intimate relationships – it is not because there are irreconcilable differences between them, per se, or because one person just won't change, or because one person is all at fault, or any of the other normal excuses. While any of those things might be a small, or surface, factor in the equation, the greater issue is nearly always something quite different.

Relationship impasses occur and grow
because one person (or sometimes two) is withholding some truth
that they know, if they speak it, would blow up the relationship.

Things that were never spoken or never admitted, at some point in the relationship only grow. They grow out of sight, well hidden. But they do grow, insidiously, quietly, at least for a while. Then they break out, infecting everything. They manifest in every unimaginable way, even as their real identity remains beyond the light of day.

It could be:
- A past affair
- Failure of hidden investments that drained the family bank account
- I'm not attracted to you anymore

319

- I was never really in love with you; and I knew it before we married
- I never wanted you
- I'm gay
- I want someone with more money
- I hate you
- I'm in love with someone else
- I'm using you for stability/security
- I don't want to have kids
- I never wanted to have kids with you
- You and your values bore me
- I'm still in love with my ex
- I don't love you anymore
- I can't stand touching you and sex with you

The withholding of all of these is driven by the simple belief, "If I show you who I really am, I fear you won't like me. I know pretty much how you'll respond. I know you'll run or lose it. I know this relationship is over. And the fear of losing the security of this relationship outweighs any hoped-for gain from telling the truth." Fear, in other words, as we've seen throughout this book, is a powerful motivator.

In fact, people will hire a therapist for individual counseling and then *lie* to the therapist (not just in couples counseling but even in individual counseling!), never even revealing their truth to the therapist, because it's too powerful to even mutter. Or, people will hire a therapist for relationship counseling and then seemingly tell everything – 99% of the truth – creating what I call 'the illusion of transparency'. Yet, all the while they're withholding:

What is known in aviation (specifically, rotocraft) as the 'Jesus Pin' (or 'Jesus Nut'):
the lone nut attaching the main rotor to the helicopter body.
In more common usage, the 'Jesus Pin' denotes
the lone component that represents a single point of failure with catastrophic consequences.

People will create the illusion of transparency while never revealing what they absolutely know is the linchpin of the relationship – the single most salient, most powerful, and potentially most destructive piece of information. Interestingly, despite the illusion of transparency, this person's partner can sense – just feeeeeel – that something is off, despite incessant protestations to the contrary.

Or, the fear of telling the real truth is so great that people will avoid counseling, avoid the truth, and blame their partner (even when they fully know they, themselves, are at fault) to avoid the humiliation and loss from telling the truth.

Or, here's the other side of it, mad as it sounds. People will blow up a relationship with a lie before they'll ever blow it up with what is really going on. People will cheat or destroy the relationship in any number of ways before they will speak their truth, because the fear is so great. The fear of being completely real and honest is the most terrifying thing in most people's lives. The fear of being seen. The fear of looking bad. The fear of retribution. The fear of loss of security, even when that 'secure' relationship is in total shambles with little hope of turning around.

I've had clients engaged in full-on affairs, taking extreme risks with the potential of getting caught. I have had clients flat-out state, "I don't care about getting caught," even when getting caught carried far greater potential cost in the inevitable, subsequent divorce, as well as carrying the stigma of being the bad guy. So great is the drift between two people that love not only turns to hate, but hate turns to indifference, to eventually hoping the spouse would get pissed and dump him. So great can relationship discontent become, so great also the fear of actually talking stuff out, truthfully and forthrightly that people will do the trippiest stuff. It's crazy what people will resort to, so as to avoid speaking that truth that is consuming their soul.

It is little different from the relationship you have (or don't have) with your own self. More often than not, the grand cause of a person's life-draining disconnect from his or her own self is the unwillingness to admit, let alone deeply look at, one or two major truths. It's what drives the mad running discussed in previous chapters. It is the fear of admitting some deeply buried life truths.

For, admitting said truths would cause the carefully constructed lie known as one's life to fall apart. That, for many, is a fate worse than death.

And yet, cliché as it sounds, the truth does set you free. I'm a huge advocate of speaking even the ugliest of truths, not because it is the only thing that can possibly truly turn your relationship with your mate around, but because it is the only thing that can possibly turn around your relationship with your own self.

What this whole spiritual life is about is relationship with your own self. Until you hear and heed your own inner vibe, feel, voice, especially when it scares you, you have no relationship with yourself. No true joy. No lasting peace. No clarity.

The heart longs to be clean, and that necessarily demands an unburdening of that which is your truth, 'warts and all,' as my 89 year-old mother often says. Warts and all.

But, alas, it is the price of revealing our warts that keeps us hidden and keeps our hearts heavy. And eventually it is the heaviness and pain of the heart that break us, breaks our fears, oddly simultaneously giving us the courage to speak and live our truth. Then we discover the unbounded joy of living with a clean heart.

The Ugly Part Of Relationships
Of course,

**The really ugly and extremely difficult part of life in relationships
is having the hard conversations
before the blowout happens.**

It's so hard to bring up the small needs, the small slights, the medium wants, and the lesser longings. It's so hard to walk into a difficult situation deliberately when there is a known and credible possibility of blowback. It's so easy to say to oneself, "It's no big deal," "I'll be alright," "I just shrug it off," or "It'll get better." It's so easy to blow off one's own needs and concerns, particularly when the specter of a negative response looms.

So, what do we do? We let stuff grow. We let the cancer of discontent metastasize, until one day when we're a bit short on sleep, or hungry, or stressed from work...and the gf or bf says just the slightly wrong thing and all the discontent, anger, and hurt come pouring out, seemingly finally justified – the camel's L3 and L4 finally giving way. It's so hard to stand up for oneself by sitting down and actually talking out what one's needs are, and then not backing down. It is far easier to just blow stuff up than to truly work at fixing it and/or walk away when it is clearly no longer working. Far easier to take the path of hiding the truth and blowing things up.

It would be very easy to mischaracterize this avoidance of the hard conversation as a communication problem in the relationship. It's not. Despite the incessant culture-wide blather to the contrary, communication is almost never the big problem in relationships. It's a courage problem. What really keeps individuals from standing in the fire and having the hard conversations is fear of the blowback, fear of hurting the other person, fear of being disliked or rejected, fear of just enduring the hardness of what's ahead, fear of not even knowing how to navigate life with this person gone, with this giant hole where they used to be. It's always fear (more unwillingness than inability to communicate, thus rendering it not a communication problem, per se) that leads to the blowups, cheating, and destruction.

CHAPTER 42

NCAA POSSESSION ARROW &
DEATH BY A THOUSAND CUTS

In relationships, people tend to compromise themselves most, not in the big things, but in the small things. If it's a big decision of whether to move to San Diego or take the job in Boston, most individuals will make their voice heard. Or if it's the big or medium-size question of whether to have a third child, where to go for vacation this year, or even should we spend the Holidays with your family or mine, people tend to make their needs and wants known.

But when it comes to those medium-to-smaller decisions, it becomes very easy to lose yourself. Friday afternoon rolls around and the conversation arises, Well what should we do tonight? Movie or dinner out? Whatever you want.

Well, my partner may say, "Let's do a movie." I tell her that sounds good, even though I had been thinking it'd be fun to try that new steakhouse.

"What movie are you interested in," I ask.

"The new Bond movie looks awesome," she responds.

Now, I love James Bond as much as anyone, but I know there's a period movie (my favorite genre) that only has a couple of weeks left at the indie theater. So, of course, I respond, "Bond sounds awesome! Let's do it!" Or, perhaps, I do actually say, "Yeah, but that indie movie only has a couple of weeks left. But y'know what, I can see that next week on my own time."

"Are you sure?"

"Yeah," I breezily respond (and how many times have you heard yourself say what I say next?), "It's no big deal."

Same thing happens with: Popcorn vs Dots? Soda vs Lemonade? Ice cream afterward vs cocktail nearby? The response is so easily, "Well, what do *you* want?"

And, pretty much always, the response coming out of your mouth is:

- What do YOU want?
- It's no big deal
- I'm flexible
- Whatever you want
- Your idea sounds great
- I'm happy with either option
- Nah, I'm cool
- All good
- No worries

And before you know it, the night is done and you've compromised yourself a hundred times. Multiply that by seven days/week, 52 weeks in a year, year after year, decade upon decade. It becomes very, very easy – basically a reflex – to compromise on ALL, or most, of the small and medium-size decisions that cross your path. It becomes so easy to make yourself liked by making the other person happy, basically purchasing them liking you by giving up most everything. "I'm going to *buy* you liking me by always doing what *you* want," the thinking goes. And so, you give THIS MUCH and they give this much.

Again and again and again. If you're a born giver, it is very easy to find yourself in a relationship with a born taker. They're happy to take and take and take. It's a great relationship; fits perfectly. And it's so easy to blame the other person for being a taker, when you're just as guilty of creating the growing unrest in your life and soul. However, your crime is in not standing up for yourself, not standing up and speaking your truth...IN THE SMALL THINGS!

The real travesty that happens when we over-compromise, repeatedly, is that we lose ourselves. In truth, you're already lost, to a large degree, if incessant compromising and incessant refusal to speak your truth is your m.o. You eventually find yourself waaaaay over there, completely beyond anything that remotely resembles who you really are. And you can feel it. Something just feels really,

really off. Yet, because we're always told to compromise in relationships, you keep compromising your life away, never even thinking that that is precisely the problem. One-sided compromising is the death of an individual (the taker is dead internally, too, but for different reasons) and indicates a relationship that was doomed before it started.

There's an old form of torture and execution from thousands of years back in China, called *lingchi*, or 'death by a thousand cuts.' In it, a person who committed a particularly severe crime had small portions of the skin and body cut or removed with a knife, over time. More a form of torture than execution, it caused slow, yet significant bleeding and eventual death, after a very long time.

'Death by a thousand cuts' is fundamentally what happens, or actually what you do to yourself, when you keep compromising, keep refusing to even speak or stand up for your truth or your desires, again and again, year in and year out. Often it happens not just within one relationship, but is carried into many/all aspects of life: work, family, friendships, and even parenting. And eventually, it slow-kills your spirit and deadens your soul.

As with nearly all things, it is a fear-driven behavior. The simple fear is that if I show you who I really am or tell you what I really want, you may not like me or may not want me. So, we over-compromise.

Your own sense of self and what *you* want become lost, over time. Even if you were asked what you wanted, you wouldn't know. Worse, you can't even state, at least not audibly, what you don't want, which is normally the easiest part of discerning who one is (and isn't). That's how lost the real you is.

It is actually far less painful, in the short term, to NOT speak your truth, at all, and just do most things your partner's way than it is to speak your truth – i.e. to put yourself, your truth, and what you really want out there – and have it rejected or negated. Far better to be rejected for a fake version of you than to show the *real* you and be rejected. That latter is far too painful. Better to just keep the real you inside than to risk that level of pain.

And so we compromise, right? Again and again. And, inch by blessed inch, our soul dies. Death by a thousand cuts.

Possession Arrow

What most couples need is something to prevent that. Granted, each individual in the relationship needs to go deep inside them to open the 3 Binary Gates, smash those core negative messages in the cement of the soul, and change the core beliefs in the operating system of the soul. But, given that work in each individual – assuming each *individual* is doing the real work of revealing the truth of what they want to be, say, do, and become – what is needed *by the couple* is some simple little tool for keeping it fair.

In 1981, the NCAA instituted a ruling in college basketball stating that possession disputes – or 'jump balls' – would be determined no longer by an actual jump ball (tossing the ball straight up and a player from each team attempts to swat the ball to his own teammates) but by a 'possession arrow' – a flip-flopping arrow on the scorer's table indicating which team gets the ball next. After each possession dispute, the arrow quietly flips to the other team. This jump ball, Michigan State gets the ball; next jump ball, North Carolina gets the ball; then Michigan State, etc.

Fueled in part by the desire to keep the tempo of the game going but, more so, by the need to eliminate any strategic advantage to teams with taller players (who have the advantage in jump ball situations and who are in high demand in this sport and tend to go to the most successful programs), the implementation of the possession arrow leveled the playing field, or court, as it were. Jump ball? Just look to the scorer's table to see who gets the ball next. Simple. Next!

Same way in relationships. You decide movie or dinner out. I decide which movie. You decide popcorn or not. I decide soda or lemonade. Etc. Granted, it can get anal-retentive if required of every last decision. Obviously, there's room for flexibility. But, it's a great little tool for keeping it fair.

I had one couple who came back to me a year after our work together. They had a few problems that needed ironing out as individuals and one biggy as a couple. The husband complained that the possession arrow was great, but not really. His wife, he reported, tended to say, Well you got to pick if we went to a movie last night, so I get to decide whose family we spend Easter with. Or, you decided what we did for our day off last weekend, so I get to choose where we go for vacation. Or, you got to pick how we rearranged the

TV room furniture, so I get to pick which car we buy. You see the problem, right?

She didn't. It was laughable, but the wife didn't see it. She felt that as long as there was a rotation, all was good. It was obvious they needed to start weighing the magnitude or gravity of the decisions, as well. Picking where to go out for dinner is not a decision equal to whether or not we buy a new boat or not. Picking what to do for the weekend is not the same as picking the family vacation spot. Small for small; medium for medium; and work out the biggies together in a spirit of fairness and kindness.

The implementation of such a tool requires a good faith agreement from both parties that neither will take advantage of it – either as an opportunity to rip off the other or as an opportunity to somehow hide without having to speak your mind, both of which were the previous problems this tool is intended to significantly reduce.

The 3-Legged Stool

There is one more important piece on the topic of compromising oneself, as it relates to finding joy in life. It's the type of compromising we do, not when we're in relationship with someone else, but in your relationship with your own self.

See, most of us define being happy in life as sort of a 3-Legged Stool. One leg is money. One leg is career. And one leg is love (relationship and family). You give most people those three things and they're happy. More pointedly, those three things are what people spend most of their time worrying about, fussing over, and just plain wanting, for most of their lives. Those are the biggies.

The problem, though, is that we seem to never have them all at the same time; or, at least, if so, not until well along in life. Or, we seem to never have enough of them to really feel happy and content. The money never has enough zeroes, the career accomplishments are never high enough, and the love never lasts long enough or always has hiccups and hardships. And because we place so much emphasis on these three biggies, we just can't seem to get happy.

Worse, even when we do have one or two of the three legs of the stool, or perhaps even all three, it is an inevitable fact of life that we will lose one or two, now and then in life. Loss is inevitable. And so, because we place sooooo much weight on money, career, and love, our happiness is ripped from us when one of these is gone.

Because we think we can only be happy when we have all three legs of the 3-Legged Stool – i.e. only when we have the big things in life and have them in big amounts – we spend much of our lives quite unhappy, always striving, never there.

But what if happiness were both possible and even likely without all three legs? What if it were possible, easily so, to stack up a bunch of books under your stool, so to speak, when one of the legs is missing, only to discover the stool is actually sturdier?

Well, it's not only possible, it's actually fun. By integrating internal happiness into one's external life, the people who have mastered happiness realize that the small and medium stuff – the books under the seat of the stool – are far more powerful and sturdy in manifesting and growing happiness than are the big stuff. They are there day in and day out. They are easily added. They're far less debilitating when one is removed. The world doesn't end.

True joy demands honoring self – not compromising one's own happiness – not just in the big stuff, but in the small and medium, as well. We mistakenly spend so much time trying to win love from other people. The way we fill our own Love Cup is by attending to our own needs in the medium and small.

Perhaps it is:
- attending to your own health and fitness:
  - Daily workouts
  - Biking regularly
  - Horseback riding
  - Taking dance classes
  - Hikes
  - Going organic in one's food buying
- spending time with family:
  - Sunday football games
  - leaf-raking parties
  - kids' soccer games

- seeking new adventures,
  - walking new routes to work
  - exploring new parts of the state
  - playing/singing in a bluegrass band or garage band
  - or even as trivial as trying a new genre of movies or music
  - volunteering at the homeless shelter
- incorporating happiness-bringing rituals into daily life
  - morning mochas at the coffee shop
  - gardening
  - one client takes the train into NYC, but makes it a ritual to daily walk through Bryant Park on the way to and from the office, because of the moment of peace and beauty it brings
  - driving the pretty way to work, rather than just the fastest way
- trying new things, even as seemingly trivial as
  - new restaurants
  - new breakfast cereal
  - adding a new, fun color to your wardrobe

There are a million different small and medium ways to add joy to your life, add peace to your life, and add meaning to your life. As these small and mediums accumulate, we find that our joy – true joy! – increases significantly. We discover a kick in our step, more laughter, and a really great feeling of happiness inside.

The small and medium stuff really do matter. And it's soooo doggone easy to neglect them. It's too easy to say, "Ah, it's no big deal," about anything that isn't a big thing. It's easy to let the small and medium stuff slide. And with it our happiness slides away too. Just like in a relationship with another person, in our own lives we lose ourselves in a death by a thousand cuts when we neglect the small and medium stuff.

What's really neat is that sometimes these small and mediums become big things – become a full-size leg on the stool, all by themselves. A dear friend of mine had always been a bit of a loner, yet had cultivated a kinship among his friends. But when he became a member of his girlfriend's big southern family, the importance of family grew exponentially for him. It became its own leg on his stool of life, bringing him a level of happiness in such a new way, like he had never known. Another example: numerous friends and clients have discovered, after a lifetime of beating up their bodies in pursuit of career, that the desire and need for good health had become a sort of fourth leg on the stool – an absolute required item for them to be happy.

The goal of life is to fill our own Love Cup – to create a life of Diamonds, a life of self-love, rather than trying to buy love from another person in a relationship. Until we can fill our own Love Cup, we are forever dependent on others for happiness, forever giving our power away, also forever waiting to get the three legs in place. Forever tenuous; never arrived. And filling that Love Cup happens best in the small and mediums. However, that requires re-orienting life from the biggies to the other stuff; or at least prioritizing some portion of life energy to those other things, allowing them to grow and become new sources of joy, peace, and meaning.

CHAPTER 43

WHEN 'SHOULD I LEAVE?'
BECOMES 'I'M DONE!'

It makes it very easy to walk away from a situation, set of circumstances, or relationship when you finally feel like you've done everything you can to make it work and yet nothing has changed. At that point, walking away becomes effortless. Having that realization 'There's nothing more I can do here. I've done everything I can. I'm exhausted' is powerful in being able to then easily walk away.

And, truth is, when it's time to walk away, you'll know. You'll just know. *Du vet!* There'll be no internal wrangling or wrestling with the options, back and forth. When it's truly time, you'll know, just like you knew when it was time to get into a relationship. You trusted the voice getting in, and it's time to trust the voice, when it comes to getting out. And, if you don't know yet – I mean, like, *really know it*, matter of factly – it ain't time. As a result, worst of all, your pain *will* get worse. Guaranteed. Change will not occur, until the pain gets bad enough. If you ain't acting, your pain isn't bad enough. And, as surely as the sun rises in the east, there's a whole new level of hurt coming your way. Your grip will be broken. Count on it.

As said above, nothing is easier than walking away when it's just done – when your commitment to 'what was' is exceeded by the pain of what it has all become – and you know there's nothing more you can do. That's why I encourage people to hold on for as long as they can, rather than suggesting they get out or try to let go, or even force themselves to let go (as if that were even possible). The more and longer you hold on, the more your grip tires and, hence, the more you're getting it out of your system. Therefore, the easier it'll be to walk away, because you'll simply know you did all you can.

And, dumb as it sounds, until you know, you don't know. You're still engaged in "Should I or shouldn't I?" Mental angst rules your life. And, as a result, you're forcing it. Until it's time, it's not time. And you'll know definitively and absolutely when it's time. Mark my words.

Journaling And Song Recommendations

Forgive me for asking the obvious questions (for your journaling), but:

1. Is it time to walk away? Are you done? Have you done everything you can do? If not, do you desire to still stay in it and keep trying? If so, why? What persistent hope keeps you in it?

2. Now, download and soak in the lyrics to **Macy Gray's**, *I Try.* https://www.youtube.com/watch?v=WEQ0l_m3Xm0ITry

3. Does this song speak to where you are, right now? Or does it speak to where you were? Are you truly ready to walk away, knowing you won't stumble, knowing your world will not fall apart?

4. If you are still in it, if you're still in that state of inner wrangling and uncertainty, always responding, 'I don't know what to do,' when asked if you're walking away yet, then let me ask you for your journaling: What is it you haven't done yet? What is it that you still have not said, or perhaps never said? What is it you still feel called to keep doing, because you still don't have clarity? At least be totally honest with yourself: even if you hate doing it, what is it that you want to keep doing, at least for a little while longer? Because, if you don't have the clarity that you know you're walking away, it means you still want to keep holding on, keep trying, keep hoping against hope. And there's nothing wrong with that. But at least be honest with yourself about it. Now, whatever you wrote as your answers to those questions, go do those things. Truth is, that's the stuff that really scares you to do or say. But until you do, you're not ready to go and you're just treading water, hoping something magically changes.

5. Now, I want to ask you this, is it really that you don't want to let go of this relationship or that you're just plain

334

terrified of being on your own? If the latter, what are you most afraid of – being alone, the voices that mock you in your head when you are alone, what people will say, or the thought that maybe no one will love you now, at your age, or is it the simple logistics of making it on your own? (Btw, you CAN make it on your own, especially as you get stronger from living your truth.)

6. Is it possible, just possible, that new love can happen? What are you feeling right now as you consider all of this?

7. How bad does life have to get before you finally let go of the toxic Raw Sewage?

CHAPTER 44

BREAKUP MYTHS:
'IT WAS MUTUAL' AND 'LET'S BE FRIENDS'

All sorts of blather gets said at the ending of a relationship, most of it very well-intentioned, some of it absolute nonsense despite being well-intentioned. Unfortunately, some of what gets said isn't outright malicious but it can be quite selfish, to the detriment of the other person and, ultimately, oneself.

This is not to say that we ought not be selfish. Truth is, too many relationships get strung out well past their freshness date, because one or two people are afraid to be a bit selfish and look out for their own spiritual and relationship needs and subsequently take honest action. However, the ugly selfishness is found, most often, not in the what or even why, but in how it is done. And often the how goes much better when we best understand the why's.

> *"It's not what you say.*
> *It's how you say it."*
> -Grandma Charlotte Erlandson

Relationships End For The Same Reason They Started
Ever been in a relationship where your partner has certain attributes that you either really liked in the early years or you simply were able to overlook, but as time went further along you found yourself disliking those attributes, more and more? Sure, we all have been in that situation.

Maybe it's that your partner:
- Never apologizes
- Never forgives
- Is a crappy communicator
- Fights a lot

- Is always crabby, not outright mean, but just crabby and insensitive
- Eats too much
- Doesn't eat
- Feels like she has one foot in and one foot out of the relationship
- Doesn't shower
- Has been taking advantage of you, for years
- Has wicked breath
- Takes you for granted
- Doesn't work
- Works too much
- Is just someone you don't respect
- Has a bold, brash family
- Has an insanely boring family
- Stays in a lot
- Is never fully present
- Goes out a lot
- Is a heavy drinker
- Doesn't drink
- Doesn't play well on the team
- Nags a lot

That notion of tolerating, or even outright liking, something at one point and then later on not enjoying it is a simple little example of the very truth that **feelings change**, even on a micro level. But, they not only change, *they change even though the behavior has not changed*. In other words, a person can be engaging in some behavior you tolerate or even like, then three years later they're doing the exact same behaviors to the exact same degree, but now, three years later, it's not cute, not fun, and doesn't feel good. In other words, they didn't change, you did.

The point I am making here is not about attributes and behavioral reasons for breakups. No, it's a larger point. It's about feeeel. Specifically, how you feeeeeel about a person is not always tied up in an action or behavior. It's tied up in forces beyond our control. It's tied up in the whim and fancy of the gods, themselves, the Universe, Cupid, God, soul. How else do you explain that the exact behaviors of your mate have not changed, yet your feeeeel toward that person – your chemistry in the relationship – *has changed*?

In other words, if how you feel about someone were solely tied up in their behaviors, then you would either never have liked them and their poor communication and nagginess in the beginning or you would still like it, today, years later. If anything, in all likelihood, their nagging and communication have actually become not as bad as they were before, because you've likely said something and they've changed, somewhat. You've worn them down a bit, shaving off the rough edges. So the problem has actually gotten better, but your feelings have gotten worse.

How the heck do you explain that?!

But I ask that question only rhetorically. The real issue I'm getting at here is that at the end of a relationship all that matters is feeeeel, not reasons. The reasons or actions are irrelevant and perhaps never changed.

**All relationships end for the same reason:
One person just doesn't feeeel it, anymore.**

**It's not about reasons, logic, or 'You did this' or 'You didn't do this and that.'
It's about the simple fact, after all the reasons and circumstances are taken into consideration,
'I just don't feel it [for you], anymore.'**

Whatever their actions are (abusing drugs, abusing me, not working for a long time, being a bad mom, just being a jerk, simple chronic halitosis, or a million other reasons), what matters is that I no longer feel it for him or her. The actions and words contribute to the feelings (or lack of feelings), but, when it comes down to it, the relationship ends because of the feelings. Whatever those feelings might be that cause you to end a relationship – maybe it's lack of security, lack of fun, too much craziness, too much heaviness, or what have you – relationships end because the feeeeel has changed. Whatever the feelings are that cause you to end a relationship, they have clearly come up and reached the point where you're walking away. You can say it's about the actions, but it's really about the feeling.

And that's why I generally recommend to couples that they not get caught up in the why's of a breakup, other than to simply say, 'I just don't feel it anymore.' Getting caught up in denouncing the other person's actions only creates neuroses in them and storylines for future relationships. They begin to define themselves by the actions you call out as negative. And it's not your business to define another person's identity. It's your job to get out of a relationship, if you no longer feel it, but not do harm on the way.

Interestingly,

Relationships end for the same reason they began:
the feel.
Not reasons, feel.

Every single one of us has been in the beginning dating stage of a potential relationship and found ourselves sitting across the table from someone who has all sorts of wonderful attributes; I mean, a really great guy or woman – smart, funny, attractive, or what have you. But, for some reason, or for no reason, at all, you just don't feel it for this person. A truly wonderful person, but no chemistry between the two of you; no feeeeel inside you for this person. Right? We've all experienced that, at some point or another. And there's nothing wrong with that. Either you feel it or you don't.

Conversely, you can sit across the table from someone who doesn't look nearly so good on paper or even in person, or doesn't meet what you thought were all your criteria, but for some doggone reason (or for no explicable reason) you both feel really drawn to each other. There's admiration, chemistry, vibe, feel, and whatever else.

We get into relationships because of feeeeel, not reasons. We get out of relationships because, in the end, it just doesn't feel good anymore, whatever the 'reasons'. But, focusing on or even articulating the 'reasons' at the end of a relationship really does no one any good.

The Courage To Break Up

Many people come to me for counseling, considering ending a relationship. Yet, very often, the thing stopping them from divorcing is that they:

- Fear looking like the bad guy;
- Fear hurting the other person;
- Fear being overwhelmed by the other person's reasoning and arguments talking them out of it;
- Fear the inevitable pain that comes from breakups – pain from ending a relationship with someone you no longer love or someone you still love but aren't in love with.

But, when we understand that breakups are really, at their core, about feelings and not reasons, it alleviates a great amount of the burden. Because, the simple fact of the matter is that you cannot control your true feelings. You cannot control whom you love. You really can't. Think about that.

We do not choose love;
love chooses us.
--Unknown

If you fear your partner overwhelming you, trying to talk you out of the break up (as they likely have done with a hundred other things, previously, else you wouldn't be afraid of them doing so, this time), getting mad, or offering some other negative response, simply keep coming back to this one thing: feel. When you simply don't feel it anymore, there is no amount of talking or cajoling that can change your feelings. They may say your feelings will change if they do x, y, or z. But the truth is that they likely won't change their actions for long (because they've not even touched the underlying beliefs driving the behaviors) and your feelings won't change, at all, because if you've reached the level of clarity of feelings that you're willing to act on them, then those same feelings are strong enough to not be swayed. You may get talked into staying awhile or going back, but, deep down, your feelings haven't changed and they won't change, despite all of your partner's pleading. Clarity of feelings is an incredibly powerful thing. So, focus on the loss of chemistry.

Keep coming back to the simple truth that you just don't feel it anymore and it has been this way for a long time, long enough for you to realize (and act on) that you just don't want to be here anymore.

> *The heart has its reasons*
> *that reason cannot know.*
> --Blaise Pascal

Regarding looking like the bad guy, you are going to look that way, at least to the other person, perhaps even to a few others. But, it is alleviated by the fact that it's feelings that you simply cannot change. You've not only done everything you can, but simply no longer feel it. It simply is what it is. There is no compromise. In fact, the giant problem in the past is that you DID compromise your feelings. And now, you're simply unwilling to compromise your feelings anymore. That is a good thing.

Regarding hurting the other person, you will. The more they're enmeshed in this relationship, the more they draft their own sense of identity from the relationship. And/or, the more they get some needed sense of security from the relationship, the more this breakup is going to hurt. But, again, the consolation to yourself, if not to them, is that this is simply how you feel and you cannot die inside anymore. The short term pain your partner will experience upon losing a relationship pales compared to the long term pain you would experience if you stayed in a relationship wherein you just don't feel it anymore, not to mention the pain they're certainly experiencing in the relationship.

Regarding the inevitable breakup pain, yeah, you're going to feel it. And it stinks. But the consolation comes from knowing you have to do this, knowing that you're honoring YOUR feelings, and knowing that despite the short term dip in feelings, the long term gain in feeeeel in your life will radically increase, if for no other reason than you're cutting a major negative energy source out of your life. (Don't tell your partner that, because he/she will think they are the major negative energy source, when in fact the negative energy source is the relationship, the lack of all-around chemistry, the absence of feel.)

The ending of relationships is clean when it focuses on feel. Things get murky and relationships get protracted when we get into reasons, actions, wherefores and whynots. That's when things get drawn out for more months and years.

But acting on feel requires trusting feel. More importantly, it requires believing that your feelings matter, which, of course, goes completely contrary to everything you've been taught about yourself your entire life. Until you give credence to your feelings, nothing changes. 'Credence' comes from the Latin 'I believe'. Until you believe in you and in your feelings, ain't nothin' gonna change. Until you believe in you and the power of the Universe speaking through your body and the feeeel of things, you will never have the courage to live deliberately, live your truth, and be/say/do/have/believe/become who you truly are.

And really, what option do you have? If you choose to *not* break up, because you don't want to look like the bad guy, don't want to hurt the other person, and/or don't want to experience that breakup pain yourself, you're basically staying in a relationship that you're not fully in. You've got one foot in the relationship (if that) and one foot out of a relationship.

We only enjoy something to the degree we're in it.

And if you've got one foot in and one foot out, you're not going to enjoy it, which means you'll be sucking life out of the relationship (or what's left of it) and out of the other person, and all because you don't want to hurt their feelings or look like the bad guy. So, basically, you're using them, so that you don't have to go through pain or look bad. You're using someone you claim to love, or at least care about. You're lying, flat out, to them, so that you don't have to do the hard work of ending something that you know for fact you're done with.

That's not just cowardice. It's malicious. What does it say about you that you would rather hurt someone you love, long term, than stand up, have courage, and hurt them short term to save them long term pain, and in fact set them free to go live and find someone who truly loves them?

See, this is why people cheat. Crazy as it sounds (and I wrote a whole book on it), it's easier to cheat and thereby blow up a relationship than it is to just end a relationship that needs to be put to death. Why? That grand fear of looking like the bad guy. And that even grander fear of having the courage to speak your truth – to look someone in the eye and simply be fully doggone honest.

Don't be that guy who uses, who chooses the coward's path. Don't be that woman. Stand up. Matter. Speak your truth. Live it.

'Let's Be Friends'

And so, because ending relationships is just doggone hard, one of the things we say to assuage the pain, either the pain in ourselves or our mate, is to say the classic line, 'Well, let's be friends.' And it's a nice thought. We're trying to let the other person down nicely.

But it never works. Never. At least not in the short term.

Why? One person is always holding on, when a relationship ends. One person is still clinging. Truth is, you wouldn't be saying 'Let's be friends' unless you sorta already knew one of you was holding on. So you say it, or they do it.

But what that seemingly nice phrase does to a break up is extend it, on and on. One person keeps thinking there's hope for reconciliation, when there really isn't. The only reason that hope for reconciliation even exists is because one person didn't have the courage to do the difficult act of bringing a hard stop to the relationship. The pain for both parties becomes protracted when one person keeps clinging and trying to weasel their way back in and when one person grows exhausted that their partner just isn't 'getting the hint.' UGH! You want them to get the hint despite the simple fact that you didn't have the courage to give a hard 'No' in the first place, leaving no room for reconciliation.

> **You're getting mad at him/her**
> **for always trying to walk through a door**
> **that you, in your cowardice, left open.**

'Let's be friends' keeps getting tried and tried by the two people, until the pain of it not working gets so bad that they blow apart, precisely as they should have, in the first place.

Perhaps two people *will* be friends, in the long, long term. Heck, it's even likely. But it almost never, ever works, short term. You're better off not even trying. It places way too much strain on the person who is still clinging, as well as on the person who is forever trying to fend off their advances in the nicest ways possible, at least until the nice ways are no longer possible.

Breakups Are Never Mutual

Like you, I've heard it a thousand times from a thousand different people about past breakups, 'Oh, it was mutual.'

Hahahahahaha. It is never mutual. It's always someone's more than the other's. Always. Yeah, one person may have gotten coerced into swallowing it. Or, one person may have gone along with it. But it's never mutual. It's always at least 51% one person's breakup (though usually far more than 51%).

So, when do you have the courage to be honest about that breakup in your past, or the one you're considering? See, you can't start being honest about your present, if you're not honest about your past. You also can't start honestly expressing your feelings and living deliberately in the present, unless you acknowledge that your feelings matter. And that requires acknowledging that you've lived as though your feelings don't matter, in the past.

Stand up. Live honestly. Just be who you are. Stop running. Stop cowering, as if who you are, your voice, and what you feel and aspire to don't matter. It's time to live.

Song Recommendation

This is one of my top five favorite songs of all time. I've been listening to it my entire life. And while I've loved it immensely, I've secretly hated it, because it's about breakups; and it's hard to have a favorite song be about breakups (much like The Carpenters, *Goodbye to Love*). But, not only is this the consummation of the early, brassy yet hardrock-edged **Chicago** sound, it's a great message in this context. We're discussing the fear of breaking up, particularly the fear of hurting the other person and looking like the bad guy.

345

But, *Feelin' Stronger Every Day*, by **Chicago**, https://www.youtube.com/watch?v=e-wHixgp2REFeelingStrongerEveryDay a great message about being the person who was broken up from. It's a message of hope. But it's also implicitly a message to the person considering breaking up from someone, 'Don't be afraid. Do the break up. They will get stronger. They will recover.' And if they have the courage to go into themselves, they will find that this 'no' from you was a passageway into a greater 'yes', both from their own self and from a new lover.

Back when I was an NCAA Strength Coach, a friend of mine, who was an assistant coach for one of the teams, told me that his favorite word as a coach was the word 'No.' "Why is that," I asked.

He explained, "Sven, 2/3 of my job is spent recruiting, not coaching. At the collegiate level, it's all about recruiting. On-field coaching is so greatly determined by recruiting. So, I spend hundreds and hundreds of hours, every year, calling high school kids and their families, trying to get them to come to our school. I may call a kid 20 or 30 times. One kid! Do you have any idea how good it feels to get the word 'No'? You'd think I'd hate it, and I do; but I also love it. Because, when I get a 'no' it means I can stop calling that kid. It narrows my list, not just whittling down my work load but clarifying my list. When I get a kid who has the guts to actually tell me 'no', rather than just string me along and let me keep calling him, I love that kid. I respect that so much, because it's a sign of respect for me and my time. 'No' is such a gift."

What's true in recruiting is true in relationships. The person on the other side of your 'no' will recover, get stronger, get clarity, and move on to a greater, happier state in life. 'No' is such a blessing. Feeeel the 'no'; feel what it will be like when it is spoken and moved past. Feeel the possibility of new life, new happiness, and new love.

CHAPTER 45

SURPRISE!

And now, at the end of it all, there's a bit of a twist to this whole Love Cup story.

The simple fact of the matter is that the ultimate goal of the spiritual life is not about having a full Love Cup. Yes, I realize that we've just spent an entire book trying to get your Love Cup emptied of crud, patched on the bottom, and filled by small, medium, and large love sources. But the end game was never about walking around with a full Cup. Yes, the goal, up to this point, was to heal a wounded life that was hemorrhaging love or completely bereft of love in the first place. But there's more, far more; in fact, something completely different.

See, the really fascinating theoretical and quite practical question is this: What happens when the Love Cup of your soul has been cleaned, scoured, patched/healed of all holes, and then filled with love by your own creation of a happy life? I mean,

What do you do with a full Love Cup?

And there's only one answer:

Poke a hole in it, of course!

In truth, you were never born to be a Love Cup, collecting love here and there, like that squirrel anxiously foraging for acorns before winter. You were created as an instrument of Divine love and power. That means, it was all meant to flow *through* you, not just pool in and around you.

Spiritual mastery is not about how much love you can collect inside you, nor even just about how much love you can pour onto others. It's about both. The problem is, most people start pouring before they ever learn how to collect, or they collect but, believing in deficiency rather than abundance, never pour. Thus, sooooo many people are on empty, all the doggone time. Yet, the spiritual path is living as an instrument of the gods – doing God's work here on earth. It's about creating a vessel, or instrument, that is:

- free of encrusted negative crud
- free of holes that were put there involuntarily
- constantly fed by life forces and love sources, AND
- able and eager to flow love *out* onto and into others.

In other words, the spiritual master is one who has become a **Love Funnel**. The advanced person on the spiritual journey is one who can control the size of the aperture at the top of his/her funnel (allowing for greater or lesser flow into it), as well as the aperture at the bottom (allowing for a wide spray of love to flow onto many or a tightened, laser-like flow of love out on to one, two, or a few). A great many people, who have not commenced the real spiritual journey, have love tumbling out of them, but it is neither deliberate nor metered. It is the result of damage, not desire or Divine flow. It is spilling out the bottom or over the edges of the top – full of rocks and hole in the bottom. That is a very different state from the one who has finally healed her Cup and then voluntarily chosen to become a Love Funnel.

The one who has truly mastered his or her own spirit can pool love, release all love, maintain a seemingly endless flow and release, or pretty much any other configuration of energy and love flow, including total shutdown to simply rest....all the while knowing that the flow of love from the Universe is never-ending and abundant, easily captured, easily released.

That's not just some hokey, New Agey cliché. Every religion of the world and every myth system, past and present, uses some form of language to express that the spiritual journey is about unblocking the energy sources in your life to live a life at full wingspan, no longer afraid, wings no longer clipped. Change the language, the message is the same.

In the long run,
You were never born to be a Cup.
You were born to be a Love Funnel.

And see, there's the odd thing about funnels. If you pour a pitcher of water through a standard kitchen funnel or pour 10W-30 through a metal funnel, after you do so you can run your finger around the inside of the funnel and notice that plenty of water (or oil) got stuck to the inside of the funnel. No matter how much passes through, some always sticks. In other words, the funnel gets the joy and total rush of all that life energy and love flowing through it, AND it gets the residue of life and love after it flows through. And, somewhere amid it all is the trust, the knowing, that the flow will come again and is always available, if you are tuned in and forever removing blockages.

But the goal is never to be full of love, per se, but to forever feel the love and energy of the Universe passing through you. In other words, the purpose of the spiritual life is to learn to let go of love just as surely as it is about creating flowing love into one's life.

But...

So, why go to all the trouble of patching and healing the bottom of your Love Cup that has a hole in it, if the grand goal is to poke a hole in it and just to be a Love Funnel, anyway?

Great question!

It was necessary for your healing and growth to lay the foundation and do the work of this entire book to come to this final and most important evolution from Cup thinking to understanding yourself to be a Love Funnel. It is necessary to, first, conceive of yourself as a Cup that holds love and *necessary to make all critical repairs to the Cup,* in order to get you to the point of the next spiritual level, so to speak, which cannot be arrived at without first destroying all the cruddy beliefs from your past. It was necessary to reconstruct a healthy and love-filled Cup and foundation of core beliefs, as well as fully opened Binary Gates.

The difference between Cup and Funnel thinking
is that one is a wound and one is choice.

One is a mentality of hurt, fear, and hoarding;
The other is a place of trust, knowing, deliberateness, and
abundance.

One is what was done to you, while the other is a necessary, yet
voluntarily chosen feature
for true life, true abundance, true joy, true and lasting peace,
and true sense of purpose.

But no, the truth is, we are not Cups. We were created to be Love Funnels, instruments of Divine love – graced to both feeeel it and give it. Both, not either/or. And you simply cannot become a Funnel without first becoming a Cup, without knowing, fully experiencing, and trusting in the fullness of love flowing in the Universe. No one can ever force another person to be a Love Funnel against their will. Further, to truly be a Love Funnel demands first knowing you are wanted, are inherently good, and truly matter. And most people have no concept of what that means; or, rather, they have no *experience* of what it feeeeeels like to know that in the depths of their soul. But to be merely a cup with a hole in the bottom is to believe none of these is true. Knowing it and living/experiencing it are two vastly different things. A Love Funnel is an instrument of power; a Cup with a hole in the bottom is merely a wounded life, forever being depleted, never fully replenished, never truly knowing the enormity of Divine power.

And why would anyone ever choose to be a Love Funnel after repairing the Love Cup and being so full of love and appreciation for one's own value? Why would someone voluntarily sacrifice the state of fullness – truly full of love? I mean, who would ever do such a thing?

This is the ultimate question!

And the simple answer is because you WANT to. The human soul, in its freest and most ecstatic state, loves giving love. That's the grand spiritual commonality of our existence. We all long to both feel love and feel the massive delight of giving love. There's no greater and lasting high than:

- Creating the beliefs infrastructure and spiritual disciplines necessary for a clean vessel and an ongoing flow of Universal energy;

- Feeling the rush of the energy of the Universe coursing through you, daily, by tapping into your intuition and deepest sense of inner knowing, fully trusting where it is leading you, each day;
- Giving passionate energy and abundant love to others;
- Knowing that you can shut it all down, close the top aperture, take any length of time off, or give away all of your love and life force....*and there'll be a complete replenishment, because the love and energy flowing into you from the Universe is always there, waiting to be tapped.*

There is simply no joy in life, no more sublime experience, than to pour it all out or spray an intense stream of life energy to another, to let it all flow through you, and to feel it replenished, feel yourself rejuvenated, and then to allow the Universe to provide you with more opportunities to do it again. There is no greater ecstasy than to be an instrument of the gods, an instrument of Divine love in the world. It is to know, after you have finally healed your wounds, that your life has meaning as you experience that giving of life energy to others, a lot, knowing you can never deplete its flow.

This is happiness. This is the consummate definition of clarity. This is inner peace. This is, in the end, true ALIVENESS! May it be yours, forever.

Song Recommendation

Could any collection of songs be complete without Michael? So perfectly appropriate to both your evolution throughout this book and the climax of this final Love Funnel chapter, I offer this MJ classic, which speaks of self-change and commitment to serving those whose need is even greater: *Man In The Mirror*, https://www.youtube.com/watch?v=PivWY9wn5psManInTheMirror by **Michael Jackson**.

And now, one final recommendation: the all-time classic that has been covered by Heart, David Foster and others. The original of *You're the Voice* written and performed by **John Farnham** was, https://www.youtube.com/watch?v=Awb_JrEvtFgYouAreTheVoice back in the 80's. It's a totally kickass song. I LOVE it. Love Foster's version. Love Heart's version. But love the original most.

Actually, the very, very best version is performed by Farnham live at the 2003 ARIA Awards. For, he includes timpani, bagpipes, orchestra, and a whole lot of energy!!! You can pull it up on YouTube. If you're looking for inspiration, this song MUST be part of your music library. So buy it!

Benediction
And now, lastly, this:

[Spirit of the Universe],
You have called your servants
To ventures of which we cannot see the ending,
By paths, as yet, untrodden,
Through perils unknown.
Give us strength
To go out with good courage,
Not knowing where we go,
Only that your hand is leading us
And your love supporting us. Amen.

--from the liturgy of *The Lutheran Book of Worship*

BONUS TRACKS

THE ROOT OF ALL DEPRESSION & ANXIETY

The thing you have to understand is that basically all spiritual unrest manifests as one (or two) of two things: depression and/or anxiety. In other words, whatever is actually going on deep inside you is one thing. But h*ow you experience it* – i.e. the way you know there is a problem – is as either depression or anxiety, which can feel like: Fatigue, lack of interest, never-ending churning of the mind, apathy, numbness and/or nervousness, busyness, agitation, fighting, lethargy, hopelessness, unrest, etc. And you know it's bad when it just doesn't stop, persisting for months or even years and decades.

And the belief of Badass Counseling®, which is my method for spiritual counseling, as opposed to psychology, religion, or life-coaching is that this is not a result of your immediate life situation, per se, or even because of some chemical imbalance or bad behaviors, but in fact causes them. My belief and the core of my work is that depression and anxiety invariably result from someone living two lives – who they really are, deep down, and who they're trying to be on the outside to either win praise or avoid criticism.

The root of nearly all depression, in fact the great fear of every person is the sheer terror of "showing the world who I really am, because if I show you, you may not like me; you may reject me; you may do or say something that would hurt....just as it hurt so much as a kid when I expressed myself and was gunned down, intimidated, criticized, or in some other way hurt. Rather than relive that hell of showing the world who I really am, it's better to keep who I really am – my authentic self – locked inside."

Of course, the downside of that way of living is that there is forever this grating, this massive internal tension and unrest, about midway between your chest and gut, where the external world you're trying to force into your whole being meets the truth of your internal, eternal self and soul. There the two meet and grind in a forever dissonant and painful scraping, like tectonic plates below ground, forever creating earthquakes on the surface.

And so, the depression and anxiety grow out of living this fake external life. And when we try to live that way, the soul grieves and bleeds any hope for future ALIVENESS. Further, the soul and life-energy of the individual are so greatly taxed in trying to keep up the facade that the soul requires constant rest, both to keep things going but also to mourn another day of truth lost, another day of self gone to the wind. Yet, the mind will scurry through days, feverishly trying to generate success of some sort – always success – to make you feel important, feel like and believe you are somebody, when inside you think you're nobody, nothing. That scurrying is the anxiety, the ever-present fear of nothingness, while trying to force somethingness.

There is a third way in which a life unlived manifests itself. And that is lack of clarity. I find that a great many of my clients seek not only the experience of feeling at peace in their being and fully alive in their experiences, but also the experience of a quiet mind – a mind that is not forever churning and churning, forever trying to solve the whole equation of their unfulfilling life.

It is this churning – this feeling completely awash in one's own untangleable thoughts, fears, drives, and wants – that leads to all manner of maladaptive, inappropriate, or destructive behaviors. Each one of these things becomes a friend, of sorts; the one thing that enables you to turn off your mind, even if only for a few hours. These things, for years, enable a person to survive the massive oppression of a full mind, even while simultaneously raping every other aspect of the individual's life, from draining bank accounts to blowing up relationships, from oppressing one's own children to killing brain cells, from driving you into reclusiveness to generating massive self-loathing, and from cooking your inner organs to – did I mention? – bleeding off all your money.

That longing for mental clarity and peace is a massive driver. Clarity and peace are natural bedfellows. Clarity is an extremely powerful tonic. Meditation is a powerful tool for quieting the mind in a positive way, as are exercise, yoga, sex, physical labor and even religious services and prayer. But, they are only temporary. The high wears off. It's like you're constantly having to put out the fires of new problems, new anxieties, new headaches and new hardships. The effects are fleeting, as the endorphins, dopamine, serotonin, and oxytocin wear off. Unless you uproot the original thoughts and beliefs that created the unrest and pain, in the first place, you'll forever be fighting this battle of trying to quiet your mind, having unrest, trying to quiet the mind, unrest, quieting, unrest, *ad infinitum*.

The big mistake people make in seeking peace is attempting to control and reduce negative external circumstances and increase positive external circumstances, as if any of that is possible without becoming totally neurotic. External circumstances are wily, slippery things, not prone to being controlled. Positive situations can never be held in place and maintained for long periods and negative situations never stop coming. Try to short-circuit either or both of those truths and your anxiety level will go through the roof and stay there.

Yes, there will always been hiccups, hurdles, and hardships coming at you from life. And thus, there will always be anxieties and sadnesses, as well as the need to release them. But the effect of daily anxieties and setbacks is far, far, FAR less when all of the other major life blows are no longer inside you. The big mistake is going outside, rather than inside; or the problem is in looking inside but not going deep enough. In other words, the real and only lasting solution is to control and reduce the internal negative beliefs and negatively charged memories, and cement (which are what's really weighing you down; not your bills, boss, or responsibilities), and simultaneously increase the positive internal beliefs. The only solution is to go down to the level of core beliefs and soul.

When a lifetime of hurt is still inside you, it only takes the smallest slight or provocation to cause a lifetime of pain to come to the surface and come spilling out. If you have a mug full to the top with piping hot coffee and then you you agitate that mug just a little bit, guess what comes spilling out onto whatever or whomever is near? Piping hot coffee. Or, add even a tiny amount more of piping hot coffee to that full, hot mug and guess what. Yep, the scalding stuff spills out and burns whomever is near. Yep, we're always burning those closest to us, not those furthest away.

And sure, it feels good to get agitated and spill out some of the burning liquid, because it feels good to not have so much burning inside. But there are other ways to empty that mug.

Further, if you empty that mug of all the piping hot coffee and *then* pour in a small, or even medium to large, amount of piping hot coffee, guess what comes spilling out? Nothing, because the cup still isn't anywhere near capacity. Or if you have a mug that has little to no piping hot coffee in it, it can take a massive amount of agitation and shaking before any hot stuff comes out to burn those people around it.

It's the same with soul pain. Imagine living with an empty coffee mug! No scalding stuff. No crud. No inner anxiety and pain. No deadened spirit. It becomes easy to deal with day-to-day trials and mishaps, or even deaths and loss, without them becoming overwhelming and totally depression-inducing. Once you remove the originating beliefs and thoughts, peace is inevitable. And thus, any new stressors that come down the pike become very easily manageable, because they are not the incessant straw breaking the camel's back, again and again. But when the mug isn't full of scalding cruddy stuff it can be filled with love and happy stuff. And when you agitate a mug of love, guess what spills out: love, not scalding pain and hurt.

To have not only peace in your heart and joy in life, but also clarity in the head is a tremendously relaxed, yet powerful place to be in life. And it is not only possible but likely, if you have the courage to go inside rather than outside, to let go of that which is no longer you. And I'm talking mainly the stuff that is in you that you think you're required to carry around – beliefs and values that are simply not you and are, thus, creating a massive amount of dissonance in your gut and mind. Life only truly begins when we have the courage to cut from our lives the very deep, true sources of depression, anxiety, and incessant mental agitation.

Journaling And Book Recommendations
1. What are the parts of you that you're most afraid to show the world? Why?
2. In your intimate relationship, what are the three things you're most afraid to show about yourself to your partner? Why?

What are you most afraid will happen? Are you afraid he/she will reject you?

3. What about in your friendships, what are the two or three things you are most ashamed of or most afraid to show people?

4. What is the one career path or life choice you most want but are most afraid to make or reveal? A) Why do you want that? What's really at the heart of wanting that? B) What is the biggest reason you're afraid to make that decision or reveal that truth?

5. How does your inner life most manifest in your outer life, as depression or anxiety?

6. Who are the 1-3 people who would most accept you and love you, no matter what you revealed about yourself? Why? How have these people won your trust?

7. Who are the 1-3 people whom you know, for fact, would most judge or criticize you, if you were to reveal more of your truths? Why? What evidence have they given you in the past that they would criticize you?

Now, if you read no other book besides this one, let it be *The Sedona Method*, by Hale Dwoskin, which details the method for discharging your past (and present) that was created and perfected by Lester Levenson. It is a very fast, highly effective method for emptying out all the pain inside and living free and imperturbable as you go on about your life.

However, do not attempt to read the book if you're not going to follow through. *The Sedona Method* is not so much a book as a workbook. It requires the daily discipline to work the very simple formula for, say, 20 minutes per day. You can do it on your morning commute to work. If you are a person who regularly works out, goes to yoga, meditates, or engages in any other form of self-discipline, you can do the Sedona Method on your own. But, you gotta do the daily work as your spiritual discipline. If you lack self-discipline or just lack time, this book may not be the best for you, even though it is a book that is one of the top-3 most life-changing books I have ever read and used. In that case, the Sedona Method is offered as weekend workshops, which I also strongly recommend and have sent clients and members of my own family to. That, too, requires turning it into a brief daily habit (for 60 days, minimum), but it's easier to keep that habit when you've laid the foundation for it over a weekend with other people and a teacher. Whichever you use, book or workshop, I simply cannot recommend this highly enough for de-charging internal memories and emptying out the scalding and cruddy stuff from inside. If it is used everyday, The Sedona Method can and will change your life!

WHY TELLING AN ADULT TO
"JUST GET OVER IT AND MOVE ON"
IS THE DUMBEST THING EVER

As seen in the early chapters, core messages received from significant people, when young, become pressed into the cement of our soul, embedded in the belief system and operating system of our entire life.

For this reason, it becomes nonsensical, even silly, when that same person becomes an adult and is struggling in one way or another, and hears from others something to the effect of, "You're an adult. You need to just get over all this. It's all just a choice now that you're an adult. Just get over it and make yourself happy." To think someone can just will her- or himself past it is beyond ridiculous. No amount of willpower or behaviors, alone, can change core beliefs.

The power of core beliefs embedded in the soul – deep impressions made in the concrete of your very identity – is so great that today's problems are not quickly and easily solved by 'just getting over it'. And any exhortations by others to do so have the effect of adding even more shame and guilt to the life of the person who just can't seem to solve his/her life problems. The beliefs that run the operating system of your life cannot be over-written with a throwaway exhortation to 'just get over it.'

Such exhortations to do so are never given by the caring soul attempting to actually help the individual. Rather, they are words of frustration, exasperation, or outright contempt spoken by someone who simply doesn't want to deal with another person's problems, or at least not anymore. The callous exhortation does nothing except hurt the other person. Isn't it reasonable to assume that if someone could simply 'get over it,' they would? So, what is solved by saying such a thing, except to make the one speaking feel better by putting down the hearer. The speaker simply has no idea what to say or how to fix the troubled person who cannot seem to right their own ship. 'Just get over it' is a blatantly obvious earmark of someone who has absolutely no clue what they're dealing with.

Interestingly, this is also why a great many therapists are ineffective – they have no idea what they're looking for or lack the ability to drill down to the core beliefs embedded in the concrete of the soul or lack the ability to smash the old concrete beliefs and create a new belief system. Like a day laborer doing demolition work on a job site, it requires some heavy blows with a sledge to break and dislodge anything cemented. And a great many people, including therapists, simply don't know how to find or address core beliefs and their power over a person, not to mention the even deeper beliefs of the Binary Gates. Further, they often shy away from the 'heavy blows', opting instead for an ongoing game of Patty Cake blather. Yet, addressing the beliefs is both necessary and incredibly powerful.

PEOPLE SHOUT LOUDEST
WHEN FEELING HEARD LEAST

Jackie came into session saying that her weekend had been a disaster. Her 17 year-old daughter, who was the family emo kid and a bit of an odd duck, had recently taken to smoking grass and was sort of off living her own life. The daughter's individuality and 'having a life' simultaneously pleased and displeased Jackie. For, only two years prior, the daughter had been in the depths of a miserable relationship and a largely friendless life. Now, Jackie's prayers (and those of the ex-husband) had been answered; the kid had a life, friends, dreams, and was even doing better in school.

But now it felt like too much. The kid was gone a bit much, worked a lot, and was spending most hours of every day with her new boyfriend. None of that, in and of itself, was bad or unmanageable. But now, with the daughter's new bf there was a fear they were smoking too much pot. The mom knew the kid was smoking it previously, but couldn't prove it. Now the child had become so brazen as to come home stoned and deny it to the mother's face.

And so, the yelling had returned to their home, at least for the weekend; that on top of the daughter's unleashing on her father in very long, excoriating letters, for the first time ever, in the week prior.

Both mom and dad came to me for counsel, at separate times, wondering what the heck to do. Digging deeper, I was able to discern that the real concern was not the pot smoking but the new level of rather severe defiance. It's not that the teen was completely pliant prior to that (she wasn't) or had never yelled (she had). No, with the father letters in particular, she had taken the ferocity to a new height. As a result, the parental frustration was at a new level, as well.

Worse, I had to share with them the ugly news, which was guaranteed to bring results but was unlikely to fit into their present belief system, which fundamentally posited blame for the daughter's behavior in the daughter's lap. I'm sorry, but I'm really not of the belief that 99% of the people under age, say 30, are doing much of anything that is causa sui, *or self-generated.* They are a product, still at that age, of the primary influences in their lives, largely mom and dad. I don't excuse crummy behavior by the child. But I also know it's easy for parent's to gang up on a kid; and parents generally have all the power, in those years. So, I gave Jackie the news:

People yell because they don't feel heard.
People yell because
they feel they don't have a voice.

Jackie's daughter was raging and unleashing because someone wasn't listening, usually the powers that be. Think about it: if a person feels heard in their normal indoor voice, why would they yell? More importantly, if a person feels their points, logic, passions, and reasons are being listened to and respected by another person, what need would they have to be more adamant, more forceful, and more loud? They wouldn't.

I have plenty of clients who have cowered before their parents their entire lives, because when they were children they were taught they had no voice. Thus, the child believes, 'My voice doesn't matter.' So now there's all this pent-up rage (and really destructive core beliefs) in adulthood. People yell; people hammer home points; people get emotionally upset when conveying points, because they feel they're not being heard by normal conversation and their former methods for making points.

Not welcome news for Jackie or the father. For, it meant, in other words, the kid ain't the problem. Jackie is her own problem, to a very large degree in this case, as is the daughter's father who received the emotionally charged letters. Sadly, the father saw fit to take the daughter out for a walk and tell her how her anger and frustration only exist because she misunderstood him. In other words, implicit in his words on that walk was the message that she was at fault; she had screwed up. Her feelings had no merit. This, of course, was an obvious indicator that he still was not hearing her. In his mind, the problem was the daughter, not him. On the walk, the kid swallowed it, suppressing her truth. Once again the father failed to hear her and accept responsibility for her unhappiness.

When I heard about the father's misstep with his daughter, I was reminded of the words of my mother when I was 13 or 14, when she began teaching me how to counsel people:

Kids want to be heard, not fixed.
(And it's generally true of adults, too.)

But when you've been fixing your kid for 15 years, it gets hard to relinquish the fixing and the control that comes with it. To listen, absent of intent to influence – that is, to begin to honor the autonomy of the individual child that is, to be perfectly honest, not yours to control – requires deliberateness and letting go. It requires changing yourself, not your child, whom you could always bend in the past to meet your own needs and values. Any parent who has a teen or post-teen kid knows how incredibly difficult that is.

Jackie, the mom, was a bit more open to hearing that the only hope for lasting, positive change in the daughter demanded a change in the mother. She knew she needed to:

- Hear the child; or, at the very least, truly listen.
- Stop rebutting.
- Stop trying to defend herself.
- Stop trying to change the child.
- Stop trying to ram her will down the child's throat.
- And, again, just close her yapper and listen; hear the kid. Really hear her.

She knew she could then convey to the child that she still may not get everything she wanted (and kid's know this). There is something powerful about being heard that will often cause the child to relinquish the immediate need to have whatever-it-is right now.

Or maybe you will choose to give them whatever it is they're shouting for. But the far greater gift you give them is the experience of feeling heard and knowing their own voice is respected. It conveys to the child, "You really matter." Listening defuses anger, diffuses anxiety, and enables the other to remove the clouds of fear and high emotion that are making her unable to hear her own inner voice and confidently act on it. Until you can treat that child's voice and that child's viewpoint as valid and as the necessary lighthouse beacon orienting her own life, neither she nor you will be happy with them and their choices.

And, what's true for Jackie in her relationship with her daughter is true for you in your own life. The anger you have been suppressing toward your own father or mother, grandpa or aunt, and attempting to deny the existence of (because you still so fear your parent, in one way or another, and thus fear standing up to him/her), is the very truth that must be given voice. You may not be able or willing to speak the truth to the parent in real life. But the truth must be spoken, even if only in a letter you never send.

Truth is, you won't be free of the fear of the parent, free of the yoke of oppression of the parent, free to be who you really are, until you consider your voice important enough to be heard, until you finally yell to the heavens what your soul longs to yell. Whether that yelling involves an actual raising of the volume of your voice is irrelevant. The point is that you're finally raising your own true voice up from the dead, up from inside your soul, up from being hidden, demanding it be heard, or not heard; mostly, demanding it be spoken.

For, it's not about anyone else hearing you, anymore. It's about YOU HEARING YOU. It's about you finally proclaiming to the world that your voice matters – i.e. that YOU matter. The revolution in your life really has nothing to do with the parent, anymore. You have to change your perception of the importance of your voice and life. Until that changes, nothing changes. Until your voice and your truth matter to you and until you make life-decisions consistent with that truth, nothing matters. Everything else is just fake and ultimately pointless.

Make no mistake, your soul is yelling to you, demanding to finally be heard. So, it boils down to a few questions:

Are you listening to your soul's voice?
Has your pain gotten bad enough that you're finally motivated to do so?
Are you ready to finally let your soul shout to the heavens the importance of your existence?

Journaling Recommendation

- What is your soul longing to shout? What is it longing to say?
- Whose voice are you trying to be heard over? Who has most stifled your voice?
- In one sentence or less, what is the one message most being spoken to you that negates what you've been trying to say or your soul has been longing to say?
- Do you live with a clean heart – that is, what is it in your life that is still unspoken and to whom have you not spoken your fullest truth?
- What would it take for you to finally have the courage to speak your truths, so that your heart might finally be clean and light? Do you have the courage to do so, even knowing the price might be high?

Song Recommendation

Here's a very well-put statement by an 80's fun group, **Tears for Fears**. It's quite fitting for this work in clearing the heart of all that weighs it down. The song is ***Shout***. Give it a listen. https://www.youtube.com/watch?v=Ye7FKc1JQe4Shout

NAMING THE BEAST IS HALF THE PROBLEM

For decades, while growing up, I would hear my mother – who was a spiritual leader and counselor working as a Director of Education and later as a seminary professor – utter the words,

"Naming the beast
is half the problem."
--Charlotte E. Erlandson

Identifying and giving words to the deepest and realest 'why' driving the equation invariably has the effect of defanging it. It loses its grip on us, freeing us to, inch by inch, mile by mile, create an entirely new life. Similarly, naming the destructive *beliefs* and Binary Gates is absolutely required before there can be long-lasting change in actions, behaviors, and life paths.

Why? Because naming something changes the power equation. It disarms that which formerly held great power. In the field of medicine, doctors used to call their patients 'Tom,' 'Karl,' 'Susie' or 'Ethel,' but the patient was still expected to call the doctor 'Doctor,' 'Doctor Bentley' or 'Doctor Wenzel.' This created a power imbalance, when one person is a person and the other is a title. The titled person has power over the named person.

Staying in the medical realm, the same is true when the affliction of the patient is no longer a bunch of symptoms but becomes a disease that is seen and given a name by the powerful doctor. In traditional cultures, the job of the shaman, medicine man, or healer was to name the affliction of the individual who was suffering. The disease loses a good amount of power over an individual, once it is correctly identified, because now it can be attacked accurately, but also because it no longer possesses the mystery of the unknown and the state of being untouchable.

This is the same reason a good many clergy and therapists do not share their own personal lives with their charges. For some, doing so punctures the illusion of having their [expletive] together. They think they lose credibility if they have any problems of their own, when, in fact, precisely the opposite is true. A healer (or what the theologian Henri Nouwen called 'the wounded healer') gains both 'street cred' and greater power for change when he has gone through suffering and is not afraid to admit it.

For other healers, it is strictly an ego thing that keeps them from sharing their own struggles with their clients, patients, or parishioners. It's nice to be looked up to, and who would want to let go of that? So, the power imbalance is perpetuated. And thus, the act of 'naming the beast,' whether inside a client or inside oneself, is never brought fully into the light, because the healer lacks the power that comes from both looking at his own afflictions and being at peace revealing them. The cleric has far more oratorical impact when his/her preaching is driven by and acknowledges his/her own spiritual wrestling. Absent that, preaching becomes dry and merely didactic, domineering, or rah-rah

The whole purpose of doing this deep-diving into your soul and the core beliefs that run your entire operating system is to discern and fully articulate what the true problem is. And the real root of the problem always, always, always lies down in the realm of core beliefs.

This is why I don't try to get a drunk to stop drinking, a bulimic to stop bingeing and purging, or a cheater to stop cheating. It's a losing battle. The vice will be eventually replaced by some new vice. Cheaters will cheat again or do some other bad thing, if the root of the problem is not found and articulated. The goal is never to get the action to stop, but to root out the faulty beliefs driving the action in the first place. Do that and the change in behavior will follow, almost effortlessly. More importantly, the removal of the action will be permanent. Whereas, attempts to change the behavior without changing the messed-up core beliefs driving the action yields temporary, fleeting results, if that.

So, yes, the main problem is discerning the root problem, the faulty core belief – i.e. naming the beast. In this effort to name the spiritual afflictions of my clients, I am forever diving with them into the realm of fear. In that vein, one of the phrases my clients hear me harp on, again and again, is,

**If you're ever trying to figure out
why someone is doing something that doesn't make sense,
or isn't doing something that it would seem they should be,
ask yourself one question:
'What is the single greatest fear driving the behavior?'
Then speculate answers and go with the one that seems to make
the most sense.**

For, everything is fear. Once that core fear gets articulated and fully looked at, a breakthrough almost invariably happens, often right on the spot. The proverbial light bulb goes on. I've seen it more times than I could ever count. I've seen illumination and immediate change happen right in front of me, week after week, year after year.

What's most powerful when that happens is that the person can never go back. The genie is out of the bottle. 'Awareness' (as the Buddhists like to talk about) of one's own destructive beliefs now springs up much more organically when confronted with situations that previously sucked one down into those maladaptive actions. Once you're aware of what you're doing and why you're really doing it, it becomes harder and harder to keep choosing it. The awareness of the problem has the effect of intensifying the pain of the problem. And it is that increased pain, discomfort, or anxiety that eventually drives a person out of the very situation in which they've felt trapped. Thus, a sort of spiritual 'breaking the fever by spiking the fever' occurs.

Journaling Recommendation
1. What is the beast in your life that is still unnamed? What are the earmarks, or symptoms, of the beast afflicting your soul? How is the affliction manifesting itself?
2. It's sometimes hard to see it on our own, to go deep enough on our own, but what can you see? What is the grand fear afflicting your life? Why?
3. What is your preferred means of running from your afflictions? Is it an eating disorder, the bottle, gambling, or what?
4. What would your life look like if you stopped running?

POURING OUT THE LOVE CUP ONTO THE GROUND

This whole conversation of filling the Love Cup with love raises the obvious theoretical question: What do you do with it when its full? Or, what do you do with the love when there's at least more than you've ever had before, even if you're nowhere near full yet? Well, that's the fun part, obviously. The giving away of love is life's greatest joy, not to mention that grand and glorious blessing of simply getting to feel all that love inside, especially when your Cup used to be perennially empty or even full of the crud of negative beliefs.

But there is another way love leaves the cup: deliberate dumping. I had never encountered this phenomenon before, until I had a client who, upon hearing my Love Cup explanation and pondering it for a few weeks, came back and said, "What do you do with a client who dumps out his Love Cup?" I had no idea what he meant and, so, asked him to explain. He continued, "Pours it out. What does it mean when someone pours love out onto the ground, basically, wasting it? I just waste it. I don't know what to do with it. I waste it. It's like it doesn't even feel right inside of me."

Hmmm. That was a new one for me. I had seen it, but never heard it stated as such. I got to thinking about it more within the context of this particular client as a way to understand it more generally. This client, though uber-successful and working at the very highest level on Wall Street, had a particular knack for blowing stuff up in his life. Like when my buddies and I would make mini-pipe bombs as kids and blow up trash cans or small stuff in the neighborhood, because we had pent-up anger (and boredom), this client had a real gift for blowing up relationships in his life, in particular, not to mention jobs or otherwise good career situations. He was ridiculously good at his work and had risen to levels of immense influence and wealth, but he just couldn't keep himself from consistently harming his own best interests, as well as those around him. He came to me because his anger kept coming out at his girlfriend, only to be followed by reconciliation and another blow-up later.

I won't bore you with the details beyond that, except to say that after drilling way down I helped him to see that he had tremendous rage toward his father that he had been burying and avoiding his whole life. His father was abusive. Eventually, after writing letters, on my prompting, to his father and mother, which he did not send, he confronted his parents, in person, instead, by his own choosing. For this titan of industry, nothing had ever scared him so much as that confrontation. It went well, insofar as it got a lifetime of pain off his chest. The parents' response was basically both irrelevant and predictable: denial and deflection. But my client said his piece and felt great, afterward. He had given back to its rightful owner the burden of pain he had been carrying all through childhood and well into adulthood. He put that 500lb bag of rocks back in the lap of the original owners.

I helped him to see, after that, that the reason he had previously poured love out, the reason he pushed away people he loved and essentially spat on those who loved him was because he simply had no room in his Love Cup for love. Agitate a full cup and it will spill out. And if it's full of dirty, filthy, stinking crud, that same stinking sh-t will spill indiscriminately onto those in the most immediate proximity, again and again.

But, love doesn't just spill out of the love cup accidentally. Some people, as my client described, deliberately, willfully poured out love. He was so full of crud – so full of hate and indifference – that, yes, the love felt good when it came in. But the experience and receiving of love went so completely contrary to the crud and self-beliefs that filled his cup and soul that he simply could not believe them. He could not accept love because it simply didn't compute. His system was so infected with un-love and hateful messages that he literally did not know what to do with love, at least not for any extended period of time. He couldn't believe it and didn't want it, even for as much as he knew he did want it.

Again, the message of love feels good, momentarily, while it comes in and even for the moment it stays inside before the self-defense blood cells of the host attack the foreign invader, so to speak. The transplant doesn't take. The host body can't recognize a good thing.

I had seen this phenomenon in lesser forms among hiding women – women who had been so burned and hurt in previous relationships that they hid behind walls, refusing to come out and open up in a new relationship, for fear of getting hurt again. But this was a Love Cup whose crud was so full and powerful that it couldn't handle love, even though it craved it. Even though people try to look perfect on the surface to make someone like them (or keep liking them), it is the imperfections that bond us to another. Think about it, friendships thrive when two people know each other's secrets and intimate, or unpretty, truths. It is not just shared history that bonds them but that they each carry a sacred part of the other's story; each is a witness to and carrier of the other's life story, especially the ugly parts.

When a person simply doesn't believe in their own goodness, when they have been filled with messages of not being good enough and not mattering, they will keep pushing real love away, simply because they can't believe it. And it is far easier to push love away than to open up and risk being left, which would be an egregiously painful, hurt-filled confirmation of what he/she has always believed. Far better (read "less painful") to be rejected for being a false version of yourself – a persona – than to be rejected after revealing the real you.

Back to my hate-filled, hurt-filled client. His contemptuous treatment of the love that was given to him was, at the core, based on distrust. And not distrust of the person offering the love. Sure, that's what he thought it was. But his real distrust was distrust of the message that he was lovable, at all, and distrust that he would ever be okay if he opened up, let the hurt out (at the persons who had first put it there), and let it be identified. His real distrust was for his own worth and the belief that life could be anything, at all, without the only thing he had ever truly known: self-loathing.

If the notion of his own worth was not believable, then anything or anyone that tried to sell him on his own worth was likewise not believable and not to be trusted. Reject their message and reject them. Keep pushing them away and hurting them, not only to reject the virus of their love, but also in an odd way to get them to shout louder at me the value of my being. And that shouting can get through and at least plant a seed that runs completely counter to the negative message in one's cement. It's a form of handicapping: push someone away in hopes they'll prove their love (and hence trustworthiness) in always bigger ways. It's not the best way (and many perfectly good relationships have been lost to this), but it can yield fruit if there's a lot of luck.

And with my client it did take root. The woman he was in love with had persisted. The pain of his life had also persisted, such that there was deep dissonance between his core beliefs and her message to him, dissonance between the hope and happiness he still fantasized about and the deep sorrow, anger, and unrest he lived in, year in and year out.

The pain won. It broke him down. With my counsel, the overwhelming pain of life broke down his resistance to admitting the real source of his pain. It also broke down his resistance to dealing with it. But also, the pain broke down his facade of supposedly having everything under control.

With my help he dumped a lifetime of crud from his Cup, choosing to return it to its rightful owner. And with that, not to mention the massive courage it required to do so and the massive confirmation of his own worth that doing so affirmed, his Love Cup could begin to fill up with good stuff. His system had undergone a sort of cleanse. His system no longer rejected the good because it was no longer host to bad, cruddy beliefs and habitualized thinking. Today, he's actually finally married to that woman and no longer blowing up her, their relationship, or his career. Depositing his pain and anger where they really belonged changed the relationships where they didn't belong.

Are you guilty of not believing love when it is poured into your Cup? When do you tend to most disbelieve love? What is the core crud message that blocks love from staying in your Love Cup?

Song Recommendation

To really sing to where you are in this space of being down, download the song and lyrics to *Away from the Sun*, https://www.youtube.com/watch?v=DDK5qGlLT8sAwayFromTheSun by **3 Doors Down**.

THE GREATEST FEARS IN LIFE

As we progress further along on the deliberate spiritual journey, we grow into greater truths, awarenesses, and epiphanies. What formerly seemed true gives way to deeper insights and gems of wisdom that seemed utterly unfathomable, in the past, or were outright hidden from our limited view. What becomes our truth looks very different from anything previous.

One of these areas of increased awareness and truth on the spiritual journey is the notion of fear, both the power of it and the recognition of which fears are underneath all others. The reason it is necessary to identify and forever root out fear is because happiness and the fear-driven life are inversely correlated; more of one means less of the other (with the obvious exception of healthy fear of physical dangers and dangers to those you love). Fear, specifically *the fear of future pain,* is what keeps people from expressing and living their true self. Always, always, always. Nothing kills more life and sucks away more ALIVENESS than fear. Fear is the killer. Of you. Of life. Of happiness. Fear in its many forms is ultimately why every client lands on my doorstep, even though very, very few are aware of it.

Thus, in the effort to move through fear and let go of fear, it is necessary to see its influence in all you do, but more so in all you believe about yourself and life. For, true and lasting change always starts at beliefs. Simply seeing it and its impact on your life, just truly *seeing* it and identifying it, is powerfully freeing, strange as that may sound. And so we begin with the big ones.

Truth is, if it doesn't scare the holy hell out of you, it's not the deepest you can go. It's not your soul work; it's you thinking about it but not truly feeling it. The deepest is the most powerful. And it's terrifying to hold, or even touch. Other than losing a child, this is the scariest stuff you'll ever encounter in life. Your greatest fears are always indicators of where your greatest desires are. As such, these fears have the greatest power to set your soul and heart free.

1. The Fear Of Being Destitute

At least on the surface, a whole lot of Americans fear being poor and living on the street more than they fear almost anything else. This drives our rush to surround ourselves with many things and possessions. This drives the saving of money. This drives aggressive investments. This drives conservative investing.

This fear masks itself as the proverbial 'fear of failure'. But it doesn't take much digging to see that failure really often means poverty. And fear of gross financial insecurity is more than most people can handle.

The fear of losing it all or the fear of having nothing also compels people to stay in ugly relationships, remain in dead-end jobs and shrinking cubicles, complain about the misery of life, and never venture into that fertile yet scary land of allowing their truest self to arise from within and live.

What keeps people from becoming themselves is money, often enough, specifically the fear of losing money. Yet, underneath this fear is also that #1 fear lurking: the Fear of the Known – i.e. what people will think and say when they see you. Sure, being destitute is no party bus, unless you're a bit of a freak or urban monk, like I was. But it can be recovered from and worked through. Yet, the real fear inside destitution is the fear of all the people who could say, "I told you so. I told you you suck. I told you you're no good. I told you your path, decisions, and ideas stink." It's the fear of people saying, "What's wrong with you," which of course confirms the belief written in your cement that something is wrong with you.

2. The Fear Of Cheating

Oh, this is a whopper. If it ain't the fear of losing everything and being destitute, most people's greatest fear – at least the one they're most aware of and can verbalize – is the fear of being cheated on by a lover/mate/spouse. Almost nothing else in life hurts like this one.

To trust someone and to have that trust betrayed is one thing. But, to trust your most intimate lover and friend with all that you are (or at least as much as you feel comfortable sharing), and to then have that person go and sleep with another or go and have an emotional affair with another is a pain too wrenching to allow. And so, every early relationship includes the cheating conversation and all the clauses that get put into the social contract between the two people regarding cheating. Further, most people fear being cheated on so much that they will deny massive parts of who they are to avoid it. They will keep their true self suppressed, out of fear that if they show their real self, their mate will wander. People will stay hidden behind walls of fear, even with someone they love, while convinced in fictional certainty that they're going to be cheated on. Some will even stay out of relationships entirely, so as to never experience it again. That's how painful infidelity is!

I wrote a two-volume book on infidelity and the power it has, not to mention what it really takes to avoid it. If there's one thing I know a little bit about, it's the power of this fear of cheating. And so many lives have been lost, while the people were still alive; so many people have squelched their own inner voices and true soul, because they feared being cheated on. Or, even more so, they feared the lies that accompany cheating. They feared the breach of trust.

And yes, once again, below the fear of being cheated on is the fear of the 3 Binary Gates. For, if you cheat on me, it confirms – just as loneliness does – that I'm no good, not good enough, or don't really matter. To be cheated on is to be slammed, face first, into the cement of your soul, on which is written those ugly truths that you're not wanted, not good enough, and ultimately don't matter. Further, it is to be thrown back into aloneness and loneliness and their messages of being no good and not mattering.

3. The Fear Of (Confronting) The Parent
On heaven and earth, there is no fear that kills more lives and hamstrings more dreams than this one. It is a subset of the great Fear of the Known. But it is its own unique animal, because it is a fear of a person; a living, breathing, particular person, from whom there could be feedback or blowback. And, unlike the Fear of the Known where you fear a response or criticism that will likely come, in this case you're actually going to the person and almost asking for that criticism. You're poking the bear.

After going through my explanation of the Love Cup, 3 Binary Gates, core beliefs, Wet Cement, and the like, this fear of confronting the parent usually becomes abundantly obvious to both the client and me. Or it becomes abundantly obvious to just me and I have to beat the client over the head with it, because they're often too afraid to even look at it. I never force a client to speak to an external power source, in person. And often, it's actually not necessary. But if it seems to me there is no other way for my client's heart to be clean and soul to be free, I will push them to vigorously and logically defend why they'll not do so. For my job is to help them know and be confident in their real truth.

Nothing generates more underlying anger in a man than the pain inflicted by a parent. Yet nothing generates more sweat, shaking, and avoidance in a man than having to stand up to his own father (or domineering mother) in adulthood, and simply speak his truth, whatever it may be, about the past, about the present, or about the future. I have had titans of finance and industry, great athletes, coaches, ditch-diggers, military officers, and musicians abjectly refuse to state their truth to a parent, even when the client could clearly see that it was the completely unresolved anger and pain from the past that was causing the pain of the present, causing him to go white-hot with a girlfriend, son or subordinate at work.

Yet, it is that truth to a parent, either in person or in writing, that must be spoken before the adult-child will ever be free or ever be truly happy, not to mention ever have a chance at living an authentic life. So many clients will then say, "But Sven, why say all this stuff to my mother or father? It won't change anything?"

"I get it," I respond, "Your fear isn't that your father will rage at you. Heck, that'd be a gift. It'd show he actually hears you and acknowledges your truth. No, your fear is – in fact, you know in advance (Fear of the Known) – that he won't even get it; that your dad or mom won't even acknowledge it. They'll be like, 'I don't know what you're talking about.' That is what you know will happen. And it scares the heck out of you, because it'll be like it never even happened, which is of course the only way the parent has for coping with the realization that he (or she) screwed his own kid. That likely response scares you because it only confirms that your truth doesn't matter; it doesn't even exist in their eyes."

"So, what's the point in doing it, Sven? I just don't see it."

The point, I tell my clients, is not that you will get a particular response from your mother or father, even though you really want one. The point is that your heart needs to say it. The heart desires to be clean. You have something weighing on your very soul. And you will never be free until it is released and given back to its true owner. You have been living with the weight of your parents' failure (even if they were good parents in other ways) and the severe negative impact it has had on your life.

There is only one reason on God's green earth why you would ever walk into that buzz saw of opening up and speaking your real truth to your mother, when you know she has zero intention of ever changing. Only one. You need to say it. Your heart needs to be clean. You need to unburden your soul. Mom put this crud inside you and you've been carrying it around for decades. Now it's time to hand it back to her, not because she needs to hear it or because she will change, but because the child who got this negative message pressed into the cement of her soul has a right to stand up for herself and tell her mother that she was wrong and that she screwed up!

Again, you're standing up and speaking your truth may very well never change a doggone thing in the other, but it represents a total shift in you. For, fundamentally, it is the bold and loud statement to life that your truth matters, if to no one else than at least you. And you are the one who most needs to be convinced that you matter. It's not your spouse or parent. They only treat you like you don't matter because you let them and likely always have.

So, once that shift happens in you, where you actually believe and act on the belief that you and your voice matter, all of your relationships change, if for no other reason than you no longer allow people in your immediate life who attempt, through word or deed, to contradict your new truth that you matter.

Living with a clean heart – speaking and living your real truth – has a radical change on every relationship you're involved in. Some people will fall away, some will grow closer, and new people will be drawn into your life. Life is never the same. To confront the person you fear most in life is just powerful, powerful juice. Other fears cease to be intimidating when the biggie is walked into and confronted.

Whomever your primary external power source has been, once you stand up and speak your full truth to that person, life is forever different. You forever walk taller. You start erecting fences around your soul, quite particular about whom you let in and whom you don't. You spill confidence into all other areas of your life. You stop tolerating crud from bosses, boyfriends, old friends, society, and even your own children.

The other thing that makes standing up to that primary power source so difficult is that it also means coming face-to-face with the realization that you will likely now never hear the primary power source say to you: "I'm proud of you," "I love you," "You're wonderful," "You are wanted," "You are good enough," and "The real you matters." It means letting go of the very thing you've spent your entire life striving for – the affirmation, love, and confirmation of your very existence from the person who was supposed to give you a solid baseline of love and affirmation, your whole life. It means you failed at what you thought you always wanted, even while it means you succeeded at what you actually most needed – winning your own approval, your own voice, and your own confirmation of the value of your existence.

Thus, it means now shaping your identity and your life's pursuits around something new, no longer around winning external approval. That is both terrifying and liberating. Before that giant chapter ends and the beautiful new chapter begins, the old you must be destroyed. That only happens by deposing the former primary power source in your life (which kept the old you the way it was) and elevating your own self to the position of primacy in your life.

As mentioned at other points in the book, I generally recommend that you sit down at your computer first and simply type out the longest letter you possible can to the parent(s) you most need to speak truth to, using the most vile and powerful language that is conjured up in you as you consider what you really feel. And don't hit the 'Send' button. Or, at the very least, don't feel pressured to send it. There is a tremendous catharsis that comes from speaking what your soul has been longing, for decades, to speak. I'm a huge proponent of letter-writing (and not sending the letters, unless absolutely necessary to the soul). I further recommend writing letters to any other external power sources in your life, speaking the truths you've kept hidden. I've found that most people need to say something, be it all of the truth or enough of the truth, so that their voice is finally heard and their heart is finally clean.

For those who choose to confront the external power source, in person, I have had clients say all manner of things to a parent that might help you:

- Where were you?
- Where were you when I needed you?
- Why did you do it?
- You're a disappointment of a human being!
- I hate you.
- Just get out of my life.
- It's all about you. Everything is always about you.
- I'm done.
- I don't want you near my children, your grandchildren.
- I was 12 years old!!!!!!
- I do matter.
- For once in my life, I'm doing what I want.
- It's my life now.
- You hurt me and you didn't even care.
- You let him hurt us.
- You let her do this to us.

You need to drill down to that one sentence (or less) that crystallizes everything you most want to say to this person (and keep coming back to, if the conversation takes a million turns). If you can't say it in a sentence or less, you haven't drilled down all the way, yet. There's still something below it, and whatever it is, is far more emotionally charged than what you're experiencing, right now. The power that comes from speaking the words you've been most afraid to speak to the person you've been most afraid to speak them to is liberating beyond anything you can possibly imagine.

The reason these words you've kept hidden are so freeing and so empowering is not just because of whom you are standing up to and not just because of the message in the cement you are crushing, but because your action of standing up to the most powerful person in your life is fundamentally a statement to life – a bold shouting to the heavens – "I matter!! Dammit, I matter!"

Once you finally matter to you, once you finally matter enough to make your voice heard and unburden your heart, you have changed you. You have changed your underlying core reality. You have reset your beliefs. You have made a new impression – pressed a new shape – into the cement of your soul.

And now, from that radically changed, cemented belief come wide open Binary Gates, radically new core beliefs, radically new principles, and radically new behavior. Just as everything grows out of the rock that is planet earth – all vegetation, oceans, humans and animals – so also everything grows out of the bedrock of your deepest beliefs. Once you finally fall in love with you enough to stand up for you and speak your deepest and scariest truth, you proclaim to the heavens and to life itself that you matter.

And everything changes.

Dad may never change, but your relationship with dad will never be the same, because you no longer choose to live in a reality that has as one of its core defining characteristics the assertion that the real you doesn't matter, that your voice doesn't matter, that your truth is insignificant or less-than, and that you're simply no good or not important. You and dad will never again interact the way you always did. He may try, but because that old way runs counter to your new beliefs, you'll respond differently or perhaps even just walk away. And when one person changes, it forces the other person to change, no matter how hard they try to hold on to the past reality. This new change in the other person may be heightened rage, distance, or dumbfoundedness, or it may be acquiescence, shriveling, and reclusiveness. But there will be some sort of changed response. It may not be the change you want, but there will be a change, and only because you changed first.

You were the one who decided that you matter. And that lone realization and accompanying action change everything. Your life will never be the same.

4. The Fear Of Consumption

Here we come to a few slightly lesser, yet still impactful fears. The first is one a great many people have, particularly those who have been taught to subjugate their needs and wants to the needs and wants of their parents, mates, friends, and eventually spouse, children, and aging parents. One recurring theme I have seen among such people when they come out of a marriage and lifetime of being overwhelmed or run by others is that, for as much as they long to fall in love, they fear being consumed, again.

They've just begun the journey of finding themselves and it feels great. Yet, they simultaneously fear losing themselves again and often don't trust themselves to become involved with someone. They know that they could too easily lose themselves inside that other person's life.

If there were ever a great reason to take time off from relationships to get used to and enjoy being alone, it is when the fears of consumption and/or loneliness are present. Both are the soul's longing to know itself. Both demand action completely different from previous beliefs and action patterns.

5. The Fear Of Nothingness

When we are alone with no one to comfort us, console us, or entertain us, we become starkly aware that we are each and every one of us alone in this world. From dust we have come; to dust we shall each return. We come from nothing, are nothing, and return to nothing. Just carbon atoms atop a rock, somewhere in space.

As a great rabbi once said,

> **"We are each simultaneously
> the center of the universe and nothing."**

In the years I lived on the street, sleeping on concrete each night, having given up all of my worldly possessions to serve and live among the destitute and the drug-addled, it was the supreme fear of my father, my two closest friends, and later my girlfriend that I was living their great fear. That was the fear not of destitution but of overwhelming aloneness: that I am truly alone in this world. Those dearest to me ached for me – for themselves, really – because they experienced through me a stark realization of their own fear of feeling all alone. Oddly, I didn't feel alone, at all, but they did by looking at my life.

It's not that I felt I was in the company of people who loved me or that I knew I had people out there in the world, far away, back home, who loved me. Instead, I simply didn't feel aloneness because I had filled my own Love Cup. Laughter and joy followed me every day on the streets. I know it sounds unfathomable, but it's true. I didn't need people to love me to confirm my existence, my value, or my feeling loved.

That feeling of being alone in the world is, at its core, different from the fear of loneliness. It's the fear of nothingness. It's that I'm not just alone but, in the end, I am nothing. None of us is anything. We come; we go. Nothing. Poof. Gone.

That is a very sobering, even terrifying reality. The only meaning we have in life is the meaning we bring to life. That nothingness grows out of feeling I am truly alone in this world. No matter how many people you surround yourself with, even in dying, you're still alone. You leave alone.

The knowledge of that and having to look at that, particularly when you're not in a relationship, is just a horrid, beautiful, absolute, unrelenting truth. It's no wonder people stay in relationships they don't like. It at least keeps them from having to confront their own nothingness. Better to perpetuate a lie than to face that ugly truth, it would seem.

It is that same fear of nothingness that propels a great amount of action and noble endeavors, as well. A great many people fear living a life that amounts to nothing. I am victim to this aspect of this fear, as well. We attempt to erect edifices to our own significance – be they buildings, masses of money, great ideas, books, even children and great families – as a way to stave off the knowledge of our own nothingness. That returning to dust thing can be pretty intimidating.

Yet, akin to the fear of dying/death, it can also be quite liberating and life-giving. To concede my own nothingness to the Universe (which always wins every battle) frees me from walking death. It frees me to simply enjoy the now. It frees me to find and follow my bliss. For, my nothingness shall return, soon enough. To cave to the fear of nothingness is to choose dust before your body ever dies. To accept nothingness and choose to live anyway, to accept rather than run from the misery of nothingness is to also accept the opportunity to live joyfully and give energy to others, so that for this brief moment we may all laugh, eat, drink, toil, and give a bit more life to those who walk with us and come after us. To live in fear of nothingness is to become nothing, again, far too soon.

6. A Quiet, Little Stifling Fear

There is another fear that stifles those who long to break free and pursue their passion, their art, or their inner truth. What holds them back is this insidious little fear that says

"Maybe I'm not as great as I always dreamed I might be."

I had a client who had made a very successful career for himself as a doctor to the stars. A very, very successful man, at least by most general cultural markers. But, his whole life he had longed not to serve the stars but to be one, specifically to be a world class poet. He would tell me, "Sven, I have art in me. I know it. I've always known it. But, to be damn honest, I've always just been scared. I so want to spend my life writing poetry. That's it. THAT is what would make my heart sing."

"And your single biggest fear?"

"Well, as you say, Sven, the whole reason I never did it in the past is that I was totally afraid of the criticism of my old man, who was very successful and marked value by success; and just what people would think by me going after something so far out. But now that I'm nearing retirement, my fear is that maybe it has been a delusion. Maybe I never was as good as I always dreamed I was. And maybe I'm still not. That's my fear."

"And what would it mean if that were true," I asked.

"That I'm nothing. That all of this – this life of mine – is nothing. And that's just too depressing to even consider," he lamented.

"So, better to not even try at all, than to have such a monstrous fear – a monstrous dual fear, really – confirmed. Right?"

"Right."

"Better to stay trapped in a life you know you hate that can at least delude you into believing it has meaning because it is 'responsible', right?"

"Right."

"And, of course, wrong. You have no choice. You have to start writing and give more and more of your life to what you love, especially now that your career in medicine is done. You're so over it. You were over medicine, years ago. You have to discover. You have to at least try. Otherwise, as you well know, your life truly is a waste and you'll regret it to your last dying day. You know it and I know it. And truth is, you're dying already, because you're not following that which makes your heart sing. Am I correct?"

Sheepishly, "Yes."

The fear of confirmation of our own mediocrity is a subset of the fear of nothingness. It's a terribly gripping fear, keeping far too many people locked in small lives of unhappiness.

The grand realization that comes from 'doing it anyway' is that life becomes happy, like it never could before. The grand realization is that it's not about the success or no-success. It's about doing the stuff you love in life, anyway. For, it is that pursuit that changes everything. Too often, it is only success in a life path you never wanted that gives you permission to finally pursue the life you'd love, not because it frees you financially but because it makes you see how hollow success-for-success's-sake is. 'Having it all' often best teaches what true emptiness is. It is not our greatness that gives life either meaning or a sense of aliveness. It is, instead, our boldness in pursuing that which electrifies the heart.

Song Recommendation

Particularly for the fear of loneliness, I strongly recommend reading the lyrics and downloading the song, *Goodbye to Love*, by **The Carpenters**. https://www.youtube.com/watch?v=jixeE8gkT-sGoodbyeToLove I love the fuzz guitar solo at the end of the song; tight! But the lyrics soooo powerfully speak to this sense of loneliness and despair that come with giving up on love and on oneself. I love, love, love the powerful melancholy this song!

THE DOG AND THE ELECTRIC FENCE

In his tight, challenging book, *The Untethered Soul*, Michael Singer offers a brilliant analogy for the effects of doing what I call 'soul work'.

So, you got a new dog – a midsize, rambunctious one that loves to tear out of the yard and run down the street. Very early on, Fido found all the other dogs that live down the street. He discovered the immense pleasure that comes from chasing cars, digging in the neighbors' trash cans, and burying bones in the park. Very early on, Fido discovered that there's a whole lot more joy to be found well outside the confines of his own yard. He loves you dearly and very much appreciates the Alpo you provide, but he wants to run and bark, and chase and play, all day.

Well, that's kind of how your soul is. Sure, it likes the security of daily Alpo, but it desires the freedom and flow of an unbound and unburdened life. Your soul *knows* what would make your heart sing. Your conscious mind is cluttered with fears and worries, but your inner soul knows your joy sources.

Back to Fido. You, being Fido's owner and the one who has to go find him every time he scampers off, decide enough is enough. You install an electric fence for the dear boy, so he won't bolt every time you let him out. After doing so, you walk Fido to the perimeter of your lot, each time showing him the effect of getting too close to the edges. Fido gets zapped at every edge and corner. And Fido discovers very quickly that getting near the edge ain't fun. More importantly, he realizes that his days of roaming and pillaging are over. Sullen, he accepts his fate, stuck in a reality that is okay, but certainly not great.

Sound familiar? Fido is you. Life has walked you to the edges of safety and zapped you when you got too close. Now, you're stuck in a reality you did not originally choose but daily keep choosing and which does not feed your soul. It may be good, but it surely isn't great. More likely, it's miserable. You're trapped in a reality you hate that goes against the very nature of who you are.

What Fido doesn't realize is that all he really has to do is lean in for about 3 feet, until he clears that electric fence. All he needs to endure is about three feet, or so, of pain and he's home free. Only a short amount of pain stands between him and the life he knows he was meant to live, three feet to freedom, joy and a life of play.

Three feet.

So very little – far less than you realize – stands between you and the joy you long for. You're convinced if you go into the pain it'll last forever and kill you, just like Fido is. But it doesn't and it won't. So very little stands between you and the freedom of your soul. Three feet to aliveness, peace, power, joy, and purpose.

I know you feel completely overwhelmed and like there truly is no hope. I understand. I have been there. I have lived it. But if you have the courage to push through some brief hard stuff, life will turn very quickly.

Three feet.

You just gotta have the courage to lean in, endure some hardship and sorrow, and then move into your new life of effortless existence.

You ready? Or do you need to live the pain a while longer? Change will not occur until the pain gets bad enough. And your pain will get worse, until you finally act. Perhaps you still need more misery before you're sure. The gods are happy to provide it, if that's what it takes. For the gods want to finally take you to abundant life and true happiness.

Book Recommendation
The Untethered Soul, by Michael Singer. Great book! Dense and strong. Much to absorb.

Song Recommendation

Let's go country! I love this song. Such a simple message. So clear and true. ***Born to Fly***, by **Sara Evans**. Download it and give it a good long listen. The message will stick in you and inspire you. https://www.youtube.com/watch?v=8xvhutWc67kBornToFly

THE PURPOSE OF THE 'WHY'

In my old line of work as a clergyman I heard many a pastor exhort people, particularly at the time of death and funerals, to not get wrapped up in the question 'why'. 'Why', whether at death, times of loss, or during major setbacks, is an unanswerable question, they would say. And thus, it was ultimately fruitless and pointless, as they saw it.

But I have never been a believer in that line of thinking. In fact, I believe precisely the opposite. Resolution never comes to anything, unless one is able to find or create some why, some frame in which to picture the events or circumstances. The 'why' may take years or decades, but it must come and does come. It may not be the why you ever thought would come. It may not be the why others would prescribe for you. It may not be a why that even makes sense to anyone else. But it is your why, and to you it makes sense, even if it's in the most upside-down way. Peace only comes when there is some sort of ordering of the cosmos and the events that triggered the unrest.

Further, to engage the why is to engage God, himself. Too many spiritual leaders frame 'why' as a statement of doubt and thus bad. But questioning, whether in daily conversation or directed to God, is a stepping toward something, not stepping away from. Spiritually, it's stepping into conversation with God. Or, for my atheist friends and clients, it is the engagement in the deepest conversation with your own soul. It is to ask yourself, and dive deeply into, the grand questions surrounding the core question of who you really are and what you really believe about life. Because, there is no resolution until you 1) do know who you are; 2) know what you really believe about life and people; and 3) know how *you* order life and the universe, despite what anyone or any religion might've sold you, previously.

The purpose of the 'why', whether at times of death or simply as one of the greatest tools on the spiritual journey (particularly in counseling and journaling), is to climb down into the cave you have most feared to enter – the cave of your own soul, the cave of your own self. Only there can true life and clarity be found. The spiritual journey demands stepping towards God, stepping into your own soul, to engage the conversation, demanding to know why, unwilling to rest until resolution is found. This is the journey to the center of your soul. This is the journey of life, itself.

NON-NEGOTIABLES, I-DON'T-GIVE-A-CRAPS, AND THE POWER OF PERCENTAGES

Another exercise I run my clients through in this giant endeavor to allow the real you to finally come out of the box deep inside, requires only a pen and a page of paper or two, to start.

This time, draw two horizontal lines, separating the page into three same-size sections. At the top of the top section write 'Non-negotiables.' At the top of the middle section write 'Want but negotiable on.' At the top of the lower section write 'Don't give a crap.' Now, you can probably see where this is going, but stick with me, because there's a twist or two.

First of all, I don't want you to do this exercise for your life, as a whole. Rather, I want you to do one of these pages for each area of your life, to really break it down. We all kind of do it already when we are considering a bf or gf, at least in our heads. But I'm telling you, the more you do this and pull the meat off the bone for each area of your life, and the more and more you just have fun with it while you're doing the work, the more and more you'll specifically tune in to who you really are.

So, off to the top left corner of this page, write the word 'Career.' Later, you can do a page for

Girlfriend/Boyfriend/Relationship,' one for 'As a parent,' and 'Finances' or even 'Buying my new house.' Truth is, you can use this exercise for anything in your life, small or large.

Before beginning, it's important to understand *why* we're doing this. Obviously, the goal is to define for yourself who you really are. But what most people don't understand is that getting it out of your head – as opposed to just thinking, stewing, and worrying about it – forces you to clarify your thinking and enables you to truly see what you believe and want. Writing it is a completely different experience from merely thinking about it. Putting thoughts into words, so that you can see it outside of you is a higher order of creation.

So, for this first 'Relationship' page begin listing that which you know. It may be that you know exactly what two of your non-negotiables are, or a few things you really don't care about that perhaps other people might care about. Or, if you know some of the things you've discovered about yourself, over the years, that you're negotiable on but do have preference for, list those in the center section.

The goal is to list as many things as you can think of to go into each of the three sections. It's to really think about the question, yes, but more so to allow yourself to feeeel the answers. It is to allow yourself to play. Play only happens when we're relaxed, and relaxation is necessary for tuning into the intuition. The answers aren't in your head; they're in your intuition, in your gut, in your sense of peace and inspiration. Let it speak it's truth to you through how it feels inside or on your skin. Does it excite you or make you grin? Does the thought of it bring you relief and peace? Those are big indicators it's a priority for you.

Additionally, nothing is too big or too small for this list. If it's important to you, it's important to you. In fact, as with life itself, it is very easy to get caught up in only focusing on the big stuff; as the saying goes, "Don't sweat the small stuff." But the small and medium stuff are often the most important. That's where your commitment to your happiness becomes most evident. For, it's in the small and medium that it's easiest to compromise yourself and neglect your intuition and yourself.

Once again, if it's important to you, it's important to you. THAT is the point! See, up 'til now, you've been filling out the priorities for your life, based on someone else's values. These pages are about YOU.

Now, a few notes:
- The non-negotiable section is precisely that. It's the deal-breakers. It's that handful of things that if they're not present, you're not in. Or, perhaps it's something that if it is present, you're out. We're always told in life, "Gee you need to compromise more." But, first of all, it's okay to have non-

negotiables. And, second, the whole point of knowing your non-negotiables is that you don't compromise on them. You honor your own wants and needs, which is for many people a whole new concept. One of my non-negotiables, after my first marriage became 'apologizes freely and forgives freely'. I do likewise and refuse to be in a relationship with anyone close to me who expects me to do all the heavy lifting – who cannot or will not concede fault and express contrition. Absolute non-negotiable.

- The bottom section can, at times, be an eye-opener, because it opens you to seeing what might be important to others in your life, or in society, or what you've been told *should* be important to you, but just isn't that important to you. Further, if necessary, it can help others better understand you, despite their own, different experiences. For instance, I had a girlfriend who was blown away when I told her that on my 'Relationships' page in my I-don't-give-a-crap section I had 'picking out my clothes.' She had only dated men who were very particular about the clothes in their closet and what they wore each day. It made no sense to her when I told her both of my ex-wives bought my clothes, if they felt like it. Back then, I really didn't care what I wore. Often what we don't care about says as much about us as what we do care about.

- The real action, however, happens in that middle "Want but negotiable" section. Here, I want you to list everything that you know you want in your career, in this case. Again, it can be big or small; nothing is insignificant.

- But here's the twist that makes this section so instructive and helpful in negotiating your decisions. After every item, in parentheses, state the percentage you want it and the percentage you don't need it.

  ○ So, for example, on my page for relationships/girlfriend, I had in this section 'She cooks'. But, a woman who cooks for me really isn't that big a deal because I have weird eating habits (lots of chips and salsa, very few vegetables; and I don't eat an evening meal, most nights). So, in parentheses after 'She cooks' I had: (20%/80%). In other words, for me, a woman who cooks is 20%

important/wanted and 80% no big deal. (You can imagine the response when I started dating a full-blooded Sicilian, whose very identity as a woman was wrapped up in cooking for those she loves! hahaha)

○ Also in the center section of my 'Relationship' page, I had 'present when listening'. In the parentheses for this, I had: (90%/10%). The ability and desire to be truly present to, listen to, and hear another human being are as close to a non-negotiable as I can get. I tend to enjoy driven, high-strung women. But they gotta value and be able to stop on a dime and instantly go into listening mode. No small trick. I just can't be in a relationship, of any sort, with someone who doesn't care enough to stop and be present.

○ Another in that section on my 'Relationship' page was 'Likes sports and the symphony'. I was in the orchestra and theater almost as much as I was in sports, growing up; both the arts and sports are part of my DNA. But, neither is something I really need in a mate, as long as she will now and then engage in them with me. That's why I state it as "Likes sports and symphony" and not "Loves sports and symphony." In fact, I pretty much prefer to not watch football with other people, but enjoy season tickets to the symphony, whether with my mate or alone. So, for me, 'Likes sports and symphony' rated this percentage: (30%/70%). I 30% want it and am 70% negotiable. I couldn't date a sports-hater or someone who is bored by classical music. But I don't need someone who is fanatical about them, either. They're just things I enjoy for myself and would only occasionally enjoy sharing.

So, now you see the importance and effectiveness of the percentages. Also, now you see how the issue of compromise in a relationship, a career, or even with your own self becomes much easier, because you can see clearly what you will not compromise on, at all; what you totally don't care about; and then what those things are that you will compromise on...and how much and when you're willing to compromise.

And see, this is critical, because far too many people compromise themselves far too much, on large, medium, and small issues. They compromise things they have no desire to compromise on and often compromise too much. (Some have the problem of compromising too little. For example, some single parents choose that course, or even choose to become single parents, precisely because it means they don't have to compromise in their parenting decisions. Often because they perceive compromise as an admission that they don't know everything and aren't perfect, which opens the door on all of their insecurities and opens the door to criticisms and questioning. Or, he/she is just so angry at the ex that he/she hates the idea of playing on a [parenting] team.) Eventually, if you do this, you lose all sense of self. You become someone near-completely different from what is written on your soul. Compelled by the banal, inaccurate societal platitude to always compromise, you give and give and give, in the form of compromise – giving up all of your own wants – then wonder why you're not happy. Every time you stand up for what you genuinely want, you are proclaiming to the heavens, 'I matter! Dammit, I matter,' and that hole in the Love Cup gets a little smaller. The Third Binary Gate begins to open.

But also, to know what is written on your soul, you must begin to allow up from inside of you the feeeeel of what is right for you, especially in the medium and small things. Who you most authentically are is a feel, not a thought. For, our thoughts become too easily infected by the thoughts, words and deeds of others, arriving into us through our ears and eyes. Remember, tuning into yourself is not so much about 'discovering' or 'finding', as if it is outside of you, but about 'allowing', because it is inside you and has been blocked for too long by your fears and debilitating beliefs. And the only way to access it is to shut the thinking mind down and begin to feel it rise up from within, begin to allow for inspiration, creativity, and intuition to speak their course for your life. This exercise is a great tool for doing precisely that.

WHEN POSITIVE ENERGY SOURCES TURN NEGATIVE

One of the things that can happen when doing the Diamonds and Raw Sewage exercise is that you may realize that some things/people/places/circumstances/beliefs/values/paths do not fall completely in one column or the other, but in fact land between, bearing both positive and negative energy in your life. There is good energy coming from it, but also rotting, heavy energy.

In this case, it is necessary to assess whether the negative energy outweighs the positive to a significant degree, for a significant amount of time, and if it holds little hope of returning to a largely positive state, such that it can be moved entirely into the Diamonds column. If the general trend of a particular aspect of your life seems to be moving slowly (or quickly), yet inexorably into the Raw Sewage column, then it either is or will be necessary to begin taking steps to remove it from your life, or at least radically reduce its presence in your life.

You may not want to admit that some formerly beloved element of your life has moved in the Raw Sewage direction or has done so to a large degree, but that doesn't change the fact that it's pretty clear what is happening and, therefore, needs to happen next.

In any case, it is helpful to understand why something makes that shift from being in the positive energy column to moving toward and fully into the negative column. Simply put, you are changing. You are growing. You are evolving. Whether you like the idea or not, we all change and evolve. As a result, things/people/residences/dreams/values/relationships/paths that fit before can begin to chafe. We outgrow things from our past. Things cease to fit.

There is no guarantee anywhere of anything being permanent. But, because we find security in that which is familiar and because we fear losing happiness if we change, we cling to that which has been in fear of that which might be. And slowly that which has been begins to slip into the Raw Sewage column. In fact, many things eventually do, big and small, if for no other reason than the Law of Diminishing Returns – more of something does not mean more happiness. If action is not taken on the sources of Raw Sewage in your life, they become fetid. They stink up your life and make you feel yucky inside. Silly as that may sound, it's 100% true. Removing the sources of stink in your life is critical to growth. Creation is invariably preceded by destruction. That which no longer gives you life energy must be destroyed, so to speak, to make room for new creations – new life.

As an aside, occasionally Raw Sewage can drift slowly into the Diamonds column. But this requires distance and/or some jarring event, so that former Sewage can be seen in a new light and felt with new openness.

Too Many Diamonds

There is another phenomenon that happens with positive energy sources in our lives. It happens when we have too many. On many occasions, I have clients who report that they have so many things they want to do that they can't find time to rest. Or, they find themselves becoming anxiety-ridden because they can't seem to complete, or actively engage in, all the good and great things they want to do.

Now that seems like an odd thing. Seemingly, adding more positive things/people/values/paths/experiences to life should only bring more positive energy. And, actually, that is true. So, how can more positive bring about the negative of anxiety?

It can happen two ways. One, as mentioned in the Diamonds/Raw Sewage chapter, is the common mistake made by those trying to get happy: they add more Diamonds without getting rid of the Raw Sewage. Life is still cluttered with the drag and drain of Sewage, effecting no room for increased Diamonds. There are only so many hours and only so much energy in the day. Spend them on the Sewage and there's less time and energy for the Diamonds. But the second way is when the pursuit of the positive energy sources – the Diamonds – is driven by something other than sheer bliss.

I had a client, Jennifer, 28, who was knocking all sorts of stuff off her bucket list – run a marathon, play in a volleyball league, take jiu-jitsu classes – on top of working 40+ hours at a job she loved, AND continuing to make time for and build a relationship with her new husband. I had not heard from Jennifer in roughly a year, when I got a call on Christmas Eve, right as I was going into church for some good singing of the Christmas classics. It ended up being a two-hour session, and I missed Christmas carols, that year. For she and her husband of three months had just had their first major blowout fight. On Christmas! How could I say 'no'?

I dug around and dug around and discovered that this bucket list was part of the problem. Jennifer readily admitted that what was driving this big push to knock so many things off the list was the further desire she and her husband had to get pregnant in the next year. Jennifer was of the belief that once she got pregnant and once she had kids in the house, she would largely not be able to do the things she still wanted to do.

I teased her a bit, gently, in her belief that the adventurous, go-get-em life ends once you have kids. She laughed. And then I stopped kidding her and said there is some truth to that, or there can be. There's only so much gas in the tank in a given day or month. But what was vividly apparent to me was that her mad quest to shrink the bucket list was driven, ultimately, by the fear, 'If I don't do these things now, I'll likely never be able to.'

And fear is not a good driver for bliss. Positive energy cannot be sought for negative reasons. Or, rather, positive energy sources will be completely undermined and drained of their joy if pursued out of fear, which is precisely what was happening to her. She had become very uptight, very time-crunched, and as a result her main relationship (with her new husband) was suffering. He had been complaining that he never gets to see her and that it's like they're already living somewhat separate lives. And, even when they were together, she either had less energy or was not fully present.

Thus, the grand effect was similar to wanting a donut for a tasty snack, then eating 11 of them and getting a serious stomach ache or throwing up. Too much of a good thing(s).

But it was the fear driving her to do it that was the real problem – the fear of never getting another donut. She could not let go of the things she wanted. She was clinging tightly, because she feared losing them if she didn't do them all now. Thus, she couldn't relax and actually enjoy them, and she was screwing over the one relationship that mattered most to her.

What I helped her see, as well, was that the negative energy rising up in herself and her relationship is the first indicator she was disconnected from her soul's voice. She was doing what she thought she should do, but at the expense of inner peace and joy. (It's interesting that a bucket list can become a 'should' or obligation, isn't it?) She had lost connection.

The solution, therefore, was two-fold. She had to re-prioritize what was really most important in her life, at this exact juncture, and give that, or those things, her best energy. That meant letting go of some of the other things on her bucket list, for now. For, her fear had caused her to force results and caused her priorities to get jumbled, creating both chaos and the anxiety that comes with chaos. Truth is, her Diamonds list had become re-shuffled. That was the disconnect from self she was experiencing in the form of anxiety, confusion, and light depression, as well as marital discord. She needed help re-finding her own highest priorities. Marriage trumped the others. It was her true non-negotiable. That required letting go of other Diamonds, or de-prioritizing them half a notch, or so, to lesser positions, for now.

Far more importantly, the solution was really that:
- She had to let go.
- She had to trust.
- She had to trust that in the re-prioritizing she would be okay.
- She had to trust that she might be able to do some of these things later in life.
- She had to trust that ,while she might lose some things for now at least, that is okay and life doesn't end because of it.
- She had to learn to trust that it will be okay, even if she doesn't get everything she wants, right now.
- In trust, she had to stop forcing life, forcing results.

When Happy Memories Inhibit Action

In a similar vein, a couple in their mid-70s, whom I counseled recently, admitted that they were considering selling the house they had lived in for 40 years. Yet, because it was the house they had raised their now-adult children in and because they had so many warm and wonderful memories tied up in that house, not to mention lots of actual mementos of all that love and those experiences, they felt guilt over considering leaving, and were quite hamstrung by it all.

I explained to them that my own parents went through something similar, a decade or so ago. The joy that they had gotten from the house and all the joyful reminders around the house began to be outweighed by the burden all those mementos and the house that held them had become. The upkeep of a good-size house, and the pics, knick-knacks, memory-laden furniture and so on was just too much for them, weighing them down, bleeding their life energy.

I told the couple that clearly too much positive had become a negative. More importantly, the fear of letting down those children they had raised kept them in a happy house that had become a burden, depleting their joy and zest for life.

We know our path in life by the energy it both brings and promises. And for this couple the positive energy would come not in the form of excitement, but in the form of relief. The gods were calling them in a new direction through the voice of their own bodily energy. They knew they would have physical relief if they downsized to either a smaller house, a two-bedroom condo, or possibly a sailboat in the marina (a lifelong dream). But, again, their fear had been keeping them locked in an increasingly negative situation.

More importantly still, what defined a Diamond now was different from what had previously defined a Diamond for them. They sought peace and relief, now, more than the highs of new experiences. They had grown. They had out-grown. They had evolved, even in their 70s. They needed me to help them see the issues. But, in the end, they needed to give themselves permission to change their values. It was they who needed to say it's okay that we are not who we were, and that who we are becoming is quite good, even if it is very different. They had to admit to themselves that relief is just as wonderful and legitimate a positive energy source as anything else.

I had to help them see that sometimes the joy of 'having' is well-exceeded by the joy of 'having less'. They admitted that their long buy-in to the societal myth that joy mainly comes from having more had grown so great that they couldn't see how much it was holding them back from the next stage of life. "If we have less things, we'll be less happy," was their myth. They needed to see that, in an odd twist of fate, precisely the opposite had become true. They needed to see that happiness is not just in having, but in doing, saying, becoming, and believing that which is reflective of your truth, today. Further, they needed to see that letting go of old positive memories could give way not only to new energies, but give room for more new positive experiences and the wonderful creating of new positive memories.

Dying For A Dying Spouse

I had an uncle, Gunnar, whom I had grown fond of, over the years. We had similar temperaments. We lived in separate cities, so we never got real close. But there was a shared fondness, nonetheless. He was a total blue-collar guy; hard-nosed. And he took care of people – neighbors, former students, friends, family – when he didn't have to, simply because he had the energy to do so and liked helping out.

I recollect visiting Uncle Gunnar, more than once, in his later years when passing through Denver. He had become largely bed-ridden, in his early-70s, ravaged by a brain tumor. Still salty as ever, however, he was not afraid to get real and call it as he saw it, whether it was about his childhood, my grandparents (his parents), his own failings, or just about anything.

So, while it wasn't completely out of character for him to say it, it still hit me strange, when he said, "Y'know Sven, caring for Doris (his wife) in her final five years as cancer killed her is what is killing me now. I know I have this tumor because I kept her at home and did it myself. It just sucked everything out of me."

"So, forgive me for asking," I tap-danced a bit, "but why did you do it?"

"It's who I am, who I was. I thought, 'I'll do it myself. I can handle it.' And I didn't want her to be alone in a facility of any kind."

"So, your very nature, then, is what's killing you, now."

"Absolutely."

Two of the very biggest Diamonds in his life – his wife and his indomitable generosity – led him down a path that created the very brain tumor that was killing him, now. I didn't ask him if he regretted it. Implicit in his even stating it was a hint of regret. Fruitless to ask a dying man if he'd do it differently if doing it again. He was just being who he was. So, to ask if he would do it differently would be to ask if longer life would be worth it if it came at the price of changing your inherent character at the last minute. I already have my own answer on that one. His Diamonds killed him and he knew it.

Finally

Bottom line in all of this is that it is easy for positive energy sources to become negative energy sources, if they are driven by fear of some sort. And the way to know if some Diamonds have slide partly to the Sewage side of the ledger is to simply feel your energy. Are you down, drained, anxious, combative, or lethargic? It is then necessary to identify and name the fear, and decide if you want to continue to live in that fear or let go of the fear, trusting you'll be okay, no matter what happens.

Effortlessness And Flow

One of the core beliefs I have in life is heretical to a great many leaders in the spiritual business. I believe in effortlessness – that when you are on your path, following your truest and deepest inner voice/vibe/feel, there is a flow, happening in your life. Life, done rightly, does not need to be forced or even toiled over, as if in a perpetual state of work. Done rightly, work is play, because it's work you love; relationships flow, because they are built upon two individuals who believe in their own mattering.

This notion of effortlessness is not to be conflated with either ease or pain-free existence. Pain is an inevitable element. It is both a great teacher and simply that which makes life life. But it does not oppose effortlessness, as the latter is a sense of clarity, of knowing you're precisely where you are supposed to be, not needing to be somewhere else or someone else, even when it's amid pain. Effortlessness may still be hard as [expletive], but it just feeeeels right. It's a place of inspired action. It may be hard, but it's inspired. Hence, there's flow.

> *"Taking fun simply as fun*
> *and earnestness in earnest*
> *shows how thoroughly, thou,*
> *none of the two discernest."*
> --David Miller, *Gods and Games*

Yes, I absolutely believe and daily experience effortlessness and flow. Work is play and things – wonderful things, big and small – rain out of the sky, things I could have never previously imagined and certainly never made happen on my own. Is every day pink bows and cotton candy? No, but darn near. That is, even the negative stuff or challenging stuff exists within the greater contexts of

- No matter what happens, I'll be okay; even when it hurts;

- This negative, or challenging, happening is the best possible thing that could happen to me, right now. I need only ask it what it is trying to teach me, even when it hurts;
- I need to calm myself, relax, and find the laughter and joy in it all, even when it hurts.

The great challenge of life, according to 20th Century mythologist Joseph Campbell, is to "walk joyfully amid the sorrows of the world." I know this sounds incredibly Pollyanna. But I've lived through hell, multiple times, and have the scars on my heart, body, and soul to prove it. Further, I'm a big believer in the transformative power of the refiner's fire that is pain. I have seen it, time and again. When clients make that turn of eliminating the Raw Sewage from their lives (particularly from within) and boldly pursue the Diamonds, blessings begin to rain out of the sky in the most unexpected segments of their lives. This isn't made up nonsense. I see it almost every single day. Clients begin to put in place the spiritual disciplines necessary to not only weather any storm but necessary to be in a state of bliss daily. (Where bliss is defined as inner peace – a felt knowing [not just believing or hoping] that life is okay, good, and even happy....even amid pain.) Yes, daily.

Further, bliss, flow and ongoing effortlessness do not always happen overnight. But sometimes they do. More importantly, the greater the velocity exerted by you to remove the Raw Sewage and courageously endeavor your Diamond pursuits, the greater the velocity of bliss and blessings flowing into your life. Solely pursuing your Diamonds vigorously is not enough. Solely eliminating your Raw Sewage sources is not enough. For, to pursue only one is to tacitly admit you fear pursuing the other, which means you're living a fear-based existence, which cannot bear fruit. Happiness and fear-based living are inversely correlated. Make no mistake, the biggest roadblock to effortlessness and flow is the refusal to eliminate Raw Sewage from life, the greatest of which is the core belief that I'm not good enough or I don't matter.

Further, if you tend to both your Sewage and Diamonds, the stunning results won't happen where you most want them and in the ways you most want, at least not initially. They'll happen in the most brilliantly unexpected ways. Further, the bigger the blockage that is removed, the greater and quicker the unexpected blessings that will flow.

With time, a momentum of effortlessness kicks in as you, more and more, make priorities out of: Removing Raw Sewage, pursuing Diamonds, relaxing, letting go of anxiety, trusting that answers will come for any existing unknowns, savoring what is in front of you right now, and knowing that this is right where you are supposed to be.

"Lift your oars.
Nothing you want is upstream.
Everything you want is downstream."
--Esther Hicks

Song Recommendation

Growing up in the 70s and 80s, I am a very big fan of the master craftsman, **Peter Gabriel**. But that love for his music is only heightened by the enormously soulful, powerful nature of his solo work, much of which came later in his career. One of my faves, so apropos to this conversation of trusting flow and the effortlessness of life that comes from doing so, is *Washing of the Water*. It's a song written, in part, about the loss of love and the longing of the soul for healing. Yet, it's simultaneously a song about this deep notion of believing in the flow of the river of life, trust in the healing of soul waters, and, ultimately, about trust.

https://www.youtube.com/watch?v=AICeVeWpMtsWashingOfTheWater

WORDS SPEAK LOUDER THAN ACTIONS,
NOT VICE VERSA

Speedy was a New York City cop who came to me because of his love life. Great guy. Older, say 60. Just a couple years from retirement. A guy who described himself as a Brooklyn meatball – an average Italian Joe, who liked serving people. He was over being a cop, so ready to retire to New Mexico. But he was also an honest, committed and genuinely good man.

Speedy was having relationship problems. Actually, as he tells it, he basically had always had relationship problems. But he was in the throes of dating a woman who, seemingly, less and less wanted to be around him. In fact, to an outside observer (me), she was flat-out rude to him. Gert was in her 50s and working three mini-careers: a family-owned restaurant, a social work side job, and teaching the occasional class at the community college. And, while her excuse was always that she was too busy, she never initiated phone calls to him, as in never. She balked at dates. Speedy had to grovel for sex. During the week, she rarely texted him. If she did, it was always in response to one of his. Too busy, Gert claimed. Yes, too busy for a 10-second text to the person you claim to love.

Aye, and there's the problem. 'Claim to love'. See, Gert and Speedy had had a wonderful start to a relationship, roughly three months before Speedy started seeing me. Dates, calls, texts, sex, and even a vacation together. Speedy was completely smitten. And, as was his nature, he gave. In fact, Speedy didn't just give to Gert. He gave and gave and gave and gave and gave. He was fawning, but not oppressive, in his attention. He regularly bought her things – from an oil change for her son to rolls of tape and boxes when Gert sold her condo. He bought her groceries. He took her to nice restaurants. He wasn't rich – he's a cop! – but he loved doting on the woman he was in love with, and he made sure she felt loved. This meatball didn't need much in return, he just loved giving. In those early months, he and Gert regularly exchanged 'I love yous.' And it made Speedy's heart sing. He was so doggone happy. To hear those words from a woman was, for him, the very apex of human experience.

But something happened on that vacation, a few months into the relationship. The change was imperceptible, yet perceptible. She came back changed. Weeks later, he got sick and was bed-ridden for weeks. She never once visited him (later claiming she didn't want to get what he had), nor even sent flowers or sent food (an easy slam dunk when her family owned a restaurant).

Yet, even after the change, even after the slow slide away from Speedy had picked up a bit of steam, they still had occasional dates. But she started guilting him over sex or even for wanting a phone call or a text each day. 'I'm too busy and tired,' was her mantra. Yet, she still gladly accepted his help loading, driving, and storing her furniture for the move, his paying for the truck, and his making sure all of her and her son's small needs were taken care of, too. Worst of all, she still occasionally uttered those words for which he lived: 'I love you.'

Mind you, 3-4 months in, he starts coming to me for counsel. So, obviously, there's some crud wrong with his relationship in his mind. Something doesn't feel good. Otherwise, why seek spiritual counseling?

Heavy Words, Light Actions

Well, first off, I dinged him on the whole 'Relationship Camel' thing he had going on. And I early on linked that tendency to over-give (and basically buy smidgens of love, in return) to his lifelong core belief that he was a bum, wasn't good enough just as he was, and that's all the love he was worth. Speedy just couldn't see what I did: he was a loving, kind, giving, not-half-bad-looking guy. He also couldn't believe what I knew: There are a ton of great, intelligent, beautiful women in their 40s, 50s and 60s who would kill to have a decent, kind, loving meatball like him, who also looked pretty good in uniform.

After that initial round of sorta shaking him by the shoulders to see he was a great guy – rattling his core beliefs – and that he needed to stop acting like he wasn't, I began what would be a long and painful (for him) process of helping him see that he was making the classic 'in love' mistake. After a month, two months, and four months of seeing Speedy weekly, he began to see and feel more clearly the pattern I had laid out for him early on:

**Speedy weighted Gert's occasional "I love yous"
as 1,000 pounds each,
but weighted her unloving, even hurtful, actions
as if each one was but a feather.
He so wanted love and so needed to hear those precious *words* of love
that he ignored all *actions* to the contrary.**

**<u>For a great many people in love,
words speak louder than actions,
even when they shouldn't.</u>**

Despite a long – and growing longer – pattern of behavior on Gert's part, Speedy just couldn't bring himself to let go. In truth, his pain hadn't gotten bad enough yet to outweigh the infrequent "I love yous" and rare text messages.

It's the same thing that happens in cases of infidelity. You sense something is up. You just *know* your mate is cheating, but you can't prove it. You feel it. You see the changes in behaviors and deviations from long-established patterns. And you even confront your mate, but they swear up and down that nothing is up. The say all the "I love yous" and "I didn't do anythings." And, despite the growth of negative actions, you believe their words, don't you? No matter how much evidence to the contrary, we weight words soooo doggone heavily.

Of course, at the bottom of the problem wasn't Gert; it was Speedy. Gert had nothing to do with it. She was the sore throat; Speedy's own core beliefs were the virus. He believed that giving feasts of love while only getting scraps of love, in return, was good enough. The notion of a woman fawning over him as much as he fawned over her was unfathomable, the stuff of fairy tales. His expectations for love were shaped by his belief that scraps were all he was worthy of.

And so, he would cling and cling and cling to a relationship that was corroded and near-dead, until the pain and his own sense of slowly growing pride gave him the strength to walk away. The subsequent letting-go wasn't easy; he cried for months. But the turn toward self-belief and wanting to be treated well by a woman had begun.

With that came the absolute requirement that, going into any new relationship, he would have the awareness to see breaks from good patterns and see when he was being treated in ways that didn't feel good or negated his importance.

Other Applications Of This Notion Of 'Words Are Greater Than Actions'

Truth is, we all implicitly know that it's human to err on the side of believing loving words over unloving actions. I mean, why else would we keep saying in therapy or in conversations with friends, "Y'know Susie, actions speak louder than words." I mean, why even *say* that, unless Susie was doing pretty much exactly the opposite? Why would we all need to keep reminding ourselves that actions speak louder than words, unless our natural inclination was to do the opposite?

We forever do that, don't we? We are forever ignoring the truth right in front of us. As the Zen proverb goes, 'The truth is obvious.' We spin ourselves around and tie ourselves up in knots trying to, supposedly, figure stuff out, when the truth of the situation is almost always glaringly obvious.

There is one more application of this notion that words can be tremendously powerful, to the point of outweighing actions. It gets back to the notion of Wet Cement and how even reasonably good parents can really screw up a child. Despite loving actions, despite providing food and clothing, despite being generally supportive and even passing the words 'I love you' on to the child, if the parent is speaking any words bearing negative messages regularly, or even occasionally, bad things can happen. Words can outweigh actions. They have the power to concretize a very destructive self-belief system inside the child, one that can be very difficult to extract. Children are such delicate creatures that extreme deliberateness is required. There must be an unwavering consistency of word and action, else destructive messages can slip out and embed themselves in the tender little soul of the child.

An Aside Regarding Speedy

Regarding that notion of awareness and being tuned in to how you're being treated, and insisting on being treated well and treated fairly and wonderfully in a relationship, you must also have the courage to simply speak when you're not being treated well. For someone of Speedy's self-loathing, speaking up when he was feeling yucky about how a woman treated him was just plain scary.

Speedy said numerous times in our work together, "I gave everything in this relationship. I deserve to have someone give back to me." And, while I applauded the sentiment affirming his worth, I had to call him out. "You didn't give everything," I said to him, amid praising him for all love he did shower on Gert.

"What do you mean I didn't give everything," Speedy inquired, simultaneously put off and confused.

"Dude, you gave a ton. You took care of her, bought her stuff, told her of your love, gave her tons of affection – when she wasn't pushing you away – and on and on. But you withheld the one most important thing, the very thing that most contributed to this whole thing getting so messy and painful. You withheld your truth. Every time she did small and medium stuff that really hurt, you didn't say squat. You did what a whole lot of guys do. You took it and took it and took it. You kept telling yourself, 'It's no big deal. It's no big deal. I can take it. I can take it,' because you have a long fuse, right? Yeah, me too. But the problem is that all those small and mediums would add up, 'til eventually you blew, right?"

"Yep."

"Yeah, you're doggone right. You were so afraid to speak up when you felt hurt, because you were so afraid that if you had any needs or expressed any of your real feelings she may not like you, might reject you, might leave you. And then you'd just be left with all your thoughts of self-loathing. You were afraid to ask the questions you really wanted answers to. You were afraid to stand up to her nastiness. So you'd back down, always. You heard the voice of your pain inside, but were terrified to act. No Speedy, this whole relationship problem got so big and monstrous because you refused to nip it in the bud when it was small, when she was dinging you with little hurts, early on. Then you just kept that pattern up, for eight months."

"You're so right, Sven," he responded, stunned, numb.

I continued, "The key to being treated well (and thereby confirming your worth to the Universe and to life) is awareness of when stuff ain't right and the courage to speak against it. You do those two things, rather than waiting for stuff to explode, and your next relationship(s) will be radically different. Granted, it's hard as heck, at least in the beginning. But it's soooo worth it, once you see people – women! – treating you differently."

Therein are two of the three cornerstones of the spiritual life: 1) Awareness – i.e. to tune in to the voice of the Universe and life speaking deep within you. That awareness is a mirror, which both convicts and compels. It shows us how we're failing ourselves, failing God, and failing life. And it compels us to action, to change; 2) Courage – to act on what you hear or feel; to walk into the fears and do the actions, anyway. Do that and everything changes. But it requires the willingness to not weigh sought-after words far heavier than truth-revealing actions. (The third cornerstone, as mentioned in previous chapters, is: Letting go of results.)

The Sheer Destruction Wrought By Fear

As mentioned, at the root of Speedy's fear of standing up to Gert and standing against her ill-treatment of him was his fear of being alone and all that happened inside him when he was alone. *He was terrified (to his very core) of the voices inside him when he was alone*: 'See, just like I was always told, I'm no good. I'm alone. And that is the clearest confirmation that I'm no good. If I were any good, I certainly wouldn't be alone.' The fear not of aloneness but of the voices inside that happen during times of aloneness drove Speedy to cling fiercely to a clearly toxic relationship. Those voices drove him to refuse to stand up to a woman who clearly was unkind to him. If he stood up to her, she might leave. And the tender soul of the child inside him simply couldn't handle the voices of aloneness again.

But stand up he did. And walk away he did. Per my prompting, he forced himself to have no contact with her, after the relationship was done. Then, a few months later, because he still had some of her furniture stored at his house, I had him text her a very brief, breezy message saying he'd like to drop the furniture off. He needed to be done with her completely. And holding on to artifacts of a relationship (be it furniture, old letters, pictures, or mementos) is an indicator of a heart still holding on to a person, to some greater or lesser degree. So he texted.

And precisely as I predicted (though not to him), she started wanting him again (or wanting to be wanted by him again). They had long talks wherein he called her out (something he had never done before), she apologized, and he stated strongly (again on my prompting) that he's not waiting forever for her to come out of her shell. She had admitted that she's still so hurting from past relationships and so has a lot of fear. He told her he has no interest in a relationship governed by fear, so she needs to start opening up, as in now. I helped him see that she has had an entire year to see his kindness, stability, extremely giving nature, and just plain decency; how much more time and proof does she need before she opens up? How much clearer of a pattern of behavior did she need (to the point where even her own parents and daughter were telling her she blew it in letting him go)?

Yet, I also forced him to look, in the subsequent months, at the fact that he had seen a clear pattern of her behavior and that she would only stop treating him poorly if he required it. She would only break from her 'I'm busy' patterns if he found the courage to do the thing he feared most: state his feelings when he was feeling them, even when they were small.

She was back in his life. He was happy. She was eager. But I was skeptical. I told him, point blank, the changes of him being strong and not taking her guff and her being invested in the relationship would not last, long term, unless the core beliefs driving the behaviors changed. And, since she had shown resistance to coming to meet with me individually, it was a reasonable assumption that her core beliefs had not yet changed. Further, since Speedy and I still had distance to go in diving deeper into his past, his core beliefs hadn't fully changed yet. Thus, having done this about a million times before with couples, I told Speedy that I didn't see them lasting a long time without slipping back into old patterns.

Well, that was enough to light a fire under Speedy. And, as of the writing of this book, they are still planning to come in individually for counseling and then later as a couple. But, what's most remarkable is the almost constant change and growth I've seen in Speedy, to the point where he commented recently, after a dinner out with Gert, "Sven, it's like those NFL quarterbacks talk about when they say the game slows down for them. It's weird, when I talk with her, I'm so happy to be with her and she says 'I love you' a bunch of times and really means it. But, it's like I'm in it and yet standing aside watching it, at the same time. *I'm aware.* I've never experienced this before. I see it happening while it's happening. I'm not just caught up in it."

"Yeah, man," I responded, "and she can see the difference. She senses, she knows, something is totally different about you. And that's the change that needed to happen in you, whether for this relationship or your next one. You had to get your butt kicked and be broken down before you were ever ready to finally change and grow. The pain had to get bad enough. And now you're a totally different person in the relationship and in life."

"It's great, Sven. I'm so aware and I'm firm enough and strong enough to act on stuff. I'm just a totally different person in so many ways. I'm not afraid, anymore. Thanks, man!"

Song Recommendation

I think **Christina Perri's** song, *The Lonely*, so so so https://www.youtube.com/watch?v=3SFErl-X-pcTheLonely brilliantly conveys the power of loneliness, making it very easy to understand how each one of us, like Speedy, can so easily spend our lives running from it. Fear of loneliness in the future (and the voices inside us that arise in loneliness) is so overwhelming as to make it easy to engage in all sorts of bad decisions within the context of an existing relationship. This song also highlights the fear of going inside to actually look at and remove the pain and fears. Download her song and soak in the powerful sound and message.

When The Soul Burps Gold

I have to be honest, there are certain things I love greatly about my work as a spiritual counselor. Well, actually, I love pretty much all of it. People ask me how I can listen to people's problems all day and go into their deepest stuff. "Don't you get exhausted?" Heck no. I'm more jacked at the end of a day of counseling than I am at the beginning. And I can't wait to wake up and do it all over again. It's the same with me when I'm writing. A 16-hour day of writing and I'm eager to go to sleep, not because I'm tired, but because I wanna do it again, tomorrow.

Well, within this realm of loving most everything about counseling, there are certain times that really make my butt pucker and put me on the edge of my seat, times when I know a breakthrough is imminent. And it's nearly always after I ask a penetrating, difficult question of a client and hear, in response, those precious three words, "I don't know."

See, those three words represent a part of a person that is either unexplored or unsolved. Thus, quite logically, it's there on that new ground, that fertile ground, that something magical is going to happen. And, boy, if you ever want to see resistance, ask a person to push through the 'I don't know' they offer when asked a deep question about him- or herself, something they've either never thought about or never found resolution to.

"Well, just give it a shot," I prod. "Pretend maybe you do know. Just take a wild guess at what the reason might be that you've done this in the past or continue to do this. Knowing you can change your answer next week or next month, what *might* the reason be?"

To which they always respond, "But I don't *know*. That's the point. I've never thought about this before (or, 'I've tried to figure it out and just can't.'). I don't know what the answer is."

"Right. Got that. But if you were to guess at what it might be like now. I mean, just totally speculate. What *might* it be?"

Sometimes this back-and-forth can go for 5 or 10 minutes, sometimes they buckle sooner. But, if I don't back down, they eventually realize I'm not backing down, then think about it or, better, blurt something out. (Blurts are awesome, because they're like a burp of the soul – just this one gaseous, bubble of truth rising up from deep in their soul, un-vetted by the ever-churning mind; it's all feeeel and no thought; and that is very, very good.). And, whether by burp or by guess, when pushed through the 'I don't know', truth is almost invariably uncovered.

The client throws out to me his or her best guess, and if it feels like there's some meat on the bone I just run with it, continuing as if it were true. And 99 times out of 100 it is. Naturally, that's when light bulbs go on over their head. Revelations of the soul. That's when breakthroughs happen and real momentum begins to take over. It's such a stunningly beautiful thing to watch.

Lives are changed, right there, right in the middle of 'I don't know.' This isn't just cutesy crapola. 'I don't know' is the phrase that pure magic is made of in my world of spiritual counseling. It's a simple trick you can use even in your own personal journaling. I use it on myself when I'm stuck or in need of deeper illumination. I just spitball what it might be, then run with it. 99% of the time, that first burp of the soul is spot-on.

Ask the question and burp whatever bubbles up from the soul; or even ruminate; speculate answers; go with the one that feels right; then let your life be changed as you get a new window into your soul. 'I don't know' is where the real gold of the soul lies. Once you discover an answer (or six) to an 'I don't know,' dig deeper, like a 7 year-old hectoring mom for facts about some important 2nd grade topic on the drive to soccer: "Well, *why*?"....."and why is that?"...."but why did that happen?"..."but what about this other thing?" etc. Keep asking why. Go deeper. Dive further into the revelation on the other side of 'I don't know.' That's where the gold is.

Journaling Recommendation

1. So, let's tinker around a bit here. This is generally something I have to do in person, because I have to be able to sniff out with my own curiosity where to go with the questioning. But let me ask you, if we were to set your *future* aside and only

look at your *present* and *past,* what are the three biggest "I don't knows" in your life? That is, what are the three biggest things from your past and/or things you still think or do in your present that you have no explanation for, or that you have always answered "I don't know" when queried about why you do that? What are the great unanswered questions of your life?

2. Now, if you were to speculate what the answer to one of those questions is, what would you say it is? Just if you were to take a wild guess, knowing you could change your mind tomorrow or next week, what would you speculate is the real reason?

   ◦ I often have people say to me, "Well, Sven, I don't know. I've never thought about this, before." I know you haven't. I'm asking you to not only think about it now, but to stay focused on it and just throw the answer out there that it might be, just off the top of your head.

3. Now do that same thing for the other two things from your past and/or present that were your other "I don't knows." Speculate. What *might* the reasons be? Now, if I were with you, I'd be able to sense whether it's deep enough or not, whether it's the 'bingo' answer or not. But you're gonna have to do this part on your own. And it requires a certain measure of intuition and sensing and feeeeeling the answer for what sorta feeeels right.

   ◦ One way to test it for veracity is to simply sit on it for a day or week. Offer up that answer and hold it. Dwell on it for a week. Let it sit back there in your head, off the front burner. Come back to it in a week and just feeeeeel again. Does it feel like that really is the answer? If you have to keep thinking about it and vacillate, back and forth, let it go. When something is right, it just feels right; there's a certain sense of knowing it's right.

   ◦ One more way to test the rightness of an "I don't know" answer is with this simple question, "Did your answer bring an epiphany? Does it feel like an epiphany? Does it feel like a 'Holy Crap!'moment? Does it give you a sense of 'Wow. Wow. Wow,' like you just stumbled upon something very real, very significant, very powerful? If not, it's not the right answer. When you hit the answer to a long-held "I don't know," you know it. You feel it. There's a serious sense of awe that you just stumbled upon something seriously ill, seriously monster.

4. What's the effect of realizing these new answers to your big 'I don't knows'? What is the vibe? Does it feel like you've just found a new door, like you've just looked inside one of the hidden secrets of life, like hardcore 'Holy Crap!'?

5. See, now's the really trippy part. Now, you gotta start spinning out the ramifications and multiple sub-epiphanies. What other revelations do your three epiphanies give birth to? What is it you realize you need to do/be/say/become/etc? What really, really, really are the course corrections that spin out of all of this? How does this re-write the story of your life, past and present? See, this is where life starts to get heavy, get real, and get deliberate. If you can dive into your own "I don't knows," you can do some serious soul-spelunking. The wisdom of life begins to not only open up to you but do so at your command. And this is when the velocity of soul work increases exponentially, when you can begin to look within, deeper and deeper, all on your own. Now is when we're getting somewhere.